TALES OF MARTIN COUNTY'S PAST

Its people, places, events, and mysteries

LENNY TVEDTEN

Dedication

I would like to dedicate this book to my wife, Carol, who encouraged me to accept the position of executive director of the Martin County Historical Society in 2001. At that time, I was uncertain as to whether or not I would consider this position. If not for her persistence in suggesting that I give careful consideration to this opportunity, I would likely not have been as fortunate as to have experienced a second career that has proven as interesting, meaningful, and rewarding as this has been for me.

Throughout the course of this experience, I have received many compliments regarding my writings and work at the MCHS. However, I am the one who should be complimenting the many people with whom I have had the pleasure of working, including colleagues, directors, our membership, and the vast number of community and business supporters in Martin County. Through all of these people, I feel that I have been truly blessed and gained far more than I have imparted. Being somewhat of a sports enthusiast, quoting Baseball Hall of Famer Roberto Clemente seems relevant: "Any time you have an opportunity to make a difference in this world and you don't, then you are wasting your time on Earth."

With that in mind, I hope that in some small way I've made a difference and that you enjoy, learn, and appreciate the segments of Martin County history that I have provided here.

Tales of Martin County's Past
Its people, places, events, and mysteries

Main resources for this book, including the source of many photos, were the *Martin County Sentinel* and the *Fairmont Daily Sentinel* and its various iterations. Text specifically cited from these publications such as headlines and quotes are reprinted here exactly as they appeared in those papers, including spelling and grammar that differ from today's standards.

ISBN:
10 9 8 7 6 5 4 3 2 1
Printed in the United States of America

Credits
Cover design and internal layout by Alan Pranke
Edited by Liz Wheeler

Publisher
Martin County Historical Society
304 East Blue Earth Avenue
Fairmont MN 56031

For additional books, contact:
Martin County Historical Society
Phone: 507-235-5178
Email: mch@frontiernet.net

CLEAN WATER LAND & LEGACY AMENDMENT

This publication was made possible in part by the people of Minnesota through a grant funded by an appropriation to the Minnesota Historical Society from the Minnesota Arts and Cultural Heritage Fund. Any views, findings, opinions, conclusions or recommendations expressed in this publication are those of the authors and do not necessarily represent those of the State of Minnesota, the Minnesota Historical Society, or the Minnesota Historic Resources Advisory Committee.

Contents

Martin County Comes Into Its Own

Industry and Enterprise in Martin County

Acknowledgements

Perhaps the most interesting aspect of my work at the Martin County Historical Society has been researching and retelling historical events and stories from the past. Consequently, this book is the culmination of organizing the majority of articles that I have submitted to county newspapers since 2003 into one succinct publication.

This retelling of history would not be possible if it were not for the meticulous and diligent recording of history as it occurred by county newspapers. Therefore, although the *Sentinel* and the archives of the Pioneer Museum would have to be credited as the primary resources for this book, all of the county newspapers were also significant resources from which to gain knowledge and information about the history of Martin County. Accordingly, I would like to acknowledge and thank all of these newspapers, some of which are no longer in existence, for the important part that they have played in recording history and providing a resource from which to present it once again. My hope is that the completion of this project into a book will positively impact the generations that may not have had the opportunity to be exposed to the interesting and informative historical events from the past in Martin County, and that it will rekindle pleasant memories from those who recall some of the events recorded in this book.

In addition, I would like to thank the Martin County Historical Society Boards of Directors who over the years have encouraged me to pursue this endeavor and who have provided a great deal of support for this project. Likewise, my colleagues, including Jim Marushin, Dona Paris, and Sandy Nuss have provided immeasurable assistance in helping to bring this project to fruition. I would also be remiss if I did not applaud the efforts of Liz Wheeler for her detailed editing and organization that was necessary to provide a sequential direction for readers of this work.

Finally, I would like to acknowledge and thank the public and many of our members who have encouraged me to pursue this venture. Their enthusiasm has been an inspiration for me to complete this project in a manner which I hope will be interesting and informative to all who enjoy local history.

I hope you take as much pleasure in reading this as I have had in creating it.

Foreword

What an incredible honor, to be asked to write the foreword for a book celebrating the history and heritage of Martin County. When I got the call from "Mr. T," I said "Absolutely!" Mr. Tvedten, to this day, still holds the dubious distinction of being my favorite teacher. That's right: fifth grade at Lincoln Elementary in Fairmont, circa 1980.

Now, as fate would have it, 1980 was the year that my family moved from our house on Interlaken Golf Course to Knollwood Drive on Hall Lake. While I was going to miss my lemonade stand on Hole 16 and sneaking into the Yacht Club's pool, I was excited about finally getting to live on the water. My family had always had a cabin in Sherburn, and we had a lot of fun boating on Fox Lake, but this was going to be different. Not only would I have unlimited swimming and waterskiing in the summer, I would have my very own hockey rink in my backyard in the winter. And that's the greatest thing about growing up in a small town like Fairmont, being able to enjoy the outdoors on our five amazing lakes.

Mr. Tvedten taught me a lot about hard work. He was the first teacher who really pushed me. He knew that I had more to give, so he challenged me. He also taught me that there are many different ways to learn. Case in point: I was no good at math. I struggled with it, and it was really affecting my self-esteem. Mr. Tvedten saw this, so he asked me to come into school early one morning. He knew I loved sports, so he brought in a newspaper, and we looked at the box scores for the Minnesota Twins. I was awful at long division, but for some odd reason, I could calculate our third baseman's batting average and slugging percentage. Once he made that connection, everything just sort of clicked. That is his gift, connecting with people and relating to them at their level. Whenever I'd get an answer right, he'd say, "Ya done good, kid." And that was just the affirmation I needed to build my confidence.

When I got older, I was able to explore Martin County from the passenger seat of the Fairmont Furniture delivery truck. This was the family business that my great grandpa, Joe Morris, started back in 1939. My grandpa, Jay Pieser, later took over, followed by my dad, Don Bernstein. I and my two brothers, Mike and Andy, were the fourth generation, and we hung out there as much as we could. It was my first real job, and that meant starting at the bottom. My daily duties included cleaning the bathrooms, assembling furniture, and unloading semi trucks. Eventually they let me go out on deliveries. It wasn't as glamorous as being out on the sales floor all dressed up schmoozing with the customers, but it certainly beat my previous occupations as bean-walker, snow-shoveler, and lawn-mower.

Our delivery schedule was pretty simple: Monday was north, which meant we'd go to Northrop, Truman and Nashville Center Township. Tuesday was west, which included stops in Welcome, Sherburn, Trimont, and Ormsby. Wednesday was south, which featured Ceylon, Wilbert, and Dunnell. And Thursdays, we headed east to Granada, Imogene, East Chain, and Guckeen.

I remember trying to figure out just where in the world these exotic locales were. It wasn't uncommon for a rural farm family to give directions to their homestead in terms of "turn right at the green pickup and then left at the barking, yellow dog...." This was obviously in the days before GPS, so you had to pull out the trusty map book and figure it out. If I needed help, I would: roll down my window and ask a farmer for directions, pull into a gas station to use a pay phone, or call back to the shop on the CB radio. "Breaker, breaker, where the heck is Bixby Corner?"

At thirteen, I got my boating permit, which allowed me and my buddies to explore our glorious chain of lakes. And while I wouldn't experience true independence until sixteen, I learned that rural living did have its advantages. It turns out that, at the age of fourteen, ag kids can get their farm permits and legally drive when doing "official farm duties." This was a serious loophole we had discovered. That meant we could now go to Bowlmor to play Space Invaders, which was followed by twist cones at the Dairy Freeze and root beer floats at A&W as long as we had a bag of feed in the trunk just in case we got pulled over.

Once we had that figured out, we'd cruise the mall. Yup, the Fairmall was the place to be and be seen in the '80s. When you got tired of driving in concentric circles over the speed bumps in front of J.C. Penney's, you could head down to Gomsrud Park.

"Goms" truly was a fantastic place. Having two swimming beaches really put us on the map. People would drive from all over to go boating, grab a burger at the Channel Inn, and just chill out. Other fun destinations included the Fox Lake Ballroom, the Martin County Fair, and the annual Enduro Race at the Fairgrounds. Ahhh, memories.

Eventually, we discovered the greatest hangout spot of them all: the drive-in theater. We'd pile into the back seat of my buddy Thad's brown Dodge Duster and cover ourselves in blankets. He'd then pull in and politely tell the ticket taker, "One, please." And then we'd all sneak out once the coast was clear. It was hilarious. This was the ultimate spot to meet the other kids from the neighboring towns. The beauty of the drive-in was that everyone wore their letter jackets. It was like having name tags. Nobody watched the movie, we'd just hang out and talk about school or sports or whatever.

For me, sports were always the common thread. It was a source of community pride, especially as the smaller schools consolidated. I remember when Truman won the Prep Bowl in '82, right when the Metrodome opened. And then East Chain won the girls state basketball title. I will never forget the sign in the paper: "Last one out, please turn off the lights." How great is that?

I left Fairmont in 1987 when I went on to attend the University of Minnesota. I always enjoy coming home though, and seeing my buddies, guys like Kent Senf, Paul Carlson and Dave Cone, who all have wonderful families and have achieved fabulous success in business.

I especially enjoy coming home to see my mom, Judi Poulson. I've always said that there are two categories of people on this planet: people who have met my mother, and people that just haven't met her…YET. She's an amazing person and loves everything about her hometown. In fact, she still hangs out with her posse: Rhoda, MaryDon, Jo, Carol, and Ginny, among others. They are members of an exclusive tennis club they created years ago that meets weekly for breakfast at Burger King. Incidentally, they actually stopped playing tennis about three decades ago.

Being the only Jewish kids in southern Minnesota, my mom wanted my brothers and me to be cultured, to be open-minded, and to give back. We traveled a lot and regularly hosted foreign exchange students. We in turn all lived abroad as well. Nowadays she lectures about world peace and tolerance and helps charitable organizations in Martin County and beyond. That's her passion. I couldn't be prouder of her and her work, she truly makes a difference.

Her ideals definitely rubbed off on me. Today I work as a professional speaker, and wherever I go around the world—from Hong Kong to Dubai to Cape Town to Sydney—I always share my story about my hometown, Fairmont. I'm extremely proud of it and wear it as a badge of honor. Heck, I even read the *Sentinel* online just to keep up on the gossip!

Martin County is a wonderful place. It has great people, great schools, and a great quality of life. It's a fun community, and it has great momentum in business of which we can all be proud. Mr. Tvedten, upon retiring from teaching, has now made it his life's work to preserve and celebrate our area's rich history. We should all be very grateful. What he has done with the Martin County Historical Society is nothing short of amazing. As a fellow historian, I can appreciate all of the hard work and research that went into this book, and it's an honor to be a small part of it. Your legacy will forever remain connected to Martin County through this work of art. Kudos, Mr. T. "Ya done good, kid."

Ross Bernstein
Proud Fairmont native, business speaker,
best-selling sports author

Introduction

When Martin County, Minnesota, celebrated its Sesquicentennial in 2007, it marked a significant juncture in the history of our county. That anniversary brought to the forefront many of the important historical events and people that, over time, shaped our county into what it is today. Some of what is depicted in our local history is very serious, some is quite humorous, some is rather insensitive, some is very important, and some may seem relatively insignificant. Nonetheless, however we choose to interpret Martin County's past, it is a part of our local history and must be remembered and recorded as a reflection of our heritage.

The content of this book includes a broad range of topics, from the early history of Martin County up to and including what has taken place in the relatively recent past. It would be impossible to document every possible historical event in a book of this nature. Rather, the intent is to include a wide range of stories about people, events, communities, entertainment, and more in reflecting the past in terms of its historical influence on the development of Martin County.

Whether you read for knowledge, for pleasure, or for other reasons, may your understanding and appreciation of the history of Martin County and its many aspects be enhanced by this book.

The Pioneers

William Hampton Budd: Pioneer, Soldier and Community Builder

In 1856, only a small portion of what is now Martin County, Minnesota, had been surveyed. At that time, East Chain, Pleasant Prairie, Center Chain and Nashville were part of Faribault County while the rest was part of Brown County.

William Budd

Soldiers passing through the area "told of the many beautiful lakes and streams, and rivers of clear pure water abounding with large quantities of fish of different kinds," along with the abundance of fowl, and fur-bearing animals, according to William Hampton Budd, one of the area's first settlers who wrote about his experience in the book *History of Martin County*.

While Native Americans had been through the area before this, following the hunting and fishing in spring and fall, it was in March of 1856 that the first white settlers, Calvin Tuttle and Mr. Rickey, made their way to the area. Within nine months, Budd reported twenty-nine men, nine women and twenty-three children living in the area during the brutal Minnesota winter. In 1857, the area officially became its own county, a year before Minnesota became a state, and got its first post office. By 1860, the area claimed 151 people as residents.

Budd settled in the Fairmont area after having moved from the east and exploring much of the Upper Midwest. Budd was born March 28, 1829, in Mount Olive, New Jersey. Having merely attended what was then known as common school, he enhanced his education with a great deal of reading and study whenever possible.

At the age of twenty-one, he moved to Dodge County, Wisconsin, and began exploring much of the new state as well as northern Iowa. At that time, there were very few settlers, and houses were spread as far as ten to twenty miles apart. Prior to becoming a permanent resident of Martin County, he also traveled over much of Minnesota, Iowa, Kansas, and Illinois.

He initially located in Mankato when there were but seven primitive houses and did carpenter work. Later, in the early part of 1856, Budd served as the assistant overseer of the Winnebago Indian Agency near Mankato. In July of that year, he traveled on foot to Martin County to assist families in securing locations in the county. Upon arriving, he decided to purchase a squatter's right for $50 to a claim that was to be in the city of Fairmont. He built his cabin at 705 Albion Avenue, on the corner of Albion and Woodland, referred to as Budd Hill.

In addition, he acted as a scout or guide to various groups which arrived in the area looking for a place to settle.

When Martin County was organized in 1857, Budd was appointed as one of the first county commissioners. He was also the first postmaster of Fairmont, which was designated as the county seat, and also served as clerk of court. He was very prominent in social, civic, and political affairs as the city of Fairmont developed.

In 1862, the great Native American massacre concerned many early Minnesota settlers and settlements. Budd, who had previously taken part in the defense of settlements in Jackson and Martin Counties during the time of the Spirit Lake massacre, enlisted in the Winnebago City Home Guards. However, they never came into conflict with any hostile tribe.

In early 1864, when troops were still stationed at Fort Fairmount in Fairmont, a call came for men to enlist in the Union Army. Budd enlisted in Company C, 6th Minnesota Infantry. Before leaving, he married Lydia Jane Swearingen-Allen, a widow. The wedding was a large military celebration that was attended by more military than civilian guests. At the conclusion of the wedding, the soldiers fired a military salute. Budd felt it an honor that this was evidently the first and only wedding in the county to be attended by a military parade accompanied with the goodwill of the soldiers as well as a military salute. Mrs. Budd had two daughters from her previous marriage; she and Budd later also had two daughters.

Budd was known as a community builder who not only made his home here but also persuaded others to do the same. Budd Lake, Budd Street, and Budd School were eventually named in his honor.

In 1897, he compiled and published his book *History of Martin County*, about the early history of Martin County based upon his personal experiences. This is no doubt one of his greatest contributions to our county.

In addition, the many positions of trust in which he served Martin County in the formative years of its development are a testimony to his honesty and integrity. He passed away on November 3, 1915, in Santa Ana, California, at the age of 86.

Information for this story came from Jan Dickinson's compiled research of newspaper articles Fairmont History 1850–1900, *a volume at the Martin County Pioneer Museum;*

Martin County Historical Society's History File 191; Budd's obituary in the November 19, 1915, Martin County Sentinel; *and Budd's book* History of Martin County.

The Fowlers: A Family of Firsts

As is often the case, early pioneers to Martin County came here for a better way of life. They wanted more for themselves and their families; consequently, they took the challenge and moved west.

One such hardy individual was Henry Holmes Fowler. Fowler's ancestors came from England and settled in Connecticut. Henry, one of ten children, was born in 1827. While in Connecticut, he learned the silver burnishing trade and also met and married his wife, Adeline Parker, in 1852.

Henry and Adeline Fowler

The east was experiencing some hard times in the 1850s; there were soup kitchens, workers rioting, and very crowded conditions. In addition, eastern cities were said to be flooded with literature promoting the fine land and conditions in Minnesota available just for settling there. This prompted Fowler to head west, eventually leading him to Minnesota and to Martin County.

Fowler, who had previously visited Minnesota, set out for the west in the spring of 1857, getting as far as Prairie du Chien, Wisconsin, by train. From there, he set out on foot.

While walking, he encountered another young man, coincidentally named George Fowler, but no relation, and the two decided to travel together to Winnebago City, which was greatly publicized back in Connecticut. However, upon reaching their destination, they were disappointed in the city which had only a few log buildings. Although Winnebago City wasn't to their liking, the region appealed to them, and Henry and George decided to continue walking to Fairmont. There they met two of Fairmont's residents, William Budd and E. Banks Hall, who told the men about the Chanyaska River, now called Elm Creek, located about ten miles north of Fairmont.

Budd and Hall said it had a substantial amount of timber and would serve as a good settlement site. The Fowlers went there and found this area much to their liking with an abundance of timber as well as wild game, fish, and many fur-bearing animals. Here, in what was later to become Westford Township, the two Fowlers each selected quarter sections of land under the Preemption Act, which was in effect prior to the Homestead Law, and agreed to pay the government $1.25 per acre of land.

After Henry had secured his land, he walked back to Connecticut to get his wife and young daughter. Then in the spring of 1858, Fowler, his wife and daughter, and several others interested in the new land, left Connecticut for Minnesota. They again went by rail to Prairie du Chien. Their travels continued by river steamboat to Mankato via St. Paul. From Mankato, Henry hired a team of horses and driver to transport them to their site on the Chanyaska River. They arrived at their new home on May 11, 1858, the same day that Minnesota became a state.

Coincidentally, one of the individuals who accompanied Henry to Minnesota was Henry Martin, for whom Martin County was eventually named. Martin was ambitious, somewhat wealthy, and very enthusiastic about this area. He entered politics and, when the county was organized, he was present at the session of the legislature when the bill was passed creating Martin County. Consequently, as a result of his enthusiastic lobbying for the passage of that bill, he was honored by having the county named after him. However, it is interesting to note that he soon left the area and went back east. Although he owned land on Martin Lake, which was also named for him, he played no further role in the development of the county and was never actually considered a true resident.

As very early settlers, the Henry Fowlers were responsible for many "firsts" in Martin County. They grew the first wheat in the county, they were said to have the first cow, and their son, Charles, was the first Caucasian boy born in Martin County. In addition, Henry, along with Budd and Benson C. Hinkle, were appointed commissioners and given the task of dividing the county into townships. Henry and his wife lived on their farm all the rest of their lives. Henry died in 1904, and Adeline died in 1921.

Descendants of Henry and Adeline celebrated 150 years on Elm Creek in Westford Township in 2007 with over 140 family members present. Today the farm is operated by Henry's descendant, Travis Fowler, and his wife, Jeanine.

For the Fowler family, their neighbors, and Martin County, one can only speculate as to how things might be different had Henry Holmes Fowler chosen a different location in which to settle back in 1857.

Sources for this included the MCHS History File 90 on the Fowler family and Mary Fowler.

The Carver–Tuttle Fight

Calvin Tuttle came to Martin County from Fort Dodge, Iowa, in March of 1856. He along with Mr. Rickey are remembered as being Martin County's first permanent white settlers. Tuttle originally located on Silver Lake. He later moved to what he named "Tuttle's Grove," which later become known as Tenhassen and was located just west of where Ceylon is today.

Sam Carver, a huge, stern character with the "voice of a bull," decided to settle in the vicinity of Tuttle's Grove in 1860. He was met by Tuttle, a giant of a man with a menacing scowl on his face. Tuttle asked what he was doing there, and Carver replied that he planned to settle in the area. Tuttle flatly stated that it was his land and that Carver should get off, and get, fast. Carver reportedly had no idea that he would encounter trouble when he tried to settle in the area, so he moved on into another wooded area nearby and set up camp once again.

Carver—Tuttle Fight Cartoons

Early the next morning, Tuttle along with his two sons, George and Columbus, both nearly as big and surly as their father, strode into Carver's camp. Tuttle snarled that he had told him to move on. Carver replied that he had and that here he would stay. It was said that Tuttle and his two sons walked away muttering threats as they left. Speculation was that they took no action against Carver at that time because of the dislike held for the Tuttles by the settlers in the area, which concerned them to some extent.

By this time in Tuttle's Grove, Tuttle had already acquired several thousand acres of land. With his sons and son-in-law, he held the area virtually by force and was considered a dictatorial land baron, stating that no man he could whip in personal combat should ever live in his empire. As a result, those that lived in the nearby community had no love for Tuttle and welcomed the arrival of Carver.

The threats continued from the Tuttle camp, and by 1862, it appeared that blood would undoubtedly be shed. At that point, Tuttle made a somewhat rash vow that if Carver could beat him in a fair fight, Tuttle and his family would depart the area leaving his entire "empire" to Carver.

The local settlers arranged where the men would meet in April 1862: a natural amphitheater cleared in the Tenhassen woods. Onlookers came from miles around to watch the big fight.

The battle began when Carver and Tuttle, both being huge men of physical prowess by standards of the time, entered the clearing. As soon as Carver raised his arms to remove his jacket, Tuttle, ignoring the prior agreement of fair play, smashed him in the face while Carver's arms were still caught in his jacket sleeves. Initially suffering fierce punishment from Tuttle's fists and boots, Carver finally freed one arm. As he fell to the ground, he managed to punch Tuttle in the groin. From that point on, nothing was barred, and the fight continued on with fingernails and teeth at times supplementing the fists of the two fierce adversaries.

Although experiencing intense pain from the kicks of Tuttle's sharp boots, Carver managed to free his other arm from his jacket and grabbed Tuttle around the legs, forcing him to the ground. The battle was said to rage on for over an hour when Tuttle, determined to put an end to the fight, rushed at Carver with his head down. Carver quickly stepped aside, and the hard charging Tuttle crashed to the ground with a thud. Carver instantly jumped on top of him, his fists battering Tuttle's head until Tuttle was heard screaming for mercy. Carver, finally the undisputed winner of the hard fought battle, was hailed by the settlers of the area as a local hero.

The Tuttles kept their word. They loaded their wagons, and the company that numbered about twenty persons moved westward a short time after the fight. They weren't heard from for some time, until word later came from Nebraska of Calvin Tuttle's death in 1882.

Carver remained in the area. His son, William, was later elected sheriff of Martin County and served in that capacity for many years. His nephew, Walter Carver, served as a deputy.

The story of this famous fight has since been told and retold, perhaps even embellished to some extent over the years, and has since been awarded its place in the archives of local history.

Sources for this included The Daily Sentinel, Martin County Sentinel *centennial edition April 16, 1958, page 3, and Dickinson's* Fairmont History Scrapbook 1850–1900.

Fort Fairmount

Shortly after the first settlers arrived in Martin County, the few citizens that comprised the population of Fairmont fled the area as news of Native American uprisings at the Lower Sioux Agency (in Morton) and New Ulm, Minnesota, spread to the area. Surrounding community residents, as well as those in Fairmont, fled to what were considered better protected settlements to the east, including Winnebago. (The land company that platted the area actually called it Fair Mount due to its location overlooking the lakes. It is not known when the town became Fairmont.)

About 300 persons began their exodus at noon on August 26, 1862, after news reached them of the attacks. The area was abandoned for more than a month. When military protection was eventually provided, some people returned while others were never heard from again.

Major General John Pope of the U.S. Army from St. Paul was sent by President Abraham Lincoln to this area as Commander of the Department of the Northwest, a somewhat hastily formed military branch, to meet the needs of the Native American threat. General Pope's forces included approximately 4,000 Civil War volunteers comprised primarily of Minnesota volunteers, five companies of the 25th Wisconsin Infantry, and about 500 men from the 5th Iowa Cavalry.

On September 23, Pope issued the order establishing Fort Fairmount. It was to become one of the protective forts on the southern Minnesota frontier. Captain Jeremiah Rusk, commander of Company K of the 25th Wisconsin Infantry who later became governor of Wisconsin, was assigned to the Fairmont and Winnebago area. The soldiers of the 25th Wisconsin Infantry built Fort Fairmount in the fall of 1862 before being ordered south for Civil War duty.

FORT FAIRMOUNT, 1862

The fort was built of logs cut from what is now the Woodland Avenue area. The courthouse of that era, a wooden log building, was entirely enclosed by the fort. The fort also included officer's quarters, barracks, and stables for horses.

In addition to Fairmont, the soldiers guarded the settlements of Elm Creek, East Chain, Twin Lakes, Tenhassen and Center Chain.

The company in Fairmont, which included about eighty officers and men, remained at the fort until ordered to move south, at which time Captain Asgrim K. Skaro and Company D, 9th Minnesota Voluntary Infantry, took over. Captain Hiram F. Bailey, commander of Company C of the 6th Minnesota Volunteer Infantry, took the next command of the fort.

The soldiers stationed at Fort Fairmount were reportedly quite happy to be there. They deemed their duty at the fort a pleasant interlude preceding their Civil War assignments, considering the quarters, location, and weather in addition to the fishing and hunting, including the buffalo spotted several times on the west shore of Lake Sisseton. They also captured animals like foxes, prairie chickens, quail, cranes, geese, and ducks. A tamed hawk was said to leave and then return to the camp in response to the bugle calls for meals. It then waited patiently to be served its ration of raw meat.

Additional entertainment involved a Fourth of July celebration in which invited relatives and guests came from Blue Earth City and St. Peter. The soldiers reportedly had good musicians among them who provided a variety of musical selections for these celebrations.

With the fear of Native American uprisings diminishing, Fort Fairmount was abandoned. Settlers used some of the logs from the fort to build homes. Albert Ward bought the old wood courthouse which he kept behind the Martin County National Bank for many years. The remains of that structure were torn down in 1902.

Today, the site of Fort Fairmount is remembered with a marker commemorating its historical significance on the grounds of the present Martin County Courthouse.

Some information for this story came from the Centennial edition of The Daily Sentinel, 1858–1868, *and MCHS History File 53.*

One Soldier's Story

The face of war has continually evolved over the years. Today's armed forces, including the National Guard and Reserves from Martin County and southern Minnesota, see action throughout the world in a technologically advanced military. From that perspective, it is interesting to go back in time and read about the experiences of those in the military of the 1860s in order to fully appreciate the advances that have been made over the years.

Lorin Cray was a soldier stationed at Fort Fairmount in 1862 and 1863. Forty years later, he wrote a letter to the *Sentinel* about his time in Fairmont, which appeared in the July 23, 1903, edition.

Cray enlisted in the army in August of 1862 for three years. His military service began at Fort Snelling in St. Paul, Minnesota. Within a few days of his enlistment, his company was ordered to march to St. Peter to address the Native American outbreak at the Lower Agency. Cray's company was made up largely of farm boys, and the only arms provided them were old Austrian and Belgian muskets which had been poorly cared for since the War of 1812, many of which were useless. He described his company at that time as resembling a squad of Missouri bushwhackers rather than Union soldiers.

Cray's company spent the winter at St. Peter drilling, picketing the town along the bluffs to the west, and scouting in the country toward New Ulm and Fort Ridgley.

In early May of 1863, one platoon from his company was ordered to Fairmont, and another platoon was ordered to Chanyaska Lake which was located eleven miles northwest of Fairmont. They marched from Judson through Garden City, Vernon Center, Winnebago City, and from there to Fairmont. Their trip was through prairie grass, as there were no roads.

Cray said his first impression when arriving in Fairmont was that of a sleepy, quiet location. The few, little homes on the lakes were hidden in the woods, and the little fort was the only evidence of man.

The fort was located in the vicinity of the present courthouse and was constructed of logs. It stood about eight feet high and was about 150 feet square. It enclosed the first courthouse, which was located in the southwest corner of the fort, which also served as a mess room. Sleeping bunks were arranged three tiers high with each bunk intended for two men.

The soldiers of Cray's company inherited three boats from the Wisconsin Cavalry that preceded them. The boats, two log canoes and one flat boat or barge, were kept on Lake Sisseton. The soldiers spent a considerable amount of time engaging in naval battles with these boats.

Their duties while stationed at Fort Fairmount consisted mainly of scouting the prairies to the west for Native Americans. There were a line of forts constructed that summer that stretched from the Iowa line well to the north. Scouting expeditions were also to the north.

However, as no Native Americans were seen that summer, their duties were light, and they had a great deal of free time. This time they spent duck and goose hunting and organizing picnics on the lakes south of Fairmont. They also fished and were said to have hauled in over 300 fish at one time with their seine, a vertical fishing net, on Hall Lake. They caught pickerel, bass, perch, crappies, and sunfish.

The soldiers also planted a vegetable garden to the east of the fort. They raised corn, potatoes, beets, onions, and peas. Many of the soldiers enjoyed working in the garden during that summer.

Cray's company boasted some good musicians, which encouraged them to plan a July Fourth celebration and dance. They invited friends from Blue Earth City to St. Peter. The barracks, which were surrendered to the ladies, were overflowing.

The celebration included an all-night dance. In preparation for the celebration, the soldiers went out on Lake Sisseton and George Lake with three boats. They killed 36 geese and caught an abundance of fish.

The usually large herds of buffalo that roamed the area at that time were broken into smaller groups as a result of the movements of the military troops and Native Americans. On several occasions, buffalo were spotted across Lake Sisseton. The soldiers organized buffalo hunting parties. In one instance, they succeeded in killing three buffalo, which served them with buffalo steak for their evening meal.

Cray related that things had been going quite smoothly for the soldiers at Fort Fairmount. As a result, the men were becoming a bit careless regarding the location of their clothing and other important items when they went to bed.

On one dark night, the drum sounded after midnight, signaling an attack. The soldiers were very disorganized and had great difficulty in preparing themselves. It took about fifteen minutes to get prepared and dressed. However, many of the soldiers were without some articles of clothing, and some did not have their guns.

The event had been a drill. The fort commander strongly suggested that, had this been a real attack, all would have been killed. The first two men ready, however, were given a reward of a six-day furlough. The remainder trained until they were able to prepare themselves for battle within two minutes from the sounding of the drum.

Cray also shared one other outstanding experience. Once, a peddler came to the fort with kegs of whiskey and beer on his wagon and opened up for business. Several soldiers became intoxicated and quarrelsome, and within a few days, there was trouble at the fort.

Several days later, it was discovered that a number of the kegs of beer had been tapped and rolled into the lake, and the faucet to the keg of whiskey had been left open. The fort's captain was very upset by this and, as a result, had the sergeant arrested. The sergeant was kept under arrest for two days; however, due to the fact that no evidence was found against him, he was eventually released.

Upon leaving Fairmont in October of 1863, Cray and the other soldiers discussed whether or not they would one day return. Many years later, Cray was the only one to ever return, as the others were either killed in battle or died at the prison stockade at Andersonville. Upon his return, he saw the progress that had been made in Fairmont during his absence.

In his memory, Cray said that he most vividly recalled the little lakes, beautiful wooded hills, and the little log fort as he remembered it forty years ago.

Sources for this included Lorin Cray's letter at the Pioneer Museum in History File 53.

The First Martin County Farmer

Martin County is well known for its farms and hard working farmers. George Murray was one of the very earliest farmers in the county, and his experiences might make us wonder why he stayed, as well as provide us with knowledge of the many hardships faced by those rugged, early pioneers.

George Murray

Murray came to Minnesota from Nova Scotia at the age of twenty-one. He and his brother Duncan eventually settled in Martin County in June of 1863. A year later, the two homesteaded government land in Rolling Green Township where Murray was the first permanent settler. Initially, he and his brother cut hay and stacked it on the north shore of Pierce Lake. They then went back to Preston in Fillmore County where his brother had lived, finished the fall's work, and started again for Martin County with twenty head of cattle for the winter.

When they returned to Martin County, they built a stable for the cattle out of poles and coarse hay. They then built a dugout in a hillside covered with poles, hay, and earth on top for them to live in during the winter. They had no stove but dug a fireplace in the bank at the end of their dugout. The fireplace was about two feet square and extended about three feet above the roof. It seemed to work quite effectively for them. The establishment of this home took place fifteen years before there was a railroad in the county and ten years before the newspaper printed its first issue.

A few days after Christmas Day 1863, it began snowing and the wind started blowing, the start of a three-day blizzard. New Year's Day of 1864 was the coldest day ever recorded in St. Paul to that point in time.

Two young men on their way to Jackson with a yoke of oxen and a wagon stopped a day before the storm. They asked if they could stay until the storm moved through the area. They put their oxen in the stable, covered the door, and brought firewood into their shanty. They then had supper consisting of pancakes and pork, as the Murrays had brought a good supply of flour and pork with them.

By the next morning, the storm had completely blocked them in, and their supply of firewood was quickly running out. Eventually, one of the men made his way through the chimney to the outdoors and was able to chop down a tree close to their dugout. He in turn dropped the split firewood down through the chimney.

After being snowed in for three days, the four men were finally able to escape the primitive hut and get to the stable. They found ten head of stock dead and one missing. The hungry cattle had eaten their way through the barn and were later found buried in the snow. Fortunately, both ox teams were still alive, and the men on their way to Jackson were soon able to continue their journey.

Duncan became disenchanted with their situation on Pierce Lake and left. He settled in Lac qui Parle County and later died during a massive snowstorm there in January of 1872.

Murray stayed in his dugout and cared for the remaining cattle until spring. During the winter and spring he caught many mink, muskrat and fox for their fur.

He continued trapping during the winters at Fox Lake until 1865. Then, after filing on his land and taking out citizenship papers, the first person in the county to do so, he enlisted in the army and went south. He was stationed in Chattanooga, Tennessee, until being mustered out in September of that year. He then returned home to his claim on Pierce Lake. During the time he resided there, he increased his land holdings to 330 acres.

Murray was married to Sarah Jones on February 28, 1867. They raised four children. Later, the family moved to Fairmont and built a home on Budd Street. However, Mrs. Murray died soon after. In 1900, Murray returned to Nova Scotia and married a childhood friend, Nellie Sutherland. They returned to Fairmont to live.

After several years, Murray and his wife moved out to the old farm and remained there until 1911. They then again returned to their home in Fairmont. They had one child.

Murray, known as one of Martin County's best loved citizens, passed away at age 99 in 1940. Murray had been a charter member of Phil Kearney Post, G.A.R.; a member of the First Methodist Episcopal Church; and a lifelong prohibitionist. Murray had also walked twelve blocks daily and, interestingly enough, never fell for the "automobile craze."

Probably the earliest pioneer farmer in Martin County, George Murray was a prime example of the early settlers in Martin County and the many hardships they endured. His life was certainly not easy, yet he never complained and was always positive in his endeavors. His efforts provided the direction for others who followed in our county and built it into what it has become today. There are certainly many difficulties in today's modern world; however, it sometimes may seem helpful to keep them in perspective in comparison to the hardships endured by our very earliest settlers.

Sources for this included the Fairmont Daily Sentinel, *July 20, 1940, and the MCHS History File 975.*

Albert L. Ward—A Martin County Leader

Albert L. Ward was perhaps one of the most influential people in Fairmont and Martin County in terms of his contributions to the area's development. Ward spent 67 years in Martin County, during which time he was a farmer, a banker, a lawyer, and a businessman, and served in a number of public offices. He was obviously an entrepreneur well ahead of his time.

Albert Ward

Ward was born in Cattaraugus County, New York, in 1842. He left New York at the age of twenty-two, after a two-year stint in the U.S. Army, and eventually ended up in St. Paul. He was told the city of Owatonna had great prospects for the future and was a fine community. Ward decided to go see for himself.

While there, he met the brother of a schoolmate who told him about his visits to other parts of Minnesota. As a result, Ward decided to head for southern Minnesota and ended up in Winnebago City for the night where he located the U.S. Land Office and selected 160 acres that he desired as a homestead. He then inquired as to how to get to Fairmont. He was told by "Trapper Johnson" that a man had come to Winnebago City a short time before with an ox team and would be heading back to Fairmont the next day.

Ward gained transportation to Fairmont with the man with the ox team and arrived in Fairmont on April 28, 1864. He was in poor health, weighed less than 100 pounds, and had no measurable financial resources. However, he recognized the opportunities and potential of this area.

Upon arriving in Fairmont, Ward's journey led him to a stockade where soldiers were watering their horses in Lake Sisseton. He was quite impressed by the beauty of the lake and the surrounding area and was won over by the Sisseton sunset. He then found lodging at the Budd Hotel, which was operated by Mr. and Mrs. James Swearingen, located at the present intersection of Albion and Woodland Avenues.

Although his army service had contributed toward his deteriorating health, the money due Ward from his military service, $85, provided him with the resources to pay the $14 filing fee for his homestead and left him enough money to buy seed, build a house, and start farming. Thus, Ward's influence on the county gradually started taking shape.

Ward's first house was made of rails banked with dirt and covered with hay. His second house was made of boards over studs with a board roof covered with sod, and a chimney of clay plastered over a wooden framework.

Having the character of a natural leader, Ward almost immediately assumed a position of prominence in the county, and he was soon holding public offices in the area. Over time, he held the titles of county attorney, county auditor, register of deeds, superintendent of schools, postmaster, and state senator. He also was a member of the 1893 World's Fair Commission.

Ward's first business venture was merchandising with his brother, Reuben Ward. However, he soon decided to pursue banking and law and left the merchandising business.

Perhaps Ward's favorite endeavor was farming. The May 29, 1931, edition of the *Fairmont Daily Sentinel* said, "Ward rarely sold any of his thousands of acres of land, after an experience in 1895 or 1896" when "someone had bid him the then large price of $30 an acre for 80 acres in Rolling Green. He accepted the offer and indicated to his friends that some 'darn fools' think land is worth $30 an acre. A few weeks later, the same piece of land was resold for $40 an acre. Ward sold no more land." He was also the largest landholder in Martin County, with between 6,000 and 7,000 acres. It was estimated that at one time he owned 17,380 acres, stretching from New York to Western Canada.

Ward sold his interest in his law firm in 1874 and concentrated his efforts on banking. He founded Martin County National Bank, which received its charter in 1875 and is now known as Profinium. In his obituary in 1931, the *Sentinel* described Ward as "a bulwark to financial institutions of this county in 1893, the year of the panic." The newspaper said that Ward loaned other banks so much money, he became short of cash. This, however, wasn't a problem for Ward. Because he was in such good standing with financial centers, he had no trouble procuring additional funds.

Ward also was the president of the Jackson County State Bank in Lakefield and the Sherburn State Bank, and was involved in other banks as well. He was also the president of two newspapers, the *Martin County Democrat* and *The Martin County Zeitung*, a German newspaper.

Ward was described as "a bundle of tireless energy." He would rise at daybreak and direct the operation of his 1,000–acre farm and be at the bank by 7 a.m. When he got things going at the bank, he would then oversee operations of his machinery warehouse. In his spare time, he would write editorials for his newspaper and practice law.

Ward married Charlotte Jennings, a New York native, in 1873. They had four children: May, who became the wife of U.J. Pfiffner of Fairmont; DeForrest, who became a lawyer; and Charlotte and Lydia.

What is the Day Farm?

Heritage Acres and the bike trail along Lake Sisseton is the area commonly referred to as the Day Farm. The farm dates back to the time when Native Americans roamed the land and prairie fires were all too common.

Reuben Ward

The farm was actually homesteaded by Reuben Ward, brother of Albert Ward, in 1867. Reuben's barn is still there and kept up by the volunteers at the Heritage Acres interpretive center. Reuben eventually passed the farm onto his daughter, Emma B. Day, so that her future might be secured. Apparently, his other children, Bertha and Beecher, were financially secure at that time.

The original Reuben Ward homestead extended as far north as the Lakeside Cemetery. However, eventually the railroad and highway took the northern portion of the farm.

The first home on the farm was a combination sod and log cabin located near the northeast corner of the farm. Ward also kept a boat on the lakeshore nearby so that his wife and children could row across Lake Sisseton to seek shelter at Fort Fairmount in the event of Native American uprisings or prairie fires.

Ward came to Martin County from New York State, traveling by water, train, and covered wagon. After establishing his homestead, his wife and children met him at Winnebago City. They then proceeded to the homestead in Fairmont by horse and wagon. The family faced many hardships in those early days in Martin County.

Reuben and Albert were both interested in acquiring land and worked together for a period of time. Eventually, however, it appears that their friendship wavered, and they went separate ways.

Reuben and Albert's parents followed them from New York to Martin County where they lived with Mr. and Mrs. Charles Gamble. Mrs. Gamble was their daughter, sister to Albert and Reuben.

Reuben was truly an entrepreneur in the early history of our county, and eventually became quite wealthy. He initially started a small store, which was later occupied in part by Dr. Fred Hunt. In a short time, Ward built a one-room home in the back of the store. He then started what was to become the very well known Ward and Cadwell store. Shortly thereafter, he built a larger home for his family. This was subsequently purchased by Dr. Roscoe Hunt, who then built the Lakeview Clinic and Hospital nearby and to the south. On a philanthropic note, he also gave the Congregational Church the necessary land so that they could build a church.

In 1965, the city purchased the homestead from Majel Habberstad of Minneapolis and her sister, Miss Doris Day of Los Angeles, Burt and Emma Day's daughters. Despite the fact the property was homesteaded by Reuben, the property has been known as the Day Farm ever since.

On a side note, Burt Day is believed to be the brother of *Sentinel* founder Frank Day.

Reuben passed away in 1891 at the age of 55. The *Martin County Sentinel* titled his obituary "Martin County's Greatest Loss." Ward was obviously a well-respected citizen of the early days of Martin County. He was known not only as a successful businessman, but also a former state senator, a man of integrity, a civic-minded citizen, and a man loved and cherished by his family.

Some information in this story came from the MCHS History File 221, the January 6, 1965, Sentinel*; the April 17, 1891,* Martin County Sentinel; *and* Martin County History *from Taylor Publishing, 1988.*

The Livingston Cabin

The Livingston cabin, currently located at Lincoln Park in Fairmont, is a historic structure significant to Martin County. The eighteen by twenty-foot structure was erected circa 1864 on North Silver Lake. It was built and originally occupied by Mr. and Mrs. W.L. Livingston who came to this area as pioneers shortly after the end of the Civil War. Mrs. Livingston, also well-known as a columnist for *The Sentinel* under the pen name Eve, named the site Tall Oaks as a tribute to the large oak trees on that site. Consequently, she named the cabin the Tall Oaks Cabin. Regretfully, a tornado wiped out the oaks, and the cabin was the last remaining reminder of those cherished trees. The Livingston log house, also known as the Livingston cabin, was believed to be Martin County's longest continually inhabited log house up to the time of its initial preservation.

In 1953, the cabin was donated to the Fairmont Parks Board by A.E. Austin who had purchased it from the Livingston family. The park superintendent at that time was quoted in the December 26, 1953, edition of *The Sentinel* as saying, "Maybe I'm getting ancient, but I believe this cabin as a part of Fairmont's pioneer history should be preserved."

Consequently, the cabin was moved from North Silver Lake to its current location in Lincoln Park in order to be historically preserved under the direction of the Fairmont Parks Board. After its move, the cabin had the newer outer siding removed as well as the inner plaster work so as to return the structure as much as possible to its original condition. Upon completion, it would be back to its original form of log construction.

In 2001, the family of Nola Livingston Brown designated $4,500 from her estate to the Martin County Historical Society to provide repair and maintenance of the cabin on an ongoing basis as needed. Once those funds were depleted, costs related to maintenance and repair became the responsibility of the city of Fairmont.

The Livingston cabin serves as a vivid reminder to everyone as to how our local society has evolved from the early pioneer days in Martin County.

Pioneer Physicians in Martin County

A number of the early settlers in Martin County included doctors.

Orville P. Chubb is considered the first practitioner of known medical ability to relocate to Martin County and was appointed the county physician in 1867.

Orville Chubb

Chubb was born in Wayne County, Michigan, in 1830. He graduated from Wesleyan College in Leone, Michigan, and then attended Cincinnati Medical College in Ohio. After graduating from medical school, he married Sarah E. Gorton and began his practice of medicine in Michigan. He and his wife had two children.

Soon after the Civil War broke out, he enlisted in the army and served as a captain in the medical corps of the 5th Michigan Regiment. He remained in the military until the war ended.

In the spring of 1865, he came to Martin County to obtain land under the Soldier's Filing Law. He returned briefly to army service and was discharged with the rank of Brigade Surgeon. In the fall of 1865, he returned to Martin County with Colonel Lounsberry after having driven a flock of sheep overland. Two years later, he built his home at 209 Lake Avenue in Fairmont, now known as the Chubb House.

Dr. Chubb was described as a very gentle and quiet individual who was disillusioned with medical practice, primarily as a result of his experiences during the Civil War.

However, as there were no other physicians in Fairmont, he willingly and skillfully provided medical service to anyone seeking it until the arrival of Dr. Winslow Hunt in 1871.

In addition to his medical practice, Dr. Chubb had abilities in a number of other fields as well. As a surveyor and co-owner of land purchased to plat the village of Fairmont, he laid out the town site of Fairmont. He also laid out the first cemetery and the first fairgrounds, and he located many claims for settlers of that era.

He also constructed bridges across creeks and rivers in the county, he examined clay at various locations to determine if any were suitable for making brick, and he built a kiln that he used for building construction. Other endeavors he was involved with included running a store out of his home for several years, starting the first drug store, building one of the first saw mills in the county, and running a grist mill with another settler, Alpha D. Cadwell. He also ran a newspaper, was a charter member of the Chain of Lakes Masonic Lodge, and served as county commissioner, Martin County Treasurer, Martin County superintendent of schools, and Fairmont postmaster. In addition, he owned a substantial amount of property here.

By 1873, Dr. Chubb felt that the community of Fairmont had become too well settled for his restless nature. As a result of this and other factors, he moved on to the frontier of Kansas, Nebraska, and other western states. He finally settled in California where he lived for many years. He never practiced medicine after 1871, and he passed away in Michigan while visiting there in 1894.

Dr. Chubb was known as an individual who put forth every effort to build up the town of Fairmont, and he was considered a worker for all that was honorable and good for the community. He was remembered for his kindness, worthiness as a friend and neighbor, and his cheerful temperament. Upon his death, his body was brought back to Fairmont and laid to rest in Lakeside Cemetery beside his wife and daughter Lottie, both of whom predeceased him.

Dr. David Winslow Hunt appears to be the first doctor to permanently settle in Fairmont.

David Winslow Hunt

Hunt was born in Mason, New Hampshire, in 1845, the son of Dr. Nehemiah A. Hunt, a "circuit riding doctor" of Blue Earth and Faribault counties in the early 1860s.

In 1862, Hunt entered the Union Army at the age of seventeen. He spent some time in a Confederate prison, endured some minor wounds, and, after a lengthy hospital stay, was discharged and returned home.

After regaining his health, which took a considerable amount of time, Hunt resumed his education. He was a teacher in Vernon Center in 1868–69. He then graduated from Ann Arbor Medical School in 1871 and moved to Fairmont that same year.

Hunt, a likable, mild-mannered man, was considered to be a good doctor. He had a long, thick mustache in contrast to the beard worn by most doctors of that era.

Hunt likely performed the first operation of any significance in Martin County. This operation, considered a "cutting" operation, took place in 1874 and involved hernia repair for John Rooney who lived in a log cabin. There were also instances of amputations made necessary as a result of hands and feet being frozen. One amputation of both feet was done in the basement of a log cabin.

An interesting article in an 1875 edition of the *Sentinel* cautioned readers as "Dr. Hunt went to St. Paul to attend a State Medical Society. He will be gone about a week and in the meantime people had better refrain from getting sick." Hunt, the only physician in Fairmont at that time, also owned and operated a drug store.

In 1882, Hunt turned his practice over to his brother, Dr. Fred N. Hunt. Hunt felt that he could no longer tolerate the Minnesota climate and, as a result, moved to California where he practiced medicine in Anaheim, Redlands, and Glendale. During his years in California, he invested much of his income in a number of speculative ventures of that time including orange orchards, walnut groves, and oil wells. Although he failed to reap the benefits of these investments, some of the land he owned on Signal Hill and Long Beach later made millionaires of many people.

Dr. David Hunt passed away in 1922 at the soldiers' home in Sawtelle, California.

Ferdinand Hunt, David's brother, was born in Illinois in 1857. He attended public school in Mankato and completed two years of college at Carleton College in Northfield. He also was a teacher and a principal in Fairmont for three years.

He attended and graduated from medical school in St. Louis. He then moved to Fairmont and took over the practice of his brother David who had become ill.

Fred was an active individual who often made trips of fifty to sixty miles or more across the pioneer prairie. He also had a great love of horses. This was a hobby many early day physicians shared as they spent long hours with the horses to which they entrusted their lives on those long trips across the winter prairie to call on ill patients.

He married Ida Cadwell, daughter of a Fairmont merchant Alpha Cadwell, in 1882. They had two sons, Roscoe of Fairmont and Rollo who became a lawyer in Duluth.

After selling his practice to Walter J. Richardson in 1893, Hunt moved to Blue Earth where he spent the next twenty-one years. In 1914, he and his son, Roscoe, returned to Fairmont and established the Fairmont Hospital. His practice in Martin and Faribault Counties spanned more than fifty years. He passed away in 1934 as a result of a head injury incurred from a fall.

Dr. Walter J. Richardson was born near Rochester, New York, in 1856. He attended Carleton College in Northfield, Minnesota, and at Amherst in Massachusetts, and studied anatomy under Oliver Wendell Holmes at Harvard Medical School. In 1885, he graduated from the College of Physicians and Surgeons of New York and then started a practice in Minneapolis. However, he soon relocated to Hutchinson before moving to Fairmont in 1892.

Walter Richardson

Richardson practiced medicine in Fairmont for approximately forty years. During that time, he was considered an excellent physician whose practice was considered "intelligent and conservative."

Although he never sought public office, he was very sincerely interested in the welfare of the community. His advice and opinions were regularly sought by others.

As with many physicians of that era, his speculative ventures often ended up as financial disasters. Probably most noteworthy of these was a Rainy Lake Gold Mine investment. After making a trip to the lake and seeing gold fished out of it, he made an investment. However, there was never any gold, as it had been planted there by unscrupulous individuals fraudulently representing their claims of gold.

He died in Fairmont in 1936 at age 79 as a result of a fractured spine. He and his wife had five children, three of whom preceded him in death.

Dr. Malcolm Farrish was born in Ontario in 1864. He graduated from Toronto University and Trinity Medical School. He practiced medicine for one year in Minneapolis, spent one year on the Iron Range in northern Minnesota, and then moved to Sherburn.

Dr. Farrish was considered a brilliant physician and surgeon with an excellent medical education. It was quite unusual at that time for a doctor of his ability and training to locate in a small town. Soon, however, his practice extended throughout the southern part of Minnesota. His first surgeries were done in homes and then in the hospital which he built.

An uncompromising life-long Democrat, he held many civic offices and attended state and national conventions. In addition, he was a talented and sought after speaker and writer.

Dr. Farrish passed away in 1915 at the age of 51 in Sherburn. He was survived by his wife and two children.

Dr. Henry Nicky Rice was another of the pioneer doctors to serve Martin County in the 1800s. Rice was born near Fort Wayne, Indiana. He entered the military at the age of eighteen and served in Company B of the 74th Indiana Volunteer Infantry from 1862–1865. He was wounded in the battle of Lovejoy Station, marched with Sherman to the sea, and spent a short time in Libby Prison.

He returned home in 1865 and taught school before marrying in 1866. Then, he moved to East Chain in Martin County and joined his father in farming and running a store.

Rice went to Keokuk, Iowa, to study medicine before continuing his studies with the "renowned and successful practitioner, Dr. Winch, of Blue Earth," according to the October 16, 1874, edition of the *Martin County Sentinel.*

Rice was described as a tall and slender man with a long black beard. He frequently drove an open buckboard and always dressed in a black coat and a black silk hat. Rice was considered a doctor with a genuine professional bearing.

His practice proved to be very successful, and as a result, he accumulated a considerable amount of property during his time in Fairmont. In addition, Rice was active in civic affairs. He served as mayor of Fairmont for several terms and served one term in the state legislature in 1876.

Upon leaving Martin County, Rice moved to California and practiced medicine there until 1907. He and his wife, Sarah Ellen, were married for sixty-six years. They had six children and twenty grandchildren. He passed away in 1935 while living in Hollywood.

Dr. Ammi Bixby was born in 1856 on a farm just east of Iowa Lake where he also spent his youth and attended country school. Bixby began his training with a physician in Estherville, Iowa, and later moved to Sherburn, becoming its first doctor.

In 1879, Bixby moved to North Platte, Nebraska, and practiced medicine there for two years. Apparently uncertain as to his career path, however, he left his medical practice and worked briefly for a newspaper in Iowa. He then left the newspaper and attended Rush Medical School. However, it seems that he felt his ultimate calling was to journalism, so he left medical school for newspaper work. Bixby worked in a number of newspaper offices and became a writer of human interest stories. Eventually he became quite popular and was sought after as a speaker, giving many lectures throughout the west.

Bixby continued to make an annual trip to Martin County to attend historical meetings at which he provided some interesting commentaries. In the May 27, 1978 edition of the *Fairmont Sentinel*, it was reported that Bixby referred to his medical practice of the past in humorous terms stating that "the only apparent good result of his practice in Sherburn was the establishment of a cemetery . . . that it had never been needed before because the people were so healthy. He said at these meetings that he saw many faces which would not have been present, he was sure, had he continued to practice."

Another pioneer physician in Sherburn was **Dr. George Harnden** who was born in Illinois in 1839. The oldest son of an old-time whaler, he also attended country school in Illinois.

Harnden and his two brothers came to Minnesota by covered wagon in 1873 and homesteaded claims east of Sherburn.

He acquired an interest in medicine as a result of the illness of his first wife when his family doctor gave him a medical book to study. He then went on to study at Wheaton College and the Homeopathic Medical School of Chicago. He received a diploma in 1884. After studying medicine in Chicago, he returned to Sherburn to practice. He later moved to Fairmont and practiced medicine until 1934.

Other pioneer doctors included:

- Dr. William H. Gough who was born in 1859 in Sioux City, Iowa, and attended medical school in St. Joseph, Missouri. He graduated in 1884. Gough entered private practice in Worthington in 1892 and moved to Sherburn in 1897. He moved to Granada to practice medicine in 1905.
- Dr. E.H. Foster who was a Sherburn doctor briefly in the 1880s.
- Dr. F.W. Weeks who practiced in Sherburn and Welcome in the 1890s.
- Dr. John Janss who practiced in Welcome for fifteen years from 1895 to 1910 before he moved to California.
- Dr. Gustav H. Luedtke who practiced medicine in Fairmont for many years beginning in 1899.
- Dr. Henry P. Johnson who practiced medicine in Fairmont from 1899 until 1935.
- Dr. Clarence C. Donaldson who was born in 1858 in Dundas, Minnesota. He attended Carleton College, studied medicine under a doctor in Northfield, attended lectures in Iowa City, Iowa, and graduated in 1887 from Western Reserve University in Cleveland, Ohio. He practiced medicine for a short time in Goodhue County and also in South Dakota. In 1890, he moved to Fairmont where he practiced for fifteen years. Donaldson was a big man, weighing over 300 pounds. He was very popular, made many friends, and had a large practice. He was also known as a great horse trader, a hobby which seemed to fit his personality. He left Fairmont and moved to Denver, Colorado, in 1905.
- Dr. Schafer who came to Center Chain in 1858.
- Dr. McDuff who served the Tenhassen area from 1862–1865, and
- Dr. Denton who was appointed county physician in 1865, the same year Dr. Orville Patterson Chubb came to Martin County.

In addition to sources already listed, information for this article also came from the May 20 and June 3,10 and 17, 1978, editions of the Sentinel, *the Martin County Centennial edition of* The Daily Sentinel, *and the Martin County Historical Society archives.*

Dead Man's Slough

The popular TV programs *Investigation Discovery, Forensic Files,* and *CSI* didn't exist in the 1800s, but if they had, Martin County's first recorded murder might have made an interesting story line. A body was found near Elm Creek.

It was August 1864 and Charles White, a trader from Yankton, South Dakota, was on a business trip traveling the Jackson Road, a well-traveled supply route through Martin County. White was on horseback and commanding a team of oxen en route from Yankton to Mankato. When he neared Twin Lakes, he left the oxen train to explore potentially shorter routes. In the meantime, his oxen team and teamsters went on to Mankato. They planned to wait for him to catch up with them there. However, after waiting for several days, they decided to continue their journey and returned to Yankton without him. They didn't know then that they would never see White again.

Death Mystery of 1864 Never Solved—Trader Slain and Robbed on Old Jackson Road—A. L. Ward Foreman of Coroner's Jury.

Headline Discussing the Cold Case of Charles White's Murder

White was described as being well-educated and a man of means. He had substantial supplies for his rather large train of twenty–four oxen, and he was a seasoned businessman in the transportation business. He was last seen alive in the vicinity of what was referred to as Dead Man's Slough located south of Monterey, now part of Trimont.

White's body, partially covered with water in a nearly dry slough, was found in November of that year by a trapper. Had it not been for a prairie fire burning the tall grass surrounding his body and the summer heat evaporating some of the water in the slough, his body might never have been discovered.

Due to the suspicious circumstances surrounding his death, the county board appointed A.L. Ward coroner and instructed him to impanel a jury and conduct an inquest. Members of that jury included J.B. Swearingen, W.W. Carrington, Giles Bartholomew, E.B. Hall, Henry Johnson, and Peter Dugaw.

The conclusion of their investigation coincided with the initial findings of the trapper. White's death was apparently caused by either a bullet or a blow to the side of his head. The body was decomposed to the point that a positive determination of exact cause of death was impossible. White had been carrying approximately $1,200 in cash when last seen; however, no money was found. In addition, the revolver and knives he was carrying were nowhere to be found. Although much of his clothing had been burned by the fire, a memorandum book was found in one of his pockets that had been left intact and other records found nearby helped to identify his remains.

Witness accounts given at the inquest showed he left the ox train in the morning of the August day on which he went missing. He had left on horseback and was noticeably under the influence of alcohol. He was next seen in the late afternoon of that same day in Fraser Township walking around a creek bottom. When approached by an individual at the scene, he waved the person off, took out his pocket book and appeared to be counting his money. He then continued walking westward. When last seen in the vicinity of Dead Man's Slough, he had no horse, and no trace was ever found of the animal.

When his wife was contacted in Yankton informing her of his demise, she showed no interest in having his body returned. Consequently, the body was buried near where it was found in an unmarked grave.

Thus, the first murder ever recorded in Martin County took place in August of 1864 and to this day remains unsolved. This crime will most likely never be considered in any cold case investigations, involve crime scene investigators, or be subject to forensic testing in an attempt to solve it. However, it provides a dramatic example of an unsolved crime committed in the early history of Martin County. Fortunately, the vast majority of those pioneering individuals settling Martin County in the 1800s made positive contributions to our local society. However, as is the case today, there remains that certain criminal element throughout society that must be constantly monitored and kept in check by the authorities, even in Martin County.

The story above is an account of the incident based upon the August 21, 1909, edition of the Martin County Independent.

The British Invasion

The British Are Coming

Before The Beatles but after the midnight ride of Paul Revere warning of their coming, another group of Brits called the English Colony played an important role in local history in the latter 1800s. They came to Martin County with a dream of becoming wealthy by growing beans. While experiencing numerous hardships, these folks made their mark on Martin County.

Connecticut lawyer Henry Shearman went on a hunting trip in Martin County in 1872. Being very impressed with the economic potential of the area, he purchased twenty-six acres of land five miles south of Fairmont for development as a model farm. He then went to England and founded the American Land Company for the sale of railroad lands in Martin County and southern Minnesota. Because England was beginning to experience a great depression in agriculture, Shearman also chose to advertise frontier farmland in America.

Being both resourceful and apparently somewhat of an entrepreneur, Shearman devised a plan to lure Britishers to Martin County. He published a pamphlet stating that investors could make their fortunes in a relatively short time by growing beans on Martin County farmland. He further stated that landowners could avoid physical labor by hiring all their work done by local residents, and that they could avoid the harsh Minnesota winters by returning to England for the social season each year. In addition, he also attempted to appeal to the English love of hunting by warning them in his pamphlet that they may well have to guard their crops from the abundance of wild animals and birds living in the Martin County area.

He began experimenting with bean crops on his model farm. Shortly thereafter, the first young English investors arrived in 1873, immediately buying land and planting beans in hopes of a quick fortune. Although Shearman's land prices were likely overpriced, they were still relatively cheap compared to land prices in England at that time. That year, they planted approximately 1,000 to 1,200 acres of beans around Fairmont in Tenhassen and Rolling Green Townships.

Most of these initial investors were recent college graduates, former military officers, clergymen, journalists, merchants, and policemen, all confident of creating a wealthy estate by raising beans. They were mostly gentlemen and brought with them their English customs and manners. None were experienced farmers.

Incidentally, one writer of the time deplored the fact that so many of the young Englishmen patronized the local saloons. He concluded that atmospheric conditions in this part of the world apparently enhanced the effects of alcohol on the British settlers to the region.

Locusts descended on Martin County in June of 1873, and in one day, they ate most of the crops. It was said that the grasshoppers came like a snowstorm, completely covering the ground.

The colonists replanted, but an early killing frost in October destroyed the second crop. Undaunted, they returned to England and recruited a large group of new investor–colonists to return the next spring.

In the spring of 1874, a new group of English colonists joined those from the previous year and hired the planting of beans on an even larger scale. However, during June the locusts hatched and once again destroyed the bean crop as well as other crops.

This plague continued for several years until, in 1877, Governor Pillsbury set aside a day of prayer and fasting. On that day, the grasshoppers flew away without depositing any of their eggs. The grasshopper plague had finally come to an end! The colonists again replanted, and this time they finally did harvest a crop in the fall.

From 1875 through 1878, more Englishmen joined the colony and faced the locust plague to varying degrees as well as partial crop failures due to the weather. Eventually, the financial losses accompanying this endeavor forced many of the English colonists to abandon their efforts to grow beans. This forced some to venture into other enterprises.

In 1877, three Englishmen developed a cooperative cheese factory in Fairmont. They encountered problems and sold the factory to a private owner who became quite successful at the business. Some attempted other business ventures, including a brewery, an ice house, a creamery, a hardware store, and a farm implement business. Others also had an interest in fine livestock, including racehorses and purebred cattle.

In that year, several English colonists became part owners in the Bank of Fairmont. Many of their countrymen soon became depositors. However, as a result of too much generosity and leniency to borrowers, as well as overextending themselves in financing the construction of a lavish building project, the Occidental Hotel, the bank failed in 1879. There were heavy colonist losses, and the bank was eventually absorbed by the rival Martin County Bank.

Despite numerous setbacks, the colony continued to expand. An exact number will probably never be known; the 1880 census indicates there were 219 Englishmen in Martin County. However, it is unclear as to how many of this number were members of Shearman's colony. The most obvious legacy of the colony was the small group of English settlers who remained around the Fairmont area.

Percy Wollaston was the premier colonist businessman of his time. He operated a 460–acre farm, a general store, a wind-powered grist mill, and the Merchants and Farmers Bank in Fairmont until he moved to British Columbia in about 1910. Although losing his 400–acre farm to the locust infestation, Cecil Sharpe remained in Fairmont where he was cashier at Merchant and Farmers Bank, which was owned by his father-in-law, Wollaston. Federick Wherland and his large family enjoyed a comfortable living on his 160–acre Belvedere Farm near Pierce Lake. Frederick A.B. Peterson, discouraged with farming, became cashier and director of the Martin County Bank, treasurer of the Fairmont Building and Loan Association, and an officer of several other organizations. The Archer-Burtons and their descendants remained in the area working at various jobs in or near Fairmont. Others who remained in the area included Harry M. Serle, W.M. Hay, Joseph Ramsdale, H.W. Sinclair, K. ff. Bellairs, A.G.T. Broum, and C.P. Cunningham.

During that time period, the influx of the English Colony's cash positively impacted the local economy through employment and spending. The colonists built a number of fine houses and buildings which were later used by local residents. The Englishmen's efforts in raising sheep may well have encouraged other farmers to acquire small flocks in later years, and Wollaston's enterprises provided services to local residents for some years after the colony's decline.

Eventually, the largest group of colonists returned to England. A second group settled in various major cities in the United States. A third group emigrated to Canada, and the smallest group remained in Fairmont where they would become merchants, bankers, restaurant owners, realtors, tradesman, and local politicians. The efforts and effects of that early group of English settlers undoubtedly shaped the direction of Martin County in those early years, and played both a colorful and significant role in the development of local history.

Sources for this included The Daily Sentinel, *Martin County Centennial edition, May 10, 1958, page 2, and September 20, 1958, page 15.*

Percy Wollaston

Considered to be the leader of the English Colony, Percy Wollaston was an early settler in Martin County who became Fairmont's first mayor and was also involved in a number of entrepreneurial endeavors in Fairmont and Martin County.

Percy Wollaston

Wollaston was born in Leeds, England, in 1825. In 1848, he married Catherine Mossop and shortly thereafter moved to the United States. They lived briefly in N Ontario, Canada, where he operated a flour mill. With the exception of one child born in Canada, all Wollaston's children were born and educated in England.

The Wollastons moved back to England in 1851, at which time he became involved in the shipping business.

Then, in 1876, they moved back to the United States and to Fairmont. Wollaston, his wife, and his thirteen children lived on Homewood Drive in Fairmont in a house built that year and described as a sixteen-room English mansion. At one time, it was considered the finest house in Fairmont.

Wollaston built a mercantile store at North Avenue and Second Street at a time when there were very few buildings in town. He continued in that business until 1891. Meanwhile, he established the Merchants and Farmers Bank in 1882, built a flour mill operated by a sixty-foot wind wheel, and was involved in farming, as he owned 460 acres of land. He is also credited with founding the Episcopal church in Fairmont.

Wollaston left Fairmont in 1896 and moved to Victoria, British Columbia, where he passed away on June 30, 1909. He was remembered as a good businessman who was punctual and orderly in his business matters and his private life as well.

He was especially remembered for his resolve involving the failure of the Merchants and Farmers Bank, of which he was the largest stockholder. It was said that he gave up all his personal property, even his home, in his old age so that all of his creditors would be fully compensated. In his July 9, 1909, obituary, the *Martin County Sentinel* said, "The world is better and happier for the possession of such men, and when they are gone there is deep sorrow and regret felt by all who knew them." Perhaps some of the titans of business and industry in today's world would do well to take a lesson from the life of Percy Wollaston, undoubtedly a man of conviction, honor, and integrity.

Captain Frederick Wherland

What's the weather going to be like tomorrow? The answer to this question is something we often take for granted today and often have predicted for us (whether accurately or no) by various means from the Weather Channel to computerized reports from around the globe.

Recording the weather in the early days of Martin County was one Captain Frederick Wherland, an English sea captain who was born in Ireland. In 1878, he settled in a rural home on Pierce Lake in Rolling Green Township because of his love of water. The Wherland home was like a typical English Colony rural mansion of that time period.

Captain Frederick Wherland

Captain Wherland was indeed a ship's captain. As master of his ship, he had varied experiences not only as the ship's commander, but also as its surgeon and chaplain. In fact, several members of his large family were born at sea. His experiences on the high seas carried him to such places as the Cape of Good Hope, and the ports of India, Australia, the Orient, and the American Pacific Coast.

The retired sea captain became Martin County's first volunteer weather observer. He brought with him a rain gauge, a thermometer, and an expensive barometer, which he had used previously in sailing the seas. Wherland took daily readings of the temperature at morning, noon, and night; he also recorded barometric pressure and measured precipitation. He then sent all original records to the weather bureau in Washington, D.C. Copies were also kept for local records. The colorful, retired sea captain diligently kept these weather records until his death in 1910.

Following Captain Wherland's death, James Lamperd, also of English ancestry, took over his work as a volunteer weather observer. Lamperd and his wife set up a weather station on their farm in Rolling Green Township, very near the Wherland estate. The Lamperd's telephone number, 1871, was well known to county residents and could be called anytime, day or night, to get the official temperature as well as precipitation amounts. The Lamperds continued their weather observances, without pay and with little public recognition, until the death of Mr. Lamperd. Eventually, age and failing health forced Mrs. Lamperd to give up her work to the Water and Light Department of Fairmont.

Two of Captain Wherland's daughters married and lived in Fairmont until their deaths. They were Sally, who at the age of sixteen eloped with Lenny Burton, and Susan, who married Otto Gimm. Another of his children, Frank, was at one time a postmaster in Welcome.

On display in the Pioneer Museum is an ancient grandfather clock that was built about 1780 by Captain Wherland's grandfather for his estate in Cork, Ireland. The twelve-foot tall clock was originally willed to Captain Wherland by a relative and shipped to America in 1900. It stood at Belvidere, the Wherland's Pierce Lake home, until the home was sold in 1912. The clock was then passed on to a number of heirs until it reached its final stop at the Pioneer Museum in 1939. A fire in the 1890s destroyed much of the Wherland's furnishings and likely damaged the clock, which was later restored by J.A. Nightingale in 1957.

Additional items displayed from the Wherland collection at the Pioneer Museum include the Tudor Ship's Log of Liverpool, England, Captain Wherland's hat, his portable writing desk, his barometer used for weather recordings, a picture of the ship *Galatea* in dry dock in London, and pictures of himself, his wife, and his two daughters.

Weather prediction, weather observation, recording of weather data, and other meteorological techniques have advanced greatly from Captain Wherland's time. However, the retired English sea captain will be remembered as a pioneer in the field and a significant part of Martin County history.

Sources for this included The Daily Sentinel, *Martin County Centennial edition September 20, 1958, page 14 and the* Martin County Sentinel, *September 7, 1910.*

Who Was Lenny Burton?

Lenny Burton, firm in his belief of the futility of his life, was one of the more colorful characters in local history. To get to Martin County, he traveled many miles from a castle on the Rhine to a log cabin here. Scion of an ancient British family, the Archer-Burtons, and a black sheep of his other relatives, Burton would become register of deeds in Martin County and a prominent citizen of this area.

Lenny Burton

His parents were British aristocrats living in Germany. His father was a high sheriff of Hampshire in 1847, and his Uncle James was killed in the Charge of the Light Brigade, made famous by Tennyson. His lineage also traces back to Robert Bruce, King of Scotland, and Robert South, a famous English divine who served as chaplain to King Charles II.

He spent his infancy in Coblenz on the Rhine, at Castle Lehneck on the Rhine, while his older brothers and sisters were living in England in the family home there.

When Burton was twelve years old, his parents sent him to Baden-Baden to a school where cadets for the German army were trained. While there, he was a schoolmate of

William Hohenzollern, later to be Kaiser Wilhelm of Germany. Burton was unsuccessful in school and decided to join the navy. However, when he went back to England for a visit, he became so seasick that he decided the navy was no longer an option.

Burton's tendencies to spend time playing with the "ragamuffins" in the streets of Coblenz coupled with his failures in school led his parents to send him off alone to the new world at the age of fifteen to join his two brothers who had gone before him.

He sailed from Liverpool. When Burton arrived in Fairmont, he described a tiny town of not more than 100 inhabitants, a few old shacks, three feet of mud and billions of flies and mosquitoes. But, the first thing he heard about was the arrival of a British sea captain, Frederick Wherland, who had arrived with his six sons and the most beautiful daughter any of the settlers had seen. Lenny and the captain's daughter would eventually marry.

Burton arrived in 1876, the year of the grasshopper plague in Minnesota. He joined his brothers and began buying land. At the age of sixteen, he was a big landowner, although he knew virtually nothing about farming or livestock. Eventually, of the 400 Englishmen who had settled in the area since 1873, nearly all had left, including his brothers. However, Burton stayed, partly as a result of his marriage to Sally Wherland.

Burton and Sally began their lives together by running away to be married by a justice of the peace in Fairmont. They went on farming together and rode horseback to town as they had no wagon. At the outset, Burton states, "Everything looked bright. She was so lovely, so beautiful, so clever, so good to me, such a wonderful mother. Her beauty was the talk of the whole county—the talk of all. We were a pair of kids."

However, being inexperienced, many took advantage of them. He started out with three farms and ended up broke, owning no land, and having five children to support. He went on to try horse trading and fur trapping but only acquired the reputation of being a good loser.

He returned to England in 1883, but the call of the west remained within him, and he returned to Minnesota again at the age of twenty-three. The money he inherited from his family was quickly gone. He worked at anything he could, including showing animals at the fair, raising chickens and keeping a zoo, The Burton Zoo, on the west bank of George Lake.

In 1909, he filed for the office of register of deeds for the first time. Although never embarking on a consistent campaign, he kept after the office for eighteen years, finally being elected in 1927 by a large majority of the voters. He was perhaps best known in later years for this position.

Fairmont Daily Sentinel editor Frank A. Day wrote of Burton, "It is not an extravagant statement to say that he has been an ideal husband, father, son and citizen all the days of his life. We do not know how to frame words to pay a man a higher compliment than is included in that sentence. Our long-time neighbor is a gentleman, a student, a scholar, a man who lives up to his highest lights and gets all the light he can. The nice thing about his is the spirit of contentment that rules his life and habits."

Yet, on Lenny Burton's letterhead is inscribed, "A Life Wasted."

Burton, a sixty-one-year beloved resident of Martin County, passed away in 1937 at the age of 76.

Sources for this included the Fairmont Daily Sentinel, *September 20, 1937 and October 23, 1940;* The Daily Sentinel, *Martin County Centennial edition, May 10, 1958, page 2; and* A History of Martin County.

Harry M. Serle

Harry Serle

Harry M. Serle, a resident of Fairmont for thirty-five years, was known as a public-spirited citizen. He was a city councilman and mayor and prominent in business affairs, and it was said he deserved greater credit than any other individual in the development of municipal improvements.

Serle was born in India in 1855 and educated in England. At the age of twelve, he began an active career at sea. In 1876, he came to America and located in Decorah, Iowa. One year later, he joined the English Colony and came to Fairmont.

He spent his first year in Martin County driving a stage from Fairmont to Winnebago. He then spent a year in railroading and also farmed in Martin County up until 1883. Later, he started an ice business which developed into a monopoly in Fairmont for some thirty years. His ice houses were located on the east bank of Budd Lake and had a capacity of 3,600 tons. He used horse-drawn delivery wagons in his business.

Serle was perhaps best known to Fairmont citizens for his efficient public service. In 1883, he organized the fire department in Fairmont. It was said that, due to his public spiritedness and energy, he developed the department into one of the most efficient in the state for towns of its size. Serle served as the chief of Fairmont's fire department, which at that time had forty-nine regular members, a team and combination wagon with a thirty-five-gallon chemical tank, 1,200 feet of hose, a Seagrave hook and ladder truck, and normal water pressure of eighty pounds with the possibility of 175 pounds when necessary. The state Firemen's Convention was held in Fairmont in 1914, quite possibly due to Serle's efforts on the local fire department.

In 1913, Serle was elected mayor of Fairmont for a term of two years. He had previously served on the city council for ten years and had also served as a voluntary deputy game warden. Serle, a Democrat, was a member of numerous clubs and organizations in the community.

He was married to Mary Goldsmith, and they had two daughters. The last local resident of the English Colony days, he passed away in 1940. He was remembered as one of Fairmont's best loved citizens.

Sources for this story included the History of Martin County Fire Departments *scrapbook at MCHS.*

The Fairmont Brewery

Although Fairmont was considered a temperance stronghold in the 1870s, it ironically became the home of a brewery. During the latter part of the nineteenth century, English settlers in the area made every attempt to maintain the "upper-class" customs from their homeland, including horse racing and boating.

Then Gideon Smales, apparently an industrious individual, arrived in Fairmont in 1877 to join his brother. Smales was certain he could profit from the English settlers through his art of brewing ale and porter, claiming that these libations were highly recommended by physicians as containing strengthening and medicinal properties, according to Doug Hoverson's *Land of Amber Waters.*

Smales' initial brewery site was a building he had purchased on the corner of North Avenue and Third Street, previously the location of a horse livery. By early 1878, Smales was advertising pure English ales and porter in kegs or bottles at what he considered reasonable rates.

In August of 1878, he felt business was brisk enough to justify construction of a new brewery at the foot of Main Street. That new facility included a large cellar, referred to as "an eighteen hundred dollar hole," Hoverson said. Smales' further expansions included an ice house and a bottling house. In all, Smales had invested approximately $1,700 in brewery improvements and additional buildings.

Regretfully, his brewery expansion may have developed a bit too rapidly. Smales, a stockholder in the Bank of Fairmont when it failed in 1879, also had an overdraft of nearly $1,700 at that time. That overdraft was deemed a contributing factor to the bank's failure. Interestingly, at the sheriff's sale held in 1879 to settle the bank's accounts, the brewery property seemed to attract the most active bidding. Consequently, the short-lived history of an active brewery in Fairmont came to a rather abrupt and tumultuous end.

Now, one might wonder what became of the actual physical structure housing the brewery. According to Claude Swanson in an article from the November 28, 1961, edition of *The Sentinel,* it was torn down in 1900 by Fairmont contractor George Hengel. Hengel described the layout of the brewery as being parallel to the lake on the northeast shore of Lake Sisseton. He also said that there were two caves, one at about lake level and the other above it. The entrances to the caves were said to be constructed of stone. Perhaps conservation was a priority at that time as the lumber salvaged from the demolition of the brewery was used to construct three houses on South Main Street.

The Mansion in the Country

The term "mansion" typically brings to mind a large, impressive, stately and opulent residence owned by the affluent and likely located within a city. Familiar examples might include the Glensheen Mansion in Duluth, the Hubbard House in Mankato, the James J. Hill House and the Alexander Ramsey House in the Twin Cities, and locally, the Wohlhueter Mansion in Fairmont. However, Martin County is the home to another, albeit lesser known, mansion located in Section 34 of Fraser Township.

This mansion was built by Charles Anthony, a highly esteemed citizen of Martin County of his era. He also happened to be a first cousin to Susan B. Anthony, the American social reformer and feminist who played a significant role in the women's suffrage movement.

It was apparently started in 1880 and completed in 1886. It was originally comprised of eighteen large rooms with high ceilings, an English style that also included a basement, two full stories, and a large attic. A house of this magnitude obviously took a number of years to complete, especially considering the time period in which it was built.

It had a full basement made of Kasota stone that included the bases for the three fireplaces that were located on the first floor. All of the basement windows had iron bars covering the windows. A hand-operated water pressure system and tank was also located in the basement. Below ground level, but not a part of the basement, was a large cistern for the collection of rain water that was routed there by gutters and down spouts. This "soft water" was used for washing clothes and bathing. At one time, an office was also located in the basement.

The first floor had a number of open porches by various outdoor entry areas into the mansion. Above these ground floor porches were porches for the second story. There were three fireplaces on the first floor, a large kitchen, a sink for washing dishes and a sink for hand washing, both having hot and cold running water. Next to the kitchen was a large pantry with counters, cupboards for storage and bins for flour and sugar.

Also located on this floor was an interesting room called the Ice Room. This room was long and narrow with thick, tin-lined interior and exterior walls that were filled with sawdust which served as insulation. It was not unlike a walk-in refrigerator and was used to store milk, butter, meat, and other perishables.

In addition, the first floor had a dining room, a parlor, and a stairway going up to the second floor. Two of the three fireplaces were located in this area, one in the dining room and another in the open stairway area. The master bedroom, located off the dining room, was quite large with an adjacent small bathroom containing a sink and toilet. Next to this room was another large room with sliding doors that incorporated the third fireplace.

The second floor was comprised of six bedrooms, a maid's quarters, and a back stairway leading down to the kitchen on the first floor. This floor also had a complete bathroom with sinks, a bath tub with hot and cold running water, and a flushing toilet. A large foyer was located at the top of the second floor open stairway.

The attic was large and unique in that there was a trap door to the flat part of the roof above. That part of the roof was enclosed with a wooden railing known as the "widow's walk," referring to where English wives who lived by the sea would watch for their husbands' ships returning home.

The mansion's grounds had an underground silo measuring fourteen by twenty feet that served as a cesspool for the collection of drainage from sinks and toilets. It held an estimated 92,000 gallons of wastewater and sewage.

The outbuildings on the grounds, modern for that era, included a very large barn, a chicken house, a corn crib, and a granary that had its own power supply. The lane was lined with elm trees, and there was a large walnut grove on the farm as well. The farm had a gravity-flow water system supplying well water to the house and outbuildings and most likely utilized gas lamps for lighting.

Over time, the farm passed through a number of owners and was eventually purchased by Henry Bents in 1916 and owned by his family until 2006. The building site was sold in 2006; however, the land is still owned by local resident Kenneth Bents.

This mansion exemplified an elegant and unique structure, having modern conveniences that were well ahead of its time. Although the mansion still stands today, it has been modified, remodeled, and added to over the years. Consequently, although still standing, it is far from its original condition.

I would like to thank Marlen Bents of Ceylon, the only person born in that old mansion, for his efforts in researching, documenting, and providing the basis of this historical account. Without the efforts of people like Mr. Bents, local history could easily slip into the past unnoticed by current generations and be therefore lost forever.

The Beginnings of Martin County

Fairmont's Lakes

Fairmont is well known as the City of Lakes for its chain of five lakes running north and south. It's attractive to visitors, businesses, recreationists, and those new to town. However, what is really known about the lakes beyond their picturesque beauty and leisure time activities? The following is a brief historical account about each of the five lakes based primarily on Arthur Nelson's book *Know Your Own County.*

The landscape of Martin County, including the notable chain of lakes, is thought to have been mostly a consequence of the last glacial period. As a result of glacial melting over long periods of time, the lakes in Martin County were formed.

Prior to 1860, Amber Lake was quite commonly called Bardwell Lake and covered about 175 acres. It was named after George Bardwell, a very early settler at the southwest corner of the lake. Then, in 1860, Ebeneezer Beers named it Amber Lake after his hometown of Amber, New York. Amber Post Office was established in 1867 in the home of George Bardwell and operated until he and his family moved away in 1879. Amber Lake covers approximately 180 acres.

Budd Lake was named in memory of William Hampton Budd, one of Martin County's most prominent settlers. Nelson's book said that Budd Lake covers close to 200 acres and is one of the deepest lakes in the chain. Budd was the first permanent settler in Fairmont, coming to Martin County on July 1, 1856.

George Lake or, as Nelson called it, Lake George covers about eighty acres and was named in the first plat of Fairmont in honor of George Tanner. His home in 1864 was at the north end of the lake. Tanner was an important figure in community affairs during his lifetime.

Hall Lake was named in honor of E. Banks Hall, also one of the first settlers in Martin County. It is the largest lake, covering approximately 500 acres. Hall came to Martin County less than four months after the county's first settler. Consequently, he had the pick of the choicest locations and wisely elected to stake a claim on the east shore of Hall Lake. Interlaken Park was at one time located at the south end of Hall.

When Father Joseph Nicollet came through the area now known as Martin County in the early 1800s, he found the Sisseton Sioux to be the only inhabitants. In mapping the region, he referred to this area as "Sisseton Country." It appears that the name Lake Sisseton, or Sisseton Lake as Nelson called it, relates back to Nicollet's designation. The last of the Sisseton villages, according to Nelson, was in the area of the lake as late as 1860. Lake Sisseton, although a smaller lake covering about 140 acres, has a prominent location near the older business district of Fairmont. Incidentally, in the first plat made of Fairmont in 1858, the surveyor called the lake Corrib; however, the name never became commonly used.

In 1891, Fairmont citizens became worried about the lakes. Their concern apparently centered on the lake levels. According to written accounts, County Surveyor Montgomery and Lawyer Lamb of the Albion Hall Committee surveyed and tested the levels of Hall and Budd Lake in June of 1891. Their findings reflected the difference in lake levels were two feet and one inch. To put the lakes on equal levels, they would have to lower Hall Lake by ten to eleven inches. Amber Lake did not receive mention. According to the written report, Amber Lake was considered, in those days, "way out tohellandgone—almost to Iowa."

What Was the Swamp Angel?

The earliest settlers of Martin County and southern Minnesota found thousands of sloughs and an abundance of lakes when they arrived, many of which have since disappeared. Much of the disappearance can be attributed to Harry Keck who organized a bull-ditching outfit in the 1880s. The goal of this bull-ditching process was to provide more fertile, crop-producing soil in the area by draining sloughs and lakes for farming.

Keck was involved with his ditching operations, in addition to his farm work, for over 30 years. He trained and used more than 40 bulls at times to pull the huge ditching machine, which became known well beyond Martin County's borders as the "Swamp Angel."

Swamp Angel

Since there were no motels or other temporary housing for his crew to stay in while on the job, Keck built bunkhouses and fitted them with bunks and locker spaces. He then mounted these bunkhouses on wagons and carried them to wherever his work called. The crew, traveling the dusty, narrow, pioneer paths of that time period, made a fascinating scene, which often stretched over a quarter-mile long. The drivers would carry long poles with attached leather thongs while walking at spaced intervals, directing the bulls as they made their way down the narrow paths to their next job.

Also included with the crew was a cook shack which was fitted with a stove and cooking utensils. The drivers and other members of the crew usually ate outdoors or, in the case of bad weather, in a large tent which served as their dining hall. Keck bought groceries and meat for the crew; however, the farmers employing the services of the bull-ditchers were expected to provide oats, corn, and hay for the bulls. In addition, the farmers were sometimes asked to allow grazing privileges for the animals.

The cost of the ditch depended upon a number of variables that included the size, width, depth, and distance traveled. The charge was on a per rod basis.

The drivers were described as tall, lean, rugged individuals who frequently risked their lives in wading through water up to their chins while driving the bulls through sloughs or lakes. The bulls could swim in spite of their yokes and, in some instances of deep water, the drivers were forced to climb on the bulls backs and crack their whips from that vantage point.

Eventually, as land became more valuable, farmers became much less likely to use the open ditch. In addition, the advent of drain tile which provided effective drainage without wasting the land associated with ditching was another blow to the bull-ditching business.

Finally, Keck quit the ditching business and sold his Swamp Angel equipment at auction on March 7, 1911.

Sources included The Daily Sentinel, *Martin County Centennial edition, June 14, 1958, page 5; and the* Minneapolis Sunday Tribune, *March 15, 1959.*

The Jackson Road

Today's travelers, whether for business or pleasure, have countless routes to consider in reaching their destinations. Travel decisions can be based upon the quickest, the shortest, the least congested, or the most scenic, and those decisions are frequently determined by global positioning navigation systems. However, in the 1850s, travel options were not that abundant and were determined by considerably different aspects. GPS was not an option.

The 1850s in Martin County saw the development of a highway that, at that time, could arguably rival today's Interstate 90 in terms of importance to the region. It did not, however, in any way physically resemble I-90.

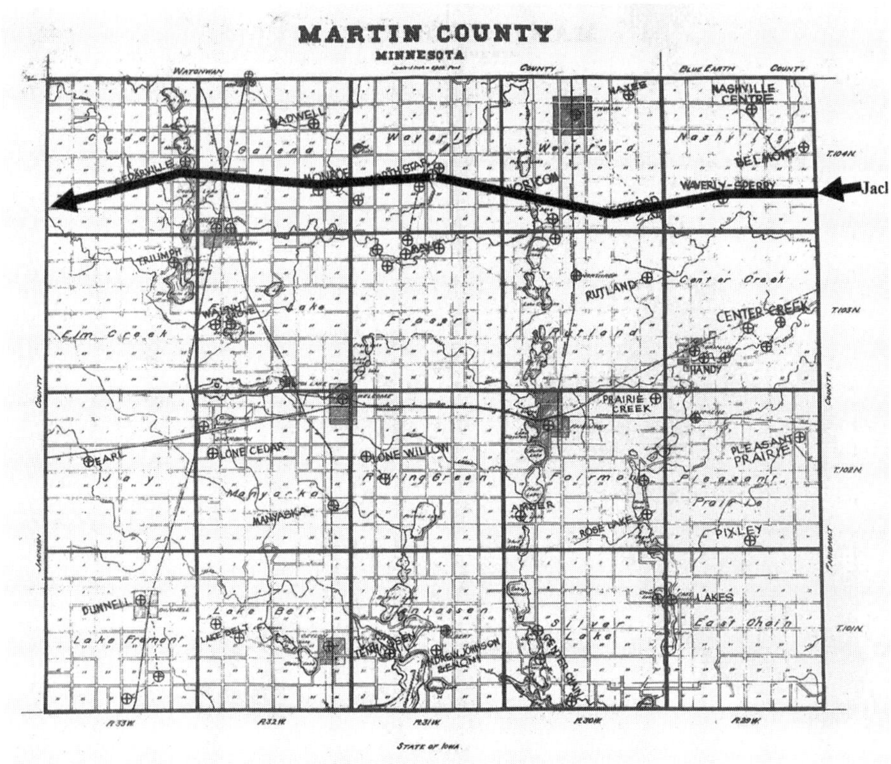

Jackson Road

The Jackson Road was established and marked by the government as the official route to the settlement on the Des Moines River called Springfield, whose name was later changed to Jackson. The road stretched from Winnebago near the Blue Earth River to Jackson near the Des Moines River.

The Jackson Road was used by stagecoaches to carry mail to the post offices along the way in making their weekly trips. Post offices being served at one time included Waverly, Westford, Horicon, North Star, Monroe, and Cedarville in Martin County. This route was also used by soldiers carrying supplies on wagon trains, settlers with ox drawn wagons, trappers, fur traders, and even Native Americans.

The exact course of the Jackson Road was quite fluid as it ran without regard to section lines or borders. It would generally follow the path of least resistance in terms of terrain, rainfall, and mode of travel being utilized. Low-lying areas were frequently avoided due to flooding, and the exact path would also change as a result of rural post offices relocating.

This "self-styled" highway of the 1850s undoubtedly saw thousands of hardy pioneers traveling west in search of a better tomorrow. Although called the Jackson Road, as indicated on the map from *Martin County Postmasters and Post Offices,* authored by

Judge Julius E. Haycraft, there was more than one account as to its actual path. Its exact path undoubtedly varied greatly as a result of many diverse changes throughout the course of its existence.

Sources for this story included MCHS History File 652.

Martin County's Second City

Back on June 22nd, 1966, then-*Sentinel* editor Claude Swanson wrote an article entitled "Martin County's Second City Lies in Silence." The title of the article was quite fascinating as one might wonder just exactly what he meant.

In the introduction to his article, Swanson said, "Ask any citizen to name Martin County's 'second city' in population and, chances are, not one in a hundred can give the correct answer. Not by several thousand." Swanson cited the census taken in 1960 indicated that Fairmont ranked first in population, Truman was second, and Sherburn ranked third.

From there, he included some population statistics. "Nowhere in the official federal census is Martin County's 'second city' mentioned, although, at the time it had more than 6,000 inhabitants, and in point of age, it is almost as old as Fairmont." Okay, that makes Martin County's "second city" rank in population second only to Fairmont.

He went on to provide some specific clues. "Martin County's 'second city' is unique in several respects. The lots are of equal size. Its inhabitants constantly face east. Its inhabitants are quiet and peaceful. They are at rest. Eternal rest, for they comprise the population of our 'Silent City' dating back to November 14, 1871, and known ever since as 'Lakeside' Cemetery." That description, of course, clearly identified what Swanson meant by Martin County's Second City, situated on fifty-eight acres on the shores of George Lake in Fairmont.

Swanson then went on to relate some early history of Fairmont, indicating that there appeared to be no record of where the deceased were buried in those very early years of Martin County history. However, he felt it reasonably safe to believe that internment was probably made at Lakeside Cemetery. The first recorded burial on this site, December 6, 1868, was a child named Carrie Waterman. George Tanner, the homestead owner of the property, had given her father permission to bury his daughter there. Five days later, former Canadian Louis LaBoute, aged 102, was buried there. Shortly after, a Mr. Howell buried his infant child at the site.

The history of the Lakeside Cemetery Association dates back to November 14, 1871, when it had its beginning at a meeting in E.W. Bird's drugstore. There appear to be no records before or after that time until November 10, 1926, although hundreds of burials were made there in the intervening years, according to Swanson's article.

Swanson's commentary goes on to state that the original tract of land was comprised of fifty-eight acres purchased from C.F. Livermore for $4,300. Of this amount, $3,300 was raised from house-to-house canvassing, and Livermore paid the final $1,000. The canvassers were headed by William H. Hay, the Fairmont theater man. Others of historical significance who participated in the campaign were H.H. Canright, G.T. Houseman, and Frank Day.

On November 10, 1926, the board reorganized at a meeting of five Fairmont citizens that included Miss Minnie Bird, A.R. Fancher, Elmore Houghtaling, Susanna Krahmer, and Henry G. Sydow. Many of these names are also recognizable in terms of their historical significance to this area as well.

The American Legion, Veterans of Foreign Wars, Disabled American Veterans, and the Vietnam Veterans built Lakeside Veterans Memorial in 1987. The upkeep of the memorial and flags is maintained by these organizations.

Each Memorial Day, morning services are held here following a parade from Veterans Park in downtown Fairmont to the cemetery by the service organizations, Fairmont High School Band, Girl Scouts, Boy Scouts, and other participants.

Swanson's article from 1966 was both interesting and informative. He was able to essentially capture the reader's interest with his headline, while gradually unraveling his story of Fairmont's "Second City" from both current and historical perspectives.

Additional information for this article came from Lakeside Cemetery's now defunct website.

Sherburn

The city of Sherburn is typical of many small communities throughout the Midwest and America, yet its history is unique.

In all probability, Sherburn's geographic location dates back to the mid-1860s. At that time, George Archer had a sod tavern on the north banks of what was then Lake Manyaska, located just south of Sherburn. Marked by a lone cedar tree, pioneer travelers used it as a rest stop as they traveled from Fairmont to Jackson. Soon there were pioneer settlers and a post office. As stage coaches from Fairmont to Jackson and St. James to Estherville crossed the area, it was concluded that there was a definite need for a settlement.

The mid-to-late 1870s witnessed the arrival of many settlers to Martin County, primarily resulting from the growth of the railroad involving Winnebago City and Fairmont. A company called Cargill, Bassett, and Hunting from La Crosse, Wisconsin, anticipated the railroad expanding west of Fairmont and, consequently, bought land in the area. Railroad engineers were at that time limited to a maximum of twelve to fifteen miles between water stops, so that was apparently the determining factor for the location of the Sherburn railroad station.

Several names were originally considered for the town site. Those suggested included Lone Cedar, Huntington, and Vestal. However, when the Southern Minnesota Railroad came through in October of 1878, the name Sherburne was accepted in honor of Sherburne S. Merrill, general manager of the Chicago, Milwaukee and St. Paul Railroad. Incidentally, the town of Merrill, Wisconsin, was also named for this man. With the railroad's influence on the area, Sherburn's growth by 1879 had grown to fifteen buildings with a total value of approximately $8,000.

Sherburn 1913

Sherburn was not without its share of excitement in its formative years. It was the site of one of the first, and deadliest, bank robberies in Martin County's history when the Bank of Sherburn was robbed in October of 1896 by two brothers. [See story on page 248.]

In 1920, several Sherburn businessmen organized the Fox Lake Park Company, issuing and selling stock to those interested in the development of the area. Much of the land along the lake was platted into lots, a dance pavilion was built, and playground equipment and picnic tables were purchased. In addition, a bath house, a diving tower, a toboggan slide, and fishing piers were also constructed. Later, a tennis court and a baseball diamond, including grandstands, were added.

Then, in 1932, the Fox Lake Golf Club was organized by ten businessmen. It started as a three-hole course, expanded to six holes, and finally became a nine-hole course. However, the Fox Lake Park Company was eventually liquidated in 1944, and the dance pavilion and park area not owned by individuals was sold. The Fox Lake Golf Club purchased the land where the golf course was located.

Sherburn's history includes a dream that all communities share but most fail to accomplish. That dream, winning a Minnesota state high school basketball championship, was accomplished by the 1970 Sherburn Raiders high school basketball team during a time when only one state basketball champion was crowned. What followed were parades and praise for the champs as they returned to their jubilant hometown of Sherburn. [For more information on this victory, turn to page 289.]

The 1979 Sherburn centennial book, A Centennial History of Sherburn, *was the primary resource for this article.*

Imogene

Imogene is a small community located approximately six miles east of Fairmont. Like all small towns in America, it has a history, a story to tell. Yet, many of us probably know very little about this tiny community. Although it's been in existence over 100 years, few of us are aware of what Imogene has added to the rich history of Martin County.

Imogene Train Depot Circa 1901

According to Minnesota Place Names, a project of the Minnesota Historical Society, Imogene was named after the daughter of Cymbeline in one of Shakespeare's plays. It was first platted in 1899 under the name Cardona; however, residents were said to have disliked the Spanish name.

Another theory on Imogene's naming was that it was named after a little girl named Imogene who had drowned in Imogene Lake. Yet another theory was that it was named by a young man with affection for a certain young lady named "Emogene," and yet another was that the name was changed from Cardona to Imogene as a result of the Northwestern Railway Line having another town named Cardona on its route.

Imogene's population was twenty-one in 1901, growing to ninety-one in 1939. However, by its centennial year of 2001, its population had dwindled back to the 1901 level of twenty-one.

Businesses in Imogene's early history included a saloon that eventually became a store, a stockyard, a water tower, an elevator, a train depot, a blacksmith shop, a barbershop, and a lumberyard. It was at one time a significant marketing location for grain and livestock due to its proximity so livestock owners could easily drive their cattle and hogs to the railroad and ship them to St. Paul and Chicago markets. Other businesses in Imogene included Blachowske Trucking, Schrock Fertilizer Plant, and R&R Rentals. It even had a post office.

In 1947, Roy and Ursula "Tootie" Loper opened Roy's Café. They sold gasoline, food, and grocery items in addition to lunches in the restaurant. The business expanded and was especially popular when Interstate 90 was being developed as the construction crews would stop for lunches and dinners. According to *A Century of Memories*, the Imogene Centennial book, "Tootie handled all the cooking by herself, with Roy entertaining the customers and farmers with many card games which lasted into the late evening hours." The business was eventually renamed The Cozy Inn and remained a popular place for locals and those passing by as well.

The Imogene Elevator was Imogene's longest running business, being in existence for ninety-nine years. Although there is no recorded information, most sources indicate that the elevator was built in 1901. The earliest record of ownership was the Nye Schneider Fowler Company on May 25, 1903.

The elevator, considered very active and competitive, was sold to William Barrett in 1937 and was named the Imogene Elevator. After owning it for a short time, Barrett sold it to Michael J. Garry in 1939. Garry grew up in Pleasant Prairie Township, graduating in 1898 from eighth grade in Fairmont at the age of 21. While attending school, Garry worked for Frank Day of the *Sentinel*. His job involved meeting all the trains and interviewing the people leaving from and arriving in Fairmont. He then brought this information back to Day for the newspaper.

Garry, who loaded the first box car of grain from Imogene, made many improvements and additions, including the erection of three large grain storage houses. He renamed it the Garry Elevator. Then, in 1950, Garry sold the business to his son, Michael G. Garry. The Garry Elevator continued to prosper. Michael G. owned the elevator for many years, and he eventually sold it in 1987 to a group of buyers. It was then again renamed the Imogene Elevator, and it conducted business until closing in 2000.

Perhaps one of the more interesting and newsworthy events to take place in Imogene happened in 1950. This involved a three-year-old boy who was trapped in a narrow, ten-foot-deep earthen well for more than three hours before Fairmont firemen and other volunteers were finally successful in digging him out.

The boy and a friend were playing in the backyard of the boy's home when they discovered a large box near one end of the garden. The youngsters, being inquisitive, pushed the box away which revealed a hole approximately a foot wide. Then, the unthinkable happened; the boy accidentally slipped and fell feet first into the hole. He was trapped and unable to free himself. Firemen were called at 12:30 p.m., and arrived shortly thereafter. Oxygen was piped down to the youngster through a rubber hose, but the space was so narrow that there wasn't enough room for the hose to reach his head. By 2:30 p.m., digging had reached a depth of nine feet, parallel to the boy's head, in what was described as hard, concrete like earth. Slowly, water was beginning to seep through the dirt and there was a very real concern that the old well might collapse, thereby burying the youngster alive. Fortunately, by 2:45 p.m. he was finally pulled up through the murky abyss by rescuers, and then rushed by ambulance to the Fairmont Hospital where he was treated for shock and then released. The youngster had no serious injuries and eventually grew up to become Fairmont's city administrator Jim Zarling.

Sources for this story included A Century of Memories *and the August 19, 1950,* The Daily Sentinel.

Historical Highlights of Truman

In about 1899, Henry Brownlee declared, "Truman is going to be the best of any of the new railroad towns in Martin County!"

The emergence of the railroad in the later 1800s served as the lifeblood of many communities throughout America, including those located in Martin County. The railroad and the Jackson Road were both instrumental to some degree in the development of Westford Township and the city of Truman.

Truman Main Street Circa 1914

How the town of Truman got its name has occasionally been questioned. It seems that it came down to two men: Truman Whited who surveyed Truman, and Truman Clark who was the son of the second vice president of the railroad company. It seems that Truman Clark is the individual primarily given credit for the city of Truman's name. Nevertheless, an article in the *Martin County Sentinel* at that time stated that the town should have been named Westford because the township and the post office already had that name.

The first train arrived in Truman in 1899, and by 1900, Truman had a population of 214. The Vandrey Brothers Store opened in 1899 and Truman erected three elevators. Those elevators were the Hubbard and Palmer, the Truman Elevator and Flour Exchange, and the Wolheuter Elevator Company of Fairmont. Then, in 1903, a group of farmers organized and raised $3,000 to build an elevator under the name of the Farmers Elevator Company. It was an instant success and, as a result, they bought out the Wolheuter Company and thus became the largest firm in Martin County.

The first school was completed in 1900. By 1901, all eight grades moved into the new brick building, and by 1912, a six-room addition was built. In 1913, Truman had its first four-year high school graduating class, albeit with just one student, Ed Olson.

The first bank in Truman was the Truman State Bank in 1900. Then, Albert Ward opened the Truman National Bank in 1902. Following that, Peoples State Bank was founded in 1906. However, it was felt at the time that three banks serving 752 inhabitants was unnecessary. Over the years, several mergers took place.

The *Truman Tribune* first rolled off the presses in January of 1900 with the cost of an annual subscription being the tidy sum of $1.50. The *Martin County Sentinel* disliked the newspaper and ran critical editorials condemning it. However, the *Martin County Independent* stepped forward to support the *Tribune* by publishing editorials sympathizing with and supporting the "just born" newspaper and asked for an apology from the *Sentinel.*

Twine Day was perhaps considered one of the largest unofficial holidays celebrated in Truman's past. Farmers would come to town to pick up twine that they had ordered, and adding to the festivities of Twine Day, the local merchants would usually show their appreciation of their customers by putting on some type of special that included food and entertainment. As a result, entire families would come to town to celebrate and take part in the festivities. [More information on Twine Day can be found on page 92.]

Truman has had many notable businesses throughout its history. There are, obviously, far too many to mention; however, a few of the following may well serve to bring back fond memories of the past: Stan and Mary Nickerson's Service and Café, the Bowl-A-Way bowling alley, Sarge's 66 Station, the Rialto Theater, Carrol's Market, Dick's Barber Shop, Ebert Hardware, the Bosshart Company, the Chat and Chew Café, Hinton Motors, and the Olson Furniture Company and Funeral Home.

The following are a few bits of history from Truman's past:

- 1857—The first settlement in Westford Township was along Elm Creek.
- 1865—The Jackson Road was built from Winnebago to Jackson.
- 1873—Grasshoppers destroyed crops.
- 1901—Otto Graf donated land for a city park.
- 1902—A production of *Old Maid's Companion* was featured at the Brownlee Opera House.
- 1918—School was closed for four weeks due to the flu epidemic.
- 1919—Edward E. Olson took over the Baker Furniture Store.
- 1921—The 800-acre Boynton Ranch sold for $200,000.
- 1923—A KKK meeting was allegedly held in rural Truman in the dead of night.
- 1924—Burglars tried to blow the safe in Truman but failed. They locked up night policeman Charles Graff in the jail.
- 1929—The Cozy Theater installed talking movie equipment.
- 1931—The Harlem Globetrotters played a team in Truman.
- 1933—Truman, Westford, and Nashville voted 188 to 78 to stay "dry."
- 1935—Jiggs, the dog, left Truman to find his previous owners who had moved to California. He found them in 1938 after a three-year journey.

- 1939—The Legion rabbit hunt ended with a game bag of 191 jacks and sixty-four cottontails.
- 1958—The Rialto Theater closed its doors.
- 1960—The grand opening of Carrol's Market was held.
- 1965—Minnesota Viking Paul Flatley spoke at an athletic banquet.
- 1966—A popular local band, The Rogues, was made up of Roger Lehr, Reid Van Brunt, Leon Barickman, and Robert Ritter.
- 1967—The first foreign exchange student arrived in Truman from Denmark.
- 1973—The last train passed through Truman.
- 1975—Local attorney Russ Utermarck died in a plane crash.
- 1982—The Truman Bluejays won the Class C football title.
- 1995—The city of Truman received $150,000 from the estate of Dr. and Mrs. Victor Vaughan.

Sources for this story include The Truman Centennial, 1899–1999 *book and MCHS History File 689.*

Martin County's Twin Cities

The Twin Cities of Minneapolis and St. Paul are a well-known metropolitan area in Minnesota. However, they were not the only twin cities in Minnesota. Martin County at one time also had twin cities.

The city now known as Trimont, located in northwest Martin County, was at one time comprised of the two communities of Triumph and Monterey. Minnesota State Highway 4 marked the boundary between the twin towns.

Triumph was platted in 1899 by the Western Town Lot Company and was initially to be called Lamholt, but that name was rejected. Consequently, it was given its name Triumph by John Steen, one of the owners of the Triumph Creamery Company. However, another account stated that the village's first post office, named Triumph, was a result of a spirited discussion deciding upon its name. Bertram H. Wetzel pounded on the table and said, "We'll triumph yet!" Another said, "Triumph, that's the name." And so, Triumph was approved, Wetzel was appointed its first postmaster, and the village grew up around the post office.

Triumph Main Street 1912

In the early years, Triumph was the home to the *Progress*, the local newspaper. Monterey also had a newspaper called the *Memorandum*. The two newspapers were often at odds, and the *Memorandum* eventually closed. By 1906, the *Monterey News* came into existence and later the *Cedar Gleanings*, both of which also eventually closed. Ultimately, the *Progress* then became the newspaper of all of Trimont.

Monterey, also founded in 1899, was named for the city of Monterey, Mexico, by a railroad employee who seemed to have a keen interest in Spanish names. At that time, railroads were an important means of transportation in the United States and played a significant role in the development of this area.

The twin communities experienced a number of interesting events as they grew. Unlikely as it might seem, Monterey experienced two bank robberies, one in 1908 and another in 1939. The following two stories summarize events as told in the May 2, 1953, *Sentinel*.

One stormy night in April of 1908, John H. Arthur and Ralph "Sheeney" Holmes took some crowbars from the railroad in Monterey and used them to gain entrance to the Peoples State Bank in Monterey.

Once inside the bank, they blew the door off the safe and made off with $1,485 in gold and bills. They went back to the railroad, took the depot agent's handcar and headed south. At some point on their escape, they tore up some letters from Sheeney's girlfriend who lived in St. Paul, dropping them near Sherburn. Consequently, Martin County Sheriff Ward found the pieces of the letter that included the name "Mack" and a St. Paul address. Sheriff Ward and a Pinkerton detective arrived in Mendota five minutes before Arthur got off the train and apprehended him. He was transported to the Martin County Jail where he pled guilty and then spent five years in Stillwater. A $200 reward was posted for Sheeney, but he was never captured.

Monterey 1908

In December of 1939, a lone bandit entered Farmers State Bank in Monterey, showing a note demanding money. After the robber was convinced he had all the money available, he escorted the two cashiers, Elmer F. Peterson and Robert Rippel, into the bank vault and slammed the door. However, a built-in safety device prevented the door from locking. They remained in the vault until they were certain the robber had left the bank. Alfred Peterson, the bank's vice president, was unaware of the robbery as he was in the back room. The bandit made off with $696.50. With the identifications made by the two cashiers, the robber was eventually captured in 1940 in Chattanooga, Tennessee.

The twin cities of Triumph and Monterey have evolved over the years, enduring many of the same hardships and obstacles faced by other small communities during the early development of Martin County. Although there was undoubtedly some competitive spirit between the two communities over the years, that was put aside in 1959 when the twin towns merged on New Year's Day.

Thus, with the merger of Triumph and Monterey in 1959, Minneapolis and St. Paul could give sole claim as "the" Twin Cities of Minnesota, no longer challenged by the twin cities of Martin County, Triumph and Monterey.

I would like to acknowledge the Trimont, Minnesota Centennial *book as a major resource for this article.*

The History of the Martin County Fair

The Martin County Fair, considered by many to be one of the finest county fairs in the state of Minnesota, has evolved from humble beginnings in the mid 1800s up to its sesquicentennial in 2015. Following is a brief account of the Martin County Fair's progression. However, readers should keep in mind that historical documentation at times presents conflicting information.

Martin County Fair 1912

The first Martin County Fair was held in 1865 at the first Martin County Courthouse in Fairmont, which was built at a cost of $200. An eyewitness account of the fair was provided by Mrs. Kate Sperry in the September 29, 1916, edition of *The Sentinel*: "I attended the fair in the fall of 1865. It was held in the old one-room courthouse on the grounds where the present courthouse stands. About all there were in the way of exhibits were in a few pumpkins and cabbages and a cow got loose and ate up part of the cabbages."

The second fair, held in 1866, was staged at the current site of Presentation College at the corner of Blue Earth Avenue and Park Street. The attendance was described as meager as were the exhibits and races that were held on First Street. Apparently, until 1869, the fair was conducted without any real organizational standards. However, that changed in November of that year when the Martin County Agricultural Society was organized and became responsible for planning and implementing the fair.

A contrasting view of these early fairs was given by Albert L. Ward. His perspective was printed in his newspaper, *The Independent*. According to Ward, fairs held prior to 1870 were presumed to be "Fairmont Fairs" and were merely forerunners to the Martin County Fair. Ward, the first secretary of the Martin County Fair, asserts that there were no accurate records of fairs held prior to 1870. Ward agrees that the first agricultural fair was held in the Martin County Courthouse, but stated that it took place in 1870, not 1865. He said that this fair included a trotting race held on Winnebago Avenue that had "many entries of all kinds of nags hitched to decrepit sulkies, two wheeled carts or any other sort of vehicle that was reasonably light." The winner was an old mare with a suckling colt, much to the chagrin and riotous protests of losing entrants crying foul. Ward believed Tom Allen to be the winner of this first big horse race in Fairmont; however, J.T. Swearingen believed E.S. Snow to be the winner. With neither an instant replay nor an appeals process available at that time, the decision regarding the winner was questionable at best.

Ward agrees that the second fair was held on the current site of Presentation College; however, his account of exhibits differs markedly from Sperry's account. He states that the stock exhibited consisted of a cow with a "freakishly crooked horn" that had grown that way since breaking it in trying to throw a rider. In addition, Ward stated that he encountered a "bellicose" woman who had taken a prize on a quilt at the first fair and insisted on entering it again in the second fair. Nonetheless, the secretary prevailed, much to the dismay of the lady, steadfastly upholding the rules of the society.

Perhaps the most spectacular event of the second fair, according to Ward, was a free-for-all fight. It involved a well-known old settler who was knocked down so hard that the top of his head was the first part of his anatomy to hit the ground. The fight caused a great deal of excitement in creating what was at that time described as a "splendid county fair."

According to yet another source, the third county fair was held in downtown Fairmont on twenty-four acres of land purchased at a cost of $600.

The fair of 1884 involved a number of interesting events, one of which was a 100-yard foot race. Entrants were blindfolded, and they used wheelbarrows. First place was a prize of $3, and second place was $2. Regarding the safety of the fairgrounds, a night watchman was on duty to protect the exhibits and a "good police force" was in attendance. Also, no "promiscuous driving" was allowed on the track in the afternoon until the close of races.

The fair of 1896 was successful despite rainy conditions. That year, Saturday's attendance was estimated to be 3,000. As usual, Judge Livermore had the largest variety of apples comprising fifteen different kinds. William Suter's big watermelon weighing forty-seven pounds was an eye-opener! Fred Houseman's freak sheep, thought by some to be a new breed, was a corker, according to the September 18, 1896, edition of the *Martin County Sentinel*.

Some events from the 1904 Martin County Fair included the Taggert family of acrobats and Professor Burton's high-diving dog. Also, Treasurer Sharpe did not have the usual struggle with privileges [concession sales], as he simply turned down the "fakirs" and "grafters," those who at that time would take advantage of fairgoers. That year's write-up in the *Martin County Sentinel* said, "There was not a game or fakir of any description on the fair grounds and if any man lost his money it was because he was so foolish as to bet on the races."

In May of 1911, the fair board advertised all of the "old buildings" on the grounds for sale to the highest bidder. The only exception was the stables for the race horses. In that same year, the fair board awarded a contract for new barns to the Fairmont Cement Stone Manufacturing Company at a cost of $3,776.

The 1911 fair was plagued with rainy weather that was said to have caused losses in the thousands, although Friday's receipts of that year amounted to nearly $100 more than the corresponding Friday of 1910. The receipts included charges for carriages, grandstand entrance and privileges sales.

The most popular feature of the 1911 fair was the "old settlers" headquarters. This was where pioneers registered, met, and exchanged stories about the experiences they had encountered over the years.

There also was the Aviation Meet. This event was to feature an airship that was to make three ascents of at least 200 feet. The aviator planned to make two short flights and one longer flight. The stage was set for a thrilling experience; however, the 500 spectators got some unexpected results. First of all, the aviator and airship failed to arrive on time. He said his train was late. Once at the fairgrounds, the aviator succeeded in climbing only to about seventy-five feet before crashing in a cornfield about half a mile from the fairgrounds. This was far from the "thrilling" event expected by the disgusted spectators.

The fair of 1912 provided what is claimed to be the very first car–pedestrian accident. The driver of the automobile was proceeding slowly when a pedestrian, attempting to dodge another vehicle, ran into and was knocked unconscious by the automobile. The victim received medical attention and was able to board a train for home that evening. Apparently, no lawsuits followed the incident.

The fair held two years later was considered a banner year as the grounds were to be lighted with electricity. This was provided by Frank E. Wade of the Fairmont Machine Company in exchange for him being allowed to erect a "large and suitable" exhibit building in which he could display products from his company. The agreement included Wade's right of exclusive use of the fair grounds on July 4 and two other dates throughout the year.

In 1949, John Livermore headed the movement toward a free-gate fair. Although unsuccessful in his first attempts, he continued his intent to "clean out the deadwood" on the fair board. Newspaper accounts indicate that after the changeover to a free-gate fair, attendance and participation greatly improved.

The fair of 1952 was highlighted by a talent show won by baritone Gene Bullard that was viewed by 700 spectators. His prize was $75. However, not far behind was the winner of the Grand Champion Corn Exhibit. The winner, Mrs. John Grathwohl, beat out 155 other contestants. The fair board and the chamber wrestled with what to do with the King Korn Days reception and crowning the winner. Would she be crowned Korn King, or Korn Queen?

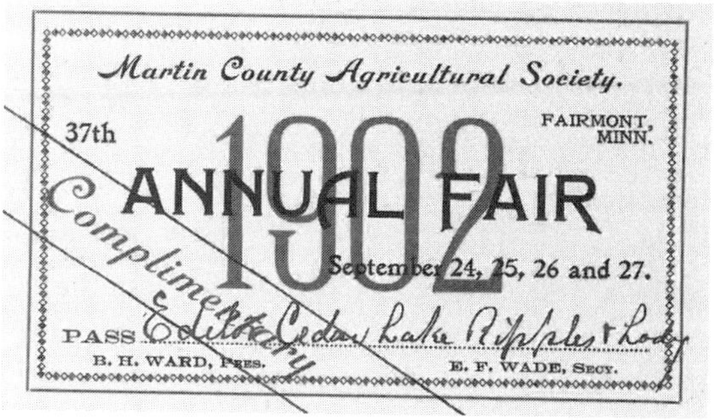

Martin County Fair Pass

In 1955, major plans included building a hog barn and floral hall. The fair board met and heard a proposal from Livermore, secretary, and Ernest Kettner, vice president, that would provide funding for the project. Livermore said that he and Kettner met with the county commissioners to propose a plan to rent the livestock hall to the county for storage of its equipment when the fair was not running. He said the county would rent the building for $200 annually for ten years and pay the total rent in advance, thereby allowing the fair board to proceed with their plans. In addition, the board planned to send at least four of its members to the Fair Short Course in Minneapolis to prepare for a bigger and better fair.

The fair of 1957 featured a grandstand wrestling event headlining the Russian Kalmikoff Brothers squaring off against George and Angus Scott. Not to be outdone, a women's match pitted Betty Hawkins against Shirley Strimple, the national TV champion, in a thirty-minute, one—fall match.

In 1964, plans were being made for a new location for the 1965 fair, which would also be the fair's centennial. The fairgrounds at that time were located at the current site of Five Lakes Centre. That site was purchased in 1877 for $500. In 1878, four additional acres were purchased there at a cost of $100.

With the exception of the articles of incorporation and a somewhat sketchy record of bylaws and amendments to the bylaws, records of the society from the early days are vague at best. An interesting aspect under the articles of incorporation encountered when the old fairgrounds were to be sold stated that "stockholders – whether living or dead, had to be in the majority before sale of the grounds could be affected." Registered notice of the election was sent to all stockholders of record. Nearly 200 letters came back marked "deceased" or "address unknown." The 200 were in the majority and counted as "no" votes. Obviously something must have been done to circumvent this obstacle as the land was eventually sold to Madsen Enterprises for $275,000 after months of searches by attorneys and engineers in finally authorizing a legal title to the grounds. The new location of the fairgrounds would be on Bixby Road on the west edge of Fairmont.

In 1965, the investment for a new location came to fruition. The new grandstand and race track were completed and considered to be, according to news reports, among the finest in southern Minnesota and northern Iowa. In 1966 and 1967, some of the improvements included adding water and sewer lines, heating some buildings, preparing buildings for the spring builders and sportsmen's shows, and a variety of other smaller projects. The grandstand was enhanced with the addition of 2,500 seats from a section of Metropolitan Stadium in Minneapolis that was being remodeled. This gave a total seating capacity at that time of 7,500.

Thus, the second century of Minnesota's Other Big Fair, the Martin County Fair, got under way in 1965. Since the first fair, whichever account you choose to believe, it has flourished and featured a wide range of attractions as well as big-name entertainers.

Sources for this story include Sentinel *stories from August 11, 1964, February 4, 1967, August 12, 1989, March 22, 1991, and a 1965 story entitled "100th County Fair Opens In New Site"; and the August 18, 1999* Photo Press.

Martin County Comes Into Its Own

Watering Holes of the Past

The word "saloons" may invoke images from the TV show "Gunsmoke" where Doc Adams, Miss Kitty, Chester, and Marshal Dillon would meet in the Long Branch Saloon to discuss the current affairs of Dodge City, Kansas. However, Dodge City wasn't the only town to have saloons, as well as colorful characters associated with them.

According to legendsofamerica.com, "The first establishment to be called a saloon was opened in 1822 in Brown's Hole, Wyoming. It was opened to serve fur trappers who were traveling through the region. The earliest saloons were not like those usually depicted in films of the Wild West. As people made their way west, liquor might be sold from wagons, and saloons might be built from whatever materials were at hand."

In looking back at the history of saloons in Fairmont, an interesting article entitled "Gentleman or Roughneck, City Had Saloon for You," appearing in the October 18, 1878, edition of the *Sentinel*, reported that "the merchants of North Avenue speak in emphatic terms concerning the drunkenness and rowdyism which is almost daily manifest upon their street. They admit that a lady cannot travel the street in safety and without being compelled, oftentimes, to listen to vulgarity, obscenity, and profanity. A good marshal is needed to restore a civilized condition of affairs."

The merchants of that era were obviously quite concerned about the effect that saloons, or at least those individuals frequenting them at the time, had on their business. It seems that in those days it was the habit or custom of some men, occasionally referred to as the "floating" population, to become intoxicated on cheap liquor and stand in front of the saloon and leer at women or make insulting remarks to whomever happened to pass by, often attempting to simply pick fights. Consequently, fights and brawls were practically a daily occurrence causing those "respectable" citizens wishing to quench their thirst to be confined to "side rooms" whereby admittance was typically based solely on the discretion of the bartender. Those of the so-called "floating" population were rarely arrested. However, if they were arrested, they were usually given a week in jail with free room and board, and when released, they were escorted to the city limits and told to move on, most likely ending up in neighboring communities causing similar problems.

According to the article, the Fairmont bar scene of the late 1800s had three distinct classes of saloons. The "third class" catered to the roughnecks, bums, and those rugged individuals who often provoked fights and brawls after consuming a few shots of cheap whiskey. In this category of saloons, falling-down drunkenness was tolerated, if not considered routine. As a result, the floors were strewn with sawdust up to one-half inch thick in order to more easily remove the remnants from any of their drunken customers who might "upchuck" on the floor.

The "middle class" of saloons served a somewhat diverse cross-section of Fairmont's society of that time. Their patrons felt that they could be exuberant and boisterous to a certain degree without fear of being thrown out of these establishments.

The bar at Rudy's Place

In sharp contrast to either the third or second class were the "first class" saloons, such as Rudy's Place and Rockwell's, which frowned upon roughnecks and "rowdyism." Their bartenders didn't hesitate to bodily remove customers if necessary.

Rudy's Place was owned and operated by Rudy Henry who was highly respected locally and considered a gentleman's gentleman in demeanor. He came to Fairmont from Chicago and was known for his dapper appearance, the diamond stickpin he wore, and his apparently unlimited financial resources. Interestingly enough, although Henry owned a saloon, he himself was not a drinker.

The bar in Rudy's Place was made of solid mahogany, which also trimmed the mirrored back bar. Just inside the entrance were two side rooms, essential in those days for a well-run saloon. It was in these side rooms where the well-known and respected business and professional men of that era would quietly enter and enjoy the liquor of their choice. These individuals usually were served by Henry himself, who did not merely serve drinks by the glass but rather by the bottle to these customers. When they finished, there was a button conveniently located in the room that could be pressed whereby Henry would come to collect his bottles and glasses as well as what he was owed.

Although Henry loved Fairmont, when the city voted "dry" in 1915, he knew that his bar, which incidentally had no sawdust on the floor, would have to close. In a matter of a few weeks, Henry moved back to Chicago saying, before he left, that he would be back. However, he passed away before having the opportunity to return to Fairmont.

Another respected saloon keeper of that period was Harry Rockwell. He was known to operate a clean, respectable place of business that also catered to what was referred to as Fairmont's most outstanding business and professional men. This was in the day when the "free lunch" was a significant feature of the so-called "best saloons."

One of the characteristics of Rockwell's lunch counter was a huge steam vat that could hold nearly a quarter of beef. Presiding at the vat was a somewhat chubby man named Eddie Smellie, whose name apparently didn't deter customers. Smellie, always impeccably dressed, was the person who would carve the beef for the customers, carefully placing a slice or slices on rye bread on a warm plate along with the customer's choice of pickles and onions. He would then ladle a cup of soup to serve with the sandwich. The customer would also most likely wash his sandwich down with a foaming schooner of beer.

Historic Hotels

In years past, Fairmont was the home to numerous hotels that no longer exist. The Fairmont of today has many fine hotels primarily in the vicinity of I-90, which would be the logical location for today's travelers. However, from the late 1800s up through the early to mid-1900s most of the city's hotels were located in the vicinity of downtown Fairmont, as that was the location best suited for travelers of that time period.

The Lakehouse was Fairmont's first hotel. It was built in 1861 by J.M. Goodrich, the first lawyer in Martin County, and was located in what is now Ward's Park. It also housed the first U.S. Post Office, the county auditor's office, the clerk of court's office, and the treasurer's office. It was later acquired by Ezra Hyatt, and the name was changed to the Hyatt House.

The Occidental Hotel, built in 1879, was located in the Flatiron Block across the street from Profinium Financial's current location on Lake Avenue. The builders were Fairmont businessman P.H. Munger and two somewhat colorful members of the illustrious English Colony, Gideon Smales and Arthur W. Lyon. The building housed district court, since the first courthouse within old Fort Fairmount had been outgrown, and the Bank of Fairmont, which failed after less than one year in existence. Ironically, one of the reasons for the failure of the Bank of Fairmont appeared to be a result of its last venture, financing the construction of the Occidental Hotel in which it was housed. A brewery owned by Gideon Smales located near the Webster Street boat landing, now Ward's Park, also closed as a result of the bank failure. The bank was eventually taken over by the Martin County National Bank and Al Ward.

The Older House was a hotel that was located between Second and Third Streets in Fairmont at the present site of the Masonic Temple and The Visual Identity Vault and where the Wallace mercantile used to be.

It was established by J.H. Older who was born in Franklinville, New York in 1824. He married Francis Caroline Chase of St. Lawrence, New York, in 1849, and in 1864, he and his family moved to a farm in Center Creek Township where he lived until he moved to Fairmont.

He bought the building from A.L. Ward, remodeled it, and converted it into a hotel. The hotel also served meals, held dances, and had a stable. It was in business in the late 1860s and 1870s.

Older passed away in 1879 leaving his wife, Francis, and nine children. His obituary notice, printed in the February 14, 1879, edition of the *Martin County Sentinel,* stated that he was one of Fairmont's old and respected citizens who was honored and beloved by all that knew him, leaving a large circle of friends who deeply mourn his loss. He is buried in Lakeside Cemetery in Fairmont.

The Bullard House Hotel

The Bullard House Hotel was also considered one of Fairmont's finest hotels and was located at 200 South Main Street. It was named after Charles H. Bullard, a native of Massachusetts. He came to Minnesota in the 1860s, enlisted in the Union Army during the Civil War, and was elected sheriff of Martin County in 1867, eventually serving four terms. He also served as justice of the peace and, with Frank Day, founded the *Martin County Sentinel.*

The hotel opened in 1895 and included an elaborate menu for their dining room. According to an article entitled "Bullard House Opening—An Auspicious Opening," from the September 13, 1895, *Martin County Sentinel,* "The formal opening and dedication of Fairmont's splendid new hotel, the Bullard House, will occur on Thursday evening, Sept. 19, when the public spirited citizens of our town will show their good will toward Col. Bullard and in a slightly more substantial manner present him with a token of their esteem."

Tickets for the occasion were listed at $5 per couple or $2 per plate. The intention was to make the affair one of the most interesting social events in the history of Fairmont. The article went on to state that "our local orators will respond to toasts, and distinguished speakers from outside will be invited. An orchestra will be on duty and the entire hotel will be turned over to the public to do with it as they see fit."

Some of the more interesting menu items were: blue point oysters, a la Peterson; boiled ham garnished, a la Hill; caneton a l'Anglaise, a la Bird; roast lamb, a la Bird; filets of bouef, a la Coult; frecandeau of veal, a la Mocedoine; roast capons, a la Fairmont; wine, a la Donaldson. The menu seems interesting, but some of us might find an interpreter helpful.

Mr. and Mrs. E.A. Luedtke of Amboy, Minnesota, acquired the hotel in 1912 and changed its name to the Edgewater Hotel. The Edgewater was for many years considered one of the finest hotels in southern Minnesota. It was demolished in 1960 in order to build a new hotel.

The Harlow House was built in 1890 and was located on North North Avenue, now Downtown Plaza, adjacent to the railroad tracks. It was a popular place for train passengers as they could easily tour Fairmont by taking a ride on the *Concord* at nearby Lake Sisseton, pay for a horse-pulled taxi ride, or rent a horse-and-buggy from a nearby stable. Prior to 1930, it was not uncommon for at least twenty passenger and freight trains to pass through Fairmont on a daily basis. The Harlow House building in time evolved into the Fairmont Packing Company and later became Building 40 of Fairmont Railway Motors.

The Interlaken Inn

The Interlaken Inn and Cottages opened its doors in June of 1916. It stretched along the high bank of Hall Lake west to the Chain of Lakes Yacht Club. The hotel was built primarily for summer use with a dining room and rooms with porch areas overlooking the lake.

Colonel Needham was hired when the inn first opened, and he brought in a chef, waiters and porters from Minneapolis rather than spend time training local persons. Sunday dinners and evening meals were seventy-five cents, and other meals were fifty cents. Dining room business was lively and bustling with as many as 200 dinners served for some meals. Conventions and banquets were quite common as well.

The Fairmont Hotel was located at 217 North North Avenue, which is now an empty lot across from the former Enderson's Clothing. The hotel was built about 1916–1917 by a farmer named Julius Reihs, a German immigrant who came to this country around 1900 with an estimated $80 to his name. He was considered somewhat eccentric in that he would always wear a cap with the earflaps down whether it was winter or summer.

In 1940, their menu had a filet mignon or a porterhouse steak for $1, broiled lamb chops were eighty-five cents, roast chicken and dressing, prime rib, roast leg of lamb, grilled ham steak, and chicken ala king all went for seventy-five cents. The meal included mashed potatoes, rolls, vegetable, coffee, tea or milk, and pudding. Guests were told to "kindly write their entire order as waitresses are instructed to serve only on written order." The hotel was well known for its excellent meals and service, and it was considered "quite the proper thing to go to the Fairmont Hotel dining room for a Sunday dinner."

The Augusta Hotel

The Augusta Hotel, located at 121 East Blue Earth Avenue, was built by Jack Croissant in the late 1920s. It had forty-four rooms and a nice restaurant. The hotel's location formerly served as a boarding house. In addition, there was a large and very popular meeting room in the basement, known as the Fiesta Room, and part of the building also included a barber shop and a beauty shop. The building was rather multi-purpose as the Fairmont Building and Loan at one time had offices there, it was the Greyhound Bus Depot for about five years in the 1930s, and Gene's Cleaners was also located in the building. The Augusta operated as a hotel until the 1970s. Its location is presently the site of First Farmers and Merchants Bank.

The Gilbert Hotel, 1200 East Blue Earth Avenue, was purchased by Harry Gilbert in 1940. It had at one time been the Ward Orphan Home; however, it had long since been abandoned. The Ward Home for Dependent Children had been built in about 1915. In 1921, Ward is said to have given up maintaining the home and, except for a caretaker, it stood empty for a long time. A 1941 *Sentinel* article informing the public of an open house at the Gilbert Hotel boasted that it had sixty-two rooms, many with two beds and fireplaces, running water, electric lights, and either a shower or tub bath. In addition, it had a coffee shop downstairs with seating for fifty people. The renovation of the Ward Orphanage into a hotel apparently sparked further expansion and building in that part of the city at that time.

Of course, there were, and are, other hotels and motels as well as those previously mentioned. There was the Heidel House located near the present site of Fairmont

Farmers Mutual Insurance on Downtown Plaza, the Lakeside Inn which occupied the former hospital site which is now the site of Albion Place Condominiums, the Wilken Motel, the Bell Motel, Colvin's Cabins, the Highland House Motel, and many more. The hotel and motel industry has played a significant role in the history and economic development of this area over the years. Their presence continues to have a positive impact today as well.

The Foster House, a Fairmont Landmark

The Foster House, built by an Englishman named Cole circa 1876, was considered one of Fairmont's finest hotels in its day and a prominent landmark. Frank Day once lived there, and some of his children were born there. Other early tenants were C.N. Peterson and Billy Hay.

In its first twenty years of existence, the Foster House was a flourishing hotel, and it was considered a real moneymaker. It was popular for the traveler both in terms of its price as well as its location near the downtown area of Fairmont. In its better days, it offered forty rooms to guests. Originally located near Second Street and Downtown Plaza near what is now Fairmont Farmers Mutual Insurance, it was moved by Hale Foster to its final location at the corner of Blue Earth Avenue and Downtown Plaza across the street to the west from the Fairmont Opera House.

Foster House

Once considered one of the top three hotels in Fairmont, it ultimately declined and became what was described as a boarding house for tilers, day laborers, and transients. An interesting aspect of this hotel was that at one time, there was a suite of rooms on the third floor that served as the meeting place for Fairmont gamblers. Interestingly enough, the gamblers did not come from the ranks of the so-called transients living in the hotel but rather involved prominent Fairmont business and professional men of the day. When their game was in session, they even had a hired lookout on watch in the event of a possible raid. The lookout resided in a small house at the rear of the hotel, next to his chicken house that supplied the hotel with chickens and eggs.

As time passed, however, the public taste in hotels gradually changed. The Foster House no longer seemed to meet the needs and wants of the traveler of that time, and it began to fall on hard times. Although considered a fire hazard in later years, no fire had ever occurred there. The hotel was eventually sold to Rudy Gimm in 1935.

At the time of its sale, the Foster House was managed by Jess Law. He found moving from the hotel to be very difficult, as he had been the hotel's proprietor for approximately twenty-one years. Law felt moving from the Foster House to be comparable to losing an old friend. In the July 29, 1935, *Sentinel*, he states, "I don't know what to do. I'd like to keep running a rooming house, but I can't find a thing except on the edge of town, and you can't expect people to stay out that far. I'm forced out of business I know, and about all I can do is to go out and find a workingman's job."

The building was slated for demolition. Law, being quite unwilling to give up the Foster House, continued to make his home in the hotel even while the building was being torn down. He had nowhere else to go, so it was agreed that he could sleep on the first floor until the building was virtually pulled down over his head. He planned to "stay with the ship," even though an inch-and-a-half of rain fell one night making it quite difficult for him to find anywhere dry to sleep. He was also attempting to keep anyone from stealing any of the building materials, although one night someone got in and stole some of the metal parts of the bathtubs.

The removal of the Foster House was completed in August of 1935 by the Hanson Brothers of Albert Lea. Among the last to finish the job was Law who then began looking for a job. The plans for the site of the former hotel included a used car lot and a possible lunchroom on the corner. What eventually became of Law is unclear; however, progress of that era appears to have taken a community landmark of its time and permanently changed the landscape of the city of Fairmont.

Sources for this story include MCHS History File 645; George Champine's Historical Fairmont in Pictures 1860–1960, Extended Version*;* The Daily Sentinel, *Martin County Centennial edition, May 10, 1958, page 6; the May 21, 1956* Fairmont Sentinel*; and the December 5, 1890* Martin County Sentinel.

Hazel Who?

Hazel-more, Hazel-less, Hazel-mere, Hazel-who? The city of Fairmont has grown over the years and spread out along its five lakes from its meager beginning in the mid-1850s. That growth included the development of areas that were once called "suburbs" of Fairmont. One of those "suburbs" was known as Hazelmere. So, just what exactly is Hazelmere, and where is it located?

Hazelmere Hotel

The Hazelmere area was noted for the Hazelmere Hotel. Located just south of Alton Street and west of Albion Avenue on Hall Lake in Fairmont, it was originally the home built by Joseph Ramsdale in 1875. The tract of land known as Hazelmere was initially purchased by Ramsdale, a member of the bean colony of English settlers to this area, from E. Banks Hall who settled the area in 1856 and for whom Hall Lake is named.

Ramsdale had been looking for a place to erect his country home and decided upon this location as he thought it to be the most beautiful spot in or around Fairmont. He built what at that time was described as a "handsome $7,000 house" on what was considered the most desirable lake farm in Martin County. It is also one of the English homes referred to in the novel *Gentlemen from England* by Maud Hart Lovelace and her husband Delos Lovelace, a fictionalized account of the English bean colony in Fairmont.

The timber and lumber for the home, which old timers of that period claimed to be vastly superior to other lumber of that era, was hauled from Winnebago, at that time the end of the railroad line. The original fourteen-room home was built with the intention of having the Percy Wollaston family live in part of the house. However, finding it unsuitable for two families, Wollaston chose to build at another location. Wollaston, also from England, served as Fairmont's first mayor even though he was an English citizen during his term.

Hazelmere was sold to Dan Alton after the Ramsdale family had lived there about twenty years. Alton later sold it in 1901 to E.J. Edwards and J.T. Swearingen for $9,000. This sale included seventy-five acres of land bordering the lake that was to be immediately platted into lake lots. It was then sold to Fred Cotton in 1904. Cotton made a number of improvements, including a dance pavilion, an open air dining area, and a number of guest cottages. The exact date when it evolved from a family residence into a hotel is unclear.

Hazelmere soon became well-known as one of the finest resorts in southern Minnesota and the Midwest where entire families could come to spend their vacations while enjoying Fairmont's lakes and other amenities, including the authentic "home cooking" for which Hazelmere had become famous.

Sundays were an especially popular day at the resort and attracted hundreds of people. Many simply enjoyed relaxing in the gentle wafting of the lake breezes while others favored the many other leisure time opportunities available in the area. Attractions the resort offered included tennis courts, bathing facilities, and a conveniently located golf course nearby. The cottages were usually filled, which in turn left waiting lists of vacationers seeking reservations. Hazelmere's appeal was further enhanced by the fact that a great deal of transportation at that time was on water via the *Concord* and other pleasure boats of that era.

It's interesting to note that the Hazelmere site had a somewhat ominous incident occur in the late 1800s when a near riot and attempted hanging took place. This incident was a result of a group of Milwaukee Railroad employees being quite disturbed by the fact that that they did not receive the pay for which they felt entitled. As a result of their discontent, the railroad employees descended upon officials of the railroad who were staying at the hotel. The intent of the railroad employees was to hang the railroad officials.

However, a posse was formed in Fairmont that intervened by descending upon the mob, marching them back to Fairmont, and holding them captive in the barn of the Older House hotel under armed guard.

In 1928, Cotton announced that the Hazelmere Hotel would be remodeled and converted into summer apartments. A February *Sentinel* article that year about the remodeling of the Hazelmere states that, "Bowing before the steady growth of the city and its suburbs, Hazelmere has changed from a summer resort to a suburban residential district," which reflected Cotton's new concept for the use of the property. This article goes on to say that, "Every convenience of a twentieth century home will be installed, including electricity, gas, and water, a great change from the early days of tallow candles, kerosene lamps, and finally gasoline lamps."

History characterizes the Hazelmere Hotel as a quiet hotel, catering to what was referred to at that time as "the better trade," apparently meaning that their clientele was considered to be of the upper echelon of local and Midwestern society. It also served as a center for numerous social functions and a meeting place for the Fairmont Whist Club, and its popular "family-style" meals further served to complement its growing popularity.

Cotton continued to operate the property until his death in 1937. Cotton's daughters, Wilhelmina and Gertrude Cotton, sold the Hazelmere property to Art Stade in 1939, and the hotel was demolished. The area where the Hazelmere Hotel once stood is now a residential area.

Sources for this story included Jan Dickinson's compiled research of newspaper articles Fairmont History 1850–1900.

Frank A. Day—Newspaperman

Frank A. Day was a very well-respected individual known for his enthusiasm for his city, his county, his state, his principles, and his friends. His presence had a significant impact on Martin County and Minnesota in the late 1800s and early 1900s.

Day was born in Attica, Wisconsin, in 1853. His family moved to Hamilton County, Iowa, after the Civil War. He didn't consider himself an ardent student. Therefore he left school before graduating from the eighth grade to pursue a position at the *Freeman* newspaper in Webster City. He was paid fifty cents a week, and he soon showed his aptitude for journalism.

Frank A. Day—Newspaperman and Politician

Day worked for a few months in Hampton, Iowa, and then, at age 18, he went on his own as a journalist and partner at the *Vindicator-Republican* in Estherville, Iowa.

Early in 1874, Day left Estherville and decided upon Fairmont as the next stop in his newspaper career. This would soon become significant for Day as well as Fairmont, Martin County, and the state of Minnesota.

Upon arriving, Day became captivated by the lakes, woods and prairie of the area. As a result of what he saw and liked, Day decided to visit Bullard at the sheriff's office. Bullard had planned to start a newspaper although three had already failed in Fairmont.

It was July 3, 1874, and the second year of the grasshopper plague, which was quickly claiming anything green in the county. Day introduced himself to the sheriff and asked if Bullard was interested in a partner for the potential newspaper. Bullard's answer to Day was a swift and resounding no.

Consequently, Day left Bullard's office and spent the night in a Fairmont hotel. The following morning, he started back to Estherville. At noon, he stopped at Cornelius Personius' tavern in Tenhassen for lunch. Bullard caught up with Day at the tavern and told him that he had changed his mind. They shook hands, rode to Mankato the following day to purchase equipment, and thus began a six-year partnership with the *Martin County Sentinel*, the forebear to our current *Fairmont Sentinel*. Incidentally, Day is said to have chuckled at the fact that, while in Mankato, he and Bullard were arrested for horse stealing. It was soon straightened out as a case of mistaken identity.

Day was first and foremost a newspaperman; however, he enjoyed politics, which he referred to as "a great game." Day had a very lengthy political career, which can be divided into two stages. Initially, he rose to prominence as a leading Republican, serving fifteen years as chairman of the Martin County Republican Committee. He also served several terms on the Republican State Executive Committee and was a delegate-at-large to two Republican National Conventions. He was elected in 1878 to his first legislative position as a member of the lower house from Martin County.

His state senate career began in the 1880s when he was elected senator from Martin and Jackson counties. He was reelected twice, and was president pro tem of the senate when Governor Knute Nelson was elected to the United States Senate. This moved David M. Clough to governor, and Senator Day was advanced to lieutenant governor.

Day appeared quite upwardly mobile in the Republican Party; however, he and several other Republican leaders of the time left the party in 1896 to follow William Jennings Bryan. Soon, Day became a full-fledged Democrat. He was a leading Democratic proponent in his newspaper, and he reentered politics in 1904 to assume the management of John A. Johnson's campaign, a fellow editor and close friend. Johnson was elected after a spectacular fight, and in turn made Day his private secretary. Day continued as Democratic State Committee Chairman and Johnson's private secretary until Johnson's death in 1909.

Following Governor Johnson's death, Day returned to private life. He briefly went to Montana, founding the *Missoula Daily Sentinel*; however, this turned out to be an unfavorable business venture. He soon sold his interests and returned to Fairmont as the editor of the *Fairmont Sentinel*.

In 1926, Day was again elected to the state senate from Martin and Watonwan counties. He was preparing for the next legislative session at the time of his death.

He was at the editorial helm at the *Sentinel* from the paper's founding until his death in July of 1928. It was said that his daily editorials had a "kick" and a "Dayesque" twist to them that made them out of the ordinary and very interesting reading, and they always "said something." In addition, he wrote the "Lake Breeze" column which appeared in the Monday edition of that time. He served one term as president of the Minnesota Editorial Association and helped to organize the Second District Editorial Association.

Day was known as a man of the people. He talked to everyone and was equally comfortable visiting prisoners in jail as well as conversing with local and state leaders in business and politics. He was perhaps best known throughout the state as a vibrant supporter and promoter of Fairmont and all of Martin County.

Sources for this story include The Daily Sentinel *Martin County Centennial edition, May 10, 1958, page 6; the December 27, 1928* Sentinel*; and MCHS History File 519.*

The *Sentinel*

The *Martin County Sentinel* started as a weekly newspaper, and it had no other newspapers as competition for its first eight years of operation. The price of the paper was at that time $1.50 annually, $1 for six months, and five cents per copy. Competitor newspapers were mostly short-lived; however, late in the century, several newspapers merged to become the *Martin County Independent*, which then became the *Sentinel's* principal competitor. Yet, major changes were about to occur.

On May 20, 1901, Day introduced the *Fairmont Daily Sentinel*. The company continued to publish the *Martin County Sentinel* on a semi-weekly basis as well and eventually purchased the *Martin County Independent* in 1929.

Day enjoyed politics and started as a Republican. He left the party in 1896 and soon thereafter became a Democrat. The *Sentinel* supplement of May 13, 1874, stated that "The Sentinel, originally launched as 'republican' in 1874, became 'democrat' shortly after the turn of the century. As time went on, it supported or opposed candidates of all parties, until it could finally be regarded as an independent newspaper." Day was succeeded by Harry Fairley as publisher whose chief contribution was his experience with metropolitan newspapers.

The *Sentinel* has had several locations during its history. Its first printing office was located in Colonel Bullard's residence across the street from the Bullard House Hotel. The hotel overlooked Lake Sisseton on Lake Avenue just south of Profinium. It later moved to the second floor of what is now Hollywood Babe and Giddyup Boutique, formerly Davidson's and Miller's Fashions. The *Sentinel's* third site was about a half-block north of First Street on North North Avenue, now Downtown Plaza. In 1897, the *Sentinel* moved to its present site which was expanded through the consolidation of an adjoining building in 1954.

Frank and Al

Not surprisingly, Frank Day and Albert Ward had interactions as contemporaries who were both quite involved in the welfare of Fairmont. It's interesting to compare the two, as they both had strong followings, yet they were in many ways exact opposites.

Day was said to have had a gregarious nature while Ward was all business. Ward was known as a shrewd businessman and was considered to be very frugal, while Day was more generous and didn't hesitate to spend. Ward was a tireless worker who had no time for anyone lacking ambition. In addition, Ward's personal habits did not include smoking, drinking, or chewing tobacco.

While Ward eventually became quite wealthy, Day, on the other hand, was considered as "poor as a church mouse" in terms of ready cash. Although very generous in nature, it seems he always "owed a little something to the bank." Additionally, it appears that he was also quite generous with other people's money and property.

A story is told of a family in East Chain that had lost its home and all its contents to a fire. Day was able to collect groceries for the family and clothing for the children. On his way to East Chain to deliver the donations, however, it was said that he consumed some of the groceries intended for the family.

Upon arriving at the scene of the fire, he jumped out of the car and said, "I am Frank Day. Too bad about the fire, but see what I brought you." Day's chauffeur subsequently asked him why he didn't give credit to those individuals and businesses that gave the groceries and clothing to the family that had lost everything in the fire. Day's comment? "Gave it?" snorted Day, "Why should they have credit? If I hadn't gone after them, those poor people wouldn't have had anything."

Another story is told of Day and his tab at the G.B. Goetz clothing store. He walked in and asked what he owed. The shop owner said he owed ten dollars. Day pulled a ten-dollar bill out of his pocket and gave it to the shop owner.

On his way out, Day asked how long he had owed the money. The shop owner said he had owed it for about ten months, at which time Day grabbed the ten-dollar bill back and said, "I haven't owed you that long enough yet," and walked out of the store.

Day and Ward were apparently at each other's throats on a fairly regular basis. Ward had the money, and Day apparently relished telling him how to use it. Day, of course, was in favor of every conceivable improvement for Fairmont that he could envision, while Ward would oppose him at every turn.

The highpoint in their ongoing feud probably reached its zenith after Day's *The Martin County Sentinel* started the *Fairmont Daily Sentinel.* It seems that the old *Democrat* and the *Martin County Independent Zeitung* newspapers were unable to repay their loans. Ward held the loans at his bank and consequently gained possession of these newspapers. This, of course, provided Ward with a vehicle from which to answer Day's verbal assaults as well as to retaliate with some of his own. From there on, Ward and Day exchanged insults in nearly every issue, and on one occasion, Ward sued Day for libel. Ward was awarded one cent in damages which in turn threw the legal costs of the trial on Day.

Ward's eccentricity can be seen in a job interview he conducted. He asked the young man being interviewed whether he went to church and Sunday school, to which the young man answered that he did attend both church and Sunday school. Ward then asked whether or not the interviewee would ever swear. The young man responded reluctantly that he did swear on occasion. To this, Ward reportedly replied, "Well, if you do. . ., you can't work for me. Swearing sounds like hell."

It could undoubtedly be said that Ward, who came to Martin County with little or nothing, became one of the wealthiest individuals in the county. At the time of his death in 1931, his fortune was estimated to be between one and two million dollars. Ward was an astute businessman and over time gained a thorough knowledge of the law. Ward was also known for his interest in politics, the Ward Orphanage, and numerous other endeavors.

However, he was not above reproach. He was said to have charged high interest rates on loans, and he did not hesitate to foreclose on those unable or neglectful in repayment of their loans.

Day and Ward, although frequently at odds, were certainly interesting, especially in their somewhat lively and exuberant exchanges over the years. Although it appears quite obvious that their beliefs and ideals were frequently in contrast, in their own unique ways, both have added a great deal to the history of Martin County.

Sources for this story include The Daily Sentinel, *Martin County Centennial edition, August 9, 1958, page 11.*

Interesting Advertisements

In looking back at newspaper ads from the late 1800s and the early 1900s, the following are some fascinating ads promoting products available at that time. It's interesting to note the unique and convincing wording coupled with the carefully crafted pictures used to promote their products.

Canright's Drug Store: Gentlemen are invited to our manicure parlors. It is just as essential that your hands and nails be clean, as it is that your linen be clean. This is especially true of all who wait on the public, such as dentists, doctors, clerks, bankers, etc.

Fred Churchyard, Auto Livery: Day or night calls promptly answered. Comfortable car, safe driver.

The Crystal: The best projection, the best vaudeville, the best pictures. Only one price, any seat—$0.10

Homer C. Jones, Furniture and Undertaking: Buying furniture of other than Homer C. Jones to save money is like stopping a clock to save time.

Fairmont National Bank: Capital $25,000, Surplus and Profits $4,000.

Bullard Hotel: Rates, $2.00, $2.25, $2.50.

Houghtaling & Coult: You never saw a saw saw like this saw saws. It is the "Flying Greyhound" brand and it has them all beaten.

Houghtaling & Coult: We have everything from $0.25 cents for the youngsters to the best $4.00 glove that can be made. We also have the hardwood ball with the double cover that has given such splendid satisfaction.

Briggs Automobile Company: The *Overland* with electric starter, electric lights, four-inch tires, magnetic speedometer, and full set of tools. Roadster: $595.00.

Wanted: 10,000 MUSK RATS: I have a big order on Rats, will pay good prices. Bring on your furs and get the top prices. I am also in the market for hides. HARRY WISHNICK, Jan. 19, 1917.

The Don Amilo has passed the experimental stage it is now demanded by many Fairmont smokers of Good Cigars. If you have never tried one call for the Don Amilo the next time you smoke. It's a cigar made in Fairmont of the finest imported tobaccos, $0.10, made by HICKS & Buelke – Fairmont. January 1917.

Wolf, Habein & Co. Grocery Department: 3 lbs coffee—$0.90, 1 can baking soda—$0.25, 2 packages Kellogg's Cornflakes—$0.30, 1 can pink salmon—$0.15.

OAKLAND, "The Car with a Conscience." Dust Proof, Unit Power Plant, 3-Point Suspension, Straight Line Drive, Skillfully Designed Frames, and Underhung Springs on rear gives the much desired low center of gravity combined with more clearance than the average high built chassis. For Sale By A. H. Welchlin, 3rd St., Fairmont. April, 1914.

FREE! A six-foot Buggy Whip with every cash purchase at TANNERS. July, 1899.

Dr. Downing, formerly of New York, now Chicago and Minneapolis. Free consultation at the Bullard House – Cures where others fail, treats middle aged and young men, ladies, and married persons. November, 1899.

Half A Bottle Cured Me! About thirty years ago I bought a bottle of Ayer's Hair Vigor to stop my hair from falling out. One-half a bottle cured me. J. C. Baxter, Braidwood, IL. September 27, 1899.

We Believe In Women's Rights! At least when it comes to labor saving machinery in the home. Maytag Power Washers at J. H. Gorman. 1915.

Fascinating! How effective would they be today?

Fairmont Social Life in the 1880s

In the 1880s, the center of some social lives was euchre, a trick-taking card game with four players who partner up.

Around 1885, several young professionals and businessmen decided to start a euchre club. Most of them were married, though there were a few romances in progress at the time. Newspaperman Frank Day, lawyer J.L. Higgins, and lumberman J.D. Young were responsible for starting the club. The club lasted for twenty years without either officers or dues.

Meetings were initially held every two weeks; however, it was later decided to meet only in the winter and with no prizes being awarded. Everyone that was a member of the club had their supper early so that play could start promptly at 7 p.m. They followed a fairly rigid schedule, as refreshments were served at 10 p.m. and the party was over at 10:30.

The food was usually quite simple, often consisting of coffee with doughnuts or sandwiches. Frank and Lucia Day once served mush and milk. Occasionally around Christmas, there was a more elaborate party that included dancing.

All the members walked to the party unless there was a storm, and then someone in town with a team and a sleigh was hired as a taxi to drive them to the meeting. The men in the club would then chip in to pay for the ride.

People attending the club wore their best clothing. Women usually purchased new dresses each year just for the club. Fifty dollars was considered reasonable for a new dress at that time, however, since styles didn't change, a woman could be well dressed with one new winter dress and one new summer dress. Last year's dresses were also considered fashionable second bests. Semi-formal dress was worn by the men in the club.

Only genuine jewels were appropriate in the women's jewelry, or they wore none at all. Costume jewelry was not worn. And women curled their own hair.

Fairmont's Euchre Club, which included a number of Fairmont's leaders of that time and their wives, was pictured in a June 1905 twentieth anniversary Hazelmere lawn party. Among the members of the club were Henry D. Gerth, J.D. Young, Henry Rippe, Frank A. Day, C.N. Peterson, William Viesselman, J.H. Quinn, George Lester, T.R. Alston, U.J. Pfiffner, E. Betz, J.L. Higgins, John W. Gorman, Harry W. Sinclair, and F.A.B. Patterson.

Sources for this story include Martin County History, *Taylor Publishing, 1988.*

The Epicenter of Entertainment in East Chain

In the early years of East Chain's existence, well before television, cell phones, and video games, there was one place that seemed to be the hub of the entertainment world for that part of Martin County, namely the Vermilya Store.

Vermilya Store

From the early 1900s, and for some time thereafter, the Vermilya Store was a hotbed of entertainment and "the" place to be in East Chain, and maybe Martin County. The lower part of the building was a mercantile; however, the upper part was known as the Woodman Hall, which was for many years the center of social activities in East Chain. At about the turn of the twentieth century, a Woodman Lodge was organized and nearly everyone in East Chain was a member. Woodman's was a group of people that bought Woodman's Insurance based out of Omaha, Nebraska. Royal Neighbors was the sister organization to the Woodman Insurance Company to which women belonged.

Between these two organizations, they served as sponsors for essentially all of the social life of East Chain as well as the surrounding area at that time. The Woodman held a dance monthly that was attended by virtually everyone in East Chain, and others from the surrounding area including Fairmont, Guckeen, and Center Chain. Admission to the dance wasn't free for the men, as they had to pay thirty-five cents. In addition, the men had to also pay fifty cents for a colored ribbon which entitled them to dance. As for the ladies, their admittance was free. Although this would not seem fair in today's world, it apparently didn't deter the men from attending.

The dances were so crowded that there was rarely room for everyone to be on the dance floor at one time. Consequently, numbers were called, and those who held the numbers called went out on the dance floor until the dance floor was full. When the dance finished, a new set of numbers was called and, consequently, the people holding those numbers were then given the opportunity to get out on the dance floor. It was rare for anyone to take a break to rest, and if they did, they were almost always quickly replaced by someone else. The dance numbers included the two-step, the three-step, the Schottish, and the square dance. The orchestra was usually Arthur and Truman Hall, including Mrs. Truman Hall. George Reigel was normally the caller.

The hall was also used for various other social activities, including basket socials. The building evolved over time and eventually served as a grocery store and a coffee shop, and had apartments upstairs.

Sources for this story include History of East Chain *by Dona Petrowiak Paris, page 19.*

Twine Day

Celebrations and festivals are integral to the flavor and identity of many small towns and rural communities. However, many of these celebrations in the past were unique to the time and place in which they occurred. One such festival apparently quite popular in the early 1900s was Twine Day, and it took place in Truman, Minnesota.

Truman Twine Day

The establishment of Twine Day came about as a result of farmers using a great deal of twine in harvesting their crops.

The Williams and Merrill hardware store that operated in Truman back then was considered a fairly large establishment at that time. It had three floors, and they advertised that they carried nearly everything in the line of hardware that a farmer might need.

The hardware store also advertised that, in addition to their hardware line, they had a first class repair shop and a competent man to repair bicycles, do tin work, plumbing, and more. They also handled hardware, farm machinery, buggies, and wagons. They were the main purveyors of twine to farmers back then.

Their method of obtaining twine was to order twine made by the inmates at the prison in Stillwater, Minnesota. Although a new approach at that time, it proved to become very popular and the store regarded it as high quality. Apparently one of their sales pitches was that by buying Stillwater twine, "the taxpayers help to remove a burden from their shoulders instead of adding more wealth to the twine trust."

In 1903, they delivered approximately 40,000 pounds of prison twine. Williams and Merrill estimated they saved the local farmers about four cents per pound, which totaled approximately $1,500. Their 1904 souvenir book said, "We have found farmers to be an appreciative class and this year they increased their orders for twine so that we had the pleasure of delivering 45,000 pounds of state prison twine."

They also stated that the savings was three cents per pound this year, and that they could have easily sold several thousand pounds more if it were available. However, Williams and Merrill was limited in that they could only supply the amount ordered, and they could not carry any inventory of twine for future sales.

So the farmers of the area pooled their twine orders, and all the twine would be shipped on a designated day. Upon arrival at Truman, the farmers could pick up their twine directly from the railroad train car.

To add to the festivities, local merchants would usually show their appreciation of the local citizens by putting on some type of special that would include food and entertainment. This would draw entire families to town to take part in the festivities. Pictures from that time show busy streets lined with many people as well as many horse and buggy rigs.

With the evolution of agriculture to what it is today, Twine Day is obviously a celebration of the past; yet Twine Day should be remembered as a significant event at the time and place in which it was celebrated.

Sources for this story include MCHS History Files 689 and "Souvenir of 1904" in MCHS History File 65; and The Daily Sentinel *Martin County Centennial edition.*

Frank Wade—Entrepreneur and Splendid Citizen

"Death took Frank Wade at the zenith of his powers and usefulness. His work, splendidly begun, was far from finished. What he might have done, what he might have been, is now idle conjecture," heralded the March 3, 1919, *Fairmont Daily Sentinel.* "Fairmont, today, stands with bowed head and heavy heart."

Frank Wade sitting in one of his company's railcars

"There is no man in Fairmont, there has never been a man among Fairmont's citizenship, whose life and deeds meant so much to every resident of the community."

Although Wade's family was originally from England, he was born in Whitehall—but not the one in the United Kingdom. He was born in Wisconsin on March 6, 1862. He attended public schools there and in rural Martin County. He also attended the Curtis Business College in St. Paul. Much of his early life was spent on a Martin County homestead where he experienced the hard conditions that faced every pioneer settler to the region.

Wade's career spanned many years and included a number of endeavors. At the age of nineteen, he became involved with G.W. Sherwood & Company, a firm that built bridges along the Mississippi River. He soon became superintendent of construction, having 370 men under him, and was placed in charge of bridge construction.

He then moved to Primghar, Iowa, and operated the Herrick & Wade General Store and then later moved to Sheldon, Iowa. Wade was also a general salesman for Fairbanks & Morse Company of Chicago where he assisted in perfecting the engines manufactured by that firm, and eventually led the company in sales.

However, Wade made the substantial portion of his fortune in the mining district of the Black Hills of South Dakota. He entered the region in 1902 and was one of the owners of the Homestake Mining Company; he was also involved with the Globe Gold Mining Company.

Wade returned to Fairmont in 1906 and took over the operation of the Water and Light Commission. That same year, he established the Fairmont National Bank and was named president. He then began to focus his attention on the Fairmont Machine Company, of which he also became president in 1909. The company manufactured the Fairmont gasoline engines, railway motor cars, and many other railway appliances. At that time, it supplied most of the railroads in the U.S. as well as many foreign markets. Wade's expertise and aggressive salesmanship was instrumental in making the company a leader in the industry.

In 1913, the city of Duluth made an attractive offer to move the Fairmont Machine Company to that city; however, the decision was made to expand and remain in Fairmont. In 1915, the company changed its name to Fairmont Gas Engine and Railway Motor Car Company, and in 1919, its name was again changed, this time to Fairmont Railway Motors, Inc.

In addition to his interests in the Fairmont Machine Company, Wade was president of the Fairmont Boat Company, a public enterprise for boating, fishing, and general outings. Other ventures included being president of the Southern Florida Land Company and vice president of the Tobacco Plantation Company, the largest sugar manufacturing plant in Mexico at that time.

Although a very successful businessman, he was also very civic minded. He was a member of the Christian Science Church. A Republican, he was a member of the State Central Committee and was elected mayor of Fairmont in 1915. It was during his term as mayor that paving was accomplished, in spite of much opposition. He also served as volunteer game warden and proved fearless in upholding the somewhat neglected laws of game resources. He found time to belong to many local and state organizations including the Chain of Lakes Lodge, the Odd Fellows, the Knights of Pythias, to name a few.

In 1915, he purchased land located south of Fairmont and developed it into one of the finest resorts in the Midwest known as Interlaken Park. It peaked in popularity in the 1920s and drew praise from as far away as New York and as close as neighboring Iowa.

Sources for this story include The Daily Sentinel *Martin County Centennial edition, July 26, 1958.*

Interlaken Park

Fairmont was the site of Interlaken Park, one of the finest resorts in the Midwest in the early 1900s. It was the brainchild of Frank Wade, who in just three years transformed the land, which he purchased for $175 an acre, into a recreational area that became an important feature of the local community.

Interlaken Park

The *Fairmont Daily Sentinel* of that era offered a weekly column devoted to Interlaken Park entitled, "Interesting Notes from Interlaken," which described the improvements taking place, happenings in the park, as well as frequently listing the hometowns of park visitors. Although most visited the park from southern Minnesota and northern Iowa, there were also many who came from the Minneapolis and St. Paul area, the Chicago area, and other parts of the Midwest.

Admission to Interlaken Park was a mere twenty-five cents in those early years, and weekend crowds often were in the neighborhood of 4,000 visitors. However, Interlaken's income was significantly less than Wade's park expenses. In 1917, Wade spent $47,000 on improvements and wages; however, poor weather significantly reduced attendance on several weekends. In addition, during the following winter, the diving pier was destroyed, and the park's pipes and faucets froze and broke and had to be replaced.

Ever the optimist, Wade continued to finance his project by adding and expanding facilities and attractions while also booking special events. The 1918 season was better than previous years, and Wade planned to continue his efforts to improve the park.

The resort had many attractions. One was the Interlaken Inn, in which vacationing families traveling to Interlaken Park could stay for weeks or months. When the inn first opened, it had a manager that imported a chef, waiters and porters from the Minneapolis area. Sunday dinner and evening weekday meals were seventy-five cents, and the inn frequently hosted conventions and banquets. Additionally, guests could choose to stay in one of the sixteen cabins near the inn.

Zoo animals were one of the attractions of Interlaken Park

The dance pavilion, one of the park's first structures, remained in use until it burned down in 1972. Some of the performing groups included the Interlaken Orchestra, the Menke Melody Orchestra, the White Hussar Band from Chicago, Harold Bachman's Million Dollar Orchestra which attracted 10,000 visitors, as well as the Fairmont City Band.

A main attraction was its zoo. Lenny Burton, one of Fairmont's more colorful and endeared individuals, was in charge of the zoo from the outset as he was experienced, having had his own zoo on the west side of George Lake. The zoo kept a wide variety of animals, including bears, deer, monkeys, owls, squirrels, seals, pheasants, eagles, foxes, swans, parrots, raccoons, skunks, ostriches, and more, including a lion at one time.

Perhaps Wade's greatest joy, however, were the Japanese Gardens. He designed them based upon his observances of others around the country. Although his plan was to expand them, those plans never materialized after Wade's death. Subsequent owners were not enthusiastic about this project, and, by the 1930s, the Japanese Gardens deteriorated and were no longer an inviting aspect of the park.

The park, at one time or another, also included a golf course, waterfront activities, special events and promotions, baseball games, pageants, a Ferris wheel, an eighteen-hole miniature golf course, a shooting gallery, and an appearance by William Jennings Bryan on July 12, 1918, who gave a speech lasting two-and-one-half hours. His appearance attracted 3,000 visitors who listened to his speech entitled, "Fundamentalism—a Plea for Patriotism, Prohibition, and Women's Suffrage." The Ku Klux Klan also used the park for rallies in the mid-1920s.

Wade's unfortunate death in March 1919 ended the vigorous growth the park had experienced up to that point.

Wade's son Harold managed the park until he sold it to John Erickson in 1923. Although the park thrived during that period of time, very few attractions were added, with the only major addition during that time being a restaurant and cabaret called the Merrie Garden.

Interlaken peaked in popularity in the early 1920s, and enjoyed praise from locals and visitors alike. In 1922, the July Fourth celebration had about 20,000 people attending.

However, problems were on the horizon. The popularity of the automobile as well as the development of northern Minnesota into a major resort area proved to have a negative effect on Fairmont's Interlaken Park.

From 1923, the park was run successfully by Erickson and his family. In 1945, Erickson negotiated a sale with a party with outside interests. The sale was eventually thwarted by a group of nineteen local businessmen who purchased the park for $60,000 in 1946. Their plan was to run the park for one year in order to give the city of Fairmont the opportunity to purchase it from them. However, the public was not convinced it was the right thing to do because of the expense and voted it down.

Over the years, the park gradually diminished and later only the ballroom remained as a reminder of those vibrant days gone by.

Little remains of Interlaken Park except the memories which are documented in *Fairmont Daily Sentinels* of the past and a well-written book entitled *The Story of Interlaken Park* by T.J. Arneson, both of which were used to write this story.

Wade passed away on March 3, 1919. The directors of the Fairmont Gas Engine and Railway Motor Car Company then elected Harold Wade president and general manager.

Frank Wade was undoubtedly one of the most influential and significant figures of his era. His accomplishments impacted Fairmont and Martin County in many ways. An entrepreneur, he was public spirited and a visionary intent on improving his community. His efforts proved instrumental in enhancing the quality of life in this area, and the positive effects of his presence were felt locally for many decades after his death. He was well-loved and respected in Martin County and throughout the state of Minnesota.

As the *Sentinel* put it, "The life of Frank Wade was a life of action."

March 6, 1862: **Frank Wade born**

1881: **Wade begins work with G.W. Sherwood & Company**

1887: **Wade moves to Primghar, Iowa, and operates a general store**

1899: **Led Fairbanks & Morse Company of Chicago in sales of its engines**

1902: **Co-owner of the Homestake Mining Company**

1902-1904: **Involved with the Globe Gold Mining Company**

1906: **Wade takes over the Water and Light Commission in Fairmont and founds Fairmont National Bank**

1909: **Wade is named president of Fairmont Machine Company**

1915: **Wade is elected Fairmont mayor and founds Interlaken Park resort**

March 3, 1919: **Wade passes away; his son Harold is named president and general manager of Fairmont Gas Engine and Railway Motor Car Company, formerly Fairmont Machine Company**

Fairmont's Excursion Boats

At one time, over a century ago, excursion boats were a common site on Fairmont's lakes. This was in the early 1900s when Interlaken, owned by Frank Wade, was in its prime. Wade, founder of the Fairmont Boat Company, also owned parks, hotels, and cabins, many of which could not be easily accessed by car as roadways were either limited or nonexistent. As a result, Wade, being the consummate entrepreneur, acquired boats for that purpose.

For a few years, these boats played an important role in transporting people to Interlaken, particularly those arriving in Fairmont by train as the train stations were only a few blocks from the Webster Street pier. The boats left every hour on the hour from that pier to go to Interlaken Park. Apparently both Bird's Bridge and the channel at Lair Road could accommodate these vessels. The trip from Webster Street went across Lake Sisseton, making stops at Oak Beach and Hazelmere Resort before docking at its destination, Interlaken.

The large boat on the far side of the dock was the Concord *which could fit several hundred people.*

There were a number of boats that navigated Fairmont's lakes during that period of time. The *Lady of the Lake* was small, about rowboat size, and was used from 1915 to 1917. Another, the *Venus*, had a four-cylinder inboard motor. The *Kildeer* was a forty-passenger boat with a canopy. The *Waubun* was fully enclosed with windows and shades and was known as the fleet's luxury boat. The *Queen* operated from 1920-1921 and measured thirty feet in length and had a capacity of twenty passengers.

The *City of Fairmont,* built by Captain Frederick Wherland, was first built for steam and later converted to a three-cycle Fairmont engine. Originally named the *Galatea*, it carried up to seventy-five people and sailed on Pierce Lake where Wherland made his home. Upon taking it to Fairmont's lakes, it was determined to be too small for the many passengers it could potentially carry. Therefore, Wherland cut through the middle and added about twenty feet. He then rechristened it the *City of Fairmont.*

When it was abandoned after Wherland's death, the city crew poured kerosene over its rotting remains on the beach of Ward's Park during the night and set it on fire. The fire was actually set out of respect as a Viking tribute to its memory.

The most famous of the fleet was the *Concord*. It was the largest boat, a double-decker, and it could accommodate several hundred people. The *Concord* was built in the winter of 1908 on the frozen ice of Lake Sisseton under the direction of Frank Wade. However, before its completion, Wade became ill. In spite of his ailing health, Wade continued to direct the construction of the *Concord* from his sickbed to his shipbuilder, George Hengel. When the ice went out in the spring, the boat floated, and the inside and top levels were then completed.

The *Concord* measured 112 feet long and twelve feet wide, and it had a flat bottom. It was first equipped with a propeller; however, according to Hengel, because it drew too much water, a stern wheel was installed. It was powered by a thirty-two horsepower Fairmont Gas Engine.

The *Concord* was available to individuals or groups and was used for summer excursions that included dances, card parties, and other social events. It was said that no trip to Fairmont was complete without a ride on the *Concord.*

Eventually, the Interlaken management found the *Concord* too expensive to operate. Another problem was that it had sunk to the mud in the boathouse several times. Ultimately, it was sold to John Lind, formerly a Welcome hotel man who later lived in Truman. He used her planks and boards for the construction of a cottage at Hazelmere and, upon completion of the cottage, still had $50 worth of lumber remaining.

As roads to Interlaken were improved and more people had access to automobiles, the demand for lake travel diminished. As a result, the Fairmont Boat Company faced extinction. In an attempt to continue its service, the city of Fairmont purchased the company in 1921 for $1,500. However, as time passed, it became obvious that the city's pursuit of maintaining the boating business was unsuccessful. The boats were being used less frequently; they fell into disrepair, and they were eventually either scrapped or sold. By 1928, the boathouse was demolished as the automobile had taken over as the primary mode of transportation.

Consequently, another colorful chapter in the rich history of Fairmont and Martin County had evolved. The days of those excursion boats on Fairmont's lakes, though relatively short lived, marked a truly unique era in our local history.

Sources for this story include The Story of Interlaken Park *by T.J. Arneson.*

Prominent Citizens of 1922

In 1922, Frank Day, *Sentinel* editor, had a close personal friend who was a cartoonist for the *St. Paul Pioneer Press.* This cartoonist, Mr. Wing, was said to be able to capture the character and personality of his subjects. Consequently, he visited Day in Fairmont and made cartoon sketches of those individuals considered prominent at that time. According to a 1964 article in the *Sentinel,* these drawings appeared in the September 10, 1922, edition of the *St. Paul Pioneer Press* and were later donated to the Fairmont Youth Center by Marjorie Pfiffner. You might note the distinct absence of "prominent" women in his drawings.

Top from left: Frank Day; H. Ward Pfiffner; Judge Julius E. Haycraft; Dr. W.L. Webb; Albert L. Ward. Middle row: Harold Wade; Judge E.C. Dean; W. Lincoln Nicholas; Robert McNab; Elmore Houghtaling; Herbert Anderson; E.J. "Teck" Edwards. Bottom: A. R. Fancher; Harry S. Fairley.

So who were these so-called prominent citizens of 1922? Each is described as follows according to the number designated to them on their likeness:

1. Frank A. Day: Founder of *The Sentinel*, state senator from Martin and Watonwan counties for two terms fifty years apart; served as Lieutenant Governor of Minnesota under Governor Clough
2. H. Ward Pfiffner: Served in the adjutant general's office at the state capitol; editor of the *Martin County Independent*; bequeathed money for the establishment of the former Fairmont Youth Center
3. Judge Julius E. Haycraft: Judge of the 17th Judicial District serving Martin, Faribault and Jackson Counties; state senator; an irreconcilable "dry" and worker for temperance causes
4. Dr. W.L. Webb: A Fairmont dentist; former Fairmont mayor; served on the park board

5. Albert L. Ward: Founder of the Martin County Bank; lawyer; state senator; land owner; had many other business interests
6. Harold E. Wade: Succeeded his father, Frank E. Wade, as president of Fairmont Railway Motors
7. Judge Ezra C. Dean: Lawyer; Judge of 17th Judicial District; known to delight courtroom spectators by leaning from his judicial chair to expectorate in a two-gallon brass spittoon
8. W.L. Nicholas: Known as "Link," he was a theater man who partnered with Billy Hay to take over the opera house, renaming it the "Haynic;" donated the land for Lincoln Park
9. Robert H. McNab: Owner of a Fairmont hotel for several years
10. Elmore Houghtaling: Beloved citizen and co-owner of Houghtaling and Coult hardware store
11. Herbert Anderson: a *Sentinel* reporter; at one time president of the Minnesota Newspaper Boy Carrier's Association; owner of Anderson Printing Company
12. E.J. Edwards: Called "Teck;" he really had no middle initial but was implored by Frank Day to have one since he was running for mayor. He was a Fairmont druggist.
13. A.R. Fancher: Owner of a general store; was elected for several terms as a judge of Martin County Probate Court
14. Harry S. Fairley: Managing editor of the *Sentinel* from 1917 until his death in 1938. Prior to that, he was the city editor of the *Minneapolis Journal* and telegraph editor of the *St. Paul Daily News.*

Many of those so-called prominent people of 1922 were in fact very instrumental in the development of Martin County as we know it today. Without their pioneering spirit and efforts, our county may not have experienced the advancements and achievements it has to date. Fortunately, and in contrast to 1922, the focus of prominent people in today's Martin County would include numerous female citizens as well.

Sources for this story include the July 18, 1964, story by Claude Swanson in the Sentinel.

Martin County's Poor Farm

What was Martin County's "Poor Farm?" While reviewing its history in newspaper accounts, it was especially interesting to see both the evolution of the facility as well as the colorful language used to describe the events and individuals associated with it.

The April 7, 1914, the *Martin County Sentinel* was headlined "County To Have Home For Poor." The county commissioners of that era planned for a building to be erected about three miles north of Fairmont on Buffalo Lake to accommodate the less fortunate. It would be a modern building for its time, consisting of a basement, a thirty-square-foot cistern, and a coal room. There would also be twelve rooms on the second floor. The first inhabitants of the facility, referred to as "inmates," moved in November 24, 1915.

Poor Farm Front

As time passed, the cost of the Poor Farm became a concern for the citizens of the county due to the expenses associated with its operation. In 1926, the county paid the cost of tobacco for the inmates, which amounted to $22.75 for a fourteen-month period. A 1928 newspaper article stated that the facility cost the county $4,776 the previous year. The breakdown of expenses showed: maintenance of the property was $4,828; the keeper's salary was $1,750; interest on the investment was $2,000; therefore, the total expenses were $8,578. Subtracting the $3,802 income determined the county's cost to be $4,776. The article further states that "the figures were without error because they were pronounced correct by county officials." Apparently the calculations of public officials were less likely to be scrutinized at that time in our history.

By 1937, the county decided to abolish the Poor Farm. The farm, consisting of 116 acres, was rented out and a tenant occupied part of the house. However, another part of the house could still be used to house poor people from the city who asked the county for living quarters.

Some reasons cited for its abolishment were that "old age pensions" and other kinds of "poor aid" would take care of the current inmates. Newspaper accounts stated that the twelve inmates of the farm were properly provided for by the commissioners. The six persons over sixty-five would be given pensions, several more had been placed "here and there" by the commissioners, and two of the younger inmates were asked to "shift for themselves" by working on farms or finding jobs in the city.

The next phase in the continuing evolution of the Poor Farm was in 1938, when it was being considered as a girls' school for the National Youth Administration. The theory was that it would provide an opportunity for training in household arts, health education, social and economic problems, recreation, and individual counseling for girls from eight counties in this part of the state. It was set to open on January 15, 1939, with the commissioners agreeing to accept rent of $35 monthly. Selection of applicants was limited to girls eligible for NYA employment, in good health, able to profit from an educational program, able to adjust to group living, and who presented no unusual problems of mental or physical health. The enrollment was limited to thirty.

The school seemed to progress fairly successfully with the girls learning washing, sewing, ironing, mending, and repair work around the house. The girls were ready for temporary placement in homes and businesses by May 15th of 1939. Their work week would consist of a maximum of ten hours, and they were to be paid no less than twenty cents per hour.

In October of 1941, the NYA School that had been in operation for less than two years was closed. The reasons cited were that it must be sacrificed for government military defense measures and that it was not a profitable venture. The Martin County School had twenty-five girls, and it was said by officials of the time that 70 were needed to make it a profitable project.

The building then became empty and posed a concern for the citizens of the county. One suggestion at that time was that it might be a good site for evacuees in the event large cities on either coast were bombed during WWII. Eventually, in 1943, it would become chartered as a youth hostel and would operate from May through October.

In 1949, the Poor Farm became the St. Joseph's Home for the Aged, a home devoted exclusively to the care of the elderly. When remodeling was completed, the facility held twenty-eight persons. Mother Lucia was the manager of the home, and she was assisted by four Catholic sisters. A new addition was added in 1956. In 1971, after twenty-two years, the St. Joseph's Home closed its doors. The Poor Farm was once again empty.

In 1973, the evolution of the Poor Farm completed its next stage and became the Chain of Lakes Halfway House. The first director was V.H. "Rocky" Baum, and it served mainly residents of Martin, Jackson, and Faribault counties.

The final chapter in the ever changing landscape of the Poor Farm was in 2004, when the Chain of Lakes Halfway House went out of existence. The site of the original Poor Farm was in operation for nearly 100 years in a variety of capacities. It was demolished in 2007.

Sources for this story include "NYA, Poor Farm, Home for the Ages" binder at MCHS.

R.J. "Bob" Wallace

Martin County has witnessed many entrepreneurs throughout the course of its vibrant history. One such individual was R.J. "Bob" Wallace.

Born in New London, Illinois, in 1885, Wallace came to Minnesota with his parents, Mr. and Mrs. Thomas Wallace. They settled in North Star, Minnesota, located between Fairmont and Sherburn. Thomas was a butter maker in a small creamery in North Star, one of Martin County's "lost towns" that was dedicated with a historical marker in 2001 by the Martin County Historical Society.

R.J. "Bob" Wallace

Wallace attended school in Fairmont through seventh grade. He also worked evenings and weekends at the Wolf–Habein store, later working full-time in the dry goods department. While working at Wolf–Habein, he met his future wife, Edna Colton, a bookkeeper for the company. They were married in 1908 and had two children, Gloria Margaret and Bruce Robert.

In 1915, Wallace opened a dry goods and grocery store in the Masonic building in Fairmont with a partner, Ed Keyes of Lakefield. Within two months of opening, however, Keyes asked to leave the partnership, and Wallace continued the operation independently. At that time, grocery and sewing needs were the largest departments. Saturday was the major day in trade and retail as customers first attended movies and then did their shopping. The store would stay open until 10 or 11 p.m. in order to accommodate its customers. Eventually, the grocery and dry goods departments were replaced with children and infants ready-to-wear as the largest departments.

Wallace eventually expanded his business by purchasing grocery stores in Sherburn and Ceylon and general stores in Granada, Winnebago, Minnesota, and Spencer, Iowa. However, in 1931, his Spencer store was destroyed by fire and was never reopened. In 1932, Wallace decided to eliminate his small businesses in the surrounding Fairmont area. Shortly thereafter, in 1933, he opened a dry goods and ready-to-wear store in Albert Lea. His son Bruce joined him in the business in 1935, and then in 1936, they opened another store in Austin.

Wallace's business motto, "The Customer is Always Right," served him well as loyal customers continued to patronize his businesses throughout the depression era of the 1930s. During that period, Wallace would drive to Chicago and load his car with fabric, discontinued fabric patterns, and other merchandise that he purchased from the Marshall Field Wholesale Division. He would then make the fifteen-to-eighteen hour drive nonstop back to Fairmont with his merchandise.

Wallace's deptartment store

Wallace, active in many organizations, including being a charter member of the Fairmont Rotary Club and a school board member, passed away in 1957 at the age of 72. His son, Bruce, then took over the business and his grandson, R.J. "Bob" Wallace, joined the company in 1967. His grandson operated the last Wallace's store, which was in Fairmont, until it closed in 1996 after eighty-one years of business. He then served as the Fairmont Area Chamber of Commerce president until his retirement in 2014.

Entrepreneurial ventures by individuals such as Wallace have proven significant in the economic development and well-being of our nation, our state, and our local region. The efforts of these creative and industrious individuals have provided goods, services, and jobs throughout our history and helped to provide a better way of life for everyone throughout our society.

Sources for this story include The Sentinel Hometown Legends, *2007 edition.*

Prohibition and the Local Response

Time marched on and with it brought about the debate on liquor.

Prohibition was a period of time in the 1920s and 1930s in U.S. history during which the manufacture, sale, and transportation of liquor was made illegal. It lasted nearly fourteen years and could be characterized by speakeasies, bootlegging, and gangsters. It was a time in which sometimes even the average citizen broke the law.

However, there were some loopholes for people to legally drink during the Prohibition Era. The Eighteenth Amendment did not mention the actual drinking of liquor and Prohibition went into effect a full year after the amendment's ratification. Consequently, many people bought cases of then-legal alcohol and stored them for personal use. Also, the Volstead Act allowed alcohol consumption if it was prescribed by a doctor. Needless to say, many new prescriptions were written.

However, it seems Prohibition was exemplified in Martin County. The county went dry five years before Prohibition was ratified. In the spring of 1915, Fairmont voted "dry" by 119 votes, Truman by three, Monterey by nine, Ormsby by two, and Dunnell by thirty-one; Triumph voted "wet" by 21 votes. However, the county became "bone dry" in 1918 when the remaining wets—Triumph, Welcome, and Ceylon—closed their saloons.

The closing of Fairmont's saloons in 1915 was preceded by what was described as a bitter "wet–dry" fight with the *Sentinel* leading the fight for drys. The dispute at one point became so contentious that an estimated 400 persons lined up from Rockwell's Saloon on West First Street to march to the *Sentinel* office in an attempt to stop the paper from running.

The *Sentinel* editor and publisher at that time, Frank Day, personally met the group amidst angry exchanges. Day led the cause for the drys; however, the wets were energized and pressured the downtown merchants, threatening to boycott any business that advertised in Day's newspaper. Business owners appealed to Day to ease off his cause, but he declined.

National Prohibition Guards

Slogan: We'll Help to Safeguard America's Future

Because I believe it to be the patriotic duty of every American to obey the laws of the land,

I hereby enroll in the Million Membership Campaign for Law Observance, promising to abstain from the use of intoxicating liquors as a beverage, and to obey the Eighteenth Amendment to the Constitution of the United States of America.

Name Martha Hannon

Date May 24th

Nat. W. C. T. U. Publishing House, Evanston, Illinois

On the eve of the wet–dry vote, interesting and perhaps ballot-changing events took place. The wets had brought a congressman from Wisconsin to address a large group of people at the Haynic Theatre. This rather stout gentleman had a raucous voice and berated the audience by holding up a five-dollar bill stating that if anyone in the audience could prove to him from the Bible that drinking should not be allowed, the five-dollar bill would be theirs. That statement angered a tall, whiskered gentleman who stood up and cried out that the congressman had no right to make a bet involving the Bible. Immediately after making his statement, the tall gentleman sank to the floor unconscious. He was carried out of the venue and died minutes later.

Ironically, what at that time appeared to be a potential eleventh-hour coup for the wets instead turned against them and the city of Fairmont voted dry.

The intensity of the issue was felt by both sides as was evidenced at the *Sentinel* office. Harry N. Brandall, a star reporter for the paper entered the office and was greeted by Frank Day. Day said, "It was a great victory, wasn't it?"

Brandall replied, "Yes, I guess it was, but I feel I must tell you I voted wet."

Day replied, "You did? The hell you did! You're fired!"

Interestingly enough, Brandall was a very talented reporter and cartoonist, earning an unheard of salary at that time of twenty-five dollars a week. His salary was equaled only by Day's. Apparently tolerance regarding one's views on that topic was limited at best.

In 1928, in California, a Los Angeles jury that had heard a bootlegging case was itself put on trial after it drank the evidence, according to a January 1928 story in *The New York Times*. The jurors argued in their defense that they had simply been sampling the evidence to determine whether or not it contained alcohol, which they determined it did. However, because they consumed the evidence, the defendant charged with bootlegging had to be acquitted. Could that constitute jury tampering by the jury?

In March of 1933, Franklin Roosevelt signed the Cullen–Harrison Act into law which allowed low-alcohol beer and wine manufacture nationally. Nine months later, the Twenty-First Amendment repealed Prohibition federally but still allowed the states and municipalities to decide for themselves whether to continue dry.

On the local scene, the legalization of alcohol sales as a result of the Cullen–Harrison Act appeared to significantly stimulate the economy, at least initially. According to archives in the Pioneer Museum, beer arrived in Fairmont on April 7, 1933. Thirsty consumers from as far away as Bancroft, Iowa, began to gather at the Crystal Bottling Plant, one of the local delivery points, around midnight. By 4:30 a.m., a truck carrying 273 cases of beer arrived. The driver barely had time to turn off the motor before all of the truck's contents were sold, mostly to private individuals with a few cases going to distant dealers rewarding them for their trip to Fairmont.

Gus Anderson, a local agent for the Hamm's Brewing Company on the north side, also experienced a rush of activity. He said they were so busy that he couldn't even guarantee delivery of the product to local establishments. He went on to say that, since there were 100 or more people standing in line, if you wanted a case you had better "stick around" and take your chances on getting one.

The city council vote on the beer ordinance, an ordinance said to be "with teeth" for the sale of 3.2 beer, passed by a vote of four to two. One alderman who actually voted in favor of the ordinance, W.L. Nicholas, said that it is ridiculous to say that 3.2 beer is non-intoxicating. He went on to say, "One quart of the stuff on an empty stomach, say about six hours after eating, will give you the peachiest jag you ever got."

In order to comply with local ordinances at that time, Sunday sales were only allowed in the afternoon and establishments offering beer had to serve food in order to acquire a beer license. As a result, pool halls appear to have had to make the greatest structural modifications. In order to comply, they would need to add booths, food counters, and kitchens. One creative pool hall proprietor may have attempted to circumvent, or at least limit, his food service requirement by providing the following menu items:

- T-Bone Steak (on the hoof) $1.25
- Fried Chicken (with or without feathers) $1.50
- Egg Sandwiches (on the nest) $0.25
- Sandwiches Toasted (slightly burned) $0.15 extra

The end result of the ordinance was that Fairmont had no more pool halls. They all became cafes.

In a vote to repeal Prohibition in 1933, the county again voted dry. Eventually, twenty years later, the county voted to allow municipal liquor. Most county municipalities then established liquor stores; however, Fairmont did not approve municipal liquor until 1957, which then passed only by a margin of twelve votes. A municipal off-sale liquor store was established in December of that year.

Consequently, the Martin County liquor drought lasted nearly forty years for the county and forty-two years for Fairmont.

Sources for this story include prohibitionrepeal.com/history/fastfacts.asp, viewed March 2, 2018; and Jan Dickinson's compiled research of newspaper articles 1930–1934.

Industry and Enterprise in Martin County

Mule Town

Farming is a driving force for the economy of Martin County today. It was significant in the past as well, and in the late 1800s, there was a large farming operation southwest of Sherburn in Jay Township known as Mule Town or Mule Farm due to the farm machinery being operated by mules.

Little is documented about Mule Town outside of one photo, brief acknowledgements in newspapers of the time, and anecdotes from people in the 1950s who recalled events from their youth regarding the farm.

What we do know is that Mule Town was developed by Cargill, Bassett and Hunting, a land company from La Crosse, Wisconsin, that had previously laid out the town site of Sherburn. Mule Town was originally managed by H.E. Anderson and later by H.M. Swarthout. Its size comprised approximately 3,000 acres originally, although some accounts indicate it was as large as 5,760 acres. The site included a two-story dwelling, a huge barn, and a large storehouse. The advent of the railroad in 1878 provided an outlet for their products.

Several hundred cattle and sheep, mules, horses, and some hogs were kept and raised for sale. The crops included wheat, corn, and potatoes. There were also hundreds of acres of hay to be cut and stored.

Mule Town employed from fifteen to twenty-five men and up to as many as forty during the peak times. It also employed two blacksmiths. Numerous girls were also hired to help; however, many failed to stay employed as a result of the strenuous work. The men were housed in a bunkhouse that included eating facilities, and the girls stayed in the main house. A large dinner bell was used to call the hired help for meals. Incidentally, the mules also responded to the call.

The archives of the Pioneer Museum provide some quite interesting accounts of the time when Mule Town was in operation. In April of 1879, H.E. Anderson planned to have Mule Town incorporated. He thought it would grow and have a larger population than Sherburn.

In March of 1880, a number of farm hands were in town, presumably Sherburn, and apparently imbibed a bit too much. On their way home, the mules became frightened and threw one of the farm hands out of the wagon. He struck his head on the frozen ground. At first it was feared that he might be seriously hurt, so he stayed in a hotel overnight rather than continuing back to Mule Town. However, he returned to Mule Town the following day with only minor bruises. No mention of medical attention was ever stated.

Representative of Mule Town

In April of 1882, Anderson left Mule Town for other employment and was replaced by Swarthout. Anderson did not necessarily leave in the good graces of Cargill, Bassett, andHunting as it had become run down and was a losing investment.

By 1885, Swarthout stated the farm was now 9,000 acres and additional buildings were built, including a cattle shed and a granary. It was also referred to at times as the Fox Lake Farm Company.

In April of 1886, all the property belonging to the farm was put up for sale, including the livestock and farm equipment. In May of 1886, Mule Farm had been sold to W.T. Hanson who planned to put the farm up for sale in small lots. However, this apparently did not transpire as the farm again came up for sale in March of 1887.

Then, in December of 1888, a disastrous fire was reported at Mule Town. That fire destroyed property, horses, cattle, grain, poultry, and farm implements, including grain and machinery stored there by other farmers. The loss was estimated to be in excess of $10,000, and there was no insurance to cover any of the losses. The owner at that time was listed as one Mr. McGovern.

This large farming enterprise at one time was a major contributor to the economy of Martin County by employing a fairly large number of people. However, careless management and poor operating practices eventually led to its demise.

Although short lived, Mule Town adds another colorful and interesting chapter to the history of Martin County.

Sources for this story include MCHS History File 178.

Henry Rippe and the Rippe Mansion

Henry Rippe, Jr., was an entrepreneur of his time who had a lasting and significant impact on Fairmont and Martin County.

Rippe was born in Dubuque, Iowa, in 1853. By the age of nine, he was buying and selling grain. When he reached the age of sixteen, he had accumulated $1,000 and began working with W.W. Cargill, buying and selling grain, auditing, and supervising forty elevators. He would go on to become recognized as an expert and leader in his field.

Henry Rippe residence

Rippe married Kay Walter in 1881, and the couple had three children while living in Grand Meadow, Minnesota. In 1891, they moved to Fairmont and established the Rippe Grain and Milling Company. Although facing stiff competitors locally, his perseverance eventually led to success. At that time, the mill had a capacity of seventy barrels of flour. It was marketed under the trade name of Rippe's Golden Leaf and was milled for family use from area wheat fields. It was operated by steam power and the locals could hear the whistle at 7 a.m., noon, and 1 p.m.

Rippe was a shrewd, successful businessman. He owned several elevators located in Welcome and Alpha, Minnesota; Armstrong, Iowa; and Bowman, North Dakota.

Rippe enjoyed a wide circle of friends. He also had an interest in politics, never as a candidate, but from behind the scenes. In 1915, he was involved in a bitterly contested county option fight involving liquor, Rippe being aligned against the "drys." He threatened that if Fairmont should go dry, the whistle at the Rippe Mill be silenced. When the final votes were tallied, Fairmont did go dry. Therefore, being true to his word, the whistle at the Rippe Mill was silent from that day forward.

Rippe was well known to the Fairmont citizens of that period, walking daily to work. Always ready with a cheerful greeting and friendly smile, he loved his work and was considered a courteous gentleman and devoted family man. He was public spirited and active in civic affairs. He helped the American Legion get a new home by making a generous donation himself as well as personally canvassing the town to raise $6,000 in merely two days. He was a member of Fairmont's first charter commission and one of the most active men and stockholders in the promotion of the Fairmont Opera House. It was said of Rippe that, although he aged, he never really grew old. He especially enjoyed movies and a game of bridge and apparently few were equal to his ability at the card table.

Perhaps as well known and documented as Henry Rippe's business ventures was his home on Woodland Avenue, the Rippe Mansion. It was one of the finest, most lavishly appointed homes of that era in Fairmont. It was located at 121 Woodland, about three blocks east of the Wohlheter mansion, both being built at about the same time. Rippe's home was said to have cost $25,000 to $30,000 when it was built in the 1890s.

The Rippe mansion was very well known throughout southern Minnesota and northern Iowa during that time. It had hardwood floors inlaid with mahogany, a fireplace boasting hand-carved hardwood woodwork, and a spacious living room and dining room separated by sliding doors. The dining room had hand-carved, glass-paneled, recessed cupboards and could seat twenty-four people at the table. The combined length of the dining room and living room, when the sliding doors were opened, measured fifty feet from wall to wall.

However, in the mid 1930s, major changes came to the home. Roy Palmer purchased the Rippe Mansion from the Rippe estate. He thought the three-story house was far too big and cumbersome. As a result, Palmer decided to cut off the second story and make another house out of it, which is now located behind that house at 126 Cedar Street. The carriage house and horse barn were also transformed into residences. The top floor of the Rippe mansion was then rearranged to make two large apartments.

Later on, Anthony Shaw, a bridegroom who had been a bachelor until age fifty-eight, was given a sales pitch to purchase the Rippe mansion for $4,600. Shaw was quite a successful farmer from Iowa who was very interested as he had previously planned to move to Fairmont. Consequently, Shaw purchased the house. The entire house was a rental for a number of years until Shaw and his wife eventually took possession of the first floor for their living quarters.

Henry Rippe, Jr., one of the early pioneering capitalists of southern Minnesota, passed away in 1930 at the age of 76. He is remembered as one of the "old-timers" who helped build Fairmont in its early years.

Sources for this article include Fairmont Daily Sentinel, *March 24, 1930, pages 1 and 4; The Daily Sentinel Martin County Centennial edition, June 28, 1958, page 4; and MCHS History File 617.*

The Family of John Allison

The compilation and recording of historical data sometimes neglects or fails to recognize those individual traits and characteristics of people who were quite likely vital to an era. An example of this to consider is John Allison, a well-known and prominent figure in Fairmont in the 1800s and early part of the twentieth century, and his family.

Mr. and Mrs. John Allison

Most local history enthusiasts will associate his name with the well-known Allison Horse Parlors of that era, which was located on North Main Street just east of where the old armory once stood in Fairmont. However, upon closer examination, there was more to Allison and his immediate family than the horse parlors.

Allison, an Englishman, came to Fairmont in the mid-1890s. His initial business venture involved livery and the importing of English horses, which evolved into the horse parlors. In addition to his horse parlor, however, he also was involved in real estate and served for many years as deputy sheriff. Due to poor health, he retired at the age of sixty-three.

According to his obituary in the December 16, 1937, edition of the *Fairmont Sentinel*, "Mr. Allison could be classed among Fairmont's favorite citizens. Genial, kindly and the soul of courtesy and consideration, he made a friend of everyone."

That same article referred to the fact that, after going west to spend the winter months, Allison told friends he was living on borrowed time thanks to his new raw food diet he had discovered while in California. When he initially left for the West Coast, he stated that he had a number of health concerns, including being overweight. Upon his arrival in California, he had to be taken off the train on a stretcher, and his doctors from Fairmont didn't think he would even be able to stand the trip. However, since being on the raw food diet, he told friends that he had lost fifty pounds, lowered his blood pressure, and had not felt this good in years. Nevertheless, he also admitted to his friends back home that he would probably be even better off if he adhered more stringently to his new diet.

Allison passed away in California at the age of 73. He was survived by a son, Jess, who was at that time the head of a large Minneapolis financial institution; a brother, Charles, in Los Angeles; and two sisters in England whom he had not seen in forty years. Allison was preceded in death by his wife, Fredrica, who was born in Wurttemburg, Germany, and a son, Ben.

Jess Allison was at one time employed by the *Sentinel* and described as a "mainstay." When Jess was leaving the *Sentinel* in August 1916 to go to Minneapolis, an article about him said, "We are going to hold a job open for him and pray that he will tire of the wicked city and come back to his first love where a lot of 'em love him." Although eventually becoming quite successful in the financial world of Minneapolis, Jess was also obviously very highly respected by the *Sentinel* and local community of that era as well.

Ben Allison attended Fairmont public schools and was a star athlete. After graduating from high school in 1921, he went on to attend Knox College in Galesburg, Illinois. He then entered law school at the University of Minnesota where he was also a starting guard on the Gopher football team. It appeared at that time that he had a very bright and promising future.

After graduating from law school, he moved to Raymondsville, Texas, where he opened a law practice. While there, he developed an impacted wisdom tooth which caused him problems and had to be removed. The extraction caused an infection which resulted in his premature and untimely death. Ben's obituary memorialized him as one who will be remembered by all who were privileged to have made his acquaintance.

It appears from written accounts in the Pioneer Museum that John Allison and the Allison family were not only well respected, but also contributed to the community in many ways. They were Martin County pioneers who helped form and shape the early history of this area.

Although they will most likely be remembered primarily for the Allison Horse Parlors, which was certainly a significant aspect of Fairmont's history, it's also important to keep in mind that there was much more to pioneering individuals such as John than strictly their business endeavors and accomplishments. Allison's presence, how he conducted himself in the community, his family, his integrity, his character, and the respect of local citizenry further serves to reveal his overall contribution to the history and development of our area, which in essence might well have actually transcended his entrepreneurial endeavors and accomplishments.

Allison's Horse Parlors

"Thanks for the buggy ride!" read the headlines of the November 19, 1926, *Martin County Sentinel.*

The equine era of our local history provided one of the most popular and thriving businesses in Fairmont's past, referred to by many as the magnificent Allison Horse Parlors. In 1898, John Allison built the horse parlors just east of where the old armory at 209 North Main once stood.

Upon his retirement in 1926, the *Sentinel,* reported that "when John Allison, who just retired and gone south and west to winter with the robins and millionaires, built these magnificent horse parlors he provided an institution that put Fairmont in the front row." The article goes on to further state that the city had the absolute best accommodations for the farmers' horses in all the surrounding area. This in turn brought many people to Fairmont, and the city profited greatly from the increased trade which resulted from Mr. Allison's business.

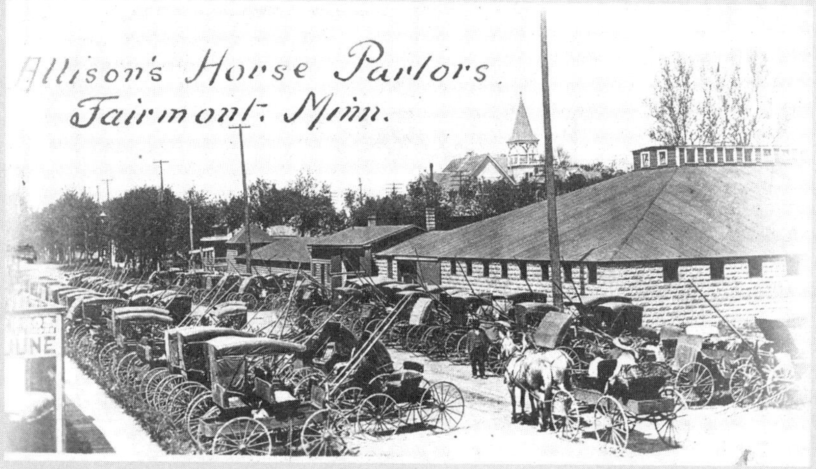

The building itself was a large structure that could accommodate up to 250 teams of horses with facilities for feeding, watering, and bedding them for the night. The stalls were arranged so that the horses faced the outside walls, and the center had another section with alleys wide enough for farmers to drive in with their teams and unhitch them out of the cold. When the stalls were filled, as was the case nearly every day, the wagons and buggies formed outside in double rows up and down the street.

The cost for use of the stable was twenty-five cents per team, or fifteen cents if you went home right after the saloons closed at 11 p.m. This price included hay, oats, and water. Thrifty farmers of that time were known to bring their own oats as they could then park their horses there all day for a dime. Mr. Allison would "throw in" the hay and water.

The barn was a popular spot, especially during the winter months, as it provided an enclosed area for public auctions of household goods and, in later years, farm machinery. In addition, it served as a gathering place for farmers, the scene of many an argument on every subject known, and a checkerboard was always present as quite a number of checker champions were developed in the feed stable office.

Allison was envied by the public as most felt he had developed a "gold mine" business. The business appeared to be at its height only a few months before the internal combustion gasoline engine made the automobile a common sight on our streets. Whether it was shrewdness or luck on Allison's part, it was at that point in time, just before the automobile put the horse parlor out to pasture, that he sold his business and eventually moved on to warmer climates.

The huge barn, once a Fairmont showplace and one of the busiest business establishments in the area, became a mere shell used for storage, an ignominious ending to a "magnificent" space.

The building was leveled by fire in the mid-1940s. Lost in the fire were music boxes, pinball machines, trucks, and automobiles. The barn had become a holding space for more modern day items, a big change from its illustrious and profitable history.

Sources for this sidebar included the MCHS History File 178.

The Changing Face of Retail

The ever-changing face of retail has taken many twists and turns as it has evolved over the years. The Walmarts, Best Buys, Targets, Costcos, and a myriad of others have created a retail landscape vastly different from those present in much of the last century, both nationally and locally. One store many long-time Martin County residents will remember is the Wolf–Habein store. Wolf–Habein, frequently referred to as Wolf's, was a popular department store located at 123 North North Avenue in Fairmont.

The history of this store can be traced back to the Wolf–Habein Corporation of Waseca, Minnesota. It was originally comprised of Orin Robert (O.R.) Wolf, William Wolf, Al Wolf, and their brother-in-law, Henry C. Habein. In 1899, they purchased the J.T. Swearingen store in Fairmont.

O.R. had general store experience in Faribault and Minneapolis, was very ambitious, and wanted to go into business for himself. Consequently, he saved $250 and borrowed $500 in order to go in with his brothers on the purchase of the Fairmont store. Al and William had stores in Faribault and Blue Earth, so the partnership consisted of three stores. After Al died in 1939, O.R. traded his interests in the other stores for full ownership of the Fairmont store.

William, O.R.'s son, was born in 1909 at 403 South Elm Street in Fairmont. He had a brother, Marland, and a sister, Wilhelmina Carey. He attended public schools in Fairmont and graduated from Shattuck in Faribault, Minnesota, in 1926. In 1930, he graduated from Knox College in Galesburg, Illinois, and obtained an MBA from the Harvard Business School two years later. William, or Bill as he was commonly known, was obviously a very well-educated individual who would also become a very capable businessman.

Bill started his career in retail when he joined Associated Dry Goods at Powers Department Store in Minneapolis. He later transferred to Hanes Department Store in Newark, New Jersey, where he became divisional merchandise manager of women's and misses accessories, silverware, books, office supplies, and yard goods. It was in New Jersey where he met his wife, Thayle Landers. They were married in 1938 and returned to Fairmont where he joined his father in running the Fairmont store. Bill and Thayle had two children, William Jr., and Dara.

Bill was quite civic-minded and very active in the community. He served as president of Interlaken Golf Club and was a member of the Chamber of Commerce, the Masonic Lodge, Fairmont Kiwanis, and Service Core of Retired Executives. In addition, in 1953, he was elected a director of The First National Bank, succeeding Frank L. McCadden.

The November 8, 1955, edition of the *Fairmont Daily Sentinel* designated a considerable amount of space to Wolf's third expansion since 1899, and the many changes that had taken place over the years. It was reported that their first expansion was shortly after WWI and included discontinuing the grocery department. Their second expansion involved more than doubling their balcony space to display merchandise, and their third was their greatest of all and involved converting their basement storage space to merchandise display space.

In that *Sentinel* article, O.R. interestingly discussed the many changes he had seen over the course of his career in retail since he started in the mercantile business in 1888. In particular, he recalled those early days in which it was customary to "throw in" a bag of candy for the kids, bargaining and haggling over price was the rule rather than the exception, it was not unusual to grant credit for as long as a year, customers always expected a discount for paying in cash, and, in the early years, a counter was a place to sit on or lean on, not for displaying merchandise. Another fascinating merchandising expectation O.R. experienced early in his career was that "it was a part of the merchant's 'duty' to entertain, keep warm, and not infrequently feed the women and children while the customer stayed at the saloon until it closed at midnight. The saloons in those days featured free lunch including pickled pig hocks, sardines, anchovies, crackers and cheese, pickles, and bread." This is one perk that has long since been discontinued.

The Wolf–Habein advertising slogan and paper goods script logo was "Wolf's, First in Quality Since 1899." It remained unchanged throughout the history of the store. In 1974, Wolf's was sold to the Ehler's Corporation, thus ending an era.

From 1899 to 1974, the Wolf–Habein Department Store was a well-known, respected, and popular retail fixture to Fairmont and Martin County residents. Since then, many locally owned establishments such as Wolf–Habein seem to have gradually evaporated and been replaced through the evolution of national retailers and department stores. Times change, but those of us who remember that era will always have fond memories of Wolf–Habein and what it represented to the local economy and community of that time.

I would like to acknowledge and thank Dara Wolf LaForce-Skelton for her contribution of historical information about her family for this article.

Fairmont's Industrial Revolution

Perhaps Fairmont's Industrial Revolution began in the early 1900s with the Fairmont Machine Company, the predecessor to Fairmont Railway Motors, which has since evolved into Harsco Rail.

Railway Motors

The company began operations in the early 1900s as a small machine shop. It began to manufacture single cylinder engines primarily for farm use for pumping water, sawing wood, and jobs such as these in 1907. Then, in 1909, it was incorporated into Fairmont Machine Company. That year marked the first time that Fairmont engines were applied to railway hand or pump cars and thereby provided their entrance into the railroad industry.

Fred Mahlman, Sr., a railroad section hand who was not employed by Fairmont Railway Motors, was instrumental in the design and development of this endeavor which eventually proved to be a driving force in establishing the company as a leader in the industry.

The business prospered and in 1913, the city of Duluth put forth an attractive offer to the company to move its offices and plant there. However, a group of concerned and interested Fairmont citizens pledged to support the company and, consequently, the directors decided to remain in Fairmont.

The company name was changed to Fairmont Gas Engine and Railway Motor Car Company in 1915. The January 11, 1915, headline of the *Fairmont Daily Sentinel* read,

"Impressionistic View of Fairmont's Greatest Industrial Enterprise." This article went on to say that the company had an international reputation, employed 155 people, and stated in detail why their engine was superior to the competition. The officers of the company at that time were: President Frank E. Wade; Vice President John P. Dunning; Secretary Arza R. Fancher; and Treasurer William M. Hay. Howard M. Starrett, Matthew Pfeiffert, and George H. Snyder rounded out the board.

Soon the company began the design and development of complete motor cars and began producing their own models in the early 1920s. In addition, during that same decade, the company began to produce and sell "maintenance-of way" work equipment that included weed burners, weed mowers, and ballast discers. In 1923, the firm adopted the name, Fairmont Railway Motors, Inc.

The 1920s saw further expansion that included an international flavor. This involved the purchase of Mudge and Company of Chicago, a railway motor car business, in 1928, and the formation of a Canadian subsidiary in 1929, Fairmont Railway Motors, Ltd., which was located in suburban Toronto.

The late 1940s saw the development of Hy-Rail vehicles that could operate either on road or rail. In addition, they could be adapted to operate on passenger cars, pickup trucks, or large railroad cranes.

The early 1960s saw the introduction of a line of lightweight hydraulic hand tools and eventually a hydraulic motor. These were used mainly for electrical transmission line construction as well as maintenance and tree trimming. This resulted in a new division called Fairmont Hydraulics.

Stockholders approved a merger with Harsco, a diversified enterprise located in Harrisburg, Pennsylvania, on June 8, 1979. The goal of this merger from a local perspective was apparently to enhance the operation of the company by providing stability and continued growth.

The company eventually sold its products to nearly every railroad in the U.S. and Canada, in addition to exporting to every other continent with the exception of Antarctica. In June of 1980, Railway Motors announced a one-million-dollar renovation and expansion project which was expected to add 62,000 additional square feet to the plant for manufacturing space and offices.

What was once a small motor car operation in the early 1900s in Fairmont evolved over time to gain an international presence and prominence in the industry. The company celebrated its centennial year of operations in 2009.

Fairmont Railway Motors evolved significantly throughout its history, experiencing layoffs, strikes, expansions, spinoffs, and mergers. Its workforce proved effective and efficient, its payroll supported many families, and in turn, many local businesses prospered. In addition, it contributed to the community and the surrounding area in an immeasurable manner. What is noteworthy is the fact that "the Motors" has been an integral part of Fairmont and Martin County for over a century. It is arguably one of the most significant industries in the history of Fairmont and Martin County.

Frank Wade, perhaps the quintessential entrepreneur of his time and the first president of Fairmont Railway Motors, Inc., would no doubt be exuberantly proud of the long-term success and economic impact his initiative has had on Fairmont and Martin County. Perhaps today's corporate executives could learn a great deal from the integrity and business acumen from a man of Wade's stature.

Sources for this article include the March 3, 1919, Fairmont Daily Sentinel*; and MCHS History File 677.*

The First Fairmont Railway Motor Car

Fairmont Railway Motors may not have developed into the company it became if not for a railroad section hand living in Fairmont who was tired of pumping his handcar by hand.

From left: Horace E. Woolery, Fred Mahlman, Sr., Melchoir Heckel, Fred Gust, and John Garowski test out Fairmont Machine Company's engine-powered railway hand car.

In about 1909, Fred Mahlman, Sr., found pumping to be a tiresome proposition, especially in inclement weather and at the end of the day. He thought it would be great to have a motor on his handcar. He saw an advertisement in a newspaper that the Cushman Company of Lincoln, Nebraska, was manufacturing a four-horsepower engine to attach to grain binders for cutting grain. He contacted them and received more information.

Shortly thereafter, he found out that what was then known as the Fairmont Machine Shop was putting out a two-horsepower upright engine. Consequently, he purchased one, tried it out for several months, and determined that it really didn't accomplish what he wanted. As a result of this, he contacted the superintendent of the machine shop and asked if they could make one to order with Mahlman supplying the specifications.

They did, and although it had more power, additional improvements were still needed. As Mahlman's ideas regarding the motor car were evolving, he and the superintendent would take it out evenings and on Sundays in order to test it and to determine potential additional improvements. Finally, they had what they considered a "pretty good motor car."

Mahlman was then asked by the superintendent of the Fairmont Machine Company to write a detailed report about the motor car. In his report, Mahlman described what he could do with the motor car, how many ties it would haul, how many miles per hour it traveled, and gas mileage details. Printed copies of this report were then sent to all the railroads.

Within a few weeks, Mahlman received so many replies that it proved impossible for him to answer them. Therefore, he took his correspondence to the machine shop office and let them handle the replies. Within a couple of years, orders were coming into the then little-known Fairmont Machine Company so quickly, they were unable to manufacture the motors fast enough.

This, at that time, proved to be a driving force in the start of Fairmont Railway Motors, Inc. From that small beginning, which was a result of a tired railroad worker who thought there must be a better way, an industry developed that could certainly be considered the most significant industry in the early history of Fairmont and Martin County. What would have happened if Mahlman had purchased an engine from the Cushman Company in Nebraska, especially since this development undoubtedly had far reaching effects on the economy of this area?

Sources for this story includes the February 26, 1941, edition of the Fairmont Daily Sentinel.

From Henry Ford to Fairmont Ford—A Century of Progress

A century of progress was marked in 2009 in Martin County. In today's world, it seems quite unlikely that a small Midwestern community can be called home to any business that has survived, no less prospered, for 100 years.

Henry Ford incorporated the Ford Motor Company in 1903 and envisioned an automobile for the average person, not merely the wealthy. His vision was accomplished by revolutionizing manufacturing through the utilization of an assembly line and creating the Model T, of which nearly fifteen million were sold in the United States alone, according to thoughtco.com.

Park Motor Co.

The heritage of the current Fairmont Ford dealership in Martin County dates back to 1909 when John Grill started selling Ford Flivvers, also known as the Model T, in Sherburn, Minnesota. At that time, the Ford Motor Company had been in existence for a mere six years. Then, in 1914, Grill opened a branch in Fairmont at the corner of Park and Third Streets. Although Fords were not sold in Fairmont until 1914, Henry Beecher Ward was the first Fairmont resident to own a "factory built" car, a Ford that he purchased in 1903. In 1920, Grill moved the dealership to a new building on the corner of Park Street and Blue Earth Avenue where it would remain for over thirty years.

In 1921, Grill sold most of his interest in the dealership to a group of Fairmont residents that included Dr. Lester Webb, Dr. R.H. Zierke, Frank Jones, and Robert Porter. The company was managed by C.W. Dammann and Ray Steelsmith during the 1920s. In 1927, Claus Kloeckner joined Park Motors as office manager. He soon became general manager and eventually became one of the owners. The company took its name, Park Motor Company, Inc., as a result of its location on Park Street and, although previous dealership names carried the manager's name, people had trouble both spelling and pronouncing Kloeckner.

Kloeckner, a German immigrant, served the American occupation forces as an interpreter in Koblenz, Germany, his hometown. He became very impressed with America due to his work with American soldiers. Consequently, after attending business college in Germany and working for an import-export firm, he made the decision that he wanted to go to America. He arrived in 1924 at the age of twenty-two.

Upon arriving in America, he was processed through Ellis Island and came to Truman, Minnesota, on October 17, 1924. He worked at several different jobs and continued his education at La Salle University in Chicago.

While employed as manager of an elevator in Granada, Minnesota, he met Porter. Porter felt Kloeckner would be an asset to the Ford dealership in Fairmont and consequently hired him as bookkeeper.

The 1950s ushered in major changes for Park Motor, primarily due to a fire. The November 3, 1952, edition of the *Fairmont Daily Sentinel* reported the Park Motor fire losses were estimated to be $200,000, the greatest in Fairmont's history up to that time. The article reported that the cause of the fire appeared to be a wrecked car that had earlier been towed into the garage. A night clerk at the Augusta Hotel, across the street from Park Motor, was the first to report the fire at 12:20 a.m. Forstrom Oldsmobile allowed Park Motor to use part of their lot to display 1953 model cars and temporary offices were set up in the Augusta Hotel.

In 1953, construction began on their new building at 700 East Blue Earth Avenue. They reopened for business at that location in 1954. In 1956, Robert Kloeckner became the second generation of Kloeckners to work at the dealership.

Robert eventually became manager of the dealership in 1976, and in 1979, the third generation of Kloeckners, David Kloeckner, became involved with the business. James Kloeckner began working full-time with Park Motor Company in 1990.

In 2003, Park Motor Company changed its name to Fairmont Ford, and the dealership went through an extensive remodeling and renovation project. That year, Robert and Kay Kloeckner were invited to Dearborn, Michigan, during Ford Motor Company's one hundredth anniversary because their dealership was the fourth oldest in the United States.

Since the day of Henry Ford, an innovator and pioneer in the auto industry, to the Fairmont Ford of today, an evolution of change has taken place as a result of the automobile that has altered the face of our society forever. Undeniably, if Ford were alive today, he would point with pride to Fairmont Ford for surviving and prospering for now 108 years, while at the same time providing quality products and service to the residents of the surrounding area. Fairmont and Martin County can be proud to be the home of businesses that have endured and created a lasting benefit to the local economy for more than a century.

I would like to acknowledge and thank the Kloeckner family and the late George Champine for the resources and historical information they provided for this story.

A Crop No Longer Harvested in Martin County

Martin County is known for its rich farmland and abundant crops. However, there is one crop no longer harvested in Martin County. Ice. Yes, at one time "ice harvesting" was a flourishing industry that contributed to the economy of Martin County.

The history of ice harvesting actually dates back to the early 1800s and a man named Frederic Tudor who became known as the Ice King. Tudor could have attended Harvard with his intellect and breeding; however, he dropped out of school at the age of thirteen.

After relaxing at his family's estate for several years, he hatched the idea of shipping and selling ice from New England to warmer climates. Gradually a demand for his product developed in places like Savannah, Georgia; Charleston, South Carolina; and

New Orleans. With the help of his foreman, he refined the process, and by 1847, about 52,000 tons of ice had been transported to twenty-eight cities in the United States. The industry grew significantly as people relied on keeping meat, milk, and other perishables fresh for future consumption.

Ice harvesting on Fairmont's lakes

Now, one might wonder how ice that was harvested in the dead of winter was kept frozen for use during the summer months when refrigerators and freezers were not yet invented or at least not widely used. The answer was an ice house and sawdust, with sawdust serving as an insulator. It was put on the ground with ice being stacked in blocks on top of it. A space between the wall of the ice house and the ice was left to be filled with sawdust. The top of the ice was then covered with about one foot of sawdust to prevent air from coming in contact with it. As long as the air didn't come into contact with the ice, it wouldn't melt.

The history of ice harvesting in Martin County is chronicled to some extent in the archives of the Pioneer Museum. In 1917, John Niesz and John Wolf purchased the Fairmont Ice Business from H.M. Serle. The new firm took possession of the ice business that included teams of horses, wagons, equipment, and ice houses. They planned to start work on the ice harvesting in January of 1917.

In 1922, Fairmont's ice harvest was said to be the best in many years. The harvest consisted of 9,000 tons of ice and the employment of thirty-two men as well as twenty teams of horses. Twenty carloads of ice from Lake Sisseton alone were shipped to southern Minnesota towns. The quality of the ice was considered exceptional as a result of the cold weather and continuous freezing that was uninterrupted by warm spells.

In 1932, the Jacobsen and Pederson ice crew began harvesting ice on Lake Sisseton in order to replace the oil-damaged crop taken out of Budd Lake. The ice crew suspected that the oil in Budd Lake was a result of drainage from the oil depots that were located in town. The ice was cut with a large circular saw attached to the shaft of an engine of an ex-Ford automobile. This was a significant advancement from either hand sawing or horse-drawn efforts.

John Livermore constructed an ice house on the Budd Lake shore at Oak Beach in 1937. Livermore had experience selling ice at the Lake Sisseton boathouses for several years. A cash-and-carry ice station was also planned for the corner of North North Avenue and Fifth Street in Fairmont by Knud Pedersen of the Fairmont Ice Company. He employed about twenty-five extra men during the ice harvest which lasted twelve to fourteen days. Pedersen estimated that it would take approximately 6,000 tons of ice to supply the ice boxes in Fairmont. Livermore supplied the Northwestern trains with ice, taking about 3,000 tons from Budd Lake.

What may have eventually doomed the "ice age" was in fact our growing dependence on ice. This dependence contributed to the creation of the very technology that ultimately led to the decline of the ice empire, namely, electric freezers and refrigerators.

During the mid 1900s, these appliances became commonplace and ice harvesting became a thing of the past. In fact, in July 1953, an automatic, round-the-clock, ice-dispensing vending machine was slated to be installed in Fairmont.

The ice industry is still huge but not nearly as dominant as in the past. Today's ice business is primarily prepackaged, direct-to-consumer ice that can be purchased in grocery and convenience stores.

Sources for this article include mentalfloss.com/article/22407/surprisingly-cool-history-ice; Sentinel *stories from January 28, 1922, December 27, 1932, December 21, 1937, March 19, 1937, January 30, 1940, and January 9, 1946; and Jan Dickinson's compiled research of newspaper articles.*

No Wife, No Job

Today's news is centered around world affairs, crime, the economy, politics, and local news. I picked a random date in local history to gain a slightly different perspective on the news of the day and to get a glimpse of what seemed important to citizens of that era.

It was March of 1917 in Martin County. The country, and county, was much younger and although the news of the day may have been somewhat different in context, it was also the same in many ways. Following are stories that appeared in the March 2 edition of the *Fairmont Daily Sentinel.*

"NO SINGLE MEN NEED APPLY TO CITY FOR JOBS" read the headline, which was followed by subtext that stated, "Majority of Aldermen Vote Against Mayor's Police Appointee Because Young Man is Wifeless." "No wife, no work" seemed to be the approach taken by municipal government of that era in an attempt to "boost the marrying game" in Fairmont. Walter Carver was appointed by Mayor Wade as night watchman for the city.

Carver, a nephew of Sheriff Carver and a sergeant in Company E, had recently returned to Fairmont and needed a job. It was said that he had the necessary qualifications of "physique and character" and although well recommended, alas, he had no wife, and thus was considered "wifeless" in the view of the city officials.

However, all was not lost as he was given a bit of a reprieve. Since the mayor couldn't appoint anyone for three days, Carver had those three days in which to get married. Of course, there was no rush, but a shotgun wedding would have solved the employment issue! In contrast to Carver's plight, it was noted that H.M. Serle was confirmed with no difficulty. It was interesting to note that he had been married for some thirty-five years at the time of his appointment.

The article also went on to criticize the council in Carver's defense by stating that Carver went away as a Fairmont soldier when there was a threat to our country. Apparently he was good enough to represent Fairmont on the battlefield but not good enough to work for the city of Fairmont. It further stated that since the council took this action, Fairmont was without a night watchman since the mayor was powerless to veto the council's "no wife, no job" stance, even though there were single as well as married men on the city's payroll at that time. In addition, there was anxiety among friends of the city engineer who were concerned for him as he too was not married. Obviously neither veteran's preference nor equal opportunity hiring practices on the part of the city played a significant role during that period in our local history.

In March 1917, the Strand Theater was showing *The Girl with The Green Eyes, Chasing Them Out In The Open,* and *A Prince In A Pawnshop.* Admission was listed as being five, ten, and fifteen cents.

Fairmont's Mayor Wade addressed the school students regarding some of the hardships encountered in life's battle. The Fairmont High School boys' and girls' basketball teams were to play at Jackson. The headline regarding their game read "We'll Lick Jackson To A Standstill."

In advertising, Canright's Drug Store was holding a "Pretty Eyes" contest. The ad read, "Which Girl or Woman in this Community has the Prettiest Eyes?" You would get one vote with any ten-cent purchase or 100 votes with each fifty-cent bottle of Lavoptik Eye Wash. The contest would last ten weeks and the winner would receive a gold wrist watch free!

Other advertisements included a Fairmont Auto and Realty Company ad for "The Oakland, The Sensible Six." Bob Wallace Mercantile advertised oranges for twenty-eight cents a dozen. The Palmer–Edwards Company was advertising a modern eight-room dwelling for $3,600. The Martin County National Bank had an ad stating that "The prudent man is prepared for sickness. He has a bank account." Men's shoes were selling for $2.98 a pair, ladies' dress galoshes were selling for sixty-nine cents a pair, women's skirts sold for $4.95, men's overalls sold for ninety-eight cents, and spring hats were priced from $1 to $1.50 each.

The classified section of the paper advertised a new café opening for business known as the Quick Meal. And finally, *Sentinel* subscriptions were priced at $4 for one year, $2 for six months, and $1 for three months, plus an additional ten cents if delivered by carrier within the city limits.

It's undeniable that times have changed significantly since the printing of that particular edition. The concepts involved in the reporting of the news appear similar to today; however, the specific topics reported, to be expected, differ somewhat which would seem likely due to the nature of the time.

There have been obvious improvements in terms of fairness and equal opportunity regarding hiring practices, in reference to the "wifeless" job applicant. That employment scenario would be laughable at best in today's world.

The economic conditions of that time were different than today as were the methods of advertising in promoting businesses and products, however, the goal was the same.

Finally, when comparing that period of time to the present, it would seem unlikely that anyone would disagree with the fact that significant improvements have been made in most, if not all, areas of our lives. Of course, with that said, it could also be argued that there were certainly some aspects of that era, if adhered to today, that would likely improve our present lifestyle as well.

Although it's enjoyable and definitely very interesting to revisit the past, would we really like to go back in time to what might be considered a simpler way of life? Maybe, if we could be assured of a swift return to the many modern conveniences that we enjoy and have at our disposal in today's world.

Fairmont Canning Company

The Fairmont Canning Company, predecessor to Fairmont's Stokely–Van Camp, was started in Fairmont in 1919. The company founder, H.H. Allison, was involved with a canning company in Nebraska but also owned 200 acres of farmland in Rolling Green Township in Martin County. He was very impressed with the quality of farmland and crops in Martin County and, as a result, decided to invest here. Consequently, Allison and fifty other Fairmont businessmen became shareholders in launching the Fairmont Canning Company on November 18.

Allison brought two Nebraska associates with him to Fairmont, A.F. Wentworth and Burr Taft. Together they decided on the site for the company, which was pasture land along the railroad right of way at East Ninth Street, then just at the edge of the city.

The original board of directors was comprised of A.R. Fancher, H.H. Canright, J.C. Musser, and Wilbur Brown, all of Fairmont. Allison, Wentworth, and Taft, all from Nebraska, rounded out the board.

The first factory was up and running by August of 1920, and the company had contracted for 1,000 acres of sweet corn from area farmers. Sixty-one thousand cases of cream-style corn were packed with a gross value of approximately $100,000.

During the early years of the company, no dividends were paid as all earnings were retained for new equipment and buildings. Allison also had a significant amount of his personal savings tied up in the company. Because he was unable to gain any immediate return on his investment, he eventually became discouraged, ill, and despondent. Consequently, he took his own life in 1921.

Fairmont Canning Co.

Leadership of the company was then transferred to A.F. Wentworth. His approach was to market their products in larger population centers such as New York and Chicago. By 1924, the company's crop acreage jumped to 5,000 acres, a second factory was added, production increased to 320,000 cases of corn, and more than 400 people were employed during their peak season.

Then, in 1926, Fairmont Canning Company began expensive experimentation with its first cooling and freezing operations in an attempt to maintain freshness and flavor quality, an industry first. During the course of their trials, the rooms and equipment were rejected, remodeled, and improved over time in order to finally meet the needs of the company.

Initially, freezing was considered merely a means of holding products fresh until canning. However, the prospect of marketing fresh, frozen vegetables soon evolved. In turn, it created new problems regarding packaging, storage, transportation, and retailing. Successful packaging took years of development, initially being suitable only for large institutions. Eventually packaging for retail trade was developed that would retain the quality and freshness of the original product.

The depression era of the 1930s saw a slowdown in production, but efforts were directed toward extending the seasonal operation and adding new products and combinations of products. This was accomplished in part by holding frozen vegetables in storage for future processing. Corn and peas were coupled with lima beans, soybeans, string beans, carrots, squash, rhubarb, and other products in advancing the operation of the company.

The advent of World War II brought rapid production demands, bringing the gross output to eight million dollars. The company also began to participate in the processing of meat, canned turkey, and army field rations for the armed forces. In addition, the shortage of prospective employees at that time resulted in importing migrant workers and utilizing the German prisoners from Fairmont's POW camp to harvest crops.

On December 15, 1955, the Fairmont Canning Company was sold to Stokely–Van Camp. The thirty-six year run of the Fairmont Canning Company, an original Martin County industry, came to an end. It was without a doubt significant to the growth and economy of this area in creating jobs while adding to the overall quality of life in Martin County and southern Minnesota.

Sources for this story include MCHS History File 1213, History of Fairmont Canning *scrapbook by Charles Meister, and "Canning Factory" in Martin County History A-Ca at MCHS.*

Soda Pop and Ice Cream

Soda pop and ice cream, two vices in which many of us indulge, were at one time products of our local economy. The Nelson Ice Cream Company and the Crystal Bottling Company served as significant producers of ice cream and soda pop products to our local region for many years.

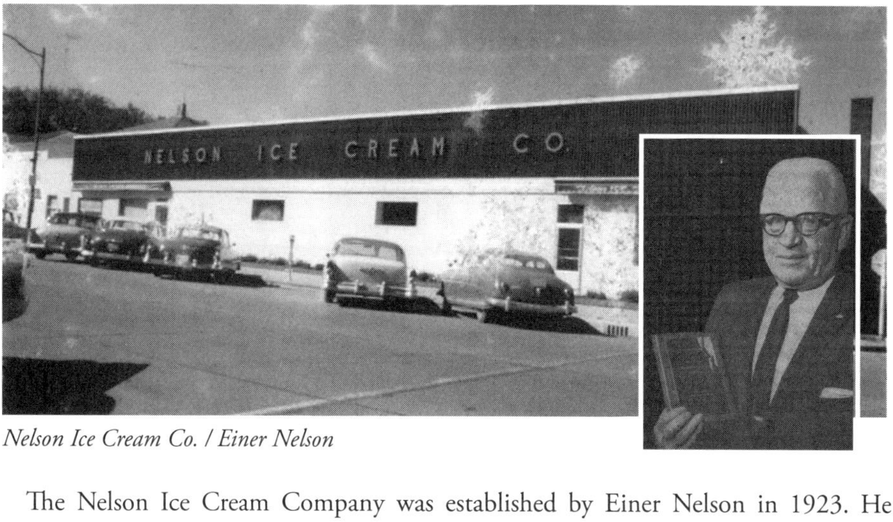

Nelson Ice Cream Co. / Einer Nelson

The Nelson Ice Cream Company was established by Einer Nelson in 1923. He originally came to Fairmont from Mankato to manage the Fairmont branch of the Model Creamery. He eventually bought out the firm's Fairmont interest and then established his own company. In the early years of ice cream production, their flavors were limited to vanilla, chocolate and strawberry. That first year, they produced 70,000 gallons.

In the mid-1950s, the Nelson Ice Cream Company had distribution centers in the Minnesota towns of Windom, Springfield, Redwood Falls, and Pipestone, and in

Iowa in Storm Lake and Fort Dodge. In 1955, the company had seventy-six full-time employees, and their ice cream output totaled 1,000,000 gallons annually.

By this time, Nelson's Ice Cream Company was producing eighteen flavors of ice cream, four flavors of sherbet, and specialty items such as drum sticks.

The plant experienced a number of expansions. It used stainless steel equipment, and could freeze 950 gallons of ice cream per hour at maximum capacity.

The distribution of Nelson's milk and ice cream products involved a fleet of thirty-three trucks. Nelson's trucks provided home delivery as well as distribution to area grocers, hotels, restaurants, and other outlets. In addition, Nelson provided his dealers with "refrigerated cabinets for ice cream storage" to ensure proper refrigeration standards. The cabinets varied in size from ten to sixty gallons and were maintained and serviced by Nelson's serviceman.

Regarding major changes in the industry at that time, in a *Sentinel* story from June 9, 1956, Nelson cited two factors that he considered significant: The first was the pattern of consumption and demand in that the only time demand diminished was in the winter when weather stopped the trucks from getting on the road, not as a result of winter temperatures. The second was that, at one time, ice cream was considered a luxury item, and by the mid-1950s, thanks to marketing, it was considered a nutritious food to be enjoyed year-round. He stated that family consumption of ice cream also influenced packaging in that one-half gallon containers were becoming common.

Fairmont also was at one time the home of the Crystal Bottling Company, a company "Built by Thirst." The original Fairmont Bottling works was established in 1894 by C.H. Meyer. Later, in 1917, Lou C. Meyer established the first Crystal Bottling plant on 111 East Third Street. At that time, the bottling of soda pop was not automated, and only limited flavors of strawberry, lemon, cream, and sarsaparilla were available. They also made a nine-ounce pop bottle called the "Interlaken Special" during the period in which Interlaken Park was popular. Telephone directories in the museum from the 1920s indicate its offices were at 111 South Main Street and a 1969 telephone directory gives its address as 115 South Main Street. It was not listed in directories after 1969.

Orange Crush was popular in the 1920s and thus became the first name-brand product bottled by the Crystal Bottling Company. In addition to bottling their own brand of beverages, they contracted with Dr. Pepper in 1939, Squirt in 1942, Nesbitt's Orange Drink in 1943, and Nu-Grape in 1955. Their own brand bottled strawberry, grape, root beer, and several other flavors.

In the 1950s, Crystal beverages were distributed throughout the southern Minnesota region from Luverne to Wells and from Le Sueur to the Iowa line. That involved ten trucks distributing from warehouses in Worthington, Jackson, Mankato, and Fairmont.

Lowell "Bud" Meyer, in the July 28, 1956, edition of the *Sentinel,* said, "The bottling business is a nice business, but believe me, it's no 'get-rich-quick' scheme. When you add such cost items as glass bottles, modern machinery at a cost of $150,000, trucks at a rough cost of $3,000 each, marketing and distribution costs, building and warehousing expenses—well, it takes a lot of thirsty people and hot weather to stay on the profit side of the ledger." One might only wonder what Meyer would think of operating the same business at today's costs.

These two businesses, at one time very significant to the local economy, no longer exist. What caused their demise? More than likely a number of factors, some of which might be considered progress. Maybe there just wasn't anyone willing to follow in the footsteps of Nelson or Meyer. In any event, although these two businesses no longer exist, their history and benefit to the county will live on.

Sources for this story include the November 3, 1956, Sentinel, *and Jan Dickinson's compiled research of newspaper articles* 1955–1957.

The Hatcheries of Martin County

Eggs are undeniably an important part of today's diet for most Americans. However, if asked where eggs come from, perhaps the most likely answer would be the grocery store. It would probably be fairly safe to say that many are unaware of the hatcheries and other businesses that were reliant on poultry and egg production in Martin County's past.

White Feather Hatchery

Egg production came into its own following World War II when meat was scarce. Consequently, Fairmont was at one time home to the White Feather Hatchery, the Kramer Hatchery, and the Mallon Egg Company. In addition, Triumph hosted Poultry Buying Days in 1911. Egg production and the chicken industry have evolved from the many separate entities of feed mills, hatcheries, farms, and processors to individual companies that now handle all aspects of production.

Locally, the White Feather Hatchery was started by Alvin and William Wilken in 1920. They shipped thousands of baby chicks to the Dakotas and Montana in the 1930s and thrived into the 1950s before poultry factory farms reduced the demand for baby chicks.

Another thriving local business related to eggs in the 1950s was the Mallon Egg Company. They employed thirty-five people and bought eggs from within a forty-mile radius of Fairmont. They had established routes to pick up eggs from their regular customers, and farmers would also bring eggs directly to the company. In addition, they provided a number of other services including culling, candling, grading, packaging, and shipping of eggs. Culling is a process whereby non-laying hens are removed from the flock, and candling of eggs is done to ascertain whether or not abnormalities exist and is done in the dark. Eggs were graded by being placed on a conveyor belt to move through automatic grading machines. These machines handled fifty cases per hour after which licensed egg graders would then grade the eggs.

Before packaging for shipment, the eggs were inspected by a full-time government inspector on duty at all times at Mallon's. After packaging, the eggs were placed on trucks that were heated in winter and refrigerated in the summer, shipping 150,000 eggs daily. Although eggs were their main business, they also bought poultry such as chickens, geese, and ducks.

The poultry industry, as with so many others, has evolved into a more centralized business, thereby eliminating the small operators. Although perhaps a more efficient business model, the local economy may have suffered as a result.

Sources for this story include the December 29, 1961, Sentinel.

J.C. Penney and Martin County

J.C. Penney's stores are well-known both locally and nationally. It's interesting to see how the company originally came into existence. However, perhaps even more interesting might be uncovering the history of the J.C. Penney store in Martin County.

J.C. Penney between 1940 and 1970 was located at 300 North North Avenue (now Downtown Plaza), now the home of Total Comfort Systems.

J.C. Penney was an American businessman born on September 16, 1875, in Caldwell County, Missouri. He worked at a dry goods store where he learned the business and eventually opened his own store in 1902. He expanded to 175 stores by the time he retired in 1917. He stayed active behind the scenes at the company to help plan the chain's future. "During the Great Depression, his stores survived by offering a good value to customers on a budget."[1] He was a member of the company's board of directors until his death in 1971.

The original name for the store that started J.C. Penney in the dry goods business was The Golden Rule. By 1912, there were thirty-four Golden Rule stores, but the following year it was changed to J.C. Penney when Penney accepted a majority ownership of the chain, William McManus still being a partner. In two years alone, from 1915 to 1917, the company grew from eighty-three stores to 175. "The chain expanded rapidly as store managers were allowed to open new stores, keeping one-quarter of the profits as soon as they were successful. This simple concept led the store's massive expansion and made it the second-biggest retailer in the country by 1970."[2]

The first J.C. Penney store in Martin County opened on September 4, 1925, at 212 North North Avenue in Fairmont. The managers of that first store were Earl Haire and Donald Campbell. The second J.C. Penney store opened in 1940 at 300 North North Avenue. Its managers were Donald Campbell, Charles Helms, and Thomas Thompson. The third store, which recently closed, opened April 15, 1970, in the then Fair Mall Shopping Center in Fairmont. The manager of the store at that time was William Krick. That store at one time also had an auto center to the north side of the lot toward Blue Earth Avenue which now houses the State Bank of Fairmont.

J.C. Penney stores were at one time found primarily in downtown locations. However, as times and retail changed, their locations have evolved into shopping mall locations as did the Fairmont store.

Sources for this story include [1]www.biography.com/people/jc-penney-38638, [2]historyofbusiness.blogspot.com/2007/03/history-of-jc-penney.html, and MCHS History File 1259.

Are You Hungry?

Eating, although a necessity for survival, can also be considered a pleasure, a pastime, a social event, an indulgence, and, at the very least, something most of us look forward to and enjoy. For many who have lived in Martin County and the surrounding area for a number of years, the thought of Kiehl's Bakery and The Oaks Inn will bring a variety of mouth-watering delicacies to mind. The Oaks had those delectable steaks as well as very good seafood, and who can forget Kiehl's champagne cake, not to mention the other exquisitely prepared offerings available at both establishments?

Kiehl's Bakery was originally opened by Art Kiehl on January 1, 1940. Kiehl had owned and operated bakeries in Nebraska but was looking for a town in Minnesota that had a population between 5,000 and 10,000. He decided to give Fairmont a try even though there were already three bakeries in town. Because of that, many didn't think his business would last six months. However, he proved those prognosticators wrong by building a thriving and extremely popular business that lasted beyond the half century mark and eventually included second and third generation family members in its operation.

Kiehl's Bakery

When Kiehl started in the bakery business, his workday was from midnight to early afternoon. He employed a crew of bread and pastry bakers. Their bread baking would be done through the night into early morning. In addition, he rarely closed the bakery. Although the workday changed over the years, the recipes remained unchanged and were enjoyed by customers for many years. The longevity of the business could undoubtedly be credited to their consistent, quality product that was passed down from generation to generation.

Kiehl's Bakery was originally located at 117 Downtown Plaza in Fairmont. He purchased the building at 214 Downtown Plaza and moved his bakery to that location. Now long closed, anyone fortunate enough to have experienced the taste of their mouthwatering offerings including cakes, cookies, rolls, and bread that they made daily for many, many years would surely long for them to be back in business.

The Oaks Inn was at one time the place to go and eat. The original Oaks Inn was started by Sumner Scott and was located in a building in the vicinity of Albion Avenue and Oak Ridge Road in the early 1940s when there was no residential development yet in that area. In 1945, the Scotts started the second Oaks Inn at 1600 Albion Avenue. They ran both businesses for a time, eventually closing the original location in the late 1940s to concentrate their efforts on the Albion location.

The Oaks Inn was probably the first restaurant in the area to have such a full and varied menu. It included many options ranging from a grilled cheese sandwich to steak and lobster tail. The Oaks was well known for its steaks, its taste coming primarily as a result of their aging process. According to Jerry McShane, one of the owners of The Oaks in the 1960s, they would cut their own meat daily and absorb any shrinkage so that the customer would not be shorted, and they made certain that all excess fat, tissue and gristle was removed.

It was considered somewhat of a gathering place, and although it only had a capacity of between forty and sixty diners, it attracted people from throughout northern Iowa and southern Minnesota. It was said to have had a relaxed appeal with a club-like atmosphere, although there was neither dancing nor entertainment, simply good food.

The Oaks Inn closed in the fall of 1980 and eventually became the site of a twin home development across from the Luedtke Slough.

Both Kiehl's Bakery and The Oaks Inn had excellent reputations for their products and services. They had a following that considered them to be without equal. Those that didn't have the good fortune to experience them don't know what they have missed!

Some information for this story was from the February 2, 1963, Sentinel.

The A&W Drive-In Restaurant

The A&W Drive-In, at one time located at 1315 East Blue Earth Avenue in Fairmont, was well known for its root beer, delicious Swiss burgers, and car hops for many years. It was a favorite restaurant for all ages.

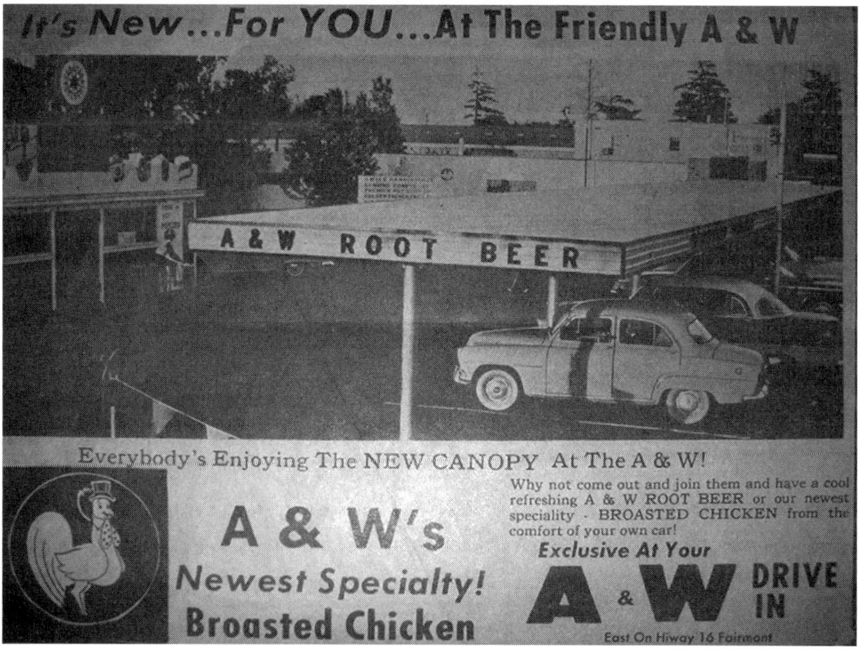

An ad announcing the addition of broasted chicken to the A&W menu

The A&W Drive-In was originally opened by James Olsen in 1946. Olsen was discharged from the Army Air Force in December 1945 as a twenty-one-year-old first lieutenant. He had a desire to own his own business and found that an A&W Root Beer franchise was available in Fairmont. Since Olsen had lived and grown up in La Crosse, Wisconsin, he felt that this opportunity in Minnesota seemed to be a good choice.

Lumber, plumbing, and electrical equipment were all extremely hard to come by during that time, which made the development of the franchise somewhat difficult. However, he was able to find enough materials to build a small building on the lot. He then obtained some second-hand root beer equipment and opened the drive-in on July 4, 1946.

Olsen made improvements to his building, initially to protect the building from the elements. The first addition was added to the front, eventually the gravel parking lot was paved, canopies were added to protect the customers, and an electronic ordering system was installed. In the early 1970s, a complete renovation took place that included the addition of a dining room. The menu was then expanded from Swiss hamburgers, hot dogs, chili dogs, and root beer to include broasted chicken, shrimp dinners, and broiled hamburgers.

During the early years of the franchise, a group of young boys approached Olsen and asked him if he would consider sponsoring them as a fast-pitch softball team. He would have to provide uniforms and equipment. Olsen agreed, and thus the A&W softball team became a reality. Fast-pitch softball was very popular during that era. It also proved to be an advertising asset by spreading the A&W Root Beer name all around surrounding counties as the team, being quite successful, participated throughout the area. The team remained in existence from 1946 to the early 1960s.

In 1955, the Fairmont Martins baseball team, managed by Jim McNulty, was scheduled to play the A&W softball team. The game was to serve as a benefit for James McNulty, Jr., who was hospitalized in Rochester suffering from polio.

The game was to be divided between each sport, softball for the first half and baseball during the second half of the game. The Martins signed Sheriff Bill Klusendorf to pitch that game. According to an August 26, 1955, *Sentinel* article, "Klusendorf is one of the few pitchers, five to be exact, to have notched a win over the strong A&W club. He tossed a four-hitter in winning 4-3 for Berchy's earlier in the season." The A&W team planned to borrow a Martins pitcher for the baseball innings to be played.

The game resulted in the Martins defeating the A&W team 3-2 in ten innings. Ironically, each team was beaten in their own sport. The Martins won the five-inning softball segment 3-1, but lost the five-inning baseball segment 1-0.

Seven hundred fans turned out for the game which resulted in a $350 benefit. Although they lost that game to the Martins, the A&W team was very successful that year, finishing 29-5 for the season and later competing in the state softball tournament in September.

Hundreds of teenage girls and five token boys held their first jobs at the A&W Drive-In. Their employment helped them pay for their education to become nurses, teachers, doctors, lawyers, and enter other professional careers as well.

The A&W franchise existed in Fairmont for twenty-five years, and when it ended, Olsen trademarked the name "Red Sun Drive-In." He continued to operate the drive-in until 1975 when it was sold. The new owners purchased another A&W franchise and continued its operation at that location for some time after that.

Sources for this story include MCHS History File 1024.

The History of Fairmont's 3M Plant

The 3M Fairmont plant has had a significant and positive effect on the area since its beginning in 1946. Its impact on the lives of its current and retired employees, as well as the overall economy of Fairmont and the surrounding area, cannot be overstated.

In 1946, the Fairmont Chamber of Commerce met with representatives of Minnesota Mining and Manufacturing who presented their needs for land, area, location, and size. Discussions were not going well and, after a long silence, Fairmont Mayor Ed Duffy leaned over to Einer Nelson and said, "Heck, me and Einer Nelson will put'em up a building."[1] They did, 3M stayed, and the rest, as they say, is history.

3M leased 3,000 square feet of the Reco KF building on Blue Earth Avenue for $150 per month beginning in 1946.

3M first began operations in Fairmont on September 23, 1946, in 20,000 square feet of rented space in the Reco Motor Building on Blue Earth Avenue. The original plant began with a payroll of thirty-three with Louis W. Bohn as plant manager. The local plant's initial operation was as an abrasive converting plant; however, this progressed so rapidly that inadequate space caused 3M to move this operation to Wisconsin. But, 3M needed a plant for its newly developed nonwoven ribbon and decided upon Fairmont for this operation.

In the fall of 1950, the gift wrap ribbon operation was moved from St. Paul to Fairmont. Production began with fifty employees in the Reco Motor Building and the newly constructed 7,500-square-foot building on Highway 15 that was leased from Duffy and Nelson. In 1955, 3M began construction of an 115,000 square foot addition on the State Street (Highway 15) location. Another 30,000-square-foot addition was finished in 1957. At that time there were 190 employees. 3M then purchased an additional nine acres in 1959 and forty more acres adjoining their plant in 1969. This location is what 3M Fairmont continues to call home for operations today.

Some of the products made in the 1960s included surgical face masks, surgical skin cleansing sponge brushes, Coban™ elastic bandages, Tarnishield™, and respirators. By 1967, the Fairmont 3M plant employed 190 with peaks of employment reaching 320.

The 1970s proved prosperous for the local 3M Plant as it was chosen as the site for Scotchmate™ manufacturing. As a result, the Fairmont plant constructed a 45,000-square-foot modification to its site. The addition of new products was significant to enhancing the economic thrust of the Fairmont plant of the 3M Corporation in the community. In the mid-70s, employment peaked to over 350 primarily as a result of two new products, Scotchmate and Bumpons™.

In the 1980s, the plant began manufacturing Dual Lock™ fasteners, urethane rollstock, bushings, and foam earplugs. In the 1990s, the plant expanded the Dual Lock™ manufacturing operations to include supply into automotive markets and added diaper fastening operations. Ribbon operations were suspended at this time.

3M Fairmont has persevered through many decades due to the people, technology, innovation, and the diversity of products and markets served. 3M's presence in Martin County has undeniably had a positive effect on the overall economic growth of the region. In addition, the 3M Foundation has provided immeasurable benefits to the community through grants and other donations serving area nonprofit organizations. It has been a stable and respected employer for seventy years with a workforce that provides quality products and, in turn, adds to the quality of life in Fairmont and Martin County.

I would like to acknowledge the Fairmont 3M plant and its employees for their input in providing accurate product information for this article. Other sources for this story include 'The Daily Sentinel, *Martin County Centennial edition 1938-1948, page 10; MCHS History File 469 and 687.*

The Corner Grocery Store

Neighborhood or corner grocery stores, at one time common fixtures in our communities, are now little more than a fading, sentimental memory. They bring to mind a kind of nostalgic reflection of days gone by. These were places where you could get almost anything, from friendly conversation to items needed at the spur of the moment for baking, cooking, or something else. They were almost always open, and they seemed to have whatever was needed that may have been overlooked or forgotten when buying the weekly supply of groceries.

A random sampling of a few of the local neighborhood grocers from a 1960s Fairmont telephone directory includes Nolte's Grocery located on North Park Street by Lincoln School, Colvin's Grocery on Lake Avenue, Park Street Grocery, Mocol's Food Market on North North Avenue, East Side Grocery on North Hampton, and Weber's Super Market on Albion Avenue. There were undoubtedly many more that came and went during the last century. However, as the major chains gradually became the predominant distributors of grocery items, the local neighborhood mom-and-pop stores could no longer compete. Fossum's Grocery and Park Street Grocery were two such stores.

Park Street Grocery

Thorvald and Hilma Fossum moved to Fairmont in 1928 and purchased a small grocery store known as Buhr Grocery. After about one year, they moved their store across the street to 801 East Fourth Street and converted the upstairs into living quarters for their family as well. Hilma, a native of Swea City, Iowa, and a 1916 graduate of Gustavus Adolphus College, was a teacher before she married. After marrying, she and her husband lived in California for a time prior to moving to Fairmont.

Shortly after their move to Fairmont, Thorvald passed away. Hilma continued to run the store while at the same time providing a home and an education for her three daughters, all of whom graduated from Fairmont High School.

During her life's work in the grocery business, Mrs. Fossum developed a great fondness of her neighborhood customers, both adults and children. She genuinely felt that the neighborhood she served had been wonderful to her. Throughout the years she learned to know her customers very well and, as a result, she developed a personal bond with each of them. It was easy to understand why her customers were devoted to her store because she always seemed to be there for their immediate needs, while at the same time knowing no real closing hours. She would sometimes be open from 6:00 a.m. until midnight. She "confided that she intentionally stayed open until midnight, especially during canning season, in the event that a housewife might run out of sugar, spices, or some other canning supplies."[1] In addition, her store was open every day of the year, including Sundays and holidays. She was committed to always being there for her customers.

However, as was the case with most of these small businesses, her little neighborhood grocery store would not last forever. Finally, on Wednesday, October 21, 1965, "the little bell announcing the arrival of a customer to her store rang for the last time."[1] Mrs. Fossum locked the door at 5:00 p.m. and quit her business after thirty-six years in Fairmont. She said her immediate plans involved taking some vacations and spending time visiting her daughters and grandchildren.

Park Street Grocery, formerly located at 717 South Park Street, was owned at different times by Rupert Rempel, Harry Miller, and Burton "Bud" Lund, who owned the store up until it closed in 1974. Park Street Grocery existed for approximately forty years and was a fixture in the Fairmont neighborhood it served. It not only provided grocery items, but also penny candy to neighborhood youngsters, delivery services to the older generation, credit for those with no cash, and friendly conversation for all. In other words, it served the entire neighborhood in more ways than might be imagined at first glance.

Lund grew up in Dunnell where his father owned a store, bar, pool hall, and barbershop combination. It was likely that experience that inspired Lund to become a store owner.

Shortly after he graduated from high school in 1935, he was hired by Harry Miller as a clerk at Park Street Grocery. At that time, his work day was frequently sixteen hours long, and his salary was a whopping fifteen dollars per week. In 1942, Lund entered the military. He returned to the store in 1945, becoming a partner with Miller in 1948.

In the early years of Lund's ownership, the store was very labor intensive as clerks were needed to serve the customers, stock shelves, bag sugar and flour, write up charge slips, and make deliveries. In 1964, the store became self-service which in turn reduced the need for labor. Park Street Grocery continued to make home deliveries, even though it was an inefficient method of doing business, as it was a tradition they weren't going to stop. In addition, regular customers were still allowed to buy on credit, paying once per month.

Lund's daughter, Susan Naumann, has many fond memories of the store. One vivid memory was when she, her father, Rempel, and her brother, Gary, all delivered groceries. At that time, in the 1960s and early 1970s, no one locked their houses and those making deliveries would simply let themselves in the house and put the items delivered in the refrigerator or freezer.

Another of her memories involves the neighborhood children coming into the store for candy. They were allowed to go behind the counter and pick out the candy of their choice. Penny candy was located on the lowest shelf, nickel candy in the middle, and dime candy on the top shelf. She also told of sacking potatoes into ten-pound bags, sorting pop bottles, and working from 6 a.m. until 8 p.m. Monday through Saturday and 7 a.m. until 12:30 p.m. on Sundays.

In the supermarkets of today, shoppers can certainly find virtually everything they need, and sometimes things they don't. The employees in these stores are always very friendly and accommodating. Nevertheless, in reflecting on that moment in time, the corner grocery store of the past will be remembered as being inherently unique in its value to the people and the neighborhoods it served. The friendly greeting, the personal attention, and the convenient location are things that those recalling that period of time will always fondly remember.

Sources for this story include Sentinel *stories from* [1]*October 21, 1965, and March 2, 1974, and Sue Naumann.*

Service Stations

Since the invention of the automobile, gas stations have been easily overlooked unless you need one. Yet, service stations occupy some of the best real estate on highly visible sites and can definitely be classified as an icon of the twentieth century.

Service stations are the most common commercial building type, according to the National Park Service's website, and "surviving, historic stations are physical reminders of the transportation revolution and the influence of increased mobility on the landscape. They are a reflection of car culture, pop culture, corporate standardization, and an era of customer service that today seems quaint."[1]

Service stations of today offer motorists the opportunity to pay at the pump and then perhaps stop in the adjoining convenience store for coffee, donuts, or a newspaper. However, washing the windshield and checking the oil are the responsibility of the motorist. While service stations of the past offered these same amenities, they also offered real "service" for the motorist, which included having an employee pump your gas, clean your car's windshield, and check the engine oil. In the 1960s through the 1970s, Fairmont and Martin County were home to many service stations that have since been replaced by other businesses.

Northside Mobil, located at the corner of State Street and Winnebago Avenue, boasted that they never closed. They were open twenty-four hours daily and seven days a week! Larsen's Conoco Service on the corner of Lake Avenue and Fourth Street offered customers free pick-up and delivery of their vehicles.

Smed's Mobil Service was located at 420 North North Avenue, the current site of Fairmont Decorating. Smed, a former Fairmont policeman, purchased the station in 1937 and, according to the July 9, 1960, edition of the *Sentinel*, he noted many changes from 1937 to the 1960s. He had a door specifically built to accommodate all sizes of trucks. Consequently, much of his business included servicing trucks.

Uptown Mobil was also located at 420 North North Avenue and provided twenty-four services. It also included auto body repair and painting, motor overhauls, car wash and polishing, and wheel alignment in addition to offering Top Value Stamps with every purchase.

Messick Cities Service was located at 115 East Blue Earth Avenue just east of the old post office and west of the site of the Augusta Hotel, now the approximate location of First Farmers and Merchants Bank. They offered a complete line of auto accessories and tune-up necessities, and one of their specialties was polishing cars with a wax applied in a spray process. Cities Service credit cards were also promoted as the June 17, 1961 story in the *Sentinel* noted that credit cards were becoming more and more popular.

Westside 66 was located at 505 Lake Avenue, now the site of the Bicycle Shoppe. They advertised that you could pull your boat up to the "new" pier, push a buzzer, and wait for an attendant to come out and fill your tank. They also offered outboard motor oil, a place to park your boat, credit card convenience, and refreshments. On the street side, cars filling with gas got all windows washed, batteries checked, tire air pressure checked, and interior floor mats swept clean.

Messick's Service Station located about where First Farmers and Merchants Bank in Fairmont is now.

Downtown 66 Station was located across the street to the west of what is now the Fairmont Opera House. This was a prime location at that time as it attracted business from downtown merchants and shoppers as well as motorists traveling along Highway 16 which is Blue Earth Avenue.

Other service stations that at one time served the public but have since disappeared include Larry's Mobil that was located at the site of the Walgreen Drug Store, Weber's Standard that is now the site of Papa Murphy's Pizza, Skaden's Standard Station at 200 South Park Street that is now the Salvation Army Corps parking lot, Fair Mall Texaco that is now the site of the Burger King restaurant, South Side Mobil that is now the site of Sommer Outdoors, the Union 76 Station that was located on the Kwik Trip corner, the Western Station and Discount Store that is now Super America on Fourth and State Street, and Erickson's Valu Center at 407 East Blue Earth Avenue, now the site of Freedom Valu Center.

As with many aspects of our society, service stations have evolved significantly from their predecessors of the early years of motoring, much of that change coming just since the 1950s.

Sources for this story include [1]https://www.nps.gov/tps/how-to-preserve/briefs/46-gas-stations.htm, and Jan Dickinson's compiled research of newspaper articles.

What's for Dinner?

Looking through Fairmont telephone directories from the past, it becomes very obvious that there were many restaurants available in or near Fairmont for a wide variety of tastes. Regretfully, many no longer exist today. There was the A&W Drive-In, The City Hub, The Oaks Inn, Club 16, the Feed Bag, the Jolly Inn, the Melody Grill on Lake Avenue, the Redwood Drive Inn Café, Ronnie's Restaurant, Serle's Café, the Sweet Shop Restaurant, the Toot-N-Tell, the Western Café, Lake Aires Supper Club, the Triangle Drive Inn, and many, many more.

Today, it might be of interest to recall the names of some more of those establishments of the past, as well as where they were located. According to a 1939 *Sentinel* article entitled "Are You Hungry? Only 45 Places To Eat Here," the following are some of the restaurants of days gone by, as well as their locations in Fairmont at that period of time in our local history:

- Roger's Eat Shop at 913 North North Avenue;
- Sooner's Café at 712 North North Avenue;
- Barney's Café at 417 North North Avenue;
- Fairmont Hotel at 223 North North Avenue;
- Lou's Café at 211 North North Avenue;
- Way Down East on Highway 16;
- Rosie's Eat Shop on First Street;
- City Drug Store on North Avenue;
- Corn Crib just south of the Nicholas Theater;
- Peglau Pool Hall at 120 West First Street;
- Chile Bowl on the corner of North Avenue and Blue Earth Avenue;
- Philips 66 Lunch on Lake Avenue;
- Jim's "Hamburger Hut" on wheels served at auctions and football games;
- Serle's Café at 209 North North Avenue;
- Augusta Hotel at 121 East Blue Earth Avenue;
- Wimpy's Pantry across from the courthouse;
- Colonial Ice Cream Company at 212 East Third Street;
- Chase & Wilson at 205 North North Avenue; and
- Brad's Café at 220 North North Avenue.

In addition, there were numerous restaurants just outside the city limits of Fairmont, such as: the Red Horse Tavern on Lair Road, Gordy's Root Beer Tap on McKisson's

Corner (where Albion Avenue and State Street meet), the Interlaken Inn at Interlaken Park, and Tubby's just west of Fairmont.

Just a few years later, an all-night café was going to open at the Bowlmor in 1946 and Sparky's Grill opened just east of the Gilbert Hotel. Koenig's Luncheonette in the Ben Franklin building on North North Avenue opened in 1947 and as a daily feature served a roast turkey dinner including mashed potatoes, vegetables, and dressing for 50 cents. The Coffeepot opened in 1948. The Gables Drive-In was located at McKisson's Corner, and Reuben and Alta Olander sold their "Nickel and Dime" eat stand business after an estimated six million hamburgers had been fried by the Olanders over sixteen years. They admitted that they almost waited too long to raise their price from five and ten-cent hamburgers to ten and fifteen cents.

Alas, in 1949 coffee was to hit ten cents a cup in Fairmont. A *Sentinel* article from November of 1949 stated, "Fairmont coffee guzzlers, hitch up your belt and dig deeper into your jeans, because effective on Thursday morning, across the counter coffee here will cost ten cents a cup." The price hike did not come without much consideration as members of "Bureau 8 of the Chamber of Commerce," restaurant owners, and other businessmen met to discuss the increase. However, it's interesting to note that a later *Sentinel* article stated that "All but two of the local food and java dispensaries chucked the decision to raise coffee to a dime a cup, for the time being at least, in the face of unfavorable public opinion."

An article from the June 11, 1952, edition of the *Sentinel* stated that the "Rainbow Café Opens Thursday." It was located at 110 West First Street and would serve breakfast, noon lunches, and dinners. Menu items included chow mein to take out and Italian spaghetti. Also, a sandwich shop was to open in the Bowlmor in 1950, Ozzie's Café had new owners, and the Beach Club, formerly known as the Merrie Garden at Interlaken, opened under new management in 1952. The Lunch Box located across from the Nicholas Theater at 210 South North Avenue had an open house in 1953, and the Toot-N-Tell was located at 1000 North State Street.

Milly's Eat Shop opened in 1955 at 117 West First Street in Fairmont. Mr. and Mrs. Leonard Milbrandt were the owners. It was said to have had five booths and thirteen stools and served steaks plus a full line of meals.

Ronnie's Café, located at 110 West First Street, opened in 1957. The café was operated by Mrs. Ronnie Jaqua, and had a staff of eleven full-time employees, including two chefs. This air-conditioned café would serve regular meals and lunches as well as Sunday dinners.

Over the years, Fairmont has certainly provided its citizens with a multitude of excellent dining establishments, each seeming to have its own unique characteristics that in turn appealed to many different tastes. Many restaurants have come and gone in Fairmont, of which many of us very likely have fond recollections of their specialties and ambiance.

The Feed Bag Drive-In

The era of the drive-in restaurant, for those of us old enough to remember, was a much simpler time. There were no drive-throughs, no computerized ordering, the employees probably didn't wear uniforms, and debit or credit cards were not used to pay for the food and beverage order. Orders were written on small pads of paper and delivered by waiters, or in most instances waitresses, known as carhops. The order was carried by the carhop on a tray that would conveniently fit on the partially rolled-up car window of an automobile.

The Feed Bag Sign with the Kickin' Chicken

The idea of a drive-in restaurant actually predates World War II, and its popularity peaked in the early 1950s, according to about.com. The first drive-in restaurant opened in Glendale, California, in 1936.

One particularly significant drive-in restaurant that many long time Martin County citizens may have fond memories of was the Feed Bag Drive-In. It was easily identified by its flashing-neon, kickin' chicken sign prominently displayed in the front of the establishment. The Feed Bag Drive-In was located at 2421 Albion Avenue in Fairmont, approximately across the street from the Hall Lake Cabins. It was originally built by Art Godfredson and called The Spot. Later owners included Gustie and Jack Croissant, Tom and Freida Rake, Ron and Nancy Milbrandt, and Gerald and Eleanor Wagner (later Eleanor Chase and Harry Chase) who purchased it in 1958 and operated it until 1977.

Several former car hops from that era, Kathy Christenson, Gerianne Izen, and Heidi Villeneuve-Schlomann, provided some perspective on that time and place in local history. They worked at the Feed Bag while attending high school during the early to mid-1970s when Harry and Eleanor Chase were the owners.

Their pay at that time was $1.45 per hour plus any tips. Their work attire didn't include uniforms, but was generally comprised of shorts, tennis shoes, and a type of carpenter's apron with separate pockets for pennies, nickels, dimes, quarters, and dollar bills. Some of the most popular foods included Danish hot beef sandwiches, french fries and later tater tots, as well as potato salad. Fried chicken-in-a-basket was a favorite of many as well. They enjoyed working at the Feed Bag because of its relaxed atmosphere, the ability to work with their friends, and their appreciation of the many regular customers.

A few unique experiences they encountered included fighting over certain customers who were known to give good tips (usually a quarter) and not wanting to dump the "slop bucket" at the end of the night.

Also, as a result of the lot being a gravel surface, a rock would frequently lodge under the screen door whch they would attempt to gently kick or nudge open as their hands were full holding the tray they were returning. This caused the door to spring right back in their faces, which they considered both hilariously funny and awful at the same time.

According to a previous owner of the Feed Bag, beverages served included Richard's Root Beer and 3.2 beer. It was at that time the only local drive-in restaurant at that time to sell 3.2 beer, which was served inside the restaurant.

Although the Feed Bag no longer exists, its memory lives on and is symbolized by the Kickin' Chicken neon sign. From 1975 to 2003, the sign journeyed to a number of different locations. It found its way to the Martin County Historical Society on loan from Warren Nelson in 2003.

The final chapter of this rather lengthy saga occurred in December of 2012, thanks to the generosity of Marlin Milbrandt who donated funding for its purchase. Consequently, it is now permanently displayed in the Pioneer Museum for the benefit of those many patrons, carhops, and others who remember it, as well as for future generations to enjoy.

Sources for this story include MCHS History File 1150 and interviews with former car hops Kathy Christensen, Gerianne Izen, and Heidi Villeneuve-Schlomann.

Remembering Fredstrom's

What began as a small Surge dairy equipment store gradually evolved into what was called in 1956 a modern "Town and Country" store. It was located at 109 South North Avenue in Fairmont, now 77 and 79 Downtown Plaza, and called Fredstrom's.

Owner and operator Fritz Fredstrom was born in Brainerd, Minnesota, and graduated from high school there. He was married in 1930 and then went to work for Gambles in Brainerd. He was later transferred to the Gamble Store in Boone, Iowa.

After becoming assistant manager of the Boone Gambles Store, he accepted a position with Montgomery Ward back in Brainerd. From there, he went to Mankato, working at a Surge distributorship, and then to Fairmont.

Fredstrom originally came to Fairmont in 1942 to manage the Mahowald Hardware Store. Then in 1944, he went into business for himself when offered the Surge Milker dealership for this territory. Being well known in all parts of the county, according to an article in the January 14, 1956, edition of the *Sentinel*, he quickly made Surge a familiar name on farms in this area. At the outset of his store ownership, he wore many hats as salesman, bookkeeper, and serviceman for his business. Although this created a rather hectic schedule, he always saved time to be active in his church and civic affairs.

"Fritz" stands in his Kelvinator range department, during the grand opening held in 1953. More than 5,000 people attended.

Fredstrom's

His business expanded with the addition of Kelvinator appliances; consequently, in 1953, he purchased the building at 109 South North Avenue which at that time housed the White Feather Hatchery. He expanded the building and it became known as Fredstrom's Surge–Kelvinator store. In the 1950s and early 1960s, Fredstrom's handled full lines of Kelvinator and Whirlpool home appliances, Surge dairy equipment, Jamesway barn and poultry equipment, and televisions made by General Electric and Stromberg Carlson. In addition, his staff was known for being well-trained, courteous and very helpful, and he had established a complete service department. Unfortunately, Fredstrom passed away in 1962 at the age of 54, ending his business ventures in Martin County.

In looking back, one can see not only the evolution of society but also the progression and development of how those conveniences attributed to making our lives easier. Although familiar to individuals who remember that era, those brand names Fredstrom carried and what they helped people accomplish may not necessarily be as readily recognizable today.

Koenig's—A Store Ahead of Its Time

Koenig's retail store and lunch counter, located at 308 North North Avenue in Fairmont, was a haven for shoppers during the 1940s and 1950s. It was so popular at that time that KSUM commentator Ev Ohrt hosted what was called "Coffee Time at Koenig's" every afternoon. Considered a hub for shoppers, people would also literally flock to the lunch counter every afternoon at 3 p.m. to be in on the radio show that consisted of Ohrt's interviews and chats with people who were present.

Koenig's

The store was owned by Emil and Vi Koenig and opened on September 13, 1941. Koenig, having little money for inventory, instructed his employees to inform him whenever a customer wanted something that he didn't stock. If someone asked for something that wasn't available in the store, Koenig would run to Woolworth's, which he referred to as his stock room, purchase the item, and then sell it to the customer for his cost. Making his customers his first priority enabled him to gain steady customers and eventually increase his inventory.

In 1943, Emil was drafted into the military, leaving his wife and one other woman to run the store, which they did quite successfully.

During a 1980 reunion of Emil and Vi Koenig with their former employees, Koenig portrayed his store as somewhat of a forerunner to stores like Target. The saying around town when his store was in operation was, "If you don't find it at Koenig's, they don't make it yet." Koenig stated that businessmen would travel from all over the country to see how he ran his business and to view his innovative displays. Also considered somewhat of a taskmaster, Koenig would often conduct fingernail and hairnet inspections of employees working in the restaurant. The Koenigs moved to Minneapolis and eventually sold their store in 1965, according to an article in the July 14, 1990, edition of the *Sentinel.*

As with the demise of the neighborhood corner grocery stores, the "mom and pop" retail stores are a thing of the past, having been unable to compete with the big retail chains of today. However, the one compelling aspect the big retail chains can't supplant is the nostalgic memories of the Koenig's store and lunch counter that many today will fondly relive in their minds. The sights, the sounds, and the aromas wafting from the restaurant stir up memories of a simpler time, a sentimental era affectionately remembered and appreciated by those who were fortunate enough to personally experience it.

Some information for this story was from the February 21, 1947, Sentinel, *and MCHS History Files 660 and 1206.*

Fairmont's New Half-Million Dollar Shopping Center

Before there was the Five Lakes Centre mall in Fairmont, there was the Tower Shopping Center, built in the late 1940s.

The year was 1948, and the new center, or what the November 3 edition of the *Sentinel* referred to as the "vast facilities of the Fairmont trade center," was set for its grand opening on Friday and Saturday, November 5 and 6. The corner, known as the Byers corner, was said to have mushroomed from a weed patch in 1936 to a new shopping district by the late 1940s.

Fairmont's New Shopping Center
Grand Opening Friday, Saturday
Wed 3 Nov 1948
Byers Store No. 3 is newest addition to east Fairmont's half million dollar shopping center. . . .

Tower Shopping Center

This location was originally the site of a fruit shack in 1941 at the corner of Blue Earth Avenue and Highway 15 and was owned by P.S. Byers. Later that year, Byers expanded and built a brick tile building for his fruit stand and enlarged it into a grocery business.

Byers launched his major expansion program in 1946 when building materials became more readily available after the war. That project provided space for the O.P. Skagg System super market, Turner Lockers, the War Surplus Store, Benson Heating and Air Conditioning System, and the Odegard Barber Shop. He had an additional and unrelated building venture that included a warehouse and apartment building on North State Street.

In addition, the new shopping center also had: Ken's Men's Store, Finley Piano Exchange, Martin County Appliance, Griffith's Bakery, Nelda's Beauty Shop, Meier's Lunch and Soda Fountain, Wash 'n Shop Laundry, Weber's Standard Service, Adam's Texaco Service and Feed Store, and Marvin Carlson Fyr-Fyter extinguishers. Byers stated that in addition to these retail businesses, offices and apartments were available for rent as well. He also said that the Mankato Jewelry Company would move into the building in the very near future.

This site eventually became known, although perhaps unofficially, as the Tower Shopping Center. It is currently the site of Kwik Trip.

Before The Five Lakes Centre

The current site of the Five Lakes Centre shopping mall in Fairmont at one time resembled anything but a shopping mall. Up until 1964, it was the site of the Martin County fairgrounds. It was also the home of the Fairmont Martins baseball field that was located in the southwest corner of that site near what is now the entrance to the U.S. Post Office.

The vision of the development of a shopping mall in this location was the brainchild of Earl Madsen of Madsen's Enterprises and his associate, V.R. (Pat) Rooney of Rooney Enterprises in Minneapolis. In 1964, Madsen's Enterprises purchased the site from the Martin County Agricultural Association for $275,000. This purchase of the yet unnamed development destined to become a shopping center proved to be the beginning of what is presently the Five Lakes Centre in Fairmont.

Plans progressed in 1965 with costs estimated to be two million dollars, in contrast to the original price tag of $1.5 million. It would be named The Fair Mall, and it would be enclosed and air-conditioned. Parking would accommodate 1,203 automobiles as compared to 722 metered parking spaces at that time in Fairmont's downtown. Those businesses making commitments were J.C. Penney, Montgomery Ward, Madsen's Super Valu, and People's State Bank of Northrop. A Texaco service station was slated for the northeast corner and Midland Cooperative was slated for the southeast corner of the site.

Finally, construction was scheduled to begin in June of 1967. Rooney and Madsen were convinced that the community needed a shopping center of this size and stated that financing was all arranged and ready to go. As of that year, additional tenants included Monty's Hallmark Shop, Walgreen's Drug Store, and Schiff Shoes. Penney's and Monty's Hallmark had been located downtown and would greatly expand their presence by relocating to the Fair Mall. Their plans at that time no longer included Montgomery Ward.

Fair Mall "shoppers can move from store to store without fearing weather."

Madsen's Super Valu would occupy more than three times the space it had at its then current location at 114 East Blue Earth Avenue, presently the site of the Salvation Army Corps building. Plans were also being made to include a "new style cafeteria" with a full-line delicatessen, bakery, and catering service, and would seat 104 persons. An automatic delivery service was being considered as well.

As is frequently the case with projects of this nature, groundbreaking did not take place until well after their initial projections. It finally happened on November 15, 1967, with Madsen, Rooney, and then-Mayor Lester Webb using a gold-colored shovel to turn the first piece of sod. The target date for completion was set at September 1, 1968. However, the grand opening was not celebrated until October 6, 1970. The project had been in the works since 1964 and was the subject of much speculation as to whether or not it would ever actually materialize. However, as everyone who has lived in this area since then knows, it did materialize and has certainly evolved in a number of ways since its inception.

Sources for this article include the area's Chamber of Commerce scrapbooks 1965-1970 containing Sentinel *newspaper articles now located in the Pioneer Museum.*

Exposing History

For those who grew up in this era of change, the '70s were unforgettable. It was a time of innocence, kids could roam the streets with their friends without fear, and families gathered together each night to enjoy a meal and talk about their day. It was a decade of simpler times, but it was also a decade of change. Not all was so innocent.

Exotic dancing as well as somewhat questionable printed material placed Fairmont at the center of a fight regarding the freedoms set forth in the First Amendment of the

Constitution. This involved the owner of the Safari Lounge and the owner of a book store in Fairmont.

The Safari Lounge was a 3.2 beer bar adjoining a bowling alley. The controversy involved the employment of female performers who would dance topless or completely nude and male performers who occasionally danced completely nude as well.

City council scene Thursday gives way to major hearing at VFW building in March

Contentious and controversial as it was, there were mixed opinions and considerable disagreement involving the issue. In February of 1974, the city council brought the topic of morality, deemed "round one," to the forefront with discussion lasting but fourteen minutes. There was some disagreement among council members, and the council chambers were said to be crammed with thirty-five to forty spectators, of which only three expressed their opinions on the matter, according to the February 8, 1974, *Sentinel*. One individual in attendance suggested that the council attend at least one session of "go-go dancing" at the Safari so that they could make an educated decision as to the merits of the proposed morality ordinance.

The owner of the Browse-a-Bit bookstore that displayed and sold what some considered objectionable material was denied a 3.2 beer license by the city council. This prompted him to file a $200,000 lawsuit against city officials, also in February of 1974, stating that he was deprived of his livelihood and was caused much distress, anxiety, discomfort and embarrassment. The case was later heard in federal court in St. Paul, but apparently it did not prevail.

In April of 1974 the Fairmont City Council passed the proposed morality ordinances by a vote of 6-2. The ordinances would outlaw topless or nude go-go dancing and ban the sale of material alleged to be obscene or pornographic. In the April 4, 1974, edition of the *Sentinel*, in arguing against the ordinance, the owner of the Safari Lounge invited members of the city council to visit by saying, "Why not come out to my place and see if you haven't seen the same thing at the beach." The council members did not respond to his request.

Petitions against the ordinances were circulated and validated in May of 1974 and signed by 232 registered voters. The petition was initiated and circulated by the owner of the Safari Lounge. That set the stage for a public referendum.

A June 26, 1974, *Sentinel* headline read "Morality ordinances pass by one-half per cent." The divergent views stated were either "it was a gratifying turnout of law-abiding citizens who want to live under the law and support morality" or "it was a disappointment that so many people would sacrifice their freedom of choice." The ordinance passed, but by a very close vote with 50.53 percent in favor and 49.47 percent in opposition. According to the article, the voter turnout was more than twice the turnout for the last municipal election. Obviously, there were strong feelings on both sides of the issue.

One year later, another *Sentinel* story reported "No nude dancing reported at Safari." On the first day the morality ordinance was in effect, Fairmont police officers were dispatched to the Safari to assure it was in compliance with the new law, which it was. Perhaps the old adage "It was a dirty job, but somebody had to do it" might be somewhat facetiously applied to this investigation.

Finally, the ordinance was appealed to the Minnesota Supreme Court in 1976 in Koppinger v. City of Fairmont which found "that the Fairmont city nudity ordinance which applied to all public dancing places and all places where tobacco was sold suffered from overbreadth and had to be redrafted because it was unconstitutional. As might be expected, the Fairmont City Council did redraft the ordinance and while you can get 3.2 beer in Fairmont, you won't get the beer in conjunction with nude dancing," according to Elton Kuderer's book *Martin County Judges, Law and Lawyers.*

The fact that the preceding events actually took place in a small, conservative, rural Minnesota community is in and of itself surprising. However, what might be even more surprising is that there was fairly strong opposition to the proposed ordinances. On the other hand, this was the 1970s, and change was definitely in the air.

The '70s was a tumultuous time defined by changes, events, and attitudes. The advancement of women's rights, technology, and music were significant to that era. People were more likely to become free thinkers while questioning the government and the status quo, thus leading it to be eventually hailed by some as the "Me Decade."

In conclusion, the "naked truth" regarding this "overexposed" chapter of local history was argued and finally settled in the courts. Democracy prevailed, nude dancers and objectionable printed material became history, and life in Martin County returned to what most would consider being normal.

It was Twenty Years Ago Today . . .

This story was originally printed in 2014.

As the lyrics in the Beatles rendition of *Sergeant Pepper's Lonely Hearts Club Band* say, "It was twenty years ago today" that Paul and Linda McCartney were the honored visitors to Fairmont. To be more precise regarding that specific event, the lyrics could be slightly altered to say "It was twenty years ago this month," as their visit took place in March of 1994.

Paul and Linda McCartney, center, do a press conference at Fairmont Foods. At left is former Minnesota governor Arne Carlson. At right is former Fairmont Foods president Larry McGuire.

Anyone unfamiliar with their 1994 visit may wonder why the famed former member of the Beatles and his wife visited Fairmont. The event actually involved a business venture that the late Linda McCartney had with a local company, Fairmont Foods. The McCartneys had at that time been vegetarians for about twenty years. She felt strongly that meatless food was better for people, and it consumed fewer resources in its preparation. In addition, she had a great love for animals.

Consequently, their visit to Fairmont was intended to launch a new line of meatless frozen foods that would be produced and marketed by Fairmont Foods called *Linda McCartney's Home Style Cooking* featuring meatless entrees. According to an article in the March 25, 1994, *Sentinel*, Fairmont Foods was to be the first American company to come out with a totally meatless line of food products. In addition, the recipes personally developed by Linda McCartney were to be included. Linda chose Fairmont

Foods because she liked its managers and felt the company had the right values. The McCartneys went on to say that their visit would also give them the opportunity to meet the people who would be preparing their line of food.

Their arrival was scheduled for Friday, March 25, by chartered jet. They planned to tour Fairmont Foods and then host an afternoon press conference that would include Minnesota Governor Arne Carlson. The event attracted television crews, Twin Cities reporters, and, as would be expected, a large crowd of sightseers.

Onlookers waited at the airport and the hotel to get a glimpse of the famous couple, some seeking autographs, and others hoping to be able to shake their hands. Many were probably thrilled just having the opportunity to be in their presence.

Reporters, city officials, and local business representatives filled a banquet room at the Holiday Inn to hear what the McCartneys had to say as a security detail stood watch at the doors. Governor Carlson welcomed the group and introduced Linda. She stated that she had launched a similar product line in England and decided against choosing a large company in the U.S. for fear of her product getting lost in the production process; consequently, she selected Fairmont Foods.

Linda's vegetarian food line produced by Fairmont Foods was relatively short-lived, lasting only slightly longer than two years, due to Linda's illness. Linda McCartney was an author, photographer, musician and social activist. She passed away as a result of cancer on April 17, 1998.

Fairmont Foods, the city of Fairmont, and Martin County can be proud of an accomplishment of this nature, although it was somewhat brief. The fact that management of Fairmont Foods was able to acquire that contract, the positive public relations generated as a result, and the work ethic of their employees speaks volumes as to the quality and ability of that local industry and labor force.

I would like to acknowledge and thank Larry McGuire, former CEO of Fairmont Foods of Minnesota, for his contribution to this story.

Progress

Fairmont Had How Many Newspapers?

Newspapers have evolved considerably over the years and faced a great deal of competition from other news sources, notably the internet and cable television. Back in the 1800s, there were quite a number of newspapers in Fairmont, many of which lasted for only a short time. Either they evolved into another newspaper or they completely disappeared. For a sense of scale, the first paper was published a year after Orville Chubb was named county physician and Reuben Ward homesteaded the Day Farm.

The first newspaper published in Fairmont was the *Martin County Atlas.* It existed for only twenty months from April 11, 1868, to December 25, 1869. The editor and publisher was C.A. Lounsberry who was the Martin County auditor. It was published weekly at the Martin County Courthouse, and its political viewpoint was Republican. In January of 1869, it moved to Wells and operated for a time as the *Wells Atlas.*

The second newspaper in Fairmont was the *Martin County Review.* It was also a Republican paper and existed from August 27, 1870, to December 20, 1872. It was published weekly with George Tanner as editor and publisher followed by Lyman F. Lent and finally the noted pioneer physician, O.P. Chubb.

The *Fairmont Chain* was the third newspaper to be printed in the county. Its initial issue was run on October 15, 1873, and continued in print until July 22, 1874, running on a weekly basis. Its political affiliation was labor-reformed and anti-monopoly. Artemus E. Ball was the editor and publisher.

The fourth county newspaper was the *Martin County Sentinel.* It was edited and published by Frank Day with C.H. Bullard as co-editor and financial backer. It was published as a weekly starting on July 3, 1874. This was the forerunner and parent newspaper of the *Fairmont Daily Sentinel,* first published on May 20, 1901, which was an offshoot of that newspaper. The *Martin County Sentinel* printed its final issue on June 28, 1929.

The fifth newspaper was the *People's Advocate.* It was a weekly paper with its political views reflecting the Greenback party. The editor and publisher was Martin V.B. Scribner. It ran from May 17, 1881, to August 10, 1881, at which time it was absorbed by the *Martin County Sentinel.*

The *Citizens Gazette* was the sixth newspaper, a weekly newspaper not affiliated with any political party. The editor and publisher was Allison Fancher. It was in print from December 20, 1881, to April 10, 1882.

THE
Citizens' Gazette.

VOL. I. FAIRMONT, MINNESOTA, MARCH 16, 1882. NO. 13.

Citizens' Gazette 1882

The seventh newspaper was the *Fairmont News,* which sometimes appeared under the title of *Southern Minnesota News.* It was a weekly which was independent of politics when it started on April 9, 1885; however, it was said to have eventually "seen the light" and became a Republican-affiliated paper. It folded on July 25, 1885. However, it came back into operation under the name *Fairmont News* until 1899 when it ceased publication.

The eighth newspaper was started by T.S. Fisk, a lawyer and auctioneer. It was known as the *Farmers' Buzz Saw.* Its first issue was printed in March of 1894, and it continued as a monthly publication until January 25, 1895. Politically, it reflected the views of the Populist Party.

The Martin County Democrat, published by Harry St. John, was the ninth newspaper in Fairmont. It merged with the *Martin County Independent* after its final issue on February 1, 1896.

The *Martin County Independent* continued as a weekly for a lengthy period of time, eventually becoming a tri-weekly and finally a daily paper. It became the tenth newspaper to serve Fairmont and Martin County. It continued publication until October 28, 1929, when it was purchased by the *Fairmont Daily Sentinel.*

The *Martin County Zeitung* was a German-language newspaper with no political affiliation. It began publication on December 1, 1893, and ran until the United States became involved in World War I and the German language became unpopular.

Providing the public with the news of the day was as important at that time in our local history as it is today.

Sources for this story include The Daily Sentinel, *Martin County Centennial Edition.*

The Fairmont Fire Department

Fire departments are essential and vital to the safety and well-being of every community, whether they are manned by volunteers or full-time firefighters. Many of the fire departments in Martin County were formed in the 1800s.

According to *The Constitution and By-Laws of the Fairmont Fire Department,* the organization dates back to 1878 with the bylaws being adopted in 1895.

Fairmont Fire Department 1900

The fire department at that time was said to be comprised of a diverse group of local residents that included the rich and the poor as well as the laborer and the capitalist. Within the organization, however, there appeared to be some turmoil as there was considerable rivalry for what was then considered to be the important positions within the department, those being foreman, first and second assistant foreman, and several other positions deemed significant by the members.

The Fairmont Fire Brigade, synonymous with fire department, considered itself to be a democratic organization made up of individuals from all walks of life. However, there were conflicting anecdotal remarks indicating that it may well have been somewhat exclusive as many potential candidates were rejected. Interestingly, the meeting minutes seem to reflect a great deal of time devoted to whether or not to accept certain applications as well as whether or not to expel or suspend some of its current members.

The collection of money from the membership was also apparently no easy task. At one of their meetings in the early years, a committee of three was appointed to contact a certain unnamed individual in an attempt to collect the money he owed the company in apparently unpaid dues. However, as of the date of that account, the individual in question remained unnamed because of the fact this gentleman had become "an honorable resident of Fairmont," and the item in question might be construed as an unfavorable reflection on his character.

Perhaps the most prominent figure in those formative years of the department was Chief Harry Serle. He was born in India in 1855 and educated in England. At the age of twelve, he began an active career at sea. In 1876, he came to America and settled in Decorah, Iowa. A year later, he joined the English Colony in Fairmont.

Serle spent his first year in Martin County driving a stage from Fairmont to Winnebago. He then worked a year in railroading and also farmed in Martin County up until 1883. Later, he started an ice business which developed into a monopoly in Fairmont for some thirty years.

Perhaps best known for his public service, Serle was instrumental in organizing the first fire department in Fairmont. It was said that, due to his public spiritedness and energy, he developed the department into one of the most efficient in the state for towns of its size at that time. He served as the chief of Fairmont's Fire Department, which consisted of forty-nine regular members, a team and combination wagon with a thirty-five-gallon chemical tank, 1,200 feet of hose, a Seagrave hook and ladder truck, and normal water pressure of eighty pounds with the potential of 175 pounds when necessary. The state Firemen's Convention was held in Fairmont in 1914, very likely due to his efforts on the local fire department.

The Fairmont Fire Brigade posted its bylaws in the June 19, 1914, edition of the *Martin County Sentinel*. Some of the more interesting excerpts from this report refer to dues, and especially fines. The following are several examples provided in that account:

- The foreman, first and second assistants, secretary, and treasurer would be fined $1 for neglecting any of their duties.
- The truck keeper would be fined $1 for neglecting to keep it in good order.
- Absences from a fire would result in a twenty-five-cent fine.
- Absences from the annual review would be a $1 fine.
- Disobeying an order would be a $1 fine.
- Speaking disrespectfully would be a fifty-cent fine.
- Losing a key to the truck house would result in a $1 fine.
- Incapable of performing duties at a meeting or at a fire as a result of "too free use of ardent spirits" would result in a fine of fifty cents for the first offense, $1 for the second, and expulsion for the third time.
- Excuses for late payment of fines and absences from fires would be heard at the regular monthly meetings.

The annual firemen's ball was considered an important event; however, the financial return was minimal at best. One such occasion in that era netted the sum of $3.50 which promptly disappeared and was unaccounted for in the treasury of the department.

Since the Fairmont Fire Department was originally organized in the 1800s, the methods, training, and fire equipment have changed dramatically. Fortunately, the evolution of fire prevention and suppression provides a much safer environment for today's citizens than what was available back then. However, as with anything, there had to be a starting point from which to advance. It's always interesting to view the origin of an organization and compare that to how it has progressed up to its present state. The members of the 1800s fire brigade would undoubtedly be in awe of the training, capabilities, and resources of our modern fire departments and fire fighters.

Sources for this story include the June 19, 1914, edition of the Martin County Sentinel, *the October 23, 1940,* Fairmont Sentinel, *and MCHS History File 644.*

A Legendary Fire Truck

Records in the Pioneer Museum indicate that Fairmont's first fire company, as it was called at that time, was organized in 1882 with fifty-four members. (Keep in mind some historical documents conflict with one another, so this data does not agree with the information in the organization's bylaws.) Early fire trucks were hand-drawn or horse-drawn and had little capacity for fighting fires as compared to today's elaborate equipment. As time went on, motorized equipment was developed and additional firefighting equipment was introduced and included with fire engines.

Locally, firefighting equipment has also evolved significantly. Looking back in time, the city of Fairmont purchased its first motorized fire engine in the early 1920s. "Fairmont Fire Engine Arrives, She's A Beauty," read the *Sentinel* headline of March 14, 1923. On that date, the Fairmont Fire Department was awaiting the arrival of an "expert" from the American La France Fire Engine Company in Elmira, New York, to instruct the Fairmont Fire Department in the use of this fire fighting machine.

The expert was expected to stay in Fairmont for about two weeks. He would also assist in moving the new fire engine, which was delivered and located at the Milwaukee Depot in Fairmont, to the Fairmont fire station.

According to the *Sentinel*, the engine was an American La France Type 75 combination pumping, chemical, and hose car, said to be the ideal type of fire apparatus for general fire protection purposes. It could pump 750 gallons of water per minute, had a forty-gallon chemical solution tank, and included 1,200 feet of hose. It also had a six-cylinder engine, two ladders, two lanterns, and two extinguishers.

A little over a week later, the newspaper covered the test results of the new engine. On March 23, the headline read, "New Fire Truck Hurls Water 30 Feet

Over Trees," emphasizing the power and efficiency of the new equipment. A cub reporter from the *Sentinel* staff was permitted to ride along on a test run of the new fire engine. He reported that it took only a few seconds to rush the department, fully equipped, to the imaginary fire, and that the fire engine could do speeds of sixty miles per hour. Their tests included taking water from hydrants on North Avenue as well as directly from Lake Sisseton.

American La France Fire Truck, now housed in the Pioneer Museum

The first real test of the new equipment, as reported by the *Sentinel* four days later, was a corn crib fire at the W.I. Boyce farm located northwest of Fairmont. It was reported that the $12,000 fire engine made the three and one-half mile run to the fire in exactly five minutes from when the whistle blew. It apparently could have been even faster if not for the fact that the regular driver of the fire engine was out of town and, as a result, there was a slight delay in getting the fire engine started.

The truck pulled out of town with eighteen men aboard on a muddy road, which it handled well, and the firemen were back in Fairmont exactly one hour after the first alarm. The fire was completely extinguished by emptying the forty-gallon tank of chemical. The estimated loss due to the fire was estimated at $300.

There have been many advances in firefighting from the time that the American La France began its lengthy tenure of local firefighting in 1923. The Fairmont Fire Department continues to do an excellent job of protecting local residents from fires, and over the years has also done an admirable job in keeping the American La France fire truck in first-rate condition.

This fire truck served the area for many years. According to Martin County Historical Society board member Randy Musser, a former Fairmont fire chief and fire marshal, one of the last fires it encountered was the Stokely–Van Camp fire in the later 1960s. It is said that the American La France literally pumped for twenty-four hours straight before being replaced by a newer truck. Shortly after that fire, it was retired.

The 1923 American La France fire truck referred to in this article, which has recently been used in local parades, is on display and can be viewed by the public in the Carlson Room of the Pioneer Museum in Fairmont. The Martin County Historical Society is grateful to the local firemen who have helped to maintain this vehicle and have kept this historic reminder of the past in superb running condition.

The "Hello Girls"

Remember Lily Tomlin as Ernestine carefully articulating "one ringy-dingy, two ringy-dingys" on the *Rowan and Martin Laugh-In* television show of the 1960s? Alexander Graham Bell was awarded the first U.S. patent for the telephone in 1876. It was perhaps at first a novelty, then a convenience, and finally it became a necessity. Today it is something far more than merely a means of communication. It would be interesting to see how Ernestine might be portrayed using modern technology and the smartphone.

Telephone communication has changed greatly from the "Hello Girls" of the early days of phone service when their pay was barely $20 monthly.

The "Hello Girls" at the Fairmont Telephone Company, 1916

The history of telephone communication started locally back in 1895. Two promoters came to Fairmont and solicited business places, proposing to install a twenty-five line switchboard and twenty-five telephones at a cost of approximately $2,500. Their proposition was accepted, and the job was completed in about two to three weeks. Ironically, not a single telephone pole was erected. Rather, wooden sawhorses were set on flat roofs of business places. Iron wire was then strung from the porcelain knobs mounted on the sawhorses.

The twenty-five line switchboard was installed in a family operated restaurant with the owner's daughter, who was also a waitress, serving as the telephone operator. The telephone service operated from 7 a.m. to 9 p.m. It was interesting to note that in the event the waitress or operator was preoccupied waiting on a "good-looking traveling man," telephone service was likely delayed or became nonexistent, perhaps comparable to the "dead zones" of cell phone service today. The mayor at that time, William Ward, acted as the first manager of the company.

In the spring of 1897, the switchboard was moved to Ed Hyde's Barber Shop. This was in the approximate location of Dee's Floral and Designs at 107 Downtown Plaza.

The next move was to the Aldrich Building. This location was in the vicinity of Edie's Restaurant at 110 West First Street. At that time, another position was added to the board, making it a two-position switch board. In 1915, it was moved to 110 North Main Street

In the early years, the telephone operators were referred to as "Hello Girls." However, it is interesting to note that in 1902, men were also hired as night operators, working the evening shift from 9 p.m. to 7 a.m. On the other hand, and certainly not to be outdone, in the 1940s, a nineteen-year-old girl working as a telephone operator volunteered to take a repair position vacated by a man who left for another job. She not only filled the position admirably, she was said to have done the "man's work" in an exemplary manner.

By the mid-1940s, there were twenty-eight telephone operators who handled about 17,500 calls per day. The staff also included five employees in the shop and four in the business office. One employee was quoted at that time as saying, "People are using the telephones much more often these days, and they spend more time talking on each call." They would undoubtedly be quite surprised by the volume of phone calls today, including cell phones, as well as the amount of time spent using these devices for a myriad of other purposes.

Telephone operators were usually female, recently graduated from high school, had a neat appearance, and had a "nice" speaking voice. They typically lasted about three years and what they disliked the most was the "funny people" or "jokers." An example would be someone randomly calling a number and asking, "Is your refrigerator running?" When the person answering said, "Yes," the caller would then say, "Why don't you go chase it?" Caller ID would probably have alleviated that problem.

The rates and fees from those earlier days were somewhat different from what customers are familiar with today, especially considering the utilization of party lines that were common at that time. In 1947, a rate increase showed an eight-party business line was $3 per month, and an eight-party residential line was $2 per month. A rural multi-party line was $1.75 per month. Long distance rates varied depending upon whether usage was day, night, or weekends.

The local telephone company grew from 1,153 phones in 1915, to 2,118 in 1932, to 3,365 in 1946, and to 4,922 in 1956. The growth went hand-in-hand with the increasing population of the area at that time. Also, the Fairmont Telephone Company was home-owned until the 1930s. However, it was sold a number of times over the years until 1957 when it became Central Telephone Company.

In 1961, the telephone got a new building at 210 North Main Street. "Modern Phone Building Shows Strides Made Since Early Days in Restaurant" was the headline in the May 19 *Sentinel.* The building opened about two weeks prior to the conversion to the dial telephone system, and an open house and tour was scheduled.

Sources for this story and from where all quotes come is MCHS History File 713 and "A History of the Fairmont Telephone Company and Telephone Operators Scrapbook."

Fairmont Pulls Itself Out of the Mud

In 1915, area residents were asked to vote on a bond for street paving. The question wasn't whether or not paving should be done, but whether it should be wood block or concrete. Those advocating wood block felt it was easier on the horses, suggesting that concrete was too hard for them which would in turn keep the farmers from coming into town. They also felt concrete would be too hard on the feet and legs of the people walking on it.

The community approved a bond issue of $60,000 for "wood block paving." The city had a population of about 3,000 at the time.

The wood blocks were treated with creosote, but there were some drawbacks to this process. The blocks "heaved" every spring and had to be re-laid, and they also had to be "retreated" with creosote each year. This made for a rather messy situation of which housewives complained quite loudly. It seems that their floors were becoming rather dirty as a result of skirts dragging on the creosote and shoes tracking it into their homes.

The first paving was eight blocks of North Avenue. The *Sentinel* of that era commented on the improvement by stating, "Progress discredits the slanders that a dry town means decay and dullness." Fairmont and Martin County had voted to not allow alcohol to be served in the area the previous year under the county option available at that time.

It appears that the exact cost of the project was a bit difficult to "nail down." Prior to the vote on the proposed improvement, the cost had been estimated at $50,000. By the time of the vote, the estimate had gone up to $60,000. Upon completion, it was listed as a $70,000 improvement.

The work was done by a crew, paid the going rate of $3 per day, from Fielding and Shepley of St. Paul. Horace "Bud" Day, the son of Frank Day, had the job of timekeeper and was paid slightly better. It was during this paving operation that Fairmont experienced its first strike; however, it lasted no longer than part of an afternoon.

That year was significant in the progress of Fairmont becoming a city. Improvements totaled $487,000, including the Strand Theater and the Fairmont Telephone exchange building.

Progress came in other areas, too.

Fairmont tolerated the wood block paving for a number of years, however, it was doomed for two main reasons. One was the constant need for treatment and repairs, and the other was that the contractors from out of town were not equipped to handle these issues. As a result, concrete paving eventually came to the forefront.

FAIRMONT PAVES — First paving in Fairmont was laid the summer of 1915 by Fielding & Shepley of St. Paul. It was wood block paving, treated with creosote. The view is on North avenue, looking north across the Blue Earth avenue intersection. In the foreground at the right was the "Haynic" — now Nicholas — theater; next was the August Krumholz feed store (now Kirsch Clothing) and the tall building with the Hicks & Goetz clothing store sign on it, was the "Sinclair Block," now the Knights of Columbus building.

A 1950s Sentinel *story looks back at Fairmont pulling itself out of the mud.*

The farmers soon had automobiles and, as a result, there was no longer a concern about their horses and the concrete streets. With the advent of rubber soles for shoes, the argument of concrete being too hard to walk on by people was also quickly resolved. And the ladies who complained about their skirts dragging over the freshly creosoted paving had also found a solution. Their answer was to shorten their skirts, and none of the men complained about that.

Some information for this story is from the Centennial edition of the Sentinel, *July 19, 1958.*

Fairmont's Carnegie Library

Fairmont was among the first cities in the state to have a library. In 1879, the Minnesota legislature passed a law enabling the council of any incorporated city to levy an annual tax for the purpose of maintaining a library. According to a 1958 *Sentinel* article, under this law, the city of Fairmont became the second city in the state to establish a city-owned library, which it did in October of 1879. Consequently, the first library began operating in 1880. Minutes of the first library board meeting were dated October 25, 1880, and included the fact that Miss Lucinda Daniels was hired as the first librarian at a salary of $10 per year.

In 1903, with the help of Frank Day and others, a Carnegie grant was obtained to build a county library. It was one of 65 public libraries built in Minnesota with funds from Andrew Carnegie and the Carnegie Corporation. Between 1899 and 1917, Carnegie, a wealthy industrialist and philanthropist, contributed close to one million dollars toward library construction in Minnesota. This made Minnesota the eighth largest recipient of Carnegie Library grants in the United States.[1]

Carnegie's decision to support the construction of libraries was a result of his personal experiences. He was born in Scotland in 1935, and, during his youth, he listened to men read aloud and discuss books borrowed from a library his father helped to create. However, the rapid industrialization of the textile trade, the industry in which his father worked, forced his family to emigrate from Scotland to America where they settled in Allegheny, a suburb of Pittsburgh. Carnegie, in his autobiography, said he felt books opened the windows "through which the light of knowledge streamed" and resolved that, should he ever become wealthy, he would make opportunities available for everyone, including the poor.

In the latter half of the nineteenth century, Carnegie, who worked for the Pennsylvania Railroad, invested in railroad locomotives, oil, and iron and steel. In 1901, he sold the business he had created, Carnegie Steel, for $250 million and devoted the remainder of his life to philanthropy. Carnegie was particularly interested in libraries, providing funding initially for construction and later for staff and training. When he died in 1919 at age 84, gifts to various charities totaled nearly $350 million, almost 90 percent of his fortune.[2]

Although the Carnegie Grant was used to construct the library in Fairmont, the local community had to provide a suitable site and tax themselves at ten percent of the grant amount. This requirement imposed by Carnegie ensured a long-term commitment for the purchase of books, staff costs, and maintenance of the building. Local residents supported the library, and land was donated for the site of the building[3] by A.C. Frey, O.C. Gould, L.H. Brosemer, and William Viesselman.

Construction of the Carnegie Library commenced in 1903 and was completed in 1904 at 118 North Park Street (the library's current address is 110 North Park Street). It opened on April 26, 1904, with Miss Minnie Bird serving as the first librarian. When she started, her salary was $100 annually, payable in four quarterly payments of $25. Her salary was later raised to $25 per month.

Fairmont's Carnegie library, completed in 1904

The city and county libraries eventually merged in the late 1960s.

After many years of service, Fairmont's Carnegie Library was eventually doomed and faced demolition in May of 1968 in order to build a new county library. The cornerstone was opened by Street Commissioner Hugh Heinrich and Irv Haertel, whose father had made the cornerstone. The cornerstone, weighing approximately sixty-five pounds, held a metal box containing a 1903 legislative manual, a picture of the new state capitol, and five local newspapers.[4] Construction of Fairmont's new $440,000 county library began in 1968. The Martin County Library opened in October of 1969.

The four granite pillars, stained glass windows, and cornerstone from the Carnegie Library are now located at the front entrance of the Pioneer Museum in Fairmont.

Sources for this story include:

[1]*www.placeography.org/index.php/Carnegie_Libraries_Tour,*

[2]*nps.gov/nr/twhp/wwwlps/lessons/50carnegie/50facts1.htm;*

[3]*nps.gov/nr/twhp/wwwlps/lessons/50carnegie/50carnegie.htm; and*

[4]Fairmont Daily Sentinel, *May 28, 1968.*

Aviation in Martin County's History

The history of aviation in Martin County goes back more than a century.

The first air activity recorded in Martin County involved a balloon ascension in August of 1894 in Sherburn. Regretfully, it ended tragically as a spectator was caught up in the ropes and fell 150 feet to his death.

The first "flying machine" to appear in Martin County appeared in Fairmont on July 27, 1911, according to an early *Sentinel* story. However, the "birdman" in the flying machine caused a degree of disappointment as he arrived too late on the agreed-upon date to provide a show. Consequently, the promoters of the event, the Fairmont Commercial Club, confiscated the machine and served papers on the owner. Sheriff Tuey Ward took possession of the plane and locked it up in J.H. Gorman's storeroom for the night. The Commercial Club then met with the owners of the plane, Mr. St. Henry and Mr. Hanlon, and worked out an agreement for a new flight date. The flight took place the next day with perfect weather conditions. The plane took off shortly after 2:00 p.m., sailed majestically into the sky, and circled to the southwest but was gradually lost from sight. Thinking there had been an accident, rescuers went off in the direction of the plane only to find the pilot had safely landed it in a meadow because of a mechanical problem.

Fairmont's first airport, circa 1930. The airport was located on the Leonard farm near McKisson's Corner, where Prairie and State Street meet.

Other air shows or air circuses, as they were frequently called, took place in the late 1920s and 1930s and included giving rides to local residents. A July 30, 1929, *Sentinel* article stated that one such circus was to take place at the Ward Home Farm located about one-half mile east of the fairgrounds. The event was to include Miss Nona Malloy of St. Paul, the "world's premier lady parachute jumper who will make the leap from her plane at 2,000 feet." Also to be included were air races, balloon busting races, bombing operations, and a complete orchestra called the Sky Riders. The headline of the August 15, 1929, edition of the *Sentinel* read "20 Pilots Do Stuff for Fairmont Crowds." The article then described the stunts and maneuvers that the many participating planes had done for the crowd of 2,500.

Fairmont's first airfield was a cow pasture on the Art Stade farm near the Interlaken Golf Course. The first airport with a landing strip was on the farm then owned by E.E. Leonard near McKisson's Corner. It apparently included a large sign visible to flyers identifying the area as Fairmont as the May 22, 1929, *Sentinel* included a note from pioneering pilot Amelia Earhart who said, "I think I can thank you, in the name of everyone who flies, for marking the city of Fairmont...Please accept my gratitude for your progressive spirit and believe your efforts are appreciated." This airport closed in the 1930s.

In the early 1940s, a state-licensed airport was in operation on the Stade farm for a number of years. The Fairmont Airport Association was established on April 3, 1944, and soon plans for a new airport were in the works. This led to a somewhat bitter dispute involving the Fairmont Airport Association, the city council, and other individuals as to the building and location of the airport. In 1948, the city of Fairmont bought land for an airport, and eventually a bond issue was passed for its construction.

"Sunday, July 22, 1951, was a day in history for the city of Fairmont. With the formal dedication of the Municipal Airport, this city is now on the air map of the world, and within fifty hours travel time of any spot on earth," reported the July 23 *Fairmont Sentinel* as it marked the milestone. Amelia Earhart, noted pioneering female pilot who crossed the Atlantic by air, wrote to thank Fairmont for marking the city for pilots.

Looking back at the history of aviation in Martin County, many names emerge. Walter Krause of Ormsby was an early flyer and test pilot and was said to be one of the most colorful pilots in early Martin County aviation. Vic St. John and Walter Ritz of Truman were the first farmers to fly to the state fair in their own airplane. Other names include Floyd Eltgroth, Roy Fuller, Jack Robinson, Ernest Thieman, Earl Gray, Dr. L.A. Degan, Carl Oltman, Reuben Swenberg, and Cora Fuller, the first female licensed pilot in Minnesota. In addition, there were a number of local individuals who attended flying schools and then returned to Martin County to train people in the art of flying.

Among these early aviators, Lloyd Alsworth is undoubtedly the most acknowledged and acclaimed individual for making aviation a significant piece of Martin County's history. Known as "Pappy," the Sherburn native is widely considered to be the father of aviation in Martin County.

Local aviation was not without its mishaps. In addition to the balloon ascension death in 1894, the first aviator to die in Martin County as a result of an airplane accident was Melvin Marple in 1940. Marple was conducting a test flight that crashed near Monterey. Marple, considered one of the most experienced pilots in Martin County, didn't seem to like this particular plane, according to the February 15, 1940, *Fairmont Daily Sentinel*. The article went on to say that "some of the people in the village described it as a death trap, but others said it had been 'okayed' by Rev. Roy K. Reed, 'flying evangelist,' who formerly lived at Sherburn but who recently moved to the west." Apparently, this "okay" preceded more rigorous FAA regulations and inspections.

Sources for this story include The Daily Sentinel *Martin County Centennial edition, 1888-1898, page 8.*

Martin County's Pioneering Pilot

Generally considered the father of aviation in Martin County, Lloyd "Pappy" Alsworth was born in 1906 and grew up on a farm in rural Sherburn. He farmed with his father and operated an airport on their farm with his brother. Alsworth took his first plane ride at a 1927 air show in Jackson and was hooked on flying from that point forward. He learned to fly in a biplane owned by Clarence Siehl of Sherburn.

In 1931, Alsworth and his brother bought their first plane together, an OX-5 Travelaire biplane that cost $375. They used a hayfield on their father's farm as a landing strip, which was also used by many other pilots who came from miles around. This acquainted them with many of the early day pilots, from whom they in turn acquired a great deal of knowledge about flying and airplanes.

Lloyd Alsworth

Alsworth quit farming and joined the Civilian Training Corp during WWII. He was assigned to flight school and, after a short training period, began instructing enlisted personnel who would become Air Force pilots. He trained fliers in Minnesota in the Twin Cities, Grand Rapids, Duluth, and Mankato. After being discharged, he moved back to Martin County where he started a commercial airport with a flight school that included general infantryman training.

In 1945, he purchased a share of Clayton Dullard's flight school located in the Stade Airport in the southwest part of Fairmont. The airport was basically a converted cow pasture across from the Jolly Inn, now known as Tami's on The Ave. He became the airport manager and trained pilots there as well as in Sherburn. In 1949, the Fairmont Flying Service was moved to the site of the present airport, which is about two miles southeast of Fairmont's business district. Shortly thereafter, Alsworth purchased Dullard's interest in the business and became the sole owner.

Alsworth was active on many fronts, one of which involved his Fairmont Flying Service that operated an air taxi service. It flew primarily within a 300-mile radius; however, Alsworth had taken passengers as far as Atlantic City, New Jersey. He was also instrumental in convincing area officials to build the Fairmont Airport and served as airport manager as well. In addition, he began crop dusting in 1947 and spraying for the Fairmont Canning Company in the early 1950s.

Alsworth was a uniquely talented individual who was actively involved in many aspects of aviation. He served as president of the Minnesota Airport Operators Association and as a flight examiner, giving check rides to hundreds of pilots of commercial multi-engine planes and sea planes. He also provided charter services for local businesses and air ambulance services when needed. Obviously, aviation was an integral and significant part of his life as evidenced by his dedicated service to the profession that included being the unpaid manager of the Fairmont Airport for over twenty-five years.

Although Alsworth's flying experiences are mostly positive, his family suffered a tragic loss when his two sons, James and Gene, aged nineteen and twenty-one respectively, were both killed in an airplane accident in 1966.

Alsworth was a respected and admired local citizen who had a positive impact on the many people who he encountered throughout his lifetime. He passed away in August of 1992 at the age of 85. He was posthumously inducted into the Minnesota Aviation Hall of Fame in 2016.

Sources for this story include "The Lloyd Alsworth Story" in the Early Aviation display at MCHS and an interview with Alsworth's daughter Kate Hawkins.

A Minnesota First

In the world of modern aviation, women are employed as pilots for major airlines and the military. They participate in space travel, they fly in air races, they seed clouds, they teach students to fly, they transport corporate officers, and much, much more. Women have accomplished many "firsts" in the history of aviation.

Some of the women who have notable aviation accomplishments are E. Lillian Todd who was the first woman to design and build an aircraft (1906), Therese Peltier who was the first woman to pilot an aircraft (1908), Blanche Scott who was the first woman to solo an airplane (1910), Raymonde de Laroche who was the first woman in the world to receive a pilot license (1910), and Amelia Earhart who was the first woman to cross the Atlantic solo in 1932, according to the Women in Aviation International association.

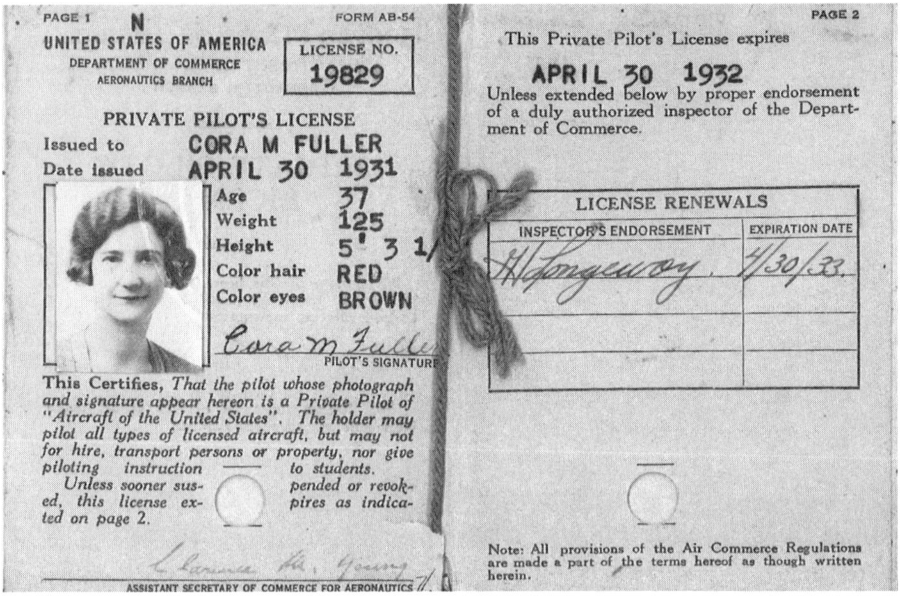

PAGE 1 N FORM AB-54

UNITED STATES OF AMERICA
DEPARTMENT OF COMMERCE
AERONAUTICS BRANCH

LICENSE NO. 19829

PRIVATE PILOT'S LICENSE

Issued to CORA M FULLER
Date issued APRIL 30 1931
Age 37
Weight 125
Height 5' 3 1/
Color hair RED
Color eyes BROWN

PILOT'S SIGNATURE

This Certifies, *That the pilot whose photograph and signature appear hereon is a Private Pilot of "Aircraft of the United States". The holder may pilot all types of licensed aircraft, but may not for hire, transport persons or property, nor give piloting instruction to students. Unless sooner suspended or revoked, this license expires as indicated on page 2.*

ASSISTANT SECRETARY OF COMMERCE FOR AERONAUTICS

PAGE 2

This Private Pilot's License expires
APRIL 30 1932
Unless extended below by proper endorsement of a duly authorized inspector of the Department of Commerce.

LICENSE RENEWALS

INSPECTOR'S ENDORSEMENT	EXPIRATION DATE
[illegible]	4/30/33

Note: All provisions of the Air Commerce Regulations are made a part of the terms hereof as though written herein.

A copy of Cora Fuller's pilot's license

Among those aviation accomplishments was a Martin County woman who became the first female licensed to pilot an airplane in Minnesota. Cora M. Fuller of Fairmont obtained her pilot's license by flying a Stinson-Detroiter monoplane solo over Hall Lake, making two trips of approximately five minutes each and attaining an altitude of 500 feet. There may have been other women who piloted airplanes in Minnesota before her; however, she was the first to be issued a pilot's license, that being on April 30, 1931.

Her preparation involved eight hours of instruction from Fairmont flyer Floyd Eltgroth. According to Eltgroth, she banked her plane masterfully and finished her flight with a perfect landing. He went on to say that she stepped off the plane as cool and collected as if stepping out of an automobile. Mrs. Fuller's log book shows she flew a total of 8,162 miles during her first year as a pilot.

She was married to Roy Fuller, also a pilot. In addition to her accomplishments in aviation, she was an ardent golfer and worked in her husband's produce company and as a bookkeeper at Paulson's Pharmacy. Fuller was born in 1893 and passed away in 1972.

Sources for this story include the "Lines by Lyle" column in the August 27, 1973, Sentinel.

Fairmont Airlines of the Past

Commercial aviation is often romanticized and has frequently been the setting for movies and novels. The handsome airline pilot, the attractive stewardess, exotic destinations, and if you include exciting experiences, all of the elements of a thrilling movie or glamorous novel seem to be in place. Could historic accounts of Fairmont's initial entry to regular airline service lend itself to at least the start of a movie or perhaps a novel?

The year was 1959, local spirits were high. A headline in the November 21, 1959, edition of *The Sentinel* was "New Airport Ticket Office Completed; Airline Stewardesses to Visit City." The story went on to detail the upcoming events and the people involved. The new station manager, Bill Vance, was characterized as an unmarried Milwaukeean who had been with North Central Airlines since graduating from high school. It went on to tell of stewardesses who were scheduled to appear at the Monday luncheon meetings with Kiwanis and Rotary members. They were to provide information about the beginning of daily air service in Fairmont. In addition, the story went on to say, "The young ladies also will be escorted to area towns where they will personally invite local dignitaries to be guests on the inaugural flights that day." The plot appeared to be thickening on the way to that first scheduled flight slated for December 1, 1959.

A North Central Airlines stewardess arrived on November 23, 1959. Her name was Miss Pat Rockstand, and her goal was to go with Fairmont officials on a tour of area towns calling on "leading citizens" and inviting them to take part in the inaugural flight. She was accompanied by two airline officials as well as C.J. Meister of the Fairmont Chamber, Fairmont Mayor John Brandenhoff, KSUM station manager Phil Solberg, and Claude Swanson of *The Sentinel.* They rode in a new twelve-passenger bus owned by KSUM called "Goliath." Although their visits were considered very successful, they were in fact late to almost every town due to the interest generated by their scheduled appearances, and they had to postpone several stops until the following day.

In a later interview with the stewardess, Rockstand explained in detail the requirements of her position with the airline. To be a North Central Airlines stewardess at that time, you had to be at least nineteen and one-half years of age, be between 5'1" and 5'6", and not weigh more than 125 pounds. In addition, a prospective stewardess must have had two years of either college or business experience. Of course, she could not be married.

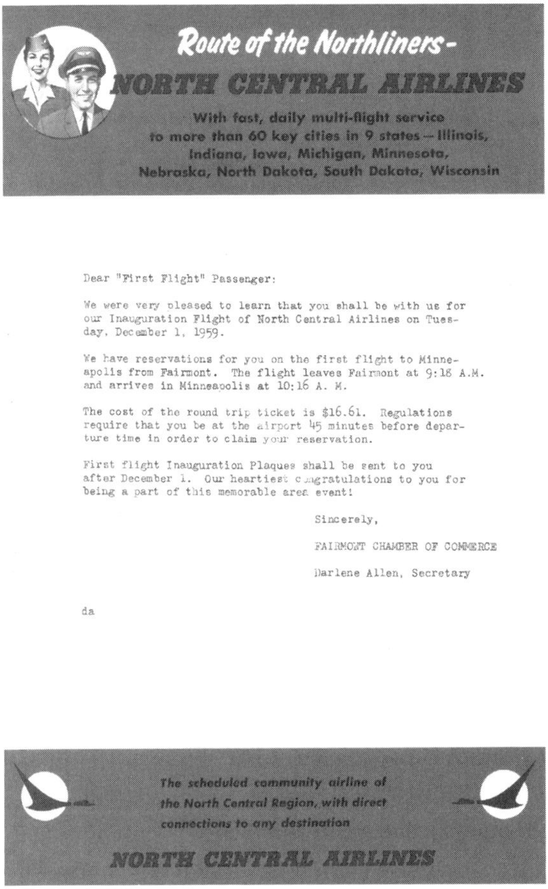

Route of the Northliners -
NORTH CENTRAL AIRLINES
With fast, daily multi-flight service to more than 60 key cities in 9 states—Illinois, Indiana, Iowa, Michigan, Minnesota, Nebraska, North Dakota, South Dakota, Wisconsin

Dear "First Flight" Passenger:

We were very pleased to learn that you shall be with us for our Inauguration Flight of North Central Airlines on Tuesday, December 1, 1959.

We have reservations for you on the first flight to Minneapolis from Fairmont. The flight leaves Fairmont at 9:18 A.M. and arrives in Minneapolis at 10:16 A. M.

The cost of the round trip ticket is $16.61. Regulations require that you be at the airport 45 minutes before departure time in order to claim your reservation.

First flight Inauguration Plaques shall be sent to you after December 1. Our heartiest congratulations to you for being a part of this memorable area event!

Sincerely,

FAIRMONT CHAMBER OF COMMERCE

Darlene Allen, Secretary

da

The scheduled community airline of the North Central Region, with direct connections to any destination
NORTH CENTRAL AIRLINES

A letter to the "First Flight" passengers from Fairmont

As the date of the inaugural flight approached, Federal Aeronautics inspectors and North Central Airlines officials gave the site of the Fairmont Airport a final checkup prior to flight approval. One of the inspectors stated, "It is one of the finest airports it has been my privilege to inspect outside of the metropolitan areas." With FAA approval in hand, the airport was now officially ready for business.

The public was informed that anyone with questions about the airport could contact Vance, station manager, by dialing 2198. He could provide information about the airport as well as schedule air travel from Fairmont. Vance stated that all travel was by reservation and that reservations could be made on connecting flights to many other cities. Concerning luggage, anything over forty pounds would cost 0.5 percent of a one-way fare. Luggage examples given included things such as binoculars, radios, cameras, and hat boxes. Ladies purses, however, were exempt regardless of size.

Vance also provided an example of airfare from Fairmont to Minneapolis in 1959, the cost being $8.69 one way and $16.61 round trip. Other examples of one-way air fares from Fairmont in 1959 included $3.85 to Mankato, $36.40 to Chicago, $80.30 to New York, and $136.18 to San Francisco.

The inaugural flight of North Central Airlines from Fairmont was scheduled for December 1, 1959. Some of those fortunate enough to be included on that passenger list were Brandenhoff, Meister, Chamber President Charles Zierke, Stokely Manager Ed Oleson, 3M Plant Manager L.W. Brown, *Sentinel* President Walter Mickelson, and a number of others referred to as local "notables" and "dignitaries." However, to the dismay of the local entourage, heavy weather grounded Fairmont's attempts to get its commercial air service off the ground on its initial endeavor.

Nonetheless, the second attempt two days later proved successful. Commercial air service finally arrived with a North Central DC-3 landing at Wold Chamberlain Air Field in Minneapolis, now known as Minneapolis–St. Paul International Airport, after having taken off from Fairmont with nineteen Fairmonters aboard headed by Brandenhoff.

Since Fairmont's initial venture into airline service, numerous airlines have served the local scene, including North Central from 1959 to 1977, Republic from 1978 to 1981, Mesaba from 1982 to 1984, Great Lakes from 1984 to 1992, and G.P. Express from 1993 to 1996.

What became of the main characters in this historic saga? The North Central stewardess, Miss Rockstand, was soon engaged to be married and, as a result, would have to leave her job as a stewardess. The status and direction of Vance was unclear. The local "dignitaries," "notables," and political figures involved at that time continued in their efforts to make improvements in Fairmont and Martin County. Flight service to and from Fairmont, including the status of the local airport, has continued to evolve.

Perhaps an imaginative mind and a little tweaking, coupled with a certain degree of nostalgic creativity and a bit of embellishment, could create the setting for an exciting novel or movie.

Sources for this story include the November 25, 1959, Sentinel *article "She Didn't 'Just Sit & Wish' to Be a Stewardess" by Barbara Blanchard, the November 28, 1959,* Sentinel *story by Ray Stougaard, and the December 1, 1959,* Sentinel.

Fairmont's Hospital

While medicine had been in Martin County for years, a formally organized hospital didn't exist until the 1920s.

What was at one time called the Fairmont Community Hospital came into existence in 1927 as a privately owned venture. The hospital was started by Dr. V.H. Gardner, a Fairmont physician who came to Fairmont from Dunnell where he had practiced medicine and surgery for four years. Originally from Cedar Rapids, Iowa, Gardner became familiar with this area as a result of his acquaintance with an Estherville, Iowa, doctor during Gardner's internship.

The hospital overlooked Ward Park and Lake Sisseton and was located on the present site of the condominiums on Albion Avenue. That lot, including the house, was purchased at that time for $15,000. Dr. H.A. Miller and Dr. A.G. Blanchard from Waseca joined Dr. Gardner in forming a corporation. Construction of the hospital began in 1927 and it opened in August of 1928. The total cost of the building and equipment was $175,000.

Gardner was with the hospital for only one year when he decided to return to private practice. That left the hospital in the hands of Blanchard and Miller.

In 1940, as a result of accumulated debt in excess of $90,000, Blanchard and Miller turned the hospital over to a group of local citizens willing to sign notes that retired the indebtedness. That group included Einer Nelson, E.E. Zemke, E.A. Thayer, Maud Brodt, J.C. Musser, and others. Their goal was to eventually turn the hospital over to the community, debt-free, at some point in the future. They operated the hospital until 1956 and successfully liquidated the debt and reorganized the hospital.

Fairmont Hospital

In October of 1956, a new board of directors was elected and a new set of bylaws was enacted. The new board hired an administrator and a professional fundraising agency to raise $500,000 to remodel the existing part of the hospital and build a new addition.

Partial funding for the hospital expansion included the support of 440 persons purchasing $25 memberships to form the Fairmont Community Hospital Association as well as a pledge of $150,000 from the county over a three-year period of time. The project, totaling close to $800,000, was completed in 1958 and included two new operating rooms, an up-to-date emergency room, and eleven additional patient rooms.

The 1960s ushered in a new era of change for the hospital. Although additional services were added, it soon became obvious that more services and space was needed than the site on Albion Avenue could accommodate. Consequently, the association board of directors voted to purchase land on the southeast edge of Fairmont for $80,000 to build an entirely new facility. A special $2,295,000 bond issue was approved by a vote of 1,958 to 71 in December of 1968. This made the projected $3.9 million dollar hospital project possible and construction was scheduled to start in June of 1970. The new hospital opened its doors to patients in September of 1972.

Around that time, Fairmont doctors and dentists formed the Fairmont Professional Building Corporation in 1969 to study the feasibility of building a medical clinic in the area.

The hospital administrator at the time, Cale Neal, told the newspaper that the venture "is something that the hospital board is really happy to see." He went on to say that the construction of a new clinic as well as hospital was very important in attracting new physicians to the community. He also added that the hospital was willing to sell two acres of land of the forty-nine-acre site to the clinic. The clinic was to be a private enterprise, and a separate corporation was also planned to operate the pharmacy.

Construction of the clinic, projected to cost between $600,000 and $700,000, was slated to begin in the spring of 1970. Although it would be adjacent to the hospital, it would be a separate entity and not connected to the hospital other than physically. The plan for the construction of the clinic was to accommodate the current physicians and dentists while providing additional space for future members to join. Each doctor would have his own office and examination rooms. In addition, a central accounting and record keeping department would be incorporated into the facility. The clinic corporation purchased five and one-half acres of land from the community hospital corporation for their venture. Although it was a separate corporation from the hospital, plans for a link physically connecting the two facilities were made at that time.

Upon completion, the clinic held an open house in September of 1971. An estimated 500–600 people were in attendance. Members of the corporation were awarded the Chamber of Commerce Enterprise Award "in recognition of their initiative, savings, resources, courage and enterprise" in establishing the corporation's facilities, according to Wayne Unze, chamber manager.

Many changes have taken place with the hospital and the health care industry as a whole since the early 1970s when private room rates peaked locally at $40 per day.

Sources for this story include Sentinel *stories from October 23, 1970, May 19, 1955, December 2, 1957, and June 30, 1959; Jan Dickinson's compiled research of newspaper articles;* Martin County History *by Taylor Publishing, 1988.*

Fairmont's Union Bus Depot

We've seen it happen many times before; buildings that once served a specific and necessary purpose and were a proven asset to the community for many years are suddenly demolished, gone and forgotten! This is the fate of one Fairmont building, now only a memory. It most recently served as the Fairmont Municipal Liquor Store on

North Park Street; however, some may recall that it at one time served the community in a much different capacity.

The building permit for this structure was taken out in 1947. It was to become the Union Bus Depot, owned and operated by Matt Dietz. As reported in the June 9, 1948, edition of the *Fairmont Daily Sentinel*, Fairmont's new Union Bus Depot was to have its grand opening the next day. It was stated that this would give Fairmont one of the finest, new, "ultra modern bus terminals in the Midwest." It boasted a restaurant that was open twenty-four hours daily, lockers, and many other modern public conveniences.

Union Bus Depot

The construction costs of the Union Bus Depot totaled $40,000. This included a modern design of the time incorporating "brick facing highlighted with the use of glass brick." The interior included what was described as a beautifully decorated lunchroom that could accommodate fifty people. The kitchen had the latest stainless steel equipment. There was also a horseshoe-shaped newsstand with ticket windows at the far end. A waiting area was located just beyond the ticket counter with nearby rest rooms, lockers, and public telephones. A large gate led from the waiting area south to the bus loading area. There was an eighteen-foot wide driveway for busses to enter from the rear and pull up for loading on the south side of the building. A canopy protected passengers from the elements while they waited for their bus.

The bus schedule was served by three bus lines. They included daily trips to Albert Lea; Worthington; Omaha, Nebraska; and Sioux Falls, South Dakota. Daily trips were also scheduled to Minneapolis and Mankato. In addition, connections to the west coast, the southwest, Chicago, and points east were available.

The Bus Depot Café's menu featured T-bone steak for $1.50, pork chops or fried ham for seventy cents, and for sixty cents you could enjoy roast beef, roast pork, spaghetti and meatballs, or hamburger steak. This included an appetizer, salad, and dessert; however, beverages were five cents extra. For the lighter appetite, hamburgers and other sandwiches were only forty-five cents. In addition, they served homemade pies and would pack lunches for anyone needing that service.

However, times changed over the years and transportation was evolving. Travel by other means was becoming more prevalent, and bus service gradually diminished in this area. In July of 1969, the bus depot had become the new home of the municipal liquor store. In 1989, an addition was built to the liquor store. Finally, in 2010 the city decided to build a new liquor store in a more favorable location. Consequently, the Park Street location was closed and demolished in 2011. It is now a parking lot serving the Fairmont Fire Department.

The times change, our priorities change, and the needs of the community change. As a result, the local landscape is also affected and continues to evolve as well.

Sources for this story include the July 14, 1948, and June 8, 1948, Sentinel.

A Slough of Controversy

Luedtke's Slough is truly a serene sight, abounding in wildlife and many diverse forms of vegetation. Today it is partially bordered by homes, but in the late 1960s and '70s, the slough was the site of a bitter controversy that made its way to the attorney general's office in St. Paul and eventually to District Court.

Luedtke's Slough

A proposal was made to use the slough as a depository for silt dredged from Fairmont lakes. The slough, categorized as a wetland, is within Fairmont city limits. The argument was whether the slough should be used as a silt disposal site, or preserved as a wetland and potentially used as a nature study. Some saw it as a way of saving taxpayer money while others viewed it as destruction of the natural habitat of plants and animals. Eventually, a number of diverse viewpoints were presented from concerned citizens, teachers, students, and city government.

The opposition to the slough as a silt depository was led by Dan Kehrberg, then a biology teacher at Fairmont High School. Kehrberg spoke to local civic organizations and, as reported in the January 19, 1971, edition of the *Sentinel*, in speaking at Kiwanis, he stated that "dredging is neither the main cause of cleaner lake water nor the algae deterrent many people believe it is." He believed that alternate methods of silt disposal should be utilized.

As the controversy intensified, the publicity expanded. A February 14, 1971, *Minneapolis Tribune* article, entitled "Teacher Leads Battle to Save a Slough," made reference to both opponents and proponents of saving the slough as a natural setting. The article refers to the late John Livermore as Fairmont's ex-officio guardian of the public purse and quoted him as saying, "Snakes alive! Now they are spending our tax dollars to tell us we need a stinking, mushy, smelly polliwag slough. . ." This article goes on to tell of a fourth grade class bombarding the *Sentinel* with letters to the editor favoring preserving the slough. It further stated that the controversy was a frequent topic on a local radio call-in program. In addition, the article included comments from individuals and groups in the community, including the city council members.

Eventually, the debate crept outside Fairmont city limits. In May 1971, the DNR became involved and recommended preserving Luedtke's Slough. According to an article in the November–December 1976 issue of *The Minnesota Volunteer*, the city of Fairmont requested that the Minnesota Water Resources Board conduct a hearing regarding filling part of the slough. However, the DNR felt that the WRB did not have jurisdiction and therefore refused to grant Fairmont the right to fill the slough. Then the city asked District Court to decide whether they should comply with the DNR or WRB.

A special public meeting was called by Fairmont in March 1974 and an agreement was reached with the DNR to allow filling the northern third of the slough and leaving the remainder in its natural state with permission from affected land owners. The compromise was reached because it was felt that continued legal wrangling could go on for years, obviously to no one's advantage.

While there was potential for lingering hard feelings, the issue helped everyone gain a better perspective and understanding of the importance of wetlands in our environment, which provide a home for wildlife and serve to enhance educational opportunities for students. Wetlands such as Luedtke's Slough provide numerous other immeasurable benefits to the environment and the landscape of our community and county as well.

The slough today is utilized as a reservoir for the east side storm sewers.

Education

A Primer on the County's Educational Past

Education in Martin County was a very important and frequently discussed topic in the area's history. In the March 10, 1914, edition of the *Martin County Sentinel*, A.N. Fancher tells the history of education in the county prior to that date.

Fancher stated that in the early days, there were few, if any, records kept of the first schools, and the state law governing the formation and maintenance of district schools was vague and uncertain. Before the territory became a state, the old township method of forming and controlling school districts was in force.

The Fairmont schools circa 1908. From left are: the elementary school, the junior high, and the high school.

In 1858, after the territory became a state, the legislature enacted the county system which was at that time regarded with a great deal of skepticism. The pioneers of Martin County had little use for school laws as they had no township or county organization and no school funds available to them. They were, however, determined not to be deprived in the area of education.

Fancher's article describes Center Chain as a leader of the time. As early as 1856, there were several children in this settlement. The children gathered together at different houses in the settlement with the women settlers acting as teachers. In 1860, a log addition was made to one of the houses, which was then made into a schoolroom. Their intent was to make it a very comfortable and desirable room for this purpose, as well as for religious and public gatherings. At that time, Center Chain was far ahead of other settlements in the county. According to Fancher's article, the entire population of what was then Fairmont consisted of Henry Pratt, his wife and four children, along with Mr. Budd, and Mr. Hinkle, both bachelors.

A joint district comprising nearly half the town of Verona in Faribault County and all of the town of Center Creek in Martin County was the first district organized in the county and the only one to be organized under the township system.

Soon after its formation, a schoolhouse was built in the district made of native boards and slabs which was covered with sod. It was located on the county line in Martin County very near Faribault County. A school term was taught there, in Fairmont, and in Center Chain. These schools were supported by private contributions with teachers receiving salaries of $10 to $12 monthly.

In 1861, the state legislature repealed existing school laws and enacted what was known as the sub-district law. This provided for a central school in each township that would be under the control of the township supervisors. They were authorized to form other districts in the township that would be known as sub-districts. This was repealed in the next legislative session and was replaced by the county system.

The Fairmont district was the first in the county to apply for organization under the new law and was thus numbered one. The schoolhouse in the joint district would have been number one; however, it was moved across the line into Faribault County and became the Huntley district.

According to Claude Swanson's column in the June 1, 1963, *Sentinel*, the first school district in Martin County was organized by the board of county commissioners in 1862. School was held in a Sibley tent borrowed from the soldiers at Fort Fairmount in the summer of 1863.

Some of the most enthusiastic workers for the cause of education in the early history of Martin County included Reverend J.C. Strong of Center Chain, and L.F. Brainerd and Mrs. Kate Sperry, both of Nashville Township.

As time passed, changes took place and buildings were erected such as:

- Fairmont's new high school in 1914 for $125,000,
- Granada's high school in 1914 for $30,000,
- A $5,000 schoolhouse in 1916 built by the Fairmont German Lutherans,
- East Chain's $40,000 structure in 1919 which included "every modern idea" for education,
- Fairmont's junior high school in 1929 built for $181,000,

- Truman's school building built in 1936 for $110,000, and
- Welcome's school addition in 1938 for $40,000.

By 1927, there were 101 rural schools in the county. By 1941, the schools had installed electric cookery. The following year a Fairmont school bus took kids to city schools from the "suburbs" of Oak Beach, Hazelmere, Shoreacres and Belle Vue. There were 91 teachers in the county then.

In 1949, the south side school was named after William Budd, and a cornerstone was laid for the Lincoln School.

Fairmont Public Schools Early History to 1931

In 1860, Fairmont was a sparsely populated region that was soon to experience rather significant population growth.

On May 21, 1860, Lorraine Swearingen signed a contract to teach school in Fairmont for the term of twelve weeks with compensation totaling $1 per week. Her salary came from a voluntary school tax paid by those who had children attending school, with the exception of Mr. Hinkle. While Hinkle had no children, he was very much interested in promoting the affairs of the then "new" community. The following individuals agreed to pay the salary of Mrs. I.B. Swearingen: Benson C. Hinkle, $2.50; A.H. Wooster, $4; J.B. Swearingen, $4; Wm. Johnson, $1; and Isaac Johnson, $1. Based on the contracted salary and the donor contributions, it appears that she received a fifty-cent bonus.

Lorraine Swearingen

The contract she signed had stipulations and stated that, "I, Lorain Swearingen, agree to teach a school of the common English branches at the town of Fairmont. School to commence on the 21st day of May, 1861, and I further agree to keep good order in said school and use only reasonable means for correcting the children in cases of necessity only."

The first school was held in a house owned by Hinkle and was thought to be located in the woods along Lake Sisseton, perhaps near the present site of the Martin County Courthouse.

News of the Sioux Uprising reached Fairmont on August 22, 1862, and caused the school year to be abruptly terminated until the following summer. Although Hinkle was a fervent promoter of schools and was actively engaged in public affairs, he became discouraged following the outbreak and left the area.

In the summer of 1863, Mrs. Swearingen was forced to hold school in a borrowed tent. Shortly thereafter, the men of the settlement built the first schoolhouse, donating materials and labor. This was a fairly crude structure built of logs, brush, and dirt. It was located in the vicinity of Main Street and Eighth. This school was used only during the summer and Mrs. Swearingen was paid $10 for that term.

In 1864 and 1865, school was held in the north part of William Budd's home located in the 700 block of Albion Avenue. The teacher, Laura H. Smith, was paid $16 per month. Up to this time, no school taxes were levied. However, with the rapid growth taking place in the mid-1860s, it was apparent that more adequate school facilities and other changes were needed.

In 1866, Reuben M. Ward, James Swearingen, and Budd were appointed to select a site for a school. The site selected was located in the southwest corner of the former Central School location, presently the home of Presentation College. It was purchased by the district in 1867 from Orville P. Chubb for $1. The east half of that lot was purchased in 1885 for $1,000.

The first building constructed on that site was a one-room building used until 1874, the first teacher being John P. Bird. A two-room building was constructed in 1875 at a cost of $2,500. Teachers in this facility included D.P. Sackett, Emma Snow, R.M. Tyler, W.A. McDonald, and Dr. F.N. Hunt. The two-room building was replaced by a brick structure in 1886.

A four-room building was constructed on the northeast corner of the Central School location in 1895 at a cost of $5,745. The high school building was built in 1900 at a cost of $13,741 and was located on the southwest corner of the Central School lot. Additionally, in 1910, a normal training department was added to the school system and was located in the elementary school on that same site.

The first Lincoln School site was purchased in 1905 for $1 with four lots added later to that for $900. The first Lincoln School that eventually became known as the Lincoln Annex was built in 1907.

The former high school and junior high school site, presently Veteran's Park, was acquired through condemnation proceedings in 1915.

Since those early years, Fairmont's schools have changed significantly in terms of their geographic location, structure, methods of delivery, and student demographics. As time passes, there will undoubtedly be more changes in many ways. Perhaps reflecting on the past will prove beneficial to enhancing the quality and direction of the future of education.

This brief historical account of the district was based in part on documentation from the first yearbook created by the Fairmont Public Schools. This publication was named The 1931 FAIR–HI–AN. *Other resources in the Pioneer Museum also contributed to this account. Incidentally, in 1931 there were 1,275 students attending the Fairmont Public Schools. Other sources for this story include MCHS History Files 244 and 730, and Jan Dickinson's compiled research of newspaper articles entitled "Martin County Schools" at the Pioneer Museum.*

Back to School

Education has changed over the years, both in theory and practice as well as with the physical structures of the many "school houses" that once dotted the Martin County landscape. In taking a glimpse back at education in Martin County, it is interesting to compare it to the world of education today and to observe the many changes that have since taken place.

In an article prepared by Mrs. M.H. O'Conner for a meeting of the Parent Teacher Association at Lincoln School in Fairmont in the 1920s entitled "Teaching in Old Days Was No Bed of Roses," O'Conner identified some of the interesting aspects of her career as a country school teacher. She said that she began teaching in a little frame box of a building with the corners resting on boulders. This, she said, gave the icy winter winds a good opportunity to swirl around the building which caused their feet to freeze. In fact, it was so cold, the water pail for drinking was often frozen, and the students had to break the ice to get a drink.

Back to school at the one-room schoolhouse in District 59

The size of her classes varied; in one instance, she had only one student in class during planting season. On another occasion, she had a class of thirty-five pupils ranging in age from four to twenty-one. Although she had little time to devote to each student, she observed, "I dare say my methods were primitive, but I believe the facts I pounded into their rather thick skulls stuck as well as though they had been inculcated by modern methods." O'Conner's assessment would probably create quite a controversy today.

Teachers of that era usually had to find boarding places if one wasn't provided for them. O'Conner said that boarding was often difficult to find and, in some cases, not always very desirable. She stated that "frequently I had to wash my face in the kitchen in the common wash basin and wipe on the roller towel with the hired men. The bed I occupied had numberless occupants who made sleep impossible." It seems that this would appear to be another somewhat controversial situation.

The country schools of that era did not have custodians. Consequently, the schools were cleaned in the middle of the school year by the teacher with the help of her students. The older boys would bring a large kettle, build a fire, and then melt snow so that they would have hot water for cleaning. The girls would bring the soap, and then all would help in cleaning the school house.

O'Conner concluded by saying that conditions improved as time went by and that country schools finally had such fine conveniences that both teachers and students should be happy and that the work might be almost ideal. As this was written in 1932, she would certainly be astounded as to the current educational systems and standards.

Another interesting account was written in the October 14, 1933, edition of the *Sentinel* by C.L. Blanchar as he wrote about Miss Maria Willard, a pioneer Fairmont teacher who had recently passed away. The writer quite eloquently articulated that "I cannot forget her kind and gentle way, for she gave me the only whipping I got in school. Even to this day of old gray hairs, I am ready to take oath before all the gods of the universe that I was innocent." Her standards of discipline apparently made a rather significant impression on that writer whether or not he was, in fact, guilty of whatever might have prompted the "whipping."

Teachers in those early years may have seemed stern and strict; however, they themselves had somewhat stringent rules to follow as well. Some rules from 1872 were that men teachers may take one evening each week for courting purposes, or two evenings if they go to church regularly; women teachers who marry or engage in unseemly conduct will be dismissed; and after ten hours in school, teachers may spend the remaining time reading the Bible or other good books. Some rules from the early 1900s specifically regarding women teachers required them to wear at least two petticoats and forbade them to go out with men or to get married while engaged as a teacher. They also were not to stay downtown in ice cream parlors too long, dye their hair, or wear dark colored clothing. Apparently some rules did not apply equally to both male and female teachers.

Ah, yes, the "good old days." There was a time when Martin County had in excess of 100 schools districts and teacher salaries approached $200 annually.

Education has evolved considerably from those days. Pupils and teachers are treated much differently than in the past. There are a multitude of opportunities available to both the teacher and the student. However, those of us who attended country schools survived, adapted to change, succeeded in spite of some of the hardships faced at that time, and became contributing members of society.

Even with all the modern technological advances, theories of education, and the many opportunities available, perhaps in some ways, today's students face as many or conceivably even more challenges than the graduates of those country schools of the past.

Sources for this story include "Rules for Teachers, 1872" posted at MCHS, and Jan Dickinson's compiled research of newspaper articles.

William Budd Elementary School

William Budd School, now merely a memory, served a multitude of students since it opened its doors back in 1950. The ceremony and cornerstone laying for Budd School took place on December 12, 1949, at 10 a.m. Sealed inside a copper box within the cornerstone were several articles of historical interest, including a copy of the school board proceedings authorizing the construction of the school, a copy of the *Sentinel* with a sketch of William H. Budd, and a list of the school board members of that time. The cornerstone was located in the extreme northwest corner of the building. In addition, the school occupied a historic site in Fairmont; the location was where the home of Mr. and Mrs. Henry Style had been. The Styles had been prominent members of the English bean colony of the 1870s.

Budd School circa 1950

Passing a bond issue for the construction of Budd School wasn't without its challenges as there was a great deal of opposition to the proposal. The initial bond issue was defeated by a vote of 531 to 394. This was primarily as a result of the citizens of the north side running advertisements in the *Sentinel* condemning the north-side Lincoln School as a fire trap. In addition, they felt it unfair that the south-siders would be getting a brand new building and, according to an ad paid for by John Livermore, the plan discriminated against the north side.

Three weeks later, a second bond issue was held calling for $500,000 to build a school in south Fairmont for $225,000 and to build a school in north Fairmont for $275,000. It passed by a vote of 599 to 246. So, as a result, Fairmont would soon have two new elementary schools.

Shortly before construction began on the new school, the name William Budd School was selected for the south side school. The name was suggested by Judge J.E. Haycraft.

According to the brochure of the dedication exercises of William Budd Grade School held on February 18, 1951, the actual cost of the school as it was equipped totaled $375,000. The school was lauded as being one of the most modern school buildings constructed in the northwest with such facilities as a visual aids room, project room, nurse's office and sick bay, library with workroom, teacher's room, intercom system, gymnasium with in-wall tables and benches to convert to a lunchroom, a serving kitchen, not to mention the many accolades related to the classrooms. The brochure also listed six members of the board of education, four members of the Parent Teacher Association, and six teachers in addition to the school principal.

In the late 1950s, the schools were becoming more crowded, and a bond issue was passed to make additions to Fairmont's schools. Students returning to Budd School in the fall of 1960 would find a new addition, three new kindergarten rooms on the ground floor of the new wing, nine new elementary classrooms on the second floor of the new wing, a new teacher's workroom, a second activity room, a band room due to the moving of the library, and new playgrounds.

In 2011, an addition was built to the Five Lakes Elementary School to house the kindergarten through second-grade classrooms, and Budd School, badly in need of expensive repairs, was demolished. In its place now stands the Fairmont water treatment plant.

Budd School served many students during its sixty-plus years in existence. Many former staff members undoubtedly have countless fond memories of Budd School as well. Although it served Fairmont's educational needs for many years, when its existence came to an end, what remained were memories and memorabilia.

Sources for this story include MCHS History File 1079, Jan Dickinson's compiled research of newspaper articles, and the March 25, 1950, Fairmont Daily Sentinel.

Higher Education in Fairmont's Past

Before there was Presentation College or the Southern Minnesota Education Campus, there was the Fairmont Business College.

Back in 1904, Professor C.R. Sweet, a graduate of Fairmont High School and the Santa Rosa Business College, opened the Fairmont Business College with approximately twenty students attending, including several graduates of another business school that was already in Fairmont.

A brochure publicizing the college called the area "picturesque," touted the city's population of 4,000, and said the area "is almost surrounded by splendid lakes where fishing, bathing, boating, steamer riding and skating can be enjoyed."

The brochure continued on saying that "Fairmont, by virtue of its surroundings and high moral standard, is considered the best school town in the state. It is a city where you can safely send your boy or girl. It is a city where they would like to live." The brochure also goes on to advise parents not to send too much money with boys attending school, as it "materially detracts from their school work."

College National Bank at Fairmont Business College

Professor Sweet's guiding principle of instruction, according to the December 16, 1904, edition of the *Martin County Sentinel,* involved conducting actual business right from the start. He advertised his system of bookkeeping as being "that of an actual business system from the start and no time wasted by laboriously copying from dry text books, no fictitious names are used, and every transaction is bona fide."

Upon entering school, students would first go to the college bank and negotiate a loan; then they would lease a store. Next they would purchase a stock of goods for their store, and finally open a set of books that "carries on an account at the bank and (the student) in every way is given an opportunity for full play of whatever commercial talent he may possess."

Sweet went on to say that, in some instances, the student prospered. He also stated that occasionally students would meet with reverses and go into bankruptcy, settling with creditors in accordance with the bankruptcy laws of the time.

The College National Bank was exactly like other national banks of its time. It was equipped with bank fixtures and an ample supply of currency and would issue pass books, checks, and drafts. It also conducted a money order post office.

One interesting aspect observed by Professor Sweet was that "the penmanship of the students is a revelation as to what the school can accomplish in that time. In every instance, the student has acquired an easy and clear business handwriting."

The tuition, payable in advance, was $50 for six months, $10 for a single month, and $10 for books and supplies. In addition, the school offered a "no risk" free trial to students. Anyone not satisfied with the school would receive a refund of their first month's tuition. The school also advertised board and lodging in private homes at a cost of $2.50 per week and up. His advertisements stated that six months should make the average student a competent and reasonably capable accountant.

Professor Clyde Sweet's school was located on the second floor of the Clark Haines building. This is where Fairmont Electric and Hardware was once located. It is now the site of the El Agave restaurant. Sweet eventually abandoned the school to run for county superintendent of schools.

In addition to the Fairmont Business College, two other business colleges started in Fairmont in the early 1900s. The first was Toland's of La Crosse, Wisconsin, which opened in 1901. However, it was short-lived.

The other, The Fairmont Practical Business College, opened by the Randall brothers from Iowa in 1916, did not last long either. It started with an enrollment of 50 students and added more during the school year, however, only two graduated.

Nearly fifty years later, Fairmont as a city began looking at higher education. Fairmont's goal of a junior college apparently started in 1965, based on a January 6 headline from the Sentinel that read, "Fairmont Buys Day Farm for Junior College Site." This piece went on to state that the city of Fairmont had purchased the 168-acre Day Farm located on the west side of Lake Sisseton as the site for a future junior college. The land was purchased from Majel B. Habberstad of Minneapolis and Doris Day of Los Angeles, the two daughters of Burt Day, brother of *Sentinel* founder Frank Day. The farm was homesteaded by the ladies' grandfather, Reuben Ward. The article also stated that the land would be paid for by profits from the municipal liquor store.

Shortly thereafter, the Fairmont Junior College Action Committee was formed. It was apparently quite instrumental in organizing meetings and dinners in which local individuals, as well as legislators and state senators, were present in extolling the virtues of building a junior college in Fairmont.

Four years later, another *Sentinel* story said the junior college might open by 1973. The story, written by Editor Roger Matz, was based on an interview with Emil Wilken, assistant to the chancellor of the state junior college system. The article started by stating, "A lakeside farm does not become an ivy-covered campus overnight." It outlined the fact that, although this ten-year dream now had $97,000 in funding and had been designated a junior college site by the legislature, answers were needed regarding what curriculum of study the college would offer and what buildings would be needed.

Another *Sentinel* article on the topic from May 30, 1969, projected what the college might become. Matz facetiously asked, "Will it come complete with student demonstrators?" He was hinting that questions like these might be more easily answered than questions about what the final product would be in terms of size and appearance. However, could his quote have also implied that there were perhaps other unwritten, but discussed, concerns about a junior college in Fairmont? In the article by Matz, Dr. Wilken estimated that the school could open in 1973 with an enrollment of 400 to

500 students. He also indicated that the JC might have several buildings serving several purposes including a science building, a library, and general classroom buildings. He added that junior colleges frequently share athletic facilities with local high schools, especially in their early stages of development.

A later article promoted the benefits to students as well as the economic benefits to the community of a junior college. It also highlighted potential class offerings and outlined necessary steps to be taken in order to establish a junior college in Fairmont.

Between 1969 and 1972, the matter seemed to essentially deteriorate. In 1972, Dr. Donald K. Harcom, who was the newly appointed president of Fairlakes Junior College, said he was anxious to move but had no idea as to where his office might be established. He went on to say that he had little information about the college but believed it would be the best in Minnesota. Obviously, things were a bit murky at best regarding the school at this juncture.

In February 1974, a *Sentinel* story entitled "After 15-year struggle, Fairlakes vanishes," seemed to toll the death knell for Fairlakes Junior College. This story stated that in December of 1973, two legislative leaders visited Fairmont in hopes of learning the key issues that concerned the people of Fairmont. During their two hours in town, they heard about everything but the junior college. What at one time had been the hottest topic in town had now seemingly slipped into obscurity. The inability of the forces surrounding Fairlakes Junior College to coalesce was due to a changing Minnesota compounded by a variety of other factors. Plans lingered beyond deadlines, state officials blamed architects, architects blamed state bureaucrats, plans were submitted to bidders months behind schedule, and bids came back $200,000 too high, causing an arduous situation at best.

Furthering the problem, college enrollments were declining and the Minnesota Commissioner of Administration impounded the Fairlakes funds. Going as far back as 1958 when a state report termed Fairmont an educational "void," the struggle ultimately reached closure in 1973. In the final analysis, had the plans proceeded in a prudent and timely manner, perhaps Fairlakes Junior College might have come to fruition. However, since it failed to materialize, one can now only speculate as to "what might have been" regarding that phase of our local history.

The acquired site for the junior college, the Day Farm, is now the location of Heritage Acres which provides a different sort of education.

Luella Keithahn, an Unsung Hero

There are many individuals who significantly impact our society and well-being in ways that most of us will never know. They quietly go about their business without fanfare or notoriety, they're neither in the news nor are they household names, yet they contribute greatly to the benefit of many within the culture in which they live. One of these "unsung heroes" of everyday life is Martin County native Luella Keithahn.

Keithahn, "twin sister to Alveda, was born on April 22, 1910. She attended rural school and then Fairmont High School," according to *The Keithahn Family in America, Volume II*, by Julian Keithahn. After high school, she attended Fairmont Normal Training School for teacher's training. This certified her to teach in rural schools until she decided to attend Winona State Teachers' College.

LUELLA MAGDALENA KEITHAHN
1974

In 1935, she decided to attend the University of Minnesota in order to complete her bachelor's of science degree, which she did, graduating summa cum laude. She went on to complete a master's of arts degree during the summers. In her early years of teaching, she taught sixth grade in Rochester; she taught as a normal school [teacher prep school] teacher in Rushford; and she served as an associate professor at Bemidji State College.

In 1948, she was asked if she would be interested in serving as an elementary and junior high principal with the U.S. Army in Germany. She interviewed, obtained a leave of absence from Bemidji State College, and accepted.

She "crossed the Atlantic in a Liberty ship that had no portholes and slept in a bunk bed in a large room in the lower part of the ship." She was destined for Bamberg, an old city east of Frankfurt with little industry, which had not been bombed much during the war. She taught in a German school of which one-half of the school was designated for American students. At first it posed some problems, particularly among American junior high boys who would pick fights with the Germans. During her vacation time, she was able to travel to many places in Europe before school was let out in June.

Keithahn then returned to Bemidji and taught for another year. However, things would soon change as she received a call to teach in Latin America. She accepted and taught in Paraguay, Guatemala, Honduras, Haiti, Venezuela, and Brazil as a technical assistant under the Institute for Inter-American Affairs Point Four Program and Alliance for Progress from 1950 to 1972.

It was apparent that Keithahn thoroughly enjoyed her time in South America. She once wrote, "I gave training courses to the teachers and visited many schools, often traveling by DC-3 plane, jeeps, or horse. The people were most appreciative of the help they were getting." According to the family history book, "She spoke and wrote Spanish and Portuguese and gave lectures in Portuguese to Brazilian teachers." During her sixteen years in Brazil, she served as a language arts advisor, worked in curriculum development, served in teacher training and adult literacy, and was an advisor on the writing of teachers' manuals and text books for elementary and secondary education.

One of Keithahn's most memorable moments in Brazil was when, on behalf of President Kennedy, she presented the Brazilian government with a check for one million dollars for the Alliance for Progress Program. The fact she was given the honor of presenting the check was indeed a testimony to the respect she had acquired in her profession.

In addition, she entertained often. In the book, *The Keithahn Family in America, Volume II,* she states: "All during the twenty-two years I worked in South America, I had a wonderful social life. Since the program was under the State Department, I was invited to many receptions. I had a full-time maid and would put on buffet dinners for up to thirty people. My menu always included Brazilian ham and apple pie. I would help with the cooking up to party time and then turn everything over to the maid and a hired waiter who would serve the drinks and dinner."

Upon her retirement in 1972, she received a special citation from the U.S. Government for her years in Brazil. The citation said, in part, "the list of your accomplishments would be lengthy but none of the items would surpass the lasting effect that you will leave resulting from your example of dedication, hard work, and humble desire to help the Brazilian children have an opportunity for a better life through education." Keithahn retired in Sacramento, California, and did volunteer work, was active in church work, chaired many boards, and traveled extensively. She passed away after a short illness in 1996. She was cremated, and her ashes are buried in Lakeside Cemetery in Fairmont.

Keithahn wasn't an influential figure on corporate boards, she didn't amass a fortune in wealth, she wasn't famous, she wasn't a prominent political figure, and she didn't provide lasting legacies within Martin County. No, she didn't do any of those things; she did far more.

She extended the values she acquired growing up in Martin County to the world, making it a better place. The positive influence she had on many lives, those she touched in her work in Germany and South America, is truly immeasurable. Her life exemplifies the lives of a great many Martin County, and American, citizens. She went about her business quietly, unselfishly making a difference in a positive manner in everything she attempted while influencing and touching the lives of many who are better off for her efforts. There is no monetary value, level of fame, or political prestige that can come close to the impact on society those individuals, such as Luella Keithahn, have made through the efforts of their lifelong endeavors. As a result, many lives have been permanently changed for the better.

Sources for this story, beyond the family history volumes, include family interviews.

Hair Today, Gone Tomorrow—Maybe

Schools and education serve as ongoing topics of discussion and opinions in all communities. Priorities and standards seem to evolve and have even been a bit controversial, having occasionally stirred up protests and sit-ins. At the junior high and high school level, controversies involving hair and clothing seem to have been, historically, some of the more common catalysts for disagreement.

Back in November of 1956, a *Sentinel* headline read "City School Officials Give 'Hitch to Students' Pants." The lead sentence to that story said, "Fairmont junior high boys seeking that long, lean, sloppy look in blue jeans got their pants pulled up by school officials." This style of attire, according to the article, was said to be the mark of "young hoodlums" in schools of some of the larger cities and was consequently outlawed by Fairmont schools. The concern was that some of the boys were reportedly sitting on their belt loops. One young man at one point apparently looked down to see his belt around his ankles! School officials quickly acknowledged that was entirely too low. The Fairmont junior high principal at that time, Gerald Barger, was quoted as saying, "I understand the so-called juvenile 'hoods' wear their trousers that way in large cities." He went on to say, "It's kind of a badge, I'm told. But it's one badge that won't be allowed in the school here."

The school previously had a long-time ban on girls' slacks or slack-type clothing, including Bermuda shorts. However, this was the first instance regarding what was considered offensive clothing worn by boys. The story said, "Up to now, a low belt meant a broken-down, middle-aged or elderly man using the belt to hold up a stomach that would look better inside a girdle." It would seem that the preceding rather colorful and uncomplimentary description might be viewed as offensive as well.

Although this phenomenon was also reported in some other schools throughout the state, it was primarily a junior high concern locally as only two incidents were reported at the high school. Apparently, the school's ability to quickly crack down on this loosely supported issue nipped it in the bud before it reached new lows.

Moving ahead to the 1970s, the hippie era, Fairmont High School experienced a sit-in protest regarding haircut policies for student athletes. The headline in the April 22, 1972, edition of the *Sentinel* read, "Meeting set to pursue issues raised at sit-in."

The senior high students staged a sit-in on a Friday morning in the gym. Included were 203 of the school's 712 students. That garnered the attention of the superintendent, high school principal, and athletic director, all of whom were present in an attempt to develop a plan to resolve the issue. The superintendent, L.H. Baumann, suggested that the students choose a representative group to meet with the district officials to discuss the matter further in order to come up with something that would represent the town and the school in an appropriate manner. That suggestion, and others, was rejected by the students. Some student comments included, "I'm not going to go out for sports if I have to get my hair cut," "We need guidelines, but not in terms of hair," "Just about all the students have long hair. If athletes have shorter hair, do they really represent the school?" Consequently, the sit-in continued and was not yet resolved by 10:45 a.m. of that day.

The following Monday, seven students and four school administrators met for two-and-a-half hours in an attempt to resolve their differences and establish a time for a public meeting. It was finally agreed that the students would form a committee to meet with school officials in setting a future meeting time and format.

Seventeen days later, on May 9, a public meeting consisting of approximately 200 attendees made up of students, school administration, and the public, was held to discuss the "hairy" topic, with students barely outnumbering the public in attendance. There was considerable give and take between all sides, including a letter signed by 100 townspeople in support of the school administration's stance; however, based on that article, no definitive resolution was reached. Consequently, whether or not hair today would be gone tomorrow was not officially resolved; nevertheless, Baumann concluded that opinions expressed would be taken into consideration for the following school year.

Although some may have bristled as to the discussion regarding individual coiffures, apparently, the "mane" concern pertaining to this "shaggy" conflict remained unresolved. Perhaps it would have been helpful to seek the insights of the follicly challenged as well in order to gain their perspective and shed more light on the issue.

What was important to those living in one era may not be nearly as significant at another time. Nevertheless, society evolves, and standards from one period in history may not necessarily be applicable to another.

Homecoming

Homecoming week and all its associated activities are an important part of the lives of high school students. There are many activities including pep fests, a homecoming parade, the crowning of a king and queen, and of course, the big football game on Friday night. It's interesting to look back a few years and see what homecoming was like in the past and how it has evolved.

In reviewing the Fairmont High School *Echo* newspapers from the past, Red and White Day in 1954 was held on October 1. It featured a parade, the homecoming game against New Ulm at 8 p.m., and a sock hop after the game. The Cardinal's record as of that date was one and one, a win against Estherville and a loss to Worthington. Admission to the dance was thirty-five cents for couples and twenty cents for singles.

At that time, the annual Snake Dance was held on Thursday and was led by the senior band. The human snake zigzagged down Third Street, through the business section, and down First Street to the fairgrounds, at that time located at the current site of Five Lakes Centre. Students held a pep fest with "flames licking at the dummy," the dummy apparently representing the opposing team. After that, students scattered to garages to put the final touches on their floats. Floats were entered by grades eight through twelve with prizes ranging from $5 for first place, $3 for second place, and $2 for third place. Half-time of the football game was scheduled to feature a unique quiz show with contestants from the Senior Band and the Cardinal Band. KSUM commentator Ev Ohrt was slated to emcee the program. Janice Meyer was crowned the 1954 Homecoming Queen out of a total of ten candidates, all senior girls.

How did things change a decade later, in 1964? Again in reviewing the *Echo*, Red and White Day in 1964 was held on October 2. Jeanne Grathwohl was crowned

Homecoming Queen and her two attendants were Betty Hamre and Marsha Ellenbecker. The coronation took place at 3 p.m. on Thursday. At 7:15 p.m., a pep fest was held followed by two FHS singing groups and a skit by the Dramatics Club taken from "The Three Billy Goats Gruff." The four best floats would be awarded prizes of $10, $7, $5, and $3.

The Homecoming Game featured the Cardinals with a one and two record facing the unbeaten Hutchinson Tigers, the only team to beat the Cardinals during the previous season. To quote a phrase from the 1964 *Echo*, "Homecoming havoc is an annual thing at FHS. The whole school has been afire this hot week. Who missed the sleep or studies? (Especially when the whole week will end tonight when our team touches off a victory.)" The halls of the high school were covered with slogans, designs, and displays, however, there was no mention of a Snake Dance or bonfire.

The Homecoming Dance featured music by the Del Rays and admission was fifty cents for couples and thirty-five cents for singles. Again, inflation was at work from 1954 to 1964 regarding both the float prizes and admission to the dance.

In 1974, according to the *Echo*, the festivities began on Tuesday of Homecoming Week when the Red and White Day queen candidates gave their skits in the auditorium. The election of the Homecoming Queen was held on Wednesday, the Red and White Day parade was on Thursday at 7 p.m., and the queen was crowned at 8:15 p.m. in the auditorium with the 1973 queen, Doreen Olson, presenting the crown to the new queen, Pam Hanson.

The 1974 Homecoming Game featured the two and two Waseca Bluejays facing the three and one Fairmont Cardinals. Coach Tom Mahoney, commenting on the Cardinal's first overtime loss in their history the previous week against the New Ulm Eagles, said, "Both teams played well on defense all through the game...However, our offense couldn't generate enough to score. And if you can't score, you can't win."

The Red and White Day dance would signal the conclusion of the homecoming festivities and featured a band from the Twin Cities, Rue Light. The dance was held from 9:30 p.m. to 1:00 a.m. with the cost being $4 per couple and $2.25 for singles. Once again, there was no mention of a Snake Dance or a dummy being burned at the stake as was the case in 1954.

Homecoming Week, as well as most aspects of our society, has certainly evolved. However, in many ways it has also stayed the same.

Natural Disasters and Diseases

Blizzards in Martin County

Deadly blizzards and snowstorms have played a dramatic, and sometimes tragic, role in the lives of Martin County residents while also creating some interesting memories.

Following is an account of some of these memorable blizzards and how they affected residents of the county.

In the latter 1800s, singing schools were quite popular social events, and people would travel long distances to attend them. On February 14, 1866, a singing school was being held at Silver Lake. A storm came up during that evening, and it became very cold. Two families of young people in attendance started for home that evening. They had an ox team and sleigh filled with blankets and hay, and they left with their backs to the storm, thinking they would get home safely.

However, the team of oxen eventually left the road and began wandering aimlessly. The boys in the group would take turns leaving the sleigh and scouting around to try to find the road or a house until the sleigh became stuck in a snowdrift. One of the boys stayed outside the sleigh trying to hear or see something while trying to keep himself warm by lying between the oxen. The storm eventually became so severe that they couldn't see anything, and they didn't dare leave the sleigh.

It was two nights and one day before the storm subsided. Finally, the next morning, one of the families' dogs came to them, and the boys in the group found their way home. However, the three boys lost hands and feet from the freezing cold, the oxen were frozen to death and, tragically, the three girls were also frozen to death sitting in the sleigh. Ironically, the sleigh was within 50 yards of a farmhouse.

Just seven years later, "the worst blizzard" hit the county. The morning of January 7, 1873, started out as a very warm day for that time of the year. The two feet of snow on the ground was rapidly melting. People were out working and away from home visiting neighboring towns, many without their overcoats due to the warm conditions.

At about 2 p.m., however, a rumbling sound like distant thunder was heard coming from the northwest until it became a white mass a hundred feet high racing across the prairie at a terrific speed. Those unfortunate individuals who were out on the prairie found themselves facing an avalanche of whirling, blinding snow coupled with an intensely cold wind. Hundreds of people and livestock across the Minnesota prairies were frozen to death by the sudden storm. Although Martin County was a sparsely populated region at the time, there were several deaths there and many others were seriously frostbitten. In closing, the article in the *Fairmont Daily Sentinel*, written in January 1903, stated confidently, "There will probably never be such a storm again in our beautiful well-settled state, and all should sincerely thank God that the possibility of such a calamity is forever passed." That was perhaps wishful thinking.

Another interesting story, probably taking place in the early 1900s, tells of a Martin County schoolteacher walking twelve miles from Welcome to Ormsby to open school in a blizzard. Hulda Hausfeld had spent the weekend with her parents in Welcome when the blizzard hit the area. School children in District 126, Ormsby, thought they were going to get several days of vacation. However, Miss Hausfeld apparently felt school should be in session.

She drove two miles in her car before becoming stuck in the snow. From there, she walked the twelve miles in the blizzard in little more than three hours to ring the school bell on time Monday morning. Miss Hausfeld was a graduate of Fairmont High School Normal Training Department. They must have already used up all their snow days!

The Armistice Day storm of 1940 was another entirely unexpected blizzard. The fall of 1940 was pleasant and mild. The war in Europe was in the headlines, the Minnesota Gophers football team was ranked number one in the nation, and winter seemed to be far from the minds of most everyone. However, that serene and tranquil autumn would soon make an abrupt transformation. One of the deadliest blizzards to ever hit the Midwest struck without warning, leaving death and devastation in its wake while carving a 1,000-mile wide path through the mid-section of the country.

By 3 a.m. on Monday, November 11, the temperature dropped, snow began falling and gale force winds began blowing.

By 9 a.m., the streets of downtown Fairmont were impassable, travel was treacherous at best due to the poor visibility and snow drifts, and outside communication had all but been cut off. Display windows were blown out of the J.C. Penney building and Braun's. Bob Wallace's fifty-foot sign was blown down and landed on a car. Al Menke's Orchestra van was stranded three miles west of Sherburn.

Especially vulnerable were the many unprepared duck hunters who found themselves in a life and death struggle for survival. The storm took its toll, killing 49 in Minnesota and 150 nationwide.

All means of communication and transportation were halted, and the city would eventually spend $500 per day in snow removal. Truman wound up with a snowdrift on highway 15 south of town that measured 300 feet long and twelve feet high. Estimated losses in the county included 9,400 turkeys valued at $18,000, 236 cattle valued at $13,960, 209 sheep valued at $1,672, 200 chickens valued at $100, one horse, and thousands of pheasants.

The November 12, 1940, edition of the *Fairmont Daily Sentinel's* headline read "Blizzard Leaves Death, Loss in Wake." It further stated "Old timers of 1960 will talk about it, measure events by it, as do those of yesterday recall the great storm of October 1880." Of course, we're well beyond 1960, and many today will likely measure snow events as compared to the historic 1975 "Storm of The Century." However, due to the sudden and unexpected onset of the Armistice Day storm, coupled with the lack of preparedness on the part of the public, the 1940 storm was extremely perilous in Martin County and throughout the Midwest.

Here's That 12-Foot Truman Drift

This is a part of the 300-foot long, 12-foot deep drift that held up traffic 1½ miles south of Truman on State Highway No. 15. The drift was opened at 8 a. m. today. Atop Mister Guckeen's car is Uno Nelson, Sentinel advertising man, who got up there to see what he could see. "Just more snow is all," was his laconic reply. He must have been impressed, as he usually doesn't waste that many words in telling things. The one word "snow" ordinarily suffices.

A Truman snowdrift from the unexpected Armistice Day 1940 blizzard

An example of this involved County Treasurer Pete Cory who had gone duck hunting with some friends near Hand's Park. He and his friends ended up spending from 8:30 a.m. until 2:30 p.m. in their car while keeping the motor running in order to keep warm. Due to the intensity of the storm, they had no idea they were a mere fifty yards from a farmhouse. Nevertheless, they felt they were lucky to have the protection of the automobile and to be alive.

Another account concerned an emergency medical situation in Truman in which Doctor E.A. Thayer, who happened to be in Fairmont at the time, left Fairmont for Truman by car. He was forced to abandon his vehicle for a horse in Northrop, and he finally abandoned the horse when he encountered a snow drift measuring ten feet deep and forty feet in length. However, he successfully made his way to Truman on foot in order treat a lady who had broken her arm.

There were also a number of unusual, if not somewhat humorous, accounts regarding the storm that were reported. One involved an incident concerning a hat on top of a snow drift at the intersection of North North Avenue and Blue Earth Avenue. Apparently, no one was concerned enough to stop to determine whether or not there was, in fact, anyone under the hat.

Another rather amusing story was told of twin daughters, referred to in the article as L'il Fatso and Peewee, who were without milk and consequently proceeded to wail without stopping during the storm, thereby causing a great deal of anguish to their parents. Their tantrum continued until their father "mushed" to the Nelson Ice Cream Company for a gallon of milk. It was said that "the way they tore into it would have been a sight for the dairy industry."

The storm also resulted in some interesting and rather peculiar clothing being worn. Included was headgear made up of gunny sacks and white sheets with holes cut in them for eyes. It was said that the white sheets resembled "Kluxers" in full regalia, an apparent reminder of the Klan presence in Martin County in earlier years.

Yet another bizarre request came to the *Sentinel* office from three men who had battled the storm for five hours to get from Blue Earth to Fairmont. After they had found a room in a local hotel, they called the *Sentinel* to see if anyone could supply them with a pint of whiskey in order to help them "warm up" a bit. Their request was unsuccessful.

More recently, I'm sure many of you recall the 1975 Storm of the Century. The storm started with a steady snowfall on Friday morning and visibility became near zero by late Friday night and early Saturday. Then the temperatures began a steady descent and the winds began to blow. By Monday, all area schools were closed and only main traffic roads were gradually beginning to open. After that January storm, the *Sentinel* reported that the Martin County area averaged a foot of snow and winds of 50, 60 and perhaps 90 mph.

The extraordinary Martin County snow storms or 1873, 1880, the Armistice Day storm of 1940, the "Storm of The Century" in 1975, and the "Halloween" storm of 1991 account for some of the most memorable and recorded snow events in Martin County's history. Nevertheless, Martin County residents are accustomed to winter storms, and they know that it's not a matter of "if," but rather "when" the next one will strike.

Some statistics of the Armistice Day blizzard are from http://minnesota.publicradio.org/display/web/200011/10_steilm_blizzard-m/. Sources for this story include Jan Dickinson's compiled newspaper articles Martin County History, A-Ca; Martin County History *by Taylor Publishing, 1988, page 125; and the February 13, 1957,* Sentinel *story "3 Girls Frozen to Death in East Chain."*

The Invasion of the Rocky Mountain Locusts

Although it's difficult to determine what might have been the greatest disaster in Martin County's history, the grasshopper infestation of the 1870s and the effect it had on crops and gardens of that time is certainly one to consider.

In early June 1873, it was reported that Rocky Mountain locusts, or grasshoppers, were working their way toward Minnesota from the Dakotas and destroying everything. Although people in this area at that time paid little credence to the threat, the insects reached Jackson County June 8. If the wind was favorable, they could make ten miles in one day.

Ten days later, they arrived in Martin County like a snowstorm until the ground was nearly covered. They took a special liking to the English Colony's beans, and it was said that within twenty-four hours, there wasn't a beanstalk left standing. Some farmers of that time grew tobacco, which was also a favorite of the grasshoppers. The grasshoppers were content to eat the tobacco and then sit on the fences while squirting tobacco juice on the ground. In addition, the grasshoppers ate off the leaves of the cornstalks and other grains. It was estimated that one-quarter to one-half of the grain crop was salvaged; however, the gardens were a total loss.

Many thought the grasshoppers would not survive the harsh winter. However, the following April, they began to hatch. In June, there were two days of heavy rain. It was predicted that this would finish the grasshoppers. But when the storm subsided, they were out in force and ready for business. By the end of June, they had cleaned out many fields of grain, including beans, corn, and even potatoes.

Many settlers of that time began to lose faith in the future of the country and left. Finally, in the spring of 1877, Governor Pillsbury set April 27, 1877, as a day of fasting and prayer for deliverance from the pests. People gathered in their respective places of worship and joined in prayer.

In the early summer of that year, when the grasshoppers had developed to the point where they could fly, they all at once rose up to the sky and left the area. Sailors on the Great Lakes and Atlantic Ocean were said to have found insects floating on the water. They had left this area without depositing any eggs, and thus ended the grasshopper years.

Sources for this story include Martin County History *by Taylor Publishing.*

Disastrous Fires

Our area has experienced nature's wrath over the years in the form of tornadoes, blizzards, droughts, hail, and flooding rain. Arguably, none have been as locally destructive and devastating as fires, of which the city of Fairmont has experienced its share throughout the course of its history.

New Year's Eve of 1914 proved to include much more than just fireworks in downtown Fairmont.

At about 3 a.m. on that cold December day, some young men returning from a dance in Granada noticed a fire in a building known as the Syndicate Block. At that time, people living in the overhead rooms had been awakened by smoke, and an alarm was subsequently turned in at 3:40 a.m.

By the time the fire department arrived on the scene, the fire was raging. To further complicate the matter, nearby fire hydrants weren't working properly.

The Syndicate Block was home to a meat market, two drug stores, a department store, a jewelry store and two doctor's offices. The building itself was owned by Dr. Johnson and Ward and Company.

It had been built in 1892 by J.W. Daniels and G.T. Houseman and was in the center of the west side of the 100 block of what is now Downtown Plaza. It was considered prime property by business owners of that time and was called "the handsome and substantial new brick business block" in the September 16, 1892, edition of the *Martin County Sentinel*.

The fire scene was very cold with the temperature hovering near zero. Spectators on the scene were noticeably suffering from the frigid conditions, and the firemen were covered with ice from head to foot.

At first, the fire seemed limited to the Barto Drug Store; however, it soon became apparent the losses would not be contained to that location. Frequent loud bangs were heard as a result of containers of drugs and chemicals catching fire and exploding, as well as the detonation of fireworks from Bomboy's Department Store, which added a somewhat unusual dimension to the atmosphere surrounding the fire.

The most effective means of controlling the fire appeared to be from the roofs of several neighboring buildings in which streams of water were used to control the flames. However, the efforts were to no avail, according to newspaper accounts of that time, as the Syndicate Block was eventually reduced to debris and ashes.

When all was said and done, thirteen businesses were destroyed, and the total loss was estimated to be $80,000, and only half was said to be covered by insurance.

The story in the January 1, 1915, edition of the *Martin County Sentinel* called it the worst fire in the history of the city.

Some recalled the prediction by a fortune-teller at the Haynic Theater (now known as the Fairmont Opera House) several months earlier that a disastrous fire would strike on North Avenue within the year. It would seem that this would have undoubtedly created an eerie uneasiness at that fire scene as the events began to unfold during that very last day of 1914.

Fire Chief Serle missed the first big fire during his service to the department as he was visiting his daughter in Ceylon. However, the *Martin County Sentinel* stated that, "The boys handled the situation well despite the absence of the *old man*."

Several nearby businesses removed their belongings for safe keeping until the situation was safe enough for them to return, and a number of chickens in crates, some suffocated and some still alive, were carried out of the meat market.

The fire continued to smolder for several more days. There was no immediate answer as to how the fire started.

A fire in July of 1949, discovered at 1:15 a.m. on a Sunday, caused damage estimated at $100,000 to Wallace's Department Store and Koenig's Ben Franklin Store. The fire was said to have been caused by an automatic electric steam iron left on in one of the stores. Firemen battled this blaze for over seven hours with an estimated 500 onlookers, some dressed only in pajamas or bathrobes. Smoke and water damage was the primary cause of losses in this fire.

In November of 1952, a fire destroyed the Park Motor Company on Blue Earth Avenue. Extensive damage was also caused to other nearby businesses, including the Style Distributing Warehouse, Thorpe Wallpaper and Paint, and Olson's Standard Service Station. Firemen battled the blaze in near-freezing temperatures for over eight hours. The fire was believed to have been the result of defective wiring in a wrecked car that had been towed into the garage earlier that day. Losses were estimated to be in excess of $200,000.

In December of 1963, fire destroyed Harold's Shoe Store on North North Avenue and ten other shops and offices located on the first and second floors of that building. According to a *Sentinel* article from December 24, 1963, the fire was reported to the police officer on duty by a teenager. Firefighters contended with ice-glazed streets and an estimated 1,000 onlookers from the Christmas shopping crowd that had been downtown prior to the fire.

Another memorable fire took place in December of 1966 involving the Stokely–Van-Camp's Plant No. 1 warehouse and canning department. The fire alarm was sounded at 2:45 p.m. on the ten-degree December day. The fire was discovered by two teenagers from Minneapolis visiting relatives in Fairmont who lived near the plant. In fighting this fire, the fire department even broke out its 1923 American La France fire truck, now located in the Pioneer Museum.

It was finally brought under control by 7 p.m. The fire, of undetermined origin as of the date of that article, resulted in the loss of work for over 100 employees.

In January of 1969, a fire described at that time as "one of the most disastrous fires in Fairmont's history" destroyed Nu-Tech, Inc., an electronics factory located at 1205 North Dewey Street. Early estimates pinned losses at $150,000 to $500,000. That same year, fire destroyed the Fairmont Junior High School.

Interlaken Ballroom, fondly remembered by many Martin County residents, succumbed to fire in April of 1972. The fire, apparently started by an electrical short in a neon light, destroyed the famed ballroom in less than an hour. The exact loss was estimated to be $100,000. The owner of the structure stated at that time that it was only partially insured. Nevertheless, this loss was perhaps far more significant to many in terms of memories and nostalgia. A number of well known musicians, including the nationally known Lawrence Welk and Duke Ellington bands, played at Interlaken Ballroom to throngs of young people over the course of its illustrious existence.

Another major fire took place that year in June which ravaged a popular downtown Fairmont landmark. The fire started mysteriously about 3 p.m. on a Sunday afternoon in the Sweet Shop Restaurant, virtually ending the memorable existence of this popular eatery. Other businesses sustaining damage included the Lake Theater, Roger's Jewelry, Ben Franklin Variety Store, and Mahowald's Hardware. Sweet Shop owner Michael Boosalis estimated his losses to be about $140,000.

These were but a few of the local disasters caused by fire over the years. Fires seem to strike quickly and unexpectedly and frequently during the most inopportune weather conditions.

For many local citizens, the losses include many intangibles, such as memories and experiences that can be neither insured nor replaced. However, perhaps most notable and assuring in all of these accounts dating back to 1914 is the unconditional willingness of local people to provide assistance to those in need in the wake of those untimely and unfortunate circumstances.

Sources for this story include "A History of Martin County Fire Departments" at MCHS, and the December 18, 1974, and September 5, 1975, editions of the Sentinel; *Jan Dickinson's compiled newspaper articles 1900-1999 and Martin County School binders at the Pioneer Museum.*

The 1918 Flu Pandemic and Martin County

Not too long ago, we were inundated by the media with information about the H1N1 Flu, also referred to, perhaps inappropriately, as the Swine Flu, and the potential of another pandemic similar to the deadly flu pandemic of 1918 which was known as the Spanish Flu. The pandemic of 1918-1919, a deadly killer of people in the twenty-to-forty age group, came in three waves. The first wave occurred when mild cases of influenza erupted in the late spring and summer of 1918. The second wave involved a severe outbreak of influenza in the fall of 1918, and the final wave took place in the spring of 1919. This pandemic left fifty million dead across the world.[1]

SCHOOLS CLOSED FOR FORTNIGHT; 4 TEACHERS ILL

This November 3, 1918, headline shows that the flu pandemic was news for weeks

In Minnesota, the Paulson family of Wells was one of the first to be sickened by the outbreak. Three of the Paulson children were in the military fighting the Great War. On September 14, they received word that one son in the military had caught pneumonia. Within three days, they were notified of his death. Shortly thereafter, another brother and a sister in the Paulson family succumbed to the flu.

By the end of September, a large number of army recruits being temporarily housed at the University of Minnesota became ill. Less than a week after influenza was first reported, Minneapolis had more than 1,000 cases. On October 10, all public meetings were banned, and by the next day, all schools, churches, theaters, dance halls and billiard parlors were closed. By the time the pandemic ended in Minnesota in 1920, 75,000 people had been sickened and 12,000 were dead.[2]

The 1918 pandemic also left its insidious mark on Martin County. The October 4, 1918, edition of the *Fairmont Sentinel*, reported that "Welcome has 70 Influenza Cases Says Physician." The article went on to state, "Spanish Influenza has broken out in Welcome, Fox Lake and Sherburn, according to Dr. W.G. Strobel who said today that there were seventy cases in and around Welcome, four in Sherburn, several in Fox Lake and others in neighboring territory." The article further stated that Fairmont physicians reported a number of cases of the usual "fall grip" but no influenza so far. However, things quickly deteriorated.

Three days later, the *Fairmont Sentinel* headline reported "Influenza Kills Two at Welcome; Mrs. Strobel Dead." This article read that the flu was rapidly spreading and that the wife of Welcome's Dr. Strobel had died from the flu, in addition to others. The situation had become so serious in Welcome that the Adjutant General had sent six medical corps men of the Fifth Minnesota Infantry. They ordered 500 gauze masks for use in Welcome, "which appears to be thoroughly impregnated with germs," according to Major Dahl of the Fifth Minnesota Infantry.

Locally, the pandemic seemed to be getting worse by the day. The October 8 *Fairmont Sentinel* headline read "Influenza Spreads Rapidly Here; 40 Cases in Fairmont." The article went on to say that Dr. Hunt and his son were treating cases in Blue Earth, Granada, and surrounding towns as well as Fairmont. Fairmont schools, churches, Sunday schools, and theaters were closed. Hay and Nicholas stated that the Strand Theater would be voluntarily closed as they did not want to be responsible for possibly spreading the disease. They also canceled a production scheduled for the Haynic.

As the fall of 1918 progressed, the following was reported in the *Fairmont Sentinel:*

- October 9, 1918: Six New Cases of Influenza Here; Huntley Hard Hit. Consolidated school closed, teachers ill and one near death, Dr. Strobel better.
- October 10, 1918: Third Death in Village of Welcome Reported, Others in Serious Condition, Few New Cases in County and Worst May Be Over.
- October 11, 1918: Truman Soldier Dies of Influenza Few Weeks After Entering Service of Our Country.
- October 12, 1918: Closing of Schools Extended One Week; Fred Johnson Dead. (Johnson was the well known and respected manager of Rippe Elevator in Welcome.)
- October 14, 1918: Influenza Takes Two More Lives; 5 Ill in 1 Home.
- October 15, 1918: Fraser Township Boy a Victim Of Influenza Plague
- October 29, 1918: Ruth Rademacher Former Fairmont Girl Is Summoned, Influenza Claims Young Woman Well Known and Esteemed in This City.
- November 2, 1918: Harry Wishnick Dies; Is Second Influenza Victim.
- November 3, 1918: Schools Closed For Fortnight; 4 Teachers Ill
- November 5, 1918: Fairmont Girl Dies in Montana–Influenza and Pneumonia Fatal to Teacher
- November 23, 1918: Health Officer Says Influenza Now Seems Over

As can be readily observed, the 1918 Spanish Flu Pandemic took a severe toll on Martin County residents, lingering beyond the fall of 1918. There were few who weren't touched by sickness or death.

However, in contrast to the many somber accounts reported on this topic, there were also some humorous findings intermingled with this rather grim subject. One involved spitting on sidewalks in Rapid City, South Dakota. This article stated that "Yesterday the Home Guards patrolling the streets were kept busy enforcing the city ordinances prohibiting spitting on sidewalks. J. Mulcaby was hauled into Judge Nystrom's court charged with flagrant violation of the anti-spitting ordinance. He entered a plea of not guilty."[3] Another article of interest quotes a doctor from Des Moines stating that he had a serum that cures flu and pneumonia. Finally, there was a report that hogs were catching pneumonia around Mason City. Despite the bad news about the flu pandemic of 1918, some of the stories that appeared to be incidentally related to that flu outbreak might seem somewhat fascinating and humorous today.

The 1918 Influenza Pandemic infected twenty-eight percent of all Americans and killed 675,000 people, ten times as many Americans as died in World War 1.[4] Influenza is obviously an illness to be respected and treated appropriately.

Sources for this story include numerous Fairmont Daily Sentinel *stories from October 1 through November 23, 1918, in addition to faribaultcountyregister.com/page/content.detail/id/522658/Historic-pandemic-hits-the-county.html?nav=5002 and*

[1]*https://www.cdc.gov/flu/pandemic-resources/basics/past-pandemics.html*

[2]*http://www.pandemicflu.gov/generel/greatpandemic2.html#minnesota*

[3]*http://1918.pandemicflu.gov/pics/newspapers/Arrested_for_Spitting.gif*

[4]*http://virus.stanford.edu/usa/*

1936—A Year of Weather Extremes in Martin County

Weather: everybody talks about it, weather forecasters try to predict it, but no one can really do anything about it.

The winter of 1936 saw record-breaking sub-zero temperatures combined with massive amounts of snow. This created what was referred to at that time as snow blockades. There were thirty-six consecutive days of below-zero temperatures in January through February. These were accompanied by what was called five of the worst snow blockades since the advent of the automobile and the improved highway systems. Snowfall for that winter up to March 1 totaled four feet and ten inches. This was in sharp contrast to the open winter of 1934 when dust storms swept through the plains states.

The first snow blockade took place in mid-January. Temperatures dropped to twenty-two below zero, closing schools. The cold snap was broken on February 2 when seven inches of snow fell; however, heavy winds following that halted rail and highway traffic.

During the month of February, the high winds created snowdrifts and, coupled with frigid temperatures, isolated many farms and even entire communities. Mail was delivered by dog team in Triumph; there were serious shortages of coal, fuel oil, and grocery items. Coal was limited to one-half ton per customer in Fairmont as temperatures dipped to twenty-three degrees below zero and was accompanied by stiff winds. From January 18 to February 22, the temperature failed to reach zero, ranging from minus two to minus twenty-six.

The spring of 1936 heralded a much different kind of weather phenomena for Martin County, and it resulted in some serious damage.

In the late afternoon of Thursday, April 30, 1936, windy and dusty conditions gradually became ominous as menacing dark clouds began to appear in the sky. Soon, a part of Martin County would be ravaged by a devastating tornado, one that never left the ground from its point of origin near Sheldon, Iowa, until it finally blew itself out near Preston in Fillmore County. It traveled over 100 miles, and cut a wide, twenty-mile swath of Martin County that included Tenhassen, Silver Lake, East Chain, and Pleasant Prairie Townships.

HERE'S PROOF!

The following official figures on the history-making cold spell of 36 days below zero in January and February, 1936, are from Weatherman James Lamperd, Fairmont, Minn. It was the longest arctic wave in the weather station's history.

Jan. 18	-12
Jan. 19	-18
Jan. 20	-22
Jan. 21	-11
Jan. 22	-30
Jan. 23	-27
Jan. 24	-17
Jan. 25	-20
Jan. 26	-21
Jan. 27	-16
Jan. 28	-14
Jan. 29	-18
Jan. 30	- 9
Jan. 31	-21
Feb. 1	-16
Feb. 2	-14
Feb. 3	- 2
Feb. 4	-20
Feb. 5	-26
Feb. 6	-18
Feb. 7	-26
Feb. 8	-14
Feb. 9	-18
Feb. 10	-17
Feb. 11	-18
Feb. 12	-15
Feb. 13	- 6
Feb. 14	-23
Feb. 15	-21
Feb. 16	-29
Feb. 17	-14
Feb. 18	-19
Feb. 19	-20
Feb. 20	- 4
Feb. 21	-20
Feb. 22	- 5

The *Fairmont Daily Sentinel* editions of May 1 through May 7 carried numerous accounts of property damage, injury, and other strange events that seem to only happen as a result of tornadoes. Reports stated that 200 farms in the four townships were hit, with 100 farms having extensive damage, and 300 farm buildings wrecked. Three persons died as a result of the tornado.

The storm tore through Hand's Park, completely demolishing the pavilion and hardwood dance floor, and scattering nearly 3,000 chickens from the Hand's Park farm over the highway and farmyard. In addition, the debris from the Gay Paree nightclub blocked the county road running from Highway 15 east to Ceylon. Also, the smell of beer, resulting from the destruction of the bar and tap, persisted in the vicinity of the Gay Paree for some time. According to the May 2 edition of the *Sentinel*, Ernest Hand, owner of the amusement park, planned to rebuild as soon as insurance adjustments were made and debris cleared away.

The city of Fairmont reported minimal damage with flooded basements. The Augusta Hotel reported nine inches of water in the basement and several windows blown out. However, one radio report falsely stated that Fairmont had been wiped out, an account called "irresponsible" in the May 2 *Sentinel.* This in turn led to many telegrams to local residents from concerned relatives and friends.

Some of the "storm stories" that came out of the event were:

- A farmer, his wife, and their seven children seemed to be right in the middle of the storm near Silver Lake. The storm moved the house about twenty feet off its foundation to which the farmer commented to his wife, "It sure rides easy."
- A horse was seen grazing in a pasture in Pleasant Prairie with its halter rope dragging a piece of the manger to which it was tied when the barn blew away. In another location, three horses were still tied to stalls, but the barn was gone.
- As one family took refuge in their basement, a horse was blown into the basement and landed on the farmer's wife and their small baby. The wife sustained minor injuries, the baby was unharmed, but the horse sustained two broken legs in the fall and had to be shot.
- One farmer watched his home and outbuildings being destroyed as he hung unharmed from a tree.
- A barn was spotted in East Chain Lake.
- One of five lonely billy goats at a Silver Lake ranch was spotted in the basement of a house gnawing on debris.
- In School District 15, Tenhassen, the school house was unscathed, although there were windrows of tree trunks and other rubbish piled up against it.
- A well-known professional man from a nearby Iowa town was seen prowling around the Gay Paree ruins. When asked what he was doing, he replied, "Just trying to find the quarter slot machine I sunk all my dough in the other night."
- Three young men from Elmore were heading east on Highway 16 in a gravel truck when the storm struck. They ended up in a farmer's yard but were unable to tell how they got there. Their truck was demolished.

It was reported that people living in the western part of the county didn't know of the storm until they "rubbered" on the telephone, hearing others talk about it the following morning. The storm prompted "old timers" to recall the "cyclone of 1892."

It was estimated that 15,000 cars and 60,000 sightseers came to the area to see the ruins. The crowd was said to be the second biggest crowd of outside visitors to Martin County, surpassed only by the 1934 National Corn Husking Contest crowd. Another report was that cars were lined up from the Hand's Park corner on Highway 15 nearly to Fairmont and moving at a snail's pace. State highway patrolmen and national guardsmen were called upon to help direct traffic and keep order in the area. Local citizens, the Red Cross, and others responded quickly and unselfishly to help their storm-ravaged neighbors.

Perhaps those memorable weather events from the past have been somewhat embellished over time; however, there is no question that the diversity of seasons in Martin County provides a distinct array of interesting weather-related experiences. It's been said that if you don't like the weather today, wait until tomorrow. The seasonal changes experienced in this part of the country seem to provide something for everyone.

Additional sources for this story included the "Snow Blockades, Winter 1936" booklet by Fairmont Printing Company in MCHS History File 15.

Going, Going, Gone?

The subject of water, specifically Fairmont's water, seems to have been a hot topic throughout the town's history. A *Sentinel* article from April 23, 1946, stated that "Fairmont lakes, Martin County's lakes, all the lakes in this region are disappearing. It is a question of just a few years and they will be gone." The focus of this 1946 article certainly posed a perplexing public concern.

Lake Sisseton

What seemed to cause those ominous predictions more than seven decades ago? It wasn't a result of drainage, evaporation, where to obtain the water, or lack of precipitation. Rather, it was the concern that the lakes were simply filling up with soil from cultivated fields that would wash down natural and artificial drains, pour into the lakes, and, consequently, settle to the bottom. Some went so far as to predict that Fairmont's lakes would be nonexistent in twenty years, or by 1966.

In order to corroborate these concerns, a survey of Budd Lake was commissioned. Budd Lake furnished all of Fairmont's water at that time as well. To objectively conduct this study, the Water and Light Commission arranged to obtain data during the winter of 1946 when the lake was frozen over. In doing so, lines were drawn on the ice from the filtration plant at 1022 Albion Avenue across the lake east and west to E.L Ballou's residence which, according to the 1946 Fairmont telephone directory, was located at 321 Budd Lake Drive. Along these lines, soundings were taken at regular intervals. These soundings disclosed the present bottom, as well as the bottom as it originally existed.

According to the 1946 study, "the startling discovery was made that the lake is practically two-thirds filled." The study further revealed that the maximum depth, before mud was encountered, was 14.5 feet, therefore, twenty-seven feet of the water's depth had already been wiped out.

The article concluded that "this certain ultimate elimination of the lakes (unless offset by continuous and expensive dredging) causes many concerns, chief of which to the people of Fairmont is the water supply in the city mains. Where will it come from in, say, 1966? That's the million dollar question with which our forward looking Water and Light Commission has commenced to wrestle."

Obviously, the prospect of the lake water being replaced by mud prompted some dire predictions back in 1946. Perhaps the most ominous was that there might eventually be, instead of the five lakes as we know them today, some kind of muddy creek or river cutting through what was predicted to eventually become the lake bottoms of Amber, Hall, Budd, Sisseton, and George. This waterway would in turn connect itself to Center Creek which, as a result, would enlarge itself to a broad, shallow river.

It is also interesting to note that, in reference to the potential use of well water as an option at that time, the article said that "small consideration can be given the alternative of pumping it from wells, something that engineering thought considers impractical." Readers were directed to view the self-explanatory pictograph stating that it certainly did not present a very pretty picture.

Obviously, the bleak predictions of 1946 concerning Fairmont's lakes and water supply did not come to pass. Significant advancements and improvements have been made regarding this issue since then. Although the time has changed, someone looking back at this era seven decades from now will, hopefully, view current decisions regarding today's water issues as being effective, efficient and appropriate.

Arts and Entertainment

The Fairmont Opera House, The Haynic, and The Nicholas Theater

The Fairmont Opera House, widely considered to be one of the finest historic venues of its kind in the Midwest, has evolved over the years from being an opera house, to a movie theater, to near condemnation. It was finally resurrected to its present stately appearance, offering quality entertainment to citizens of Martin County and beyond.

The history of the Fairmont Opera House dates back to 1901 at which time a group of citizens determined the area needed an "assembly hall." A group of seventy-two individuals came together to form what was to be known as the Fairmont Opera House Association. The site at the corner of Blue Earth Avenue and North North Avenue was purchased for this purpose.

A week before the grand opening, Frank Day, *Sentinel* editor, used his newspaper to implore every businessman, professional, city and county official, teacher, and anyone owning a thousand dollars worth of real estate to purchase a ticket to the grand opening because its purpose was for the enhancement of the local area. It seems his efforts proved successful as 400 tickets at $5 per ticket were sold out in one hour!

Fairmont Opera House, circa 1928

The grand opening on February 11, 1902, featured the comic opera *The Chaperones,* perhaps considered a bit risqué for Fairmont standards and values of the time, yet was still reviewed as "a very pleasing comic opera" in the *Sentinel's* lengthy story covering the opening.

It was said that all of Fairmont was in its finest attire and the *Sentinel* critic in attendance was convinced that Fairmont would never again have "as large and as brilliant an array of artists to entertain" in this area, according to the February 14, 1902, *Sentinel.*

In the account of opening night, the Fairmont Opera House was described in great detail with emphasis on the beautifully designed walls and the brilliant and varied electric lighting, in addition to the descriptions of the rich and fashionable costumes of the ladies scattered throughout the body of the theater which in turn made a scene "never to be forgotten." The author of this article went on to say, "While the seating portion of the new play house was a scene of brilliancy and beauty, it was only a somber background to set off the wonderful stage effects, which, for sparkling beauty and splendor of scenery, are rarely eclipsed in the large cities." This was obviously a significant event within a uniquely created structure in a small Minnesota community of the early 1900s.

Although it was noted that a number of the leading members of the cast were ill and that understudies filled in for them, the reporter wrote, "The *Sentinel* critic does not feel equal to attempting a criticism of the entertainment. There is a suspicion that the fifty elegantly costumed beauties upon the stage caused every man in the audience to lose his head. The dramatic editor is only human, and a man at that. He can criticize nothing intelligently with which he is delighted, hence floats with the tide of enthusiasm for Perley (the producing manager of the company) and his bevy of beauties." He was obviously quite impressed by what he witnessed that evening it seems, especially by, as he so eloquently stated, the "bevy of beauties."

The writer went on to say that he would not attempt to give a description of the many elegant gowns worn by the ladies of Fairmont in attendance. Although he felt that he could perhaps pick out more beautiful women in the audience than on stage, which admittedly could be challenged, he concluded that "the beautiful gowns and pretty wearers on this occasion will have to be preserved only in memory." Maybe that was the easy way out for him.

Next was a rather elaborate description of the performance, a two-act play that takes place in Paris. The writer concluded that, "As a comic opera we do not see how the *Chaperon* [sic] could well be improved."

Perhaps one of the more interesting aspects of this historical account was the in-depth analysis of those in attendance. "Scattered all through the audience were well-to-do farmers of Martin County, with one or more members of their families...It shows that not only the people of Fairmont to be prosperous but the farmers as well, and that so many of them showed their loyalty to Fairmont by helping so materially to fill the new opera house at $5 a seat is very gratifying to all," it said. In addition to the support of the locals, the attendees from out-of-town communities were not only acknowledged but also mentioned in many instances by name and profession. It seemed to appear like a "Who's Who" in Martin County and the surrounding area of that time.

This account of the opening night of the Fairmont Opera House concluded with references to the firemen stationed in the Opera House, which was directed by state law at that time, and the receipts from the sale of tickets. Regarding the firemen, their stationed locations were mentioned, including the following: "Nick Hengel was monarch of all he surveyed behind the scenes with the chorus girls." Apparently, Fireman Hengel had the "choice" duty of the evening bravely protecting the chorus girls backstage from the somewhat remote possibility of fire.

Finally, the receipts for the opening night totaled $2,500. The cost of the entertainment was $1,000, which left the Opera House with a profit of $1,500 for its first performance.

In 1903, William W. Ward, later Fairmont's mayor, took over the management and control of the Opera House. The theory was that perhaps private enterprise would be more successful than committee management. However, Ward kept his lease for only about a year, and then volunteer management again took over. The building was at that time used primarily for repertory groups, local talent productions, political speeches and rallies, and high school commencement exercises.

In 1912, the board of directors accepted a proposition from Billy Hay and W.L. Nicholas to rent to them. It was renamed the Haynic Theater.

Nicholas and Hay decided to show moving pictures in the Haynic. Hay was quoted as saying that "the moving picture has come to stay." However, live shows also continued. Later that same year, a refrigerator plant for cooling the Haynic Theater was installed. It was an elaborate system of drawing fresh air into the basement piped through twelve-inch tile over ice chambers to provide cooling.

Hay and Nicholas continually stressed the comfort and cleanliness of their venue, perhaps implying to some extent that its competition was lacking in both areas. It may have had an effect as, within a short time, the other two theaters that had been operating for at least a year, the Bijou and Crystal, both closed. As an added attraction, the Haynic Orchestra, consisting of five pieces, played at all the movies that were shown every night of the week but Sunday. Shows lasted about an hour, and admission was five to ten cents.

In 1914, a competitor named Harry Gilbert built a movie theater called the Strand, later to be named the Lake Theater. Soon after the Strand opened in 1915, Gilbert sold its lease to a Mason City firm. Within a month of that transaction, the Mason City firm turned the lease over to Hay and Nicholas. Hay and Nicholas invested $5,000 in the Strand to set it up as the chief movie house in town, thereby allowing the Haynic to be used primarily for live entertainment.

In 1919, the Opera House witnessed a heated exchange between A.L. Ward, one of its largest stockholders, and members of the board of directors, especially Nicholas, charging that there was a conspiracy to prevent the sale of the property. Following

Ward's charges, Nicholas offered Ward a check for "100 cents on the dollar." Ward declined the offer, prompting hearty laughter from those present.

The interest in silent movies had caused the popularity of road shows to decline. Consequently, in 1920, Hay and Nicholas purchased the theater, showed movies on Saturday and Sunday nights and occasionally a vaudeville show or minstrel show. However, the Opera House did not thrive as the novelty of movies waned.

Then, in 1926, Hay suddenly died. Nicholas bought Hay's share in ownership from his estate and later partnered with Finkelstein and Ruben, a large theater and entertainment corporation in Minneapolis. The Haynic was then renamed the Nicholas Theater.

In 1928, Nicholas made a startling announcement that Fairmont would be the smallest city in the United States to offer "talkies." The opening of the talkies was held on July 4, 1929. The next day's *Sentinel* reported The Nicholas was continually filled with groups of 300 spectators for a grand total of 3000 during the event, some traveling from as far as 100 miles away.

From the late 1920s until 1980, the Nicholas Theater was exclusively a movie theater. The building was closed in 1980, and it appeared that its life may have come to an end. However, a group of volunteers led by Dr. Robert Arneson and his wife, Mary, spearheaded the restoration of the building. Since that time, many volunteers and donors have been able to maintain and enhance the structure, as well as its offerings, to its current state.

The information here is based upon historical documentation in the Pioneer Museum including the book ...And The Curtain Rises *by Thomas Arneson.*

The Theater Men of Fairmont

Fairmont has seen quite a number of movie theaters in its history. Those movie houses of the past included the Haynic, the Strand Theater, the Lake Theater, the Nicholas Theater, the Fair Mall Cinema, the Family Drive-In, and today we have the Five Lakes Cinema. However, the pioneers of this industry in Fairmont, namely Billy Hay and W.L. Nicholas, made their mark on Martin County in more ways than just promoting movies and their theater business.

Both Billy Hay and Willie Lincoln Nicholas were born in England, eventually becoming residents of Fairmont and Martin County. Both had an interest in the theater business, were considered honorable and well-respected citizens of this community, and were very civic-minded.

Hay came to America from England at the age of eighteen. He originally settled with other English colonists in the Rose Lake area and later moved to Fairmont.

During the forty-eight years Hay lived in Martin County, he was active in a number of endeavors. He farmed in Fairmont Township, was a bookkeeper for Ward Implement Company, was an abstractor for H.W. Sinclair Company, and was treasurer for Fairmont Railway Motors. Civically, Hay served on the Fairmont City Park Board for sixteen years, was a member of the Fairmont Heating Commission for six years, and served as secretary of the Fairmont Cemetery Association for twenty-five years. He also was in the theater business, which eventually became his life's work. It's obvious he was interested in more than his personal gain.

Theatre man Billy Hay

Nicholas was born in Bridgewater, Somersetshire, England, in 1874. Nicholas' father deeply admired Abraham Lincoln, so he named his own son Willie after Lincoln's son who died while Lincoln was in office. According to the August 8, 1947, edition of the *Sentinel,* Nicholas was admirably known as "Linc" to his many friends and acquaintances.

In 1889, his father, a cabinet maker, brought his family to America a second time, and settled near Emmetsburg, Iowa. While there, Nicholas attended school and later took a position with the American Investment Company of Emmetsburg. He worked there until 1895 when he moved to Fairmont.

Upon moving to town, he worked for the Martin County National Bank. In 1897, he was appointed as a court reporter for the Seventeenth Judicial District.

Hay and Nicholas formed a partnership in 1912 when they opened the Haynic Theater, which had previously operated as the Fairmont Opera House. In 1915, they purchased the Strand Theater and later purchased all remaining shares of the Fairmont Opera House.

Nicholas continued as court reporter until 1922 when he resigned to devote his attention to the moving picture business which he and Hay developed.

Being a civic-minded individual, as well as having an ardent interest in Fairmont's parks, Nicholas agreed to serve as chairman of the park board for several years. He was also elected alderman, and then, in 1935, mayor of Fairmont.

While serving as mayor, the city's parks remained his special interest. During his tenure, Mrs. Nicholas donated a substantial amount of land to Lincoln Park and funded a shelter house for it.

Nicholas also had a keen interest in politics. He served as chairman of the Martin County Republican Central Committee from 1933–1945. He was also past commander of The Knights of Pythias, a charter member of Kiwanis, and a member of a number of fraternal and civic organizations locally, statewide, and nationally.

Upon his death in August of 1947, the *Sentinel* wrote, "No man who has held office in the City of Fairmont contributed more generously of his time and effort toward the betterment of the city than did the deceased during his tenure of office. He was also generous in his contributions to the churches and other civic organizations." The August 8 article eulogized Nicholas saying, "Fairmont never had a better, more useful citizen."

Hay preceded Nicholas in death when he died in 1926 while shoveling snow at his home. He was sixty-six. The *Sentinel* said of him in a December 9, 1926, obituary, "Few citizens of Fairmont were as beloved and respected as Mr. Hay, whose long career here is without blemish. Truly, he was everybody's friend."

Remembering a Local Showman

In the early 1900s, theaters were not exactly as we know them to be today. In those early days, movies were somewhat rare, and theaters frequently booked road shows or stock companies for their performances. When early movies made the scene, they were generally accompanied by organ or piano music until the "talkies" became available.

Karl Lindstaedt, a vaudevillian, began his theater career in Martin County. He could truly be characterized as an original showman, a vaudeville artist, and a very successful theater manager.

He was born in 1897 and grew up in Fairmont. According to an article in the March 14, 1948, edition of the *St. Paul Pioneer Press,* he got his start in Fairmont at the age of ten peddling handbills for the Haynic. Lindstaedt gradually moved up to being an usher-janitor during his high school years and was content seeing all the shows free of charge in place of being paid for his work.

According to the May 31, 1951, edition of the *Fairmont Daily Sentinel,* in 1915, a movie entitled *The Birth of a Nation* played two performances daily in Fairmont for one week when Lindstaedt was working there. The performances, which were about the Civil War, were sold out and cost $1.50 instead of the usual fifteen cents. A thirty-five piece orchestra accompanied the film along with a sound effects crew working backstage. This brought many spectators to the theater who had never before seen a movie.

Then, in 1917, Lindstaedt ventured into vaudeville after meeting Rita Bell, a piano student, while he was studying voice at a Twin Cities music school. Bell's uncle urged them to go into vaudeville "purely as an educational and travel opportunity." They were warned that they wouldn't make a fortune. Lindstaedt confirmed this upon returning to Fairmont after thirteen months with the sum of two cents jingling in his pocket, athough he admitted that he did get an education.

Lindstaedt went to work for the Strand Theater in Fairmont after his vaudeville experiences, according to an article in the September 1, 2008, *Austin Post-Bulletin*. At the Strand, he operated the player-piano as music was used before sound films made their debut in order to enhance the drama of the movies. Then, in 1924, Lindstaedt went to Duluth to manage a remodeled theater. About Lindstaedt's departure, the *Fairmont Daily Sentinel* said, "Fairmont will regret to lose Karl. He is one of her most popular and hard working boys. He has gone as far as he can in the theatrical game here, however, his friends will welcome his advancement in a larger city." That theater eventually failed due to the closing of an iron mine.

From Duluth, he returned to Fairmont, then to Rochester to manage the Chateau Theater then to Austin to manage the Park Theater. An April 6, 1929, headline in the *The Fairmont Daily Sentinel* read "New Austin Theater Costs $150,000—Lindstaedt, Fairmont Boy, Manager." The theatre was to open in August and replace one that had been destroyed by a tornado. It was to seat 1,003 persons and was said to have Movietone and Vitaphone equipment. That theater was apparently a benchmark for its day with modern equipment of the time.

The various newspapers recounted some of the specific stories Lindstaedt told. One he shared was that of parents using the theater as a babysitter. In some instances, they would bring their children to the 1 p.m. show, leave them there with a packed lunch, and return to pick them up at 8 p.m. that evening. On one occasion, he informed parents attempting to leave their children for the day that leaving them for seven hours at a cost of thirty-six cents would get him in trouble with the babysitters union. Perhaps a bit of humor helped to make his point.

He also spoke of high school students and some of their antics. Around the time they would have their annual class play, students would sneak backstage at the theater where the plays were being held. They would arrive in the morning and hide in the loft until the evening performance. Then, during a romantic scene, they would drop confetti from the ceiling and walk across the stage wearing heavy coats and pulling a dogsled, obviously creating a scene in distinct contrast to the scheduled performance.

On another occasion, a tempermental Irish tenor who was performing at one of Lindstaedt's theaters demanded that a special onstage dressing room be built for him, including carpeting and a stagehand guard. Lindstaedt, with his friend who just happened to be the sheriff, went to the performer and "persuaded" him to back off his requests—which he quickly did.

An incident in Fairmont when *Shepherd of The Hills* was playing proved quite fascinating. The scene involved a shepherd, played by an elderly, bearded, white-haired man seated by a fireplace that depicted his cabin in the Ozarks. During the performance, a shepherd dog casually walked down the aisle of the theater looking for his master who happened to be a local farmer. The dog made his way onstage and laid down beside the actor, as if the actor was his master. The actor continued, unperturbed, as if the dog was in fact meant to be included in the scene. Although the local newspaper ran a story explaining to whom the dog belonged, most seemed to believe that this incident was actually meant to be a part of the performance.

Lindstaedt retired in 1967 after fifty years in the movie business and passed away in 1988 at the age of 90.

He was honored posthumously in August of 2008 with the unveiling of a bronze bust displayed at the Paramount Theater in Austin where he managed for forty years. A quote from his niece, Janette Horman of Minneapolis, printed in the September 4, 2008, edition of the *Austin Daily Herald*, reflects Lindstaedt's devotion to his job: "He would come home every Christmas Day and request the family have dinner at precisely 11:30 a.m. so he could get back to work (in Austin) for that evening's performance." Horman said, "For that reason, I never really knew him. He was always on the go."

Lindstaedt was obviously dedicated, well respected, and greatly admired.

I would like to acknowledge the Austin Daily Herald, *the* Austin Post–Bulletin, *the* St. Paul Pioneer Press, *the* Sentinel, *and especially Janette Horman, Karl Lindstaedt's niece, as resources for this article.*

The Voice of Martin County—KFVN Radio

"The voice of Martin County," as reported in the July 3, 1925, edition of the *Martin County Sentinel*, was Martin County's first radio station, KFVN. The radio station, called a "sending station" at that time, was established in 1924 and was located in Welcome, Minnesota. It was said to put Welcome more prominently on the map than she ever dreamed of being while at the same time making the world a smaller place.

The radio station was the dream of Carl Bagley, known then as Welcome's electrical wizard, with the help of Fairmont resident C.F. Gaarenstroom. Bagley first consulted then-attorney Gaarenstroom to join him in operating a radio station. Gaarenstroom agreed, although somewhat apprehensively, and soon the project moved forward.

Bagley built a sixty-foot wooden tower all by himself and installed the heart of the station in his own living room, which also served as both studio A and studio B. A Dunwoody Institute broadcasting set was purchased for the station at an estimated cost of $3,400. It was rated a very high-powered sending set that was said to have been heard by every state in the union. Bagley was known to play Bach and Beethoven on his piano as he didn't have any phonograph records in the early days of the station.

The dedication ceremony of KFVN included noted speakers of the time and local entertainment and music lasting for more than two hours. Some of the speakers present included former St. Paul Mayor Larry Hodson, Hennepin County Attorney Floyd B. Olson, Larry Ho of Minneapolis, attorney C.F. Gaarenstroom, and *Sentinel* Publisher Frank A. Day. It was reported that Pete Corey, the announcer, had to chase Day around the living room as he paced like a caged lion addressing his remarks to everyone and everything in the room except the microphone.

The station proved interesting in many ways. At 9 p.m., KFVN's operator would hold the single microphone outside Bagley's living room window and broadcast to listeners the screech of the village curfew. The first test program resulted in more than seventy-five telephone reports bringing words of both encouragement and criticism to the station.

HOME OF WELCOME RADIO STATION IN 1924—This is the Carl Bagley house where KFVN was born and first breathed life over the air waves back in 1924. Notches on the windowsills testify to electrical equipment once used. In the basement are other relics of one of the earliest radio stations in the country, now extinct for more than 23 years. The house is now owned and occupied by the Arnold Sandersfeld family. — Guckeen Photo Engraving.

Test programs included local speakers and musical talent from throughout the county. Criticism was solicited, as the station acknowledged, because, "a slight adjustment to the microphone or some other of the thousand and one mysterious parts around a broadcasting station may double the entertainment value of the selection given."

The goal of the station was to provide listeners with the best broadcast quality, talent, and entertainment in the county. All the artists were Martin County residents. Advertisers could buy timc for $25 and sometimes heard their product plugged all night. Prizes were awarded to the first person to call in who received the program and to those receiving the program from the longest distance away.

Callers to the station commented on the good reception. They also voiced complaints of too much talking by the announcers and not enough entertainment. During its heyday, the station once drew 1,500 people to the Fairmont armory for a hog calling contest. However, much to the dismay of the station operators, something went wrong with the wiring, and the broadcast never went out over the airwaves.

It was reported in an article paying tribute to the station in the March 5, 1952, edition of the Fairmont *Daily Sentinel* that Bagley eventually became restless and couldn't stay put. He was upset when a $27.50 tube blew out and the replacement was more than KFVN had in the treasury. Gaarenstroom concluded in the article, that "Bagley was a genius with a dream which he made come true. We never understood where the money came from, or how he lived. Now we know. He rented his own house and used the money for the station. During it all, he lived on crackers and milk."

The station eventually moved to Fairmont and became known as KFVN, The Royal Penn Station of the Southern Minnesota Oil Company. The station's goal and purpose was primarily for the improvement of the community spirit of Martin County. In 1926, Bagley and Gaarenstroom were offered $5,000 to sell the station as authorized wave lengths were in short supply at that time; however, they refused, stating that "we are going to keep our station for Martin County." Shortly thereafter, the station owners soon began to drift away, and KFVN went out of existence.

Community Treasures

Martin County is known for beautiful parks, some of which are located in Fairmont. Each park is unique in its own special way, and the summer months find them teeming with a variety of activities.

Fairmont City Band 1914

Fairmont's oldest park is Sylvania Park, located on the northeast corner of Lake Sisseton. It dates back to 1888; however, the city did not acquire the land title until 1894. Once known as The Grove, the park was initially sold or donated in a total of four parcels. The first parcel was sold by Sylvan S. and Julia M. Huntting for $1,500.

Besides its natural beauty, the park is probably best known for its legendary Singing Oak, its landmark band shell, and the many splendid performances of the city band.

The Singing Oak, tied to a Native American legend which has since been retold by Major Arthur Nelson [see page 293], stood in the northwest corner of Sylvania Park at a time when it was a wilderness area inhabited by the Sisseton Sioux.

The realization of a band shell in Sylvania Park began in 1925 when the city of Fairmont purchased the plan for $150 from George Pass and Sons of Mankato. The construction contract went to Andrew Christiansen Lumber and was constructed in 1926 at a cost of $3,135. Interestingly, the project was assisted by a number of additional people including some rather unwilling inmates from the local jail, one of whom was a woman serving a sentence for attending a flapper party.

Although construction was not fully complete, the first concert was held on June 10, 1926. Following initial construction, a number of additional improvements were completed over the years. An extended apron was added to the stage in 1951; extensive shoreline reinforcement was done in 1993 to prevent damage due to soil erosion; landscaping and reseeding was done in 1995; a new audio system was installed in 2001; new risers and wiring were completed in 2002; and, in 2003, a secure room was added for band equipment storage. The band shell has superb acoustics and an exceptionally large stage, and has served as a focal point for many local activities.

Fairmont's City Band, although having disbanded and reorganized itself on numerous occasions over the years, has been in existence since 1873. The "old band" broke up in 1945 as a result of many of its members being in the military. Then in 1951, under the leadership of the new high school band director, Dick Scherer, the band was reorganized.

It has served the public continuously since that time while maintaining an average band membership of forty to sixty musicians. Band members are not necessarily professional musicians but rather people who enjoy playing for those who enjoy listening. High school band students who have completed tenth grade and adults who have played an instrument at any time in their lives are generally welcome to become members. The annual summer concert series is sponsored by the city of Fairmont in conjunction with the Fairmont Area Schools.

Sylvania Park, the band shell, and the city band are all priceless community treasures. They serve as rich cultural resources for the citizens of Fairmont, Martin County, and other visitors.

Sources for this story include the April 15, 1995, Sentinel, *and a Fairmont City Band brochure.*

A Famous Actress and a Martin County Connection

Gail Garber was an accomplished singer, dancer, and actress born in Manhattan; however, she had a distinct connection to Martin County.

As an accomplished comedienne, she began her career in acting at the young age of three or four in the play *Lilac Time,* starring Gary Cooper. She later moved to

California and worked with "Our Gang." During her lengthy career, she teamed with Jackie Gleason, Bert Lahr, Clark Gable, Robert Young, Debbie Reynolds, Lucille Ball, Dick Van Patten, Dan Daley and many other notable entertainers of that era in show business. She also appeared on the "Ed Sullivan Show" and the "NBC Theater."

Gail Garber

Perhaps her most noteworthy accomplishment in show business was her humorous lead role in the play *Burlesque* during the 1940s. The play ran for five years, including three on Broadway. It featured Lahr, perhaps best known for his role as the cowardly lion in *The Wizard of Oz*, and was coupled with Garber's comedic role as the wife of Bozo, played by Billy Barry. In addition to being in movies and the theater, she entertained the troops during World War II.

Garber was frequently mentioned in a number of New York entertainment and gossip columns. Walter Winchell's column once told of her having a red cross on her dressing room door instead of a star. This was emblematic of her being a registered nurse as well as an actress, and she periodically worked as a nurse at Metropolitan General Hospital in New York. Another of Winchell's columns referred to Garber as a comedienne who was witty and comical, even without a script, and with a straight man being a welcome satirist. She was also mentioned in Louella Parsons' column regarding her then upcoming marriage to Lieutenant John Crawferd.

An interesting incident regarding Garber took place while she was in Boston. While attempting to sleep late in a Boston hotel one morning, she was continually annoyed by someone playing a violin in an adjoining room. She telephoned the room and asked the person who answered the phone to either "learn how to play the fiddle or throw it out." She soon heard a knock on her door and the individual responsible for playing the violin apologized profusely for disturbing her. Ironically, the "fiddle" player was none other than Jascha Heifetz, the world-renowned violinist.

Gail Garber's birth name was Jacqueline Briggs. She frequently visited her grandmother who lived in Fairmont. She was so fond of this area that she eventually chose to retire here. She passed away in 2004.

Sources for this story include the Gail Garber scrapbook of photos and newspaper clippings at MCHS.

The Big Band Era

The Big Band Era of the 1930s and 1940s, led by Duke Ellington, Tommy Dorsey, Benny Goodman, Glenn Miller, Woody Herman, and others led the country out of the grip of the Great Depression and left a permanent mark on American popular music. Not only was this true nationally, but locally as well. One of those individuals who made a significant and lasting impact on the local music scene was Lynn Kerns, a well-known and respected musician with a multitude of musical talents.

Lynn Kerns

Kerns was born in Amboy, Minnesota, in 1908. He took guitar lessons at a young age and moved to Sherburn with his family in 1922.

Kerns became interested in the printing business while in high school and, after graduating, got a job as a printer's devil, eventually becoming the night linotype operator at the *Fairmont Sentinel.* During that time, he continued pursuing his love of music and taught himself to play the banjo when he was off work. In 1928, he married Katherine Krumholz.

An opportunity arose for him to fill in for another musician with Al Menke's orchestra, a known swing band of the day. He later joined Gordon Cole and Eva Benton in starting a lounge trio that would eventually evolve into an eleven-piece orchestra in 1934 known as the Rhythm Club Swing Band. A 1937 *Fairmont Sentinel* article describes the group as "...a strictly home town organization that developed from the melting pot of lodge dance trios, 'old-time' aggregations and the like, into a popular 11-piece organization."

As they were all employed in or near Fairmont, the orchestra's cooperative agreement stated that they would not play anywhere that would jeopardize any band member's regular job. The article quoted one of the band members as saying, "We do pretty good. We don't play every night, you know, and we do a tall job of sleeping Sundays. Also, we sleep in the bus on the way home after dances. If you work in the daytime and play a program in the evening, you can sleep almost anywhere, you know. We usually get to bed by 2 or 3 o'clock and snatch five or six hours, even after playing."

"You see, we have a business of our own, and it's a serious business with us, not just an idle hobby. Yes, we have tolerant wives and girl friends."

The band at that time in the late 1930s played Thursdays, Fridays, and Saturdays, and, in the summers, they also played Sundays. They used a thirteen-passenger bus previously used by Al Menke's orchestra with Frank Van Draska serving as the driver. In 1937, the group included Vern Nolte, Gordon Cole, Lawrence Nelson, Ed Vollrath, Merle Malherek, Serle Zalesky, Kerns, Jack Furtney, Robert Wickstrom, Bill Schliecker, Fritz Williams, and Van Draska. Some of the employers of the band members included the McCarthy Grain Commission Company, the Ford Garage in Truman, and Peerless Cleaners. An itemized earnings statement for 1936 showed that their gross earnings from playing at 160 dances was $6,140.03, with the highest paid member of the group grossing $433.60 for the year.

In addition to Lynn Kerns and the Rhythm Club Swing Band, other local groups included the Al Menke Band, Amby Meyer and his Orchestra, and Fred Kielblock of Freddie Frederic and his Orchestra. These bands played at Interlaken Ballroom, Fox Lake, Storm Lake, Spirit Lake, and many other locations within about a 200-mile radius.

Besides the popular and talented local groups, nationally known groups also performed in this area. According to a November 15, 1991, *Sentinel* article, "Interlaken Park hosted Lawrence Welk, Count Basie, Glenn Miller, and even the patron saint of swing himself, Duke Ellington." Also of interest is the fact that Dick Dale, of Lawrence Welk fame, got his start playing tenor sax with the Rhythm Club just after graduating from Algona High School in Iowa at the age of sixteen. He also played for a short time with the Six Fat Dutchmen in New Ulm before going with the Lawrence Welk Orchestra for thirty-two years. Dale passed away in 2014. He was posthumously inducted into the Iowa Rock 'n Roll Music Association Hall of Fame in 2015.

By 1940, as the band became ever more popular, Kerns was faced with a decision. As written in the February 16, 1960, edition of the *Fairmont Daily Sentinel*, the managing editor of the *Sentinel* at that time gave him an ultimatum of sorts. "Either you fiddle or set type. You can't do both." This was not a reflection on his performance at the newspaper, as he was doing an excellent job; however, the managing editor felt Kerns was overworked doing both jobs.

Kerns decided, after being reassured that he could return to the *Sentinel*, that he would go full-time into the dance band business. According to this article, Kerns became the part-owner, leader, soloist, and emcee of the Rhythm Club Orchestra. In addition, he was the father of Betty, Marcia and Barbara who became the Kerns Sisters, the featured singing trio with the band.

Eventually, after twenty-seven years, Kerns hung up his baton in 1960. He continued working at the *Sentinel* until 1963 when he and several colleagues formed the Fairmont *Photo Press*.

He passed away in 1996 at the age of 87.

The era in which Kerns was a well-known, respected, and talented musician is certainly nostalgically recalled by many yet living in Martin County. The music, the dance halls, the entertainers, the bands, and that era have long since passed. However, there are likely many vivid and fond memories of those times that linger on in the hearts and minds of those lucky enough to have experienced those days gone by.

Sources for this story include MCHS History File 1011.

Corn Husking Contest Brings National Spotlight to Fairmont

On November 8, 1934, the National Corn Husking Contest drew between 50,000 to 100,000 people to Martin County, the largest turnout for that event ever up to that date. The event even brought out national print and television media.

The contest was held where the airport is presently located in Fairmont. The Associated Press estimated that there were 50,000 people in attendance while the Minnesota Highway Patrol estimated 100,000. So the *Fairmont Daily Sentinel* news department decided to split the difference and make the headline read 75,000 for its vivid account of the contest. The state patrol also estimated there were 20,000 cars and trucks parked in the field near the event.

Ted Balko, the corn-husking victor in 1934

The crowd was said to be almost "beyond description" as not even the most enthusiastic supporter expected the kind of response witnessed by residents of Martin County for this. There were an estimated 800 policemen, 250 guardsmen, 20 traffic policemen, and 400 legionnaires and others directing traffic. The traffic from 9 a.m. to noon was so heavy that highway patrolmen were forced to send it toward the contest in a double line.

Returning from the event was next to impossible. Numerous bent fenders and bumpers were reported in traffic jams due to sudden stops and some motorists trying to pull in and out of traffic lanes. Due to the many cars coming from the west, reportedly approaching three abreast, Highway 16 was made a one-way by patrolmen on the scene. Four airplanes also hovered over the area, eventually landing near the contest.

People began converging on Fairmont, referred to as the "contest city," at 4 a.m., and by 8 a.m., there were several thousand cars in and near the grounds, most belonging to officials and others who were involved in some way with the event. Stands selling hamburgers and coffee were doing "land office business" and had to make frequent trips into town to replenish supplies.

The national corn husking entrants were officially welcomed at a banquet served at the American Legion hall the night before. It was presided over by Judge J.E. Haycraft with other dignitaries in attendance. Champions of nine states were recognized by publishers of farm newspapers which sponsored contests. The following day, there was a parade that included eleven National Guard companies from neighboring towns and the American Legion Drum and Bugle corps from Mankato.

The contest was sponsored by the *Wallace Farmer* and was designed to show the athletic skills of young farmers. It was broadcast by NBC. The managing editor of the *Farmer* and *Farm, Stock and Home* gave a history of previous contests and described the upcoming contest. He also explained the work involved in putting on the biggest event of its kind ever held in Minnesota to date. The winner of the contest was Ted Balko of Redwood County, four-time Minnesota champion. His net was 25.78 bushels.

Sources for this story include the November 24, 1934, The Farmer. *Quotes are from the November 8, 1934,* Sentinel.

King Korn Days

Community celebrations of various kinds are held throughout Minnesota. One local event, known as King Korn Days, was at one time a major festival in Fairmont and Martin County. It flourished during the 1950s and 1960s and was briefly resurrected in the 1980s.

Included in the festivities were parades with floats and bands, various forms of entertainment, singers, dancers, instrumentalists, magicians, novelty acts, notable celebrities, and banquets. In addition, there were King Korn queen candidates from throughout Martin County.

A *Sentinel* article in 1952 regaling the celebration's events reported that "Fairmont is wearing its gay festival clothes today, with queens, parades, kings and corn on its mind as the gigantic 1952 annual King Korn Days festival begins to unfold in all its golden, harvest splendor." The story goes on to state that "everything is in place—bunting, corn exhibits, gifts for the public, eat stands, a carnival, reservations for notables, even purple robes for the Queen and Korn King. Corn—no matter which way you spell it—will be everywhere Friday and Saturday. Eleven thousand ears of corn will be served to the public Saturday." Included in the advance festivities were a "bevy" of five clowns selling balloons to advertise the event. That pretty well sets the stage for what was undeniably at one time one of the largest and best attended festivals in the local area.

In that same edition of the *Sentinel*, another article read "Somewhere in Fairmont is a young lovely Miss who tonight will be named 1953 King Korn queen to represent the community throughout the state…Three professional 'queen selectors' will know by early tonight but they won't disclose their choice until a special public radio broadcast later in the evening from Interlaken ballroom." Wow, professional queen selectors! One might wonder how they got that job. Actually these judges, or queen selectors, were Aquatennial Queen Betty Barnhart, Frank Matson of St. Paulites, Inc., and Miss City Club Jeri Demick. They were apparently well-qualified for the task at hand.

King Korn Days 1967

There were twenty-five King Korn queen candidates that year, each sponsored by a local business. Newspaper accounts included pictures and detailed personal information involving height, weight, hobbies, home addresses, and future plans, some of which might seem incredibly inappropriate in today's world.

The queen selection was to be made during the queen's dinner at which time two princesses and one queen would be chosen. At that point, the judges would "wrinkle their brows some more at the queens" as they struggled to make their final decisions. After the dinner, the queen candidates were to be escorted to their homes to change into formals for the Queen's Ball.

The grand finale, the crowning ceremonies, would begin at 10:30 p.m. in order to allow enough time for the fans watching the Fairmont–New Ulm football game to attend. The Chamber of Commerce planned to present the candidate selected as queen $100 to purchase a new wardrobe to be worn in celebrations she would attend in the next year. Each princess would also receive $10. In addition, the Korn Queen and all queen candidates would ride in what was described as the "mammoth" 1952 King Korn parade on Saturday. The winning candidate for the 1953 King Korn Queen was Betty

Harris, daughter of Mr. and Mrs. John Harris. Coincidentally, the coronation took place on her father's birthday, and her parents' wedding anniversary, which were all on the same day.

Moving ahead to 1967, King Korn Days of that year featured a number of activities and events. The Fairmont Chamber planned to serve 10,000 free hot dogs, the corn show was to be held in the youth center, the King Korn races were scheduled for Saturday, and the King Korn parade route would wind through town.

A near record, 462 entries, for the corn show was displayed in the Fairmont Youth Center, suggesting that a big fall harvest was in store. The overall grand champion of the Fairmont King Korn Days three-foot-tall corn show trophy was Walter Reinke of Truman. He won the trophy in 1966 and was champion of the professional class in 1965.

Vic Dicks of Jackson defended his King Korn car racing title, winning a hotly contested race at the Fairmont Speedway. Trophies were presented by Kathy Kay Kittleson, Miss Fairmont of 1968.

Newspaper articles indicated that Fairmont's 1967 King Korn festival may have set a record with the 10,000 hot dogs being devoured by 1 p.m. and an estimated crowd of more than 10,000 people watching the parade. Closing events included 415 youth attending the teen dance at the youth center and a standing-room-only crowd at the adult dance at the Legion Hall. In addition, the carnival was also well-attended as a result of advance ticket sales giving ten rides for a dollar.

During the 1985 King Korn Days festival, there was a parade, Enduro car races, a chicken and sweet corn feed, and perhaps most significant was the Minnesota State 1985 Corn Husking Contest. The contest was slated to begin at 9 a.m. on a twenty-five acre site across from the Martin County Fairgrounds. It included six classifications based upon age. Men's and women's categories were also included. Although not expecting anything near the 75,000 to 80,000 spectators the 1934 event attracted, the chamber predicted 5,000 to 6,000 would attend.

The contest fielded sixty contestants ranging in age from seven to ninety-four. However, the rainy and cold weather conditions apparently affected the turnout as only 1,500 to 2,000 spectators watched, considerably less than originally anticipated.

Although King Korn Days provided an important and fun-filled function for the county during its life span, as is frequently the case with community festivals, it gradually evolved and was replaced by something else. However, those that remember King Korn Days will most likely consider it to have been one of the premier festivals held by any county in the state of Minnesota.

Sources for this story include the September 21, 22, 23, and 25, 1967, editions of the Sentinel.

The Voice of Fairmont

Annabel Webb, recognized by her friendly voice as well as her flamboyant attire, was well-known for her KSUM radio show, "A Date with A. Webb," which she did for more than thirty years. Her family was directly involved with her work as her morning show was broadcast live from the kitchen in her home at 705 Albion Avenue on weekdays until she retired in 1980.

Annabel Webb

Webb was born and raised in Faribault, Minnesota. She attended and graduated from Carleton College and became a teacher. She taught in Ellendale, Minnesota, then came to Fairmont as an English and Latin teacher, and later taught in Granada. Fairmont is where she met and married Dr. Howard Webb, a local dentist. As her family grew, she eventually left teaching and soon became active in the community. In the years that followed, she proved to be instrumental in making a lasting and positive influence on Fairmont and Martin County in many ways, perhaps most notably through her radio program.

Webb, known as the "Queen of Segue" because of the ease with which she went from interview to commercials, interviewed a wide variety of personalities from high profile movie stars to regular, everyday citizens. Some of her more prominent interviews included actress Joan Crawford, actors Gig Young and Bob Newhart, pianist Liberace, and Minnesota Senator Hubert H. Humphrey. It was well known that regardless of whom she interviewed, they were all treated with the utmost of kindness and respect.

Perhaps one of her most interesting and unforgettable broadcasts originated in her bathtub. She had decided to do a program on bathtubs after seeing a book about the history of bathtubs that had sparked her interest. Annabel thought it would be fun to put one of her children in the tub to splash around while pretending she hadn't gotten up in time for the show and was just getting ready to broadcast her program. Frank Endersbe, KSUM station manager at that time, heard the splashing on his car radio and promptly sent a telegram telling Annabel to get out of the tub before she electrocuted herself.

Similar stunts, which were actually not the least bit uncommon for her, once involved a broadcast from an airplane where she stated, "So far, nothing has come up but conversation," in reference to her queasy stomach, as quoted in a *Sentinel* article from February 16, 1980. Another time, while broadcasting from her home, the family dog was having puppies, and her children announced each new arrival on the air. In addition, her Christmas morning broadcast became a local holiday tradition and also involved her family. It included her three children reading from the Bible and the family singing Christmas carols.

She had what might be considered somewhat eccentric traits as well. In addition to never learning to drive a car, she was recognized for her many hats and later for adding exotic sunglasses to her repertoire. It was said that she would first buy a hat and then find suitable attire to match it.

Webb felt that the secret to her success was attributable to her listening to people and being well aware of the fact that everyone has a story to tell. She felt that to be successful, it was important to think about the person being interviewed, not yourself or your next question.

Webb's activities were not limited to radio. She was a talented singer and actress. She was part of the original group that started the Civic Summer Theater and performed in a number of its productions as well. In addition, she was elected Community Queen in a Jaycee-sponsored event in 1940.

Upon her retirement in 1980, the *Sentinel* quoted Elizabeth Woodward who said, "There's no one that can replace Annabel. She's really been a very unique, unusual individual who is game for anything, a great personality and a warm person. It's kind of a tough thing for all of us."

Webb was unmistakably unique in the somewhat unconventional delivery of her entertaining interviews to the listeners in Martin County and beyond over the course of her thirty years in radio. It is very evident that she had the character and creativity to develop her program in a distinctive manner which obviously created a great deal of interest in her many listeners over the years. She was undeniably one-of-a-kind, a distinctive and gifted individual whose legacy will long be remembered. Martin County can be proud to share her legacy.

Sources for this story include the Sentinel Hometown Legends *2007 magazine.*

Remembering Fairmont's Youth Center

When we adults think back to our youth, what did we do to occupy our free time before the advent of soccer fields, aquatic and skateboard parks, video games, computers, cell phones, texting, community ed programs, camps for aspiring athletes, and the myriad of other activities available in today's world? Maybe, if we go back far enough, some may recall Fairmont's Youth Center.

Back in 1961, well before the whole host of activities available today, the city of Fairmont created a youth center aimed at providing area teens a fun place to congregate with their friends. The establishment of the youth center was a result of a $48,000 bequest from Harold Ward Pfiffner to the city of Fairmont for that purpose. It was named after his mother, May Ward Pfiffner.

Its location at 124 East First Street, the corner east of the Fairmont Photo Press, had been the site of the American Legion Hall. The Legion had previously rented the hall from the city for many years.

Mayor John P. Brandenhoff described the youth center as the "best equipped and most beautifully decorated center reserved exclusively for young people that could be found anywhere in the Midwest," according to the September 15, 1961, *Sentinel.* He went on to state that the center had everything up to and including an intercom system which would permit communication throughout the building, even extending to the restrooms.

Youth Center Fairmont

The center consisted of a main auditorium for dancing with built-in benches along the walls for spectators. Remodeling made the stage larger, and new, improved lighting was installed. The stairs leading up to the game room were enlarged and handrails were added. Some of the game room activities included pool tables, ping pong, and pinball games. The size of the restrooms was increased with the girls' restroom described as having a battery of mirrors, even including a full-length mirror. The kitchen was equipped with all modern equipment, stairways were covered with slip resistant material, and the color scheme was lavender, grey, light green and pale blue.

The youth center, of course, had its rules of conduct conspicuously posted for all to see. Those posted "Rules of Conduct" seem to exemplify the era from which they evolved.

In reflecting on that time, today's society might consider the venue and its rules more than a bit antiquated. Although change and perceived progress is inevitable, the youth center of that period of time in our local history undoubtedly served its purpose in providing many young people a place to call their own while bringing back fond memories for many who experienced it firsthand.

Sources for this story include Jan Dickinson's compiled research of newspaper articles.

Live Entertainment Hits Martin County

Throughout history, including local history, there are people, groups, and events that seem to shape the memories and time in which they were prevalent. The Mozart Marching Society might fit that category quite well. It was a very popular performing group from about 1965 to 1975. The founder and director of the group was Mrs. Betty Nelson Kurtz, the daughter of the late Einer Nelson, well-known Fairmont entrepreneur and former mayor.

The Mozart Marching Society, directed by Betty Kurtz

Kurtz was musically inclined from the age of five when she began playing the piano. She played the pipe organ by age twelve and, by high school graduation in 1939, had participated in virtually every extra-curricular activity available to students at that time. She was the first Fairmont majorette to be allowed to wear a skirt instead of slacks and, in addition, she was a member of the drum section of the high school concert band. After graduating from high school, she attended Stevens College in Columbia, Missouri, where she majored in drama.

In 1943, she joined the Marines and served as a flight and radio navigation instructor at Santa Barbara, California. Two of her pupils became quite well known and famous, fighter pilots Joe Foss and John Glenn.

Her marriage to Jerry Kurtz took her to Detroit where she was director of a singing group similar to the Mozarts. Then, in 1966, she and her husband returned to Fairmont as Jerry purchased Lasker Men's Clothing store. Very soon after her return, she began to organize the Mozart Marching Society, much to the pleasure of Martin County citizens.

The Mozart Marching Society began as a women's chorus that initially included only four singers. It grew fairly rapidly and, in 1969, became a mixed chorus, adding male tenors and basses including a percussionist, Dick Scherer, well-known FHS band instructor. The group averaged forty performers and included a total of 123 singers and instrumentalists involved with the productions over the years.

While traveling to a performance, it was said that Betty would "plant" herself in the center aisle of the bus and direct. When returning from a performance, they would often stop for a sandwich and coffee. The entourage of thirty-five ladies in blue dresses with sequins and large rhinestone earrings coupled with twelve men in white jackets invading a restaurant would serve as quite a surprise to the diners. However, they would soon be more than delighted as the group would often break into song.

In 1971, the Mozart Marching Society was featured for an evening of entertainment at The Sweet Shop Restaurant. It was advertised as an "Uptown Evening . . . Downtown" in combining an evening of wine and lobster tail with fine live entertainment.

The event was hailed as the birth of live entertainment with liquor-by-the-ounce as The Sweet Shop's liquor license was only the second issued in Fairmont after 104 years of being a "dry" town. The performances included servings of Mike Boosalis' lobster tail, prime rib, and Cornish hen. Incidentally, there were no complaints about the cost of $12.50 per couple.

The Mozart Marching Society performed throughout dozens of towns in both Minnesota and Iowa. The performers especially enjoyed their Christmas presentations and even collaborated on a production with the Summer Civic Theater in 1973. Although the group was made up primarily of amateur musicians, they were truly professional in their performances. They created an atmosphere of appreciation; they were energetic, skilled, and provided the area with entertainment the public sought after, enjoyed, and applauded during that era.

I would like to acknowledge and thank Norma Jean Berg for providing the Pioneer Museum with a wonderful scrapbook that details the illustrious history of this marvelous group and its many fabulous performances. The information and pictures in her scrapbook provided the content for this article.

The Family Cue

A Family Cue ad as it appeared in the Sentinel

Recreation is a somewhat nebulous term, depending upon one's definition. However, it would probably be safe to assume that it is something everyone longs for in one form or another. Various forms of recreation seem to come and go. The Family Cue Recreation Center, most often referred to as the Family Cue, was at one time the setting for several forms of recreation located in downtown Fairmont.

Little information on the business is available. The archives of the Pioneer Museum have provided several newspaper accounts dating back to the 1965–1966 time period. According to that information, the Family Cue was located at 116 South North Avenue, adjacent to the *Sentinel* newspaper office.

An article from the December 2, 1965, Fairmont *Sentinel* announced that the Family Cue, which had been opened only six months prior by Eldon Brockman, had been sold and was to become a hobby shop while retaining some of its billiards and pool facilities. The new owner was Bill Druck, Jr., from Lewisville, Minnesota, who had previously operated an auto agency and service station.

A new innovation provided by Druck included a track for slot racing model electric cars, operated by remote control, which had a raceway of eight eighty-foot lanes that replaced two snooker tables and three regular pool tables. Druck stated he would also have model cars for sale and for rent.

It appears that this business venture was short-lived as well. A May 16, 1966, business headline announced "Family Cue Reopening Set Friday." Now referred to as the Family Track and Cue, it would be reopening under the ownership of Welcome-native Bill Klusendorf, a former Fairmont police officer and Martin County deputy sheriff who had previously operated a night club in Peoria, Illinois.

Klusendorf said he planned to cater to adults and families. Apparently Klusendorf's approach would be very similar to that of the previous owner, however, he said, "It will not be a loitering place...I plan to ask the cooperation of young people in keeping this a respectable, well-ordered business, and I am sure they will." Did that statement imply there were problems or concerns with those frequenting the establishment? Did the fact that there were pool tables and snooker tables imply something other than simply recreation, perhaps a less than wholesome environment? It's of course impossible to make that determination, but the existence of the race track and Klusendorf's comment seem to indicate underlying concerns. If that were the case, all of the owners were obviously making every effort to provide an environment conducive to the best interests of their customers that likely included many young people.

Recreational opportunities have expanded and evolved significantly from the era of the 1960s. That might make one wonder whether or not an establishment similar to the Family Cue would survive in today's recreational environment.

Sources for this story include Jan Dickinson's compiled research of newspaper articles.

Warren Nelson and The Tenth Story Window

The year was 1968, a time of social turbulence and change; the Vietnam war was unpopular, campus unrest was in the news. This was an era which many of us now approaching Medicare and Social Security lived through and entered adulthood. We can probably conjure up many memories from that time as a result of some of the top movies of 1968, like *The Graduate* and *Guess Who's Coming to Dinner.* Other memories may surface through the music of 1968. Some of the popular songs were "Judy in Disguise" by John Fred and His Playboy Band, "Green Tambourine" by the Lemon Pipers, "The Dock of the Bay" by Otis Redding, and "Mrs. Robinson" by Simon and Garfunkel, among others.

O.J. Simpson won the Heisman Trophy in college football, the Green Bay Packers beat the Oakland Raiders in Super Bowl II, the Detroit Tigers beat the St. Louis Cardinals in the World Series, Rowan and Martin's *Laugh-In* was the top-rated TV program, the USS *Pueblo* was captured by the North Koreans, Robert Kennedy and Dr. Martin Luther King, Jr., were assassinated, and Richard Nixon was elected president of the United States.

But what happened locally in 1968? What do we recall that entertained us in Fairmont, Martin County, and southern Minnesota?

A local group from that era, The Tenth Story Window, was gaining popularity throughout southern Minnesota and beyond. The group, formerly known as Nellie's Folk, "Nellie" being a nickname for Warren Nelson in elementary school, was headed up by Nelson and included at one time or another Tom Messerli, Petra Marquardt, Greg See, Dennis Murphy, Dave Nordby, Sharla Nelson, Sandra Sorenson, Richard Orem, Valerie Engkjer, Rex Loker, John Larsen, and brothers Bob and Ron Lundquist. Many of the group's members were local; however, the Lundquists were from St. Paul, and Loker was from Wisconsin.

The group had its start in Nelson's home. They played locally at weekly band concerts, the Exchange Club, and Interlaken Golf Club. They also played at the GOP nominating convention in Minneapolis which was televised by KROC–TV in Rochester.

Can you spot "10th Story Window" up in lights?

Originating in 1966, the group evolved from Nellie's Folk to The Tenth Story Window while gaining popularity and eventually gained a contract to play at the Depot House in Rochester. A *Sentinel* article from July 16, 1968, entitled "10th Story Window wins pact" quoted Nelson saying it was "the biggest break we've had." The Depot House supper club was at that time considered to be one of the best, if not the best, night club in Rochester. The group presented three forty-five-minute shows in the lounge of the club, which was a renovated train depot. The audience response to the group was terrific as diners watched, clapped and tapped their fingers in tune.

In the coming years, their popularity exploded. They were booked in college concert halls, night clubs, hotels, and festivals throughout the Midwest. Soon they were appearing in Las Vegas, California, Arizona, Texas, Ohio, and beyond. John Larsen served as road manager while keeping the books in order and the hectic travel schedule running smoothly and efficiently.

The group created many fond memories for local residents and well beyond Martin County, including the International Hotel in Las Vegas. Who would have ever thought that a local group would perform in the same venue that Elvis, Petula Clark, Burt Bacharach, and others of that caliber had?

Almost Famous

Throughout the course of Martin County's history, there have been many individuals who have made significant accomplishments in a variety of fields and professions. There are, however, very likely many more who have been productive members of society but who may not have reached the pinnacle of their respective professions, and therefore have lived without the fanfare and recognition that the most gifted in their fields and professions might receive.

One person who might fit that characterization is Martin County native Paul Willson, a comic actor and improv artist. Born on Christmas Day 1945 in Fairmont, he is the son of Doris and Lee Willson. His father worked a variety of jobs that included real estate, magazine advertising, and public relations which eventually led his family to the San Francisco Bay area in 1952.

According to an article from the *San Francisco Chronicle*, Willson said of himself, "I was shy as a boy; I was afraid to say anything that might be wrong." He apparently never thought as a youth that he would become an entertainer. However, he had an ongoing love for comedy and performers such as Steve Allen and Ernie Kovaks. As a result, he eventually became involved with an improv workshop which appeared to have been a turning point in his life. Improv, or improvisational theatre, is spontaneous and unscripted acting that sometimes incorporates audience suggestions into the performance.

It is very possible you have seen Willson on either television or the big screen. He is likely most well-known as the guest character Paul on the television show *Cheers,* which he also reprised in the *Cheers'* spin-off *Frasier.* He was also Garry Shandling's neighbor Leonard Smith on *It's Garry Shandling's Show* from 1986–1990.

In addition, he has numerous film credits, including being one of "The Bobs" in the 1999 movie *Office Space* with Jennifer Aniston, the man in the ticket line in *The Sting,* Grimsdyke in *My Best Friend Is a Vampire*, and a coal executive in *Straight Jacket.* Television appearances include Bill in *Empire*, Dennis Taylor in *Fast Times (at Ridgemont High)*, Deputy Zajac on *George and Leo*, and *Malcolm in the Middle.*

So, would this Fairmont native be considered "famous?" Willson has a lengthy resume of work in the entertainment industry. Although perhaps not as readily recognizable as many of the more "famous" actors, he has certainly appeared in numerous supporting roles with many of those noteworthy Hollywood personalities. Without the inclusion of his skills, they too would probably not have been nearly as successful, as well known, or as "famous."

For fun, you can check out more information on Willson's acting credits at www.imdb.com and www.filmreference.com/film/51/Paul-Willson.html.

Law and Order

Law and Order in Martin County

The history of sheriffs in Martin County dates back to 1857.

There were ten sheriffs in Martin County from 1857–1877; however, there is not a great wealth of information about these early sheriffs. Isaac A. Lewis was Martin County's first sheriff and served from December of 1857 to July of 1858. He became sheriff when Minnesota Governor Samuel Medary appointed commissioners to establish both Martin County and a county seat. B.F. Lilly served as sheriff from 1858 to 1859.

Willard Harrison served as sheriff from 1860–1863. During his tenure, jurors were selected for criminal action against an individual for burning another resident's cow barn, and $200 was appropriated for the first Martin County courthouse. At that time, Martin County had a total of eight farms and a population of 151.

Hosea A. True served as sheriff from 1864–1865, during the time Native American uprisings were reported in the area. He was originally from New Hampshire, and he had also worked across the county on a government survey crew.

Richard James served from 1865–1866. He was sheriff when the body of Charles White was found. White, of Yankton, South Dakota, owned a store and transportation business. Trappers found White's body near Twin Lake with a bullet hole in his head. It was the first reported murder in Martin County. [See story on page 41.]

E.D. Walker, Amasa Bowen, David Bates, and Oren Prentice served during the years 1866–1868.

Charles H. Bullard served four terms as sheriff from 1869–1876. He also served as justice of the peace for four years. He was been born in Massachusetts in 1833 and came to Minnesota in 1866. Before serving as sheriff, Bullard served as a second lieutenant in the National Guard in Fairmont.

When Bullard was sheriff, three men from Faribault County stole a yoke of oxen near East Chain. Upon being captured in Iowa, they were returned to Fairmont.

However, Fairmont did not have a jail, and since keeping them in Mankato seemed too expensive, it was decided that they would be held in Fairmont and watched by a deputy at all times. One day, when the sheriff was out of town, the three tried to escape. However, before they could get away, they were confronted by the sheriff's wife who was holding a revolver. She held them at bay until the sheriff returned.

In 1874, he and Frank Day started the *Martin County Sentinel.* He also served as postmaster for one term until being removed by a Democratic president. He was later appointed by President Harrison as collector of customs for the state of Alaska, and later returned to Fairmont in 1894 to begin construction of the Bullard Hotel.

William Bird, Jr., who moved here from New York, served as sheriff of Martin County from 1876–1884. It was during this time that Fairmont had its first recorded suicide when a man poisoned himself in 1879.

Also during his watch, a body was discovered near the home of A.M. Welcome. Officials were unable to determine the cause of death, the identity, or where the man came from.

Another incident involved a man being arrested on a criminal warrant sworn out by his wife for slander as he said she was a woman of "easy virtue." Additionally, a warrant was issued for an individual keeping a house of "ill fame," and $300 was stolen from the Occidental Hotel in Fairmont.

Sheriff Sommerville Hill

Two brothers, Sommerville and Washington P. Hill, also served Martin County as sheriff. They were the sons of James Hill who had come to Martin County in 1866. Sommerville, also Fairmont's first chief of police, served as sheriff from 1885–1892. Washington served after him for five years. Some notable incidents at that time included a man from Jackson falling 150 feet to his death from a balloon and the Sherburn bank robbery of 1896 in which two men, an employee and a customer, were killed. [See the Sherburn bank robbery on page 248 for more details.]

E.E. Ward, who had been deputy sheriff under Washington, served as sheriff from 1899–1912. During his term, the skeletal remains of a man and a canine were discovered during the construction of the new Martin County Courthouse in 1906. Also, the Peoples State Bank of Monterey was robbed of $1,485. And, in front of Wallace's Clothing Store, Sheriff Ward shot and killed a man attempting to escape after being charged with sexual assault.

From 1913–1926, William S. Carver served as sheriff. He was the son of Sam Carver, well known for the famed Carver–Tuttle fight near Ceylon in 1862. During his service as sheriff, John Monk of Welcome was made a motorcycle patrolman by Minnesota Governor Burnquist in 1917. The National Bank of Truman was robbed when seven men captured the Truman Village marshal and locked him in the village jail.

The criminals tried to blow the safe at the bank and eventually escaped with $300 as well as an undetermined amount from safe deposit boxes. It is also of interest to note that Sheriff Carver was at one time a high ranking member of the Ku Klux Klan. He lost his bid for reelection in 1926 because of his association with the Klan, even though he publicly stated his Klan involvement was a mistake and he had a high rate of conviction for bootleggers.

Sheriff Gus Jorgenson

Gus H. Jorgenson, who served as sheriff from 1927–1931, was the first Martin County law enforcement officer killed in the line of duty. On September 8, 1931, Jorgenson was called to a farm in Nashville Township where the farmer and his wife stated they had been threatened by a beet worker.

When Jorgenson arrived, he was directed to the "shack" where the beet worker was. The beet worker, Nicholas Rodriquez, greeted Jorgenson at the door, then shot him and pushed him out the door.

Jorgenson staggered to the farmer's house, collapsed, and died on the steps leading to the farmhouse. A posse of local law enforcement and National Guardsmen was formed. Tear gas was used to get Rodriguez out of the shack. He came out shooting with two weapons and was consequently shot and killed by the posse.

William L. Roehler was the Martin County sheriff from 1931–1946. During his term, the 1936 Hand's Park tornado took place, three Welcome businesses burned, and a plane crashed in Monterey, killing one person. Roehler also was involved with the capture of two men who had escaped from a Nebraska prison.

From 1947–1950, A.R. Batterman served as sheriff. William Musegades was appointed deputy sheriff in 1947, and in 1948, the State Bank of Ceylon was held up by two men who made off with $5,000.

Musegades served as sheriff from 1951–1971. When elected, he couldn't immediately take office because he was on active duty in the military, and William Klusendorf acted as sheriff until he returned in August of 1951. Musegades' wife, Velma, cooked for the prisoners and was also deputized. She later served on the Governor's Crime Commission.

During his service as sheriff, a grand jury was called for a triple murder, and one of his deputies, Lester Uhrhammer, was killed in the line of duty. One September evening in 1955, Deputy Uhrhammer and a friend were on their way to a dance at Interlaken when they noted an individual driving erratically. Uhrhammer recognized the individual and noted that his license had been previously revoked.

They followed the vehicle and made a stop four miles north of Sherburn. While Uhrhammer was searching the vehicle, his gun discharged, hitting him in the hand

and face and killing him. The grand jury voted 17 to 6 to return a "No Bill" verdict, meaning charges would not be brought against the driver of the vehicle.

From 1971–1978 Richard H. Evanson served as sheriff. The yet unsolved murder of JoAnn Bontjes took place in 1975.

The other sheriffs to serve Martin County include Larry Willard from 1979–1982; Gerald Nutt from 1983–1994; Robert Meschke from 1995–2002; Brad Gerhardt from 2003–2010; and Jeff Markquart, elected in 2010.

I would like to acknowledge and thank Martin County Deputy Sheriff Jean Vath for her help in providing historical information and research for this article.

The Good Ol' Days?

Tragedies in the news make us think, "What is this world coming to?" and we long for the good old days. Life moved at a slower pace, people were more respectful, violent crime didn't happen around here. Or did it?

It was January 1895. The place was Rolling Green Township, Minnesota. This was the date of perhaps one of the most vicious crimes to ever occur in Martin County. The headline in the January 25, 1895, edition of the *Martin County Sentinel* read: "Bloody Tragedy!" "Three People Atrociously Assassinated in their Own House." The newspaper account of this event covered four full columns and read like a detective novel.

MRS. S. J. HOTELLING, THE MURDERED WIFE.

This violent crime involved S.J. Hotelling, 36, and his young wife, Flora Whitney, who were married less than a year before, on February 5, 1894. They were cousins, and the Whitney family was very much against their marriage. The newspaper account indicated that "their brief marriage was far from being happy."

Hotelling was said to be a very quiet person. Few in the area knew him well and he apparently had no close friends. He had recently traveled to many parts of the South and West, and upon his return to this area, his parents were dismayed at his behavior and language. The article stated that "he had a wild look and his talk was somewhat disconnected."

One evening, Julia Whitney, Flora's eighteen-year-old sister, came to the Hotellings' house to babysit their infant child. Mr. Hotelling didn't approve of Julia's visit and abruptly and rudely told her to leave. Julia left and was closely followed by her sister, Mrs. Flora Hotelling who took her infant son with her. The two sisters walked to the home of their parents, Mr. and Mrs. Whitney.

S. J. HOTELLING, THE MURDERER.

Later that evening as the Whitneys were gathered around the fire, they heard a knock on the door. When Mr. Whitney answered the door, he was immediately shot and killed by Hotelling. Mrs. Whitney tried to close the door and was killed.

Flora and Julia fled to the pantry and tried to bar the door. Julia stepped back and accidentally dropped through a small opening in the floor that led to the cellar, which had been covered by loose boards and carpeting. Hotelling finally forced his way into the pantry, killed his wife, and continued looking for Julia who had fled through an outside entrance to the cellar and run nearly a mile to a neighboring house.

Other neighbors soon heard the news and went to the Whitney home only to find the carnage. According to the newspaper account, "T.B. Whitney and wife were highly respected, quiet old people, the former aged 68 and the latter 61." They were originally from New York and moved to Martin County from Wisconsin in 1873. The only survivors were the infant and Julia.

The news of the tragic event was brought to Fairmont by William Wherland. Deputy Sheriff Ward, Constable Miller, H.M. Serle, and S. Hill went to the Whitney home.

Hotelling had taken refuge about three-quarters of a mile away where he and his wife occupied the upstairs level of a house. When the police arrived, they notified members of the family who owned the home and lived downstairs to leave, which they did. The police then tried to determine a way to capture Hotelling.

Hotelling was ordered to surrender. Finally, his response was, "I'm fixed for you—have got a Winchester repeating rifle and a revolver—you can't take me alive!" At that point, he fired down the stairs through the door. The police determined there would very likely be many lives lost if they tried to enter the home. Instead, they sent a messenger to Fairmont to obtain a supply of militia rifles.

Before morning, reinforcements and a supply of twenty-five rifles arrived. When Hotelling again refused to come downstairs, the order was given by the police to begin firing.

Round after round of gunfire poured into the house. Finally, Hotelling gave a loud, defiant yell, which was followed by a single gunshot. There were no more shots fired from the house. Shortly thereafter, the police cautiously made their way up the stairs of the house to find that Hotelling had taken his own life.

About 300 shots struck the building during the standoff. It was estimated that it would cost about $150 to make the necessary repairs to the house as a result of the gun shots.

Hotelling left a penciled letter in which he tried to excuse his conduct and place blame on members of the Whitney family.

The funeral for the three members of the Whitney family was held in the Methodist church in Fairmont. Over 1,000 people attended, and hundreds were turned away as there was no more room in the church. The family is buried in Lakeside Cemetery where a monument gives their dates of birth, but no date of death.

This was, undoubtedly, one of the most tragic events to ever occur in Martin County. Were "the good old days" all that good?

The "Most Dastardly" Bank Robbery of 1896

"Sherburn, the scene of the most dastardly crime in the history of Minnesota, one of the blackest deeds in the annals of crime," was the opening line of a story in the *Martin County Sentinel* on October 16, 1896, which described the events of a bank robbery in which two men were killed.

Relics from the Sherburn robbery

Two men entered the Bank of Sherburn and, without warning, shot and killed assistant cashier George Thorborn and Olof J. Oestern of Luverne. One eyewitness, Mrs. George R. Browning, gave the following account of the crime: "I was on the sidewalk opposite the bank and saw two young men about twenty-five years of age walk briskly across the street and enter the Bank of Sherburn, which was on the west side of the street. I was standing where I could see through the front window to the back window. I heard two shots in quick succession, and saw the flash of revolvers, and saw one man fall at the same time. I saw a man leap through the paying window over the counter and in an instant saw the back window raised and two men jump out the back window. They cut the screen that was on the outside and dropped the knife used to cut it."

The robbers, brothers Hans and Lew Kellihan, headed west and then northwest out of town on bicycles. An estimated one to two thousand dollars was taken from the bank, although the robbers dropped $2,000 while leaving the bank. Over $2,000 in gold and silver in the till was not touched.

They were pursued by Sheriff Washington Hill and Deputies Miller and Peddie. Citizens of Fairmont and surrounding towns turned out in force to try to find the robbers, and Sheriff Dunn of Jackson had a posse of 200 men scouring the area from Jackson, Minnesota., to Estherville, Iowa.

"Sensation follows sensation in the now famous Sherburn double murder and bank robbery," stated the *Martin County Sentinel* as the pursuit of the criminals continued in southern Minnesota and northern Iowa. At a farmhouse about fourteen miles east of Elmore, Hans was surprised by a posse. He opened fire, killing Sheriff William Gallion, marshal of Bancroft, Iowa. The robber, although wounded twice, tried to escape on his bicycle. Deputy Sheriff E.E. Ward of Martin County again wounded the fugitive. At that point, the robber put his weapon to his head and killed himself.

Lew was captured the next day in Lake Mills, Iowa. He was recognized by Marshal Ruby of Lake Mills as Lew walked past the marshal's residence. Upon being captured, Lew made a complete confession to the robbery while stating that his brother had killed the two people in the Bank of Sherburn.

Martin County Bank Robberies

Today's criminals frequently utilize sophisticated methods in their attempts to achieve their illegal goals. Before the advent of these contemporary methods involving white collar crime, identity theft, and a variety of cyberspace crimes, there were a number of bank robberies that took place in Martin County the "old fashioned" way, meaning face to face with robbers brandishing weapons. Many of their unlawful efforts were met by the less sophisticated methods of law enforcement of the era, which most times prevailed.

Monterey, the "mont" part of what is now Trimont, experienced two bank robberies in the early part of the last century. The first occurred in 1908 when the bank was entered at night and the safe door was blown off its hinges. The robbers made off with $1,500, escaping on a three-wheeled hand cart stolen from a railroad section house at Monterey and abandoned in Sherburn. Sheriff E.E. Ward's investigation found torn scraps of a picture and a letter near the abandoned hand car. The letter, a love letter, had come from one of the robbers' girlfriends, and it had a St. Paul return address. Sheriff Ward meticulously pieced the letter together, and then went to St. Paul. Within a few days, he arrested one of the suspects who pleaded guilty and was sentenced to five years in Stillwater.

Three decades later, a headline in the December 12, 1939, edition of *The Fairmont Daily Sentinel* read, "Monterey Bank Holdup Brings FBI Sleuths." The article went on to say, "G Men, state, and county officials today in search for a lone, armed bandit who held up the Farmers State Bank of Monterey Monday and escaped with $700.00 after forcing Elmer F. Peterson, cashier, and Bob Rippel, assistant cashier, into the vault." The bandit had a note stating the following: "This is a stickup. No false moves. Or else. Put the money in there." Elmer Peterson stated, "I never knew a gun looked so big from the small end." A.E. Peterson, vice president, missed the excitement as he was in the washroom during the robbery and was quite surprised when he came out to find what had happened. Elmer stated, in giving his account of the robbery to the *Sentinel,* "It was the first loan we ever made without getting a note for it." This was the first armed holdup of a bank in Martin County since the Bank of Sherburn robbery in 1896, and was the second bank robbery in Monterey.

Another daring bank robbery occurred in Ceylon in 1948 when two young Martin County men held up the Ceylon State Bank and escaped with $5,000. One of the men robbed the bank while his accomplice, who watched from a nearby café, was drinking coffee with his family. According to the May 22, 1948, edition of *The Fairmont Daily Sentinel,* a lone bandit masked in a dirty white handkerchief and holding a large nickel-plated revolver entered the bank and stated, "This is a stick up. Put 'em up and let's have no monkey business." Next, the young man forced the bank employees into the vault and then forced another employee to then lock the vault. Although the bandit made off with $5,000, he failed to notice $1,674 in a cash drawer and another $3,500 in another vault.

His accomplice conveniently left the cafe, commandeered the getaway car, and picked up the robber around the block after he left the bank. Within two hours of the robbery, one of the robbers returned to the bank and informed one of the bank employees that his revolver, which had been purchased at Colvin's Store in Fairmont, had been mysteriously stolen. Deputy Bill Musegades, who was in the bank at that time, felt this story to be somewhat suspicious. Consequently, he kept the suspect under surveillance, eventually approaching him and asking where the money was hidden.

Shortly thereafter, Sheriff A.R. Batterman and a bank employee drove to the farm of the parents of the suspect. There it was learned that the two young men had in fact divided the $5,000 at that location and that the money was hidden in the barn on the farm site and in a tree by a creek. Upon their apprehension, the two boys pleaded guilty. They were sentenced to forty years in jail; however, because they were minors, they were remanded to the custody of the Youth Conservation Committee.

No "Horsing Around" in Martin County

Before the automobile made its way into the lives of Martin County citizens, the preferred mode of transportation involved horses. And there were those who would attempt to acquire the preferred method of transportation unlawfully by stealing horses. From that, the term "horse thieves" was derived.

Those hardy Martin County pioneers decided that the theft of horses was not to be tolerated; consequently, they formed the Martin County Anti-Horse-Thief Association, known by the somewhat cumbersome acronym as the MCAHTA. This was no loosely knit organization. In the archives of the Pioneer Museum exists the constitution of the MCAHTA that included their bylaws, membership requirements, and the fact they held a meeting at the Martin County Courthouse the first Saturday of December annually.

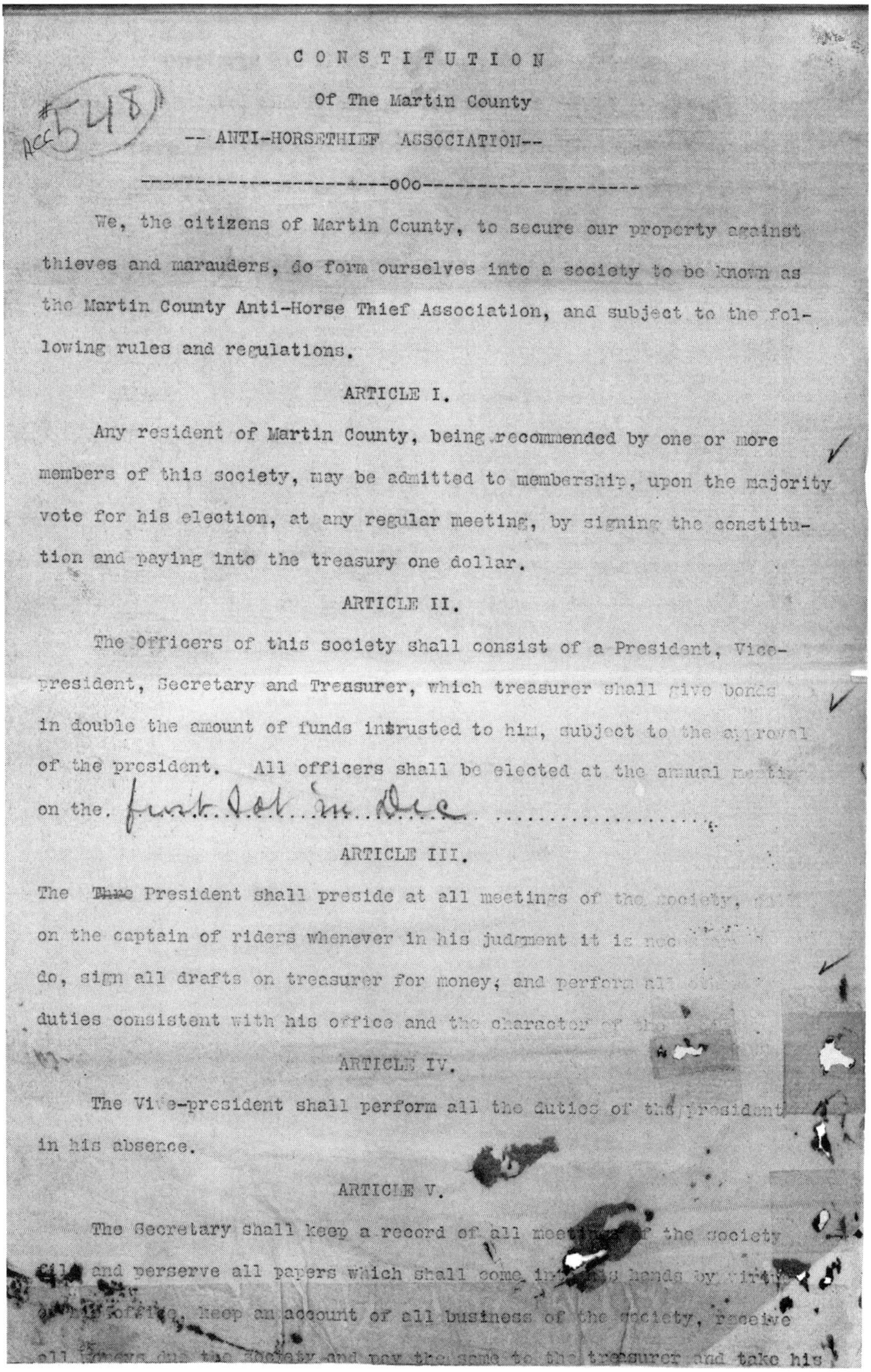

#548 Acc

CONSTITUTION

Of The Martin County

-- ANTI-HORSETHIEF ASSOCIATION--

---------------------oOo---------------------

We, the citizens of Martin County, to secure our property against thieves and marauders, do form ourselves into a society to be known as the Martin County Anti-Horse Thief Association, and subject to the following rules and regulations.

ARTICLE I.

Any resident of Martin County, being recommended by one or more members of this society, may be admitted to membership, upon the majority vote for his election, at any regular meeting, by signing the constitution and paying into the treasury one dollar.

ARTICLE II.

The Officers of this society shall consist of a President, Vice-president, Secretary and Treasurer, which treasurer shall give bonds in double the amount of funds intrusted to him, subject to the approval of the president. All officers shall be elected at the annual meeting on the first Sat in Dec ....

ARTICLE III.

The ~~Thee~~ President shall preside at all meetings of the society, call on the captain of riders whenever in his judgment it is nec[illegible] do, sign all drafts on treasurer for money; and perform all other duties consistent with his office and the character of the [illegible]

ARTICLE IV.

The Vice-president shall perform all the duties of the president in his absence.

ARTICLE V.

The Secretary shall keep a record of all meetings of the society and perserve all papers which shall come into his hands by virtue of his office, keep an account of all business of the society, receive all moneys due the society and pay the same to the treasurer and take his

There were several items in the bylaws that were significant regarding membership. Apparently, the association didn't admit just anyone who applied and was able to provide the tidy sum of $1 for their annual dues. The applicant also had to prove he was of good moral character and that he had never been convicted of stealing property or associating in any way with thieves. There was no mention of how proof of these terms would be provided. In addition, those membership requirements would lead one to wonder the amount of time necessary to run a thorough background check in the late 1800s or early 1900s, or even how one would be accomplished with any degree of accuracy.

Another interesting aspect of their constitution involved Article VIII of the MCAHTA. It clearly states that "there will be two riders from each township and organized village who shall hold themselves in readiness at all times to start in pursuit of stolen property of any kind, exceeding fifty dollars in value, belonging to any member of the society." In addition, the riders ordered into service by the president or captain of the riders shall receive the sum of $1.50 per day for their services.

An additional incentive was that the rider or riders who capture a horse thief shall receive $100 of the state bounty for the capture and conviction of such thieves with the balance of the bounty going into the MCAHTA treasury. However, in sharp contrast, any member ordered to pursue a thief who refused to serve would be fined $2 unless a reasonable justification was provided. There was no mention of what might constitute a reasonable excuse. It also seems that if not a member of the MCAHTA, and you had something stolen of value in excess of fifty dollars, you were out of luck.

The MCAHTA Constitution bears the signatures of 92 Martin County citizens, some of whom were considered quite prominent in their day. Signatories included Frank A. Day, John Hilken, E.J. Potter, George Eaton, N.C. Dahl, John Steen, Thomas Gately, and A.S. Graves.

The "good guys" and the "bad guys" are still at odds in today's society; however, the means of accomplishing their goals from both perspectives has evolved significantly. Regarding the MCAHTA, there is little information other than their constitution as to its success or longevity. In any event, it has provided another interesting piece of local history that no longer exists.

Who Just Got Arrested?

Law enforcement is undeniably a challenging profession that has recently been under a great deal of scrutiny. As with all professions, and society in general, it has evolved and procedures have changed over the years. However, some situations are more challenging than others. Following is one experience of Sheriff William S. Carver gleaned from the pages of July 1924 issues of the *Truman Tribune* and the *Fairmont Sentinel* regarding his attempt to carry out an out-of-state extradition.

"Sheriff Carver Arrested in Iowa, Martin County Sheriff is Charged With Kidnapping, Assault, and Carrying Concealed Weapons" read one headline. The saga started with an Iowa man having a little too much fun at Hand's Park. He was described as being "lit up" and causing some problems. As a result, the individual in question, a resident of Buffalo Center, Iowa, was arrested, sentenced, and given a fine. He agreed to pay the

$49.50 fine if allowed to go to Guckeen to get the money. When he returned from Guckeen, he gave Deputy Parker a check. Deputy Parker warned him that, "If this isn't good, we'll be after you." He assured the deputy that it would be good.

Sheriff William Carver

However, the individual stopped payment on the check as soon as he got back to Buffalo Center. The *Truman Tribune* newspaper article cited this as his "first mistake." The article went on to state that his "second mistake" was refusing to return to Fairmont with one of Sheriff Carver's deputies, and what was characterized as his "third mistake" was refusing to go when "Big" Bill himself came with extradition papers. This is where the story became interesting as well as exasperating for the sheriff.

It seemed the perpetrator in this instance made every effort to resist arrest. He and his father both wielded butcher knives in the direction of Sheriff Carver in an attempt to avoid being taken into custody. "Sheriff Carver pulled out his six-shooter and cautioned father and son that if there was any 'monkey business, he would use his gun", according to the July 23, 1924, *Sentinel.*

The July 24 headline of the *Fairmont Daily Sentinel* read "Drunk Sues Carver For $10,000." An attorney was hired who, as was stated in the *Truman Tribune*, had "trumped up criminal charges" in filing a damage suit against Carver in an attempt to prevent him from taking his man back to Minnesota. If the preceding events weren't infuriating enough, Carver himself was also arrested and charged with kidnapping, assault and battery, and carrying a concealed weapon in addition to the charge that he had no jurisdiction or power in Iowa.

When the Iowa sheriff and county attorney began reading their warrants to Carver, Carver asked if he was under arrest. They hesitated and, interestingly enough, said they didn't know. As a result, Carver was allowed to proceed. Apparently, the Iowa sheriff and county attorney weren't particularly anxious to exercise their authority in light of the fact that Carver had extradition papers signed by the governors of two states. Obviously, Carver wasn't going to back down, and he was determined to "get his man."

Subsequently, justice was finally served as the individual was finally returned to Fairmont and sentenced to twenty days in jail. When his sentence expired, he was faced with a charge of grand larceny for having stopped payment on his check. Bail was set at $1,000. Only cash would be accepted this time.

From all accounts, Carver appeared to be a well-liked and respected law man. However, even after his heroic and determined efforts in apprehending his man in Iowa in 1924, Carver lost his bid for reelection in 1926. That loss was attributed primarily to what would appear to be conflicting factors: one was his high conviction rate of bootleggers and the second was his association with the Ku Klux Klan. His plea to the electorate that his Klan involvement was simply a mistake did not seem to sway public opinion. Consequently, it would seem that his connection with the Klan, coupled with the opposition mounted by bootleggers, sealed his fate for reelection.

What Killed the Chief?

The National Law Enforcement Officers' Memorial is the nation's monument to law enforcement officers who have died in the line of duty. Dedicated on October 15, 1991, the memorial honors federal, state and local law enforcement officers who have made the ultimate sacrifice for the safety and protection of our nation and its people. In that respect, there may be a former Fairmont police chief who qualifies for this honor.

One evening, back in October of 1930, at about 10:15 p.m., beloved fifty-four-year-old Fairmont Police Chief August "Gus" Haase took time to help a stranded, homeless stranger find a place to stay. The chief took him to the sleeping quarters in the jail at city hall and allowed him to stay the night.

Shortly thereafter, Fairmont Patrolman Henry Plenge noticed from the First National Bank corner that the lights were on in the city jail. Patrolman Plenge entered the jail and was informed by the person given lodging that another officer had given him permission to stay.

As Plenge was about to leave, he heard the chief call for him. According to the account provided by the October 15, 1930, edition of the *Fairmont Daily Sentinel*, Chief Haase was quoted as saying, "Come in Henry, I want to have a talk with you." Plenge entered the room and Haase continued, "I've been wanting to have a talk with you for quite a while. It is all quiet around town, isn't it?" Plenge assured him that all was well.

Chief Haase went on to say, "No need for you to be walking around all the time. You know I have been disgusted with the way things have been going for quite a while and believe I will quit. You have been doing fine work since you were appointed."

Plenge then said, "Why, what's the matter Gus?" Plenge next asked if the chief wasn't feeling well. At that, Chief Haase replied, "No, I am sick, I . . . . . ." These were last the words uttered by Haase as he slowly slumped over from his chair. At that point, Patrolman Plenge caught him and gently eased him to the floor. Dr. Hunt and Dr. Zemke were called and responded immediately. However, there was nothing that could be done. They pronounced him dead at 10:27 p.m., less than fifteen minutes after providing the stranger on the street a place to stay for the night.

The headline in the October 15, 1930, edition of the *Fairmont Daily Sentinel* read, "Police Chief Gus Haase Drops Dead at City Hall." Haase was a highly respected and very well-liked member of the Fairmont Police Department. The local citizens were understandably distraught at his sudden death. A Fairmont mother reported her children cried when they were told the news. Chief Haase had helped Central School children cross the street every day at Park Street and Blue Earth Avenue. But the lingering question remained, what caused his demise?

Three physicians performing the autopsy determined that Chief Haase had been stricken with a heart attack as a result of overexertion in the recent arrest of a long-time, chronic drunk in town, a baker at the Town Pump Cafe.

Since the arrest two days prior to his death, Haase had been complaining of chest and arm pain. The baker, who was arrested for intoxication, was chastised by Justice Harry M. Serle who said, "You have caused more trouble in Fairmont than any man I've known in fifty years. You are an undesirable citizen. I am going to give you all the law will let me." The baker pleaded for leniency; however, Justice Serle stated that he had given him plenty of previous opportunities.

Serle went on to say that he had told Haase not to struggle with the baker but to use his club and to use it hard. Serle added, "Instead of coming with him as you should have done, you gave him a rough and tumble, and I am sure that it is what resulted in his death."

The baker was consequently sentenced to sixty days by Justice Serle. If the baker was truly the cause of Haase's death, this would certainly seem to be a lenient consequence for his lack of cooperation.

So was the death of Chief Gus Haase a direct result of actions taken by him in the line of duty that would in turn qualify him for a spot on the National Law Enforcement Officers' Memorial, or was it simply a medical condition that would inevitably cause his death and eventually happen anyway?

An article in the October 17, 1930, edition of the *Fairmont Daily Sentinel* regarding Haase's autopsy stated: "The doctors expressed the belief that the violent exertion made by Chief Haase in the arrest of the baker hastened his death. With his heart condition, he might have lived considerably longer had he kept clear of overexertion and excitement."

Justice Serle summed up the tragedy when he told the baker, "We lost a mighty good citizen last night, and I lay the death of Mr. Haase to you." That statement alone would weigh heavily on the conscience of most!

It's a Jungle Out There!

It was the early 1930s; Herbert Hoover was president, and the country was in the midst of the Great Depression, which affected Martin County as well. One consequence of the economic stagnation of this era was that Fairmont became home to Jungleland, located in the vicinity of the southwest shore of George Lake.

Jungleland may evoke mental images of various types of exotic animals in the pleasant and tranquil setting of a picturesque zoo. However, Jungleland was the name given to an area of Fairmont that served as a home to hoboes and transients. Although it didn't house exotic animals, it may have been home to what might be considered somewhat exotic characters.

In 1932, a July *Daily Sentinel* headline read "Fight at 'Jungles' Brings Cleanup." The group in question was described as "the toughest gang of hoboes, transients and questionable characters that had invaded Fairmont in years."

FIGHT AT "JUNGLES" BRINGS CLEANUP; 30 HOBOES DRIVEN OUT OF FAIRMONT

Jungleland, Sentinel, July 6, 1932

The cleanup of Jungleland was prompted by a call to the police informing them of a fight involving ten men. Upon arriving on the scene, the police found that about a dozen men were involved, including several who were drunk. The apparent ringleader was arrested and taken to jail.

A man injured in the melee wasn't immediately found but was later located and gave the police an account of the incident. He stated that there were initially four on each side; however, once the fight began, his three friends quickly abandoned him. Consequently, he was left alone and became the recipient of a sound beating that included a broken jaw. The cause of the fight was not determined.

The roundup, which began in earnest at 5:30 p.m. on July 5, 1932, involved the police officers combing the "jungles" on the west edge of town. It was said to have been an extremely tedious task, with the hoboes hiding in the long weeds and grass as well as literally burrowing into the earth. In addition, the men had devised a new type of hut constructed of sections of old boxes made into small rooms with the aid of brush and rubbish. Several of them were under the trees on the shores of George Lake. The cleanup also found many empty bottles and cans of Bay Rum and canned heat. Retailers were advised not to sell denatured alcohol to "questionable characters."

Plenge, along with officers Shea and Batterman, rounded up some thirty men of various ages and nationalities. They were then loaded into a departing Northwestern train cattle car heading west.

The burly ringleader, blamed for starting a near riot at the camp, stubbornly refused to get on the train when ordered to do so by police. He said that he liked this town and intended to stay. At that point, Chief Plenge rapped him across the back with his club and again ordered him on the train. That was apparently enough incentive for him to agree, and he entered the cattle car with the other hoboes, according to the July 6 article. Where they ended up is an unknown.

In carrying out the cleanup, Plenge received permission from the city council to go through all the jungles and destroy the huts, cooking places, and camping sites. In addition, all the tall grass was ordered cut down in order to provide no further hiding places for the transients. The findings in the cleanup of Jungleland concluded that there were also a few "honest, unemployed" men looking for work in addition to some of the regular transients who resided in Fairmont during both good and bad times.

Apparently Fairmont's problem at that time was effectively resolved by simply placing those transients and hoboes from Jungleland on a train heading west. It would seem that this form of 1930s problem-solving, perhaps labeled as simply "kicking the can down the road," wouldn't be a viable long-term solution. However, might this method of problem-solving still be in use to some extent today in our modern society? You be the judge.

Remembering George Cavers

Martin County has had many people who have positively impacted its history. One of those individuals was George Cavers.

Cavers with a Thompson submachine gun

Cavers was born in North Dakota but moved to Martin County with his parents when he was seven years old. After graduating from Fairmont High School in 1929, he spent a short time with the highway department. After that, he served in the Navy, and later joined the Fairmont Police Department in 1936.

Cavers spent thirty-two years with the police department, including eighteen as chief of police before retiring in 1968. He was also very active in the community. He served on the safety council from 1938–1988, was a county commissioner for ten years before retiring from that position in 1980, and was a member of the American Legion and the Knights of Columbus.

Throughout his lifetime in Martin County, Cavers was probably most well known as being a member of the Fairmont Police Department and being chief of police, succeeding Henry Plenge.

Cavers, a graduate of the Federal Bureau of Investigation Academy, received two letters of commendation from legendary FBI Director J. Edgar Hoover. The first letter was in 1950, congratulating Cavers on his appointment as Fairmont chief of police. The second letter from Hoover came in 1953, congratulating him on his election as president of the Southeastern Minnesota Peace Officers Association. Letters of commendation from the FBI director would certainly be distinguishing events in the career of any police officer.

In addition, it is widely believed, although not officially documented, that the Thompson Submachine Gun, presently in the possession of the Fairmont Police Department, was a gift from Hoover to Cavers. To add veracity to this theory, the Martin County Historical Society has pictures showing Chief Cavers with the submachine gun. Whether it was actually given to Cavers by Hoover is unverified, but it certainly makes for an interesting conversation regarding local history.

During his career in law enforcement, as might be expected, Cavers had a number of interesting experiences, including a potentially deadly situation when the department received a call from a concerned citizen about a neighbor who was drunk and brandishing a gun.

When five police officers, including Chief Cavers, arrived on the scene, the man threatened them. It was a standoff for about an hour until Cavers decided to shoot a tear gas cartridge through a basement window where the man was located. Just as it was discharged, the man came out of the house and Cavers disarmed and handcuffed him.

Upon being taken into custody, the individual stated that he had intended to shoot Cavers. Fortunately, the event ended without bloodshed or injuries to anyone involved.

Chief Cavers also investigated a relatively minor shoplifting case at the former Red Owl grocery store that exposed a series of interesting findings. The shoplifting inquiry Cavers conducted involving the theft of a mere $1.79 in groceries led to the recovery of $135 in merchandise from J.C. Penney's, Wallace's Department Store, Wolf's, Georgia's, and Miller's Fashions. In talking about the shoplifter, Cavers was quoted as saying, "The girl put up a good story but it didn't hold water." The sum of $135 was a fairly substantial amount of money in that era of our local history.

Another incident involved a trio of gangsters who assaulted Fairmont resident Charlie Potter in his home and robbed him of money and jewelry amounting to $12,000. The robbers overpowered the homeowner and his wife and even subdued Cavers when he arrived on the scene. Cavers, oblivious to the robbery taking place, entered the home, believing the car parked outside belonged to Sheriff Batterman. Consequently, being unaware of the impending danger, he was caught off guard by the intruders who then proceeded to handcuff him to the stair railing.

George Cavers is an example of another Martin County citizen who dedicated his lifetime to serving and making our community and county a better place in which to live. His efforts, as well as those of others like him, have enhanced the quality of life in Martin County. He exemplified the definition of service through his profession, his actions, and his community involvement.

Sources for this story include the May 24, 1961, and April 26, 1948, editions of the Sentinel, *and the* 2007 Hometown Legends *special to the* Sentinel.

Remembering the Chief

The city of Fairmont has had a number of well-known police chiefs over the years. Some of these include Fred Lindstaedt, George Cavers, H.C. Plenge, Erwin "Butch" Thiel, Vic Hillmer, Greg Brolsma, and currently Mike Hunter. Each of these individuals, in their own unique manner, has carried out the mission of law enforcement for the citizens they served.

A May 9, 1983, *Sentinel* article reflected on then-Fairmont Police Chief Vic Hillmer's thoughts on his career in law enforcement as he was nearing retirement.

Hillmer entered the profession in a very different era, serving in the Fairmont Police Department from 1958 until he retired as police chief in 1983. He began as a patrolman with the police department at age thirty-one, stating that his only regret was not entering law enforcement at an earlier age. Prior to that, he served in the Navy, worked as a greens keeper, an auto mechanic, and a time keeper and parts manager for Stokely–Van Camp.

Police Chief Victor Hillmer is retiring the "hottest seat" in Fairmont. Bob Schroeder

Hillmer: 25 years on police force an unending education

He advanced from patrolman to sergeant and was appointed police chief in October 1968 and served in that position for fourteen years. However, Hillmer emphasized the importance of education while also stating that experience was indeed vital to the job. He reiterated that being the police chief was an ongoing education in and of itself. He cited the importance of classes he took in social sciences, administration, firearms, and what he learned while attending the FBI Academy. Hillmer considered these opportunities to be excellent educational experiences and essential to his position as chief of police.

Hillmer went on to reflect on the many changes that had taken place in law enforcement since he began in the profession. He referenced Supreme Court rulings, the computer age, improvements in two-way radio communication, record systems, and police officers. His perceptions were that community relationships were good and that Fairmont was fortunate to not have to deal with the big city problems. Although there was the possibility of some sort of organized crime operating in the area at that time, perhaps including gambling, it apparently never developed into any significant concern. He emphasized that the community was too small to support issues such as those and that they were not what might be considered immediate concerns at that time.

Hillmer was involved in many organizations including Immanual Lutheran Church, Lee C. Prentice American Legion, Minnesota Police Chiefs Association, and the Northwest Chapter of the Federal Bureau of Investigation National Academy. He also was a board member of the Fairmont Policemen's Benefit Association. He passed away in March of 1997.

The role of the police chief, whether in a big city or a rural community, has certainly evolved. The requirements and training have changed significantly and the tools available to law enforcement would undoubtedly astound the police departments of fifty years ago. However, in contrast to the advances that have been made, the problems faced by the police have certainly multiplied as well.

Chief Vic Hillmer will be remembered for his unquestionable integrity, his sound leadership, and the indisputable confidence the public placed in him as chief of police. He was an authentic and positive role model for the community.

Martin County at War

Martin County's Benjamin Franklin

When the name Benjamin Franklin comes up, most of us will undoubtedly conjure in our minds a man in Pennsylvania from colonial times flying a kite, writing in a newspaper, publishing *Poor Richard's Almanac*, or perhaps being involved in politics. However, there was another, somewhat lesser known, Benjamin Franklin who had a Minnesota connection during the 1800s. Although he was far less prominent than the Ben Franklin most of us are familiar with in terms of historical significance, this Benjamin Franklin had a very unique story to tell as well.

Ben Franklin, circa 1866

Benjamin Franklin was an unfortunate soldier. He lost all of his extremities while crossing the plains from Fort Wadsworth, Dakotah Territory, to Fort Ridgley in Minnesota, as a result of freezing temperatures. While making this ill-fated journey with four of his comrades, they were caught in a ferocious winter storm. They were without food or fire for warmth for eight days. Franklin nearly starved to death until he was found by two Native Americans after the storm had subsided. Unfortunately, the fate of his four fellow soldiers was sealed as they all perished.

Having lost both his hands and his feet, Franklin was at that time the only quadriplegic soldier in the United States. In order to support himself, he attempted to sell photographs of himself for twenty-five cents each for at least twenty years.

Franklin briefly served at Fort Fairmount and at one time lived in Blue Earth.

Sources for this story include Blizzard Ordeal of a Minnesota Cavalryman *by Marlin Peterson, 2014.*

Martin County in the Spanish–American War

The patriotism of Martin County citizens became evident once again during the Spanish–American War. Martin County's National Guard infantry, Company D, had an intense interest in becoming involved in the Spanish–American War, so it began a rigorous recruiting campaign in April of 1898. At that time, Fairmont had no state armory, and a large barn-like structure was erected for this purpose. The armory was cold and poorly suited for the needs of the soldiers; therefore, J.W. Daniels, owner of the Daniels Hall, permitted the use of his building for Company D's nightly drills.

Shortly after recruiting began, Company D, made up of about 100 local citizens, received its call to duty. Approximately 3,500 people at the railway station saw the boys off. This included the entire population of Fairmont as well as many people from other parts of the county as a large portion of the men were from other communities in the area.

Company D

The first stop was Camp Ramsey at the state fairgrounds in St. Paul. The stay there involved intensive training and was the first experience of this nature for most of the volunteers. Finally, on May 8, the company of raw recruits was mustered into federal service for the period of the war, and the members took their oath on May 9.

Company D, then made up of 80 men, was sent to Camp Thomas at Chickamauga Park in Georgia. Camp Thomas was considered a good training ground and had the largest mobilization of troops the United States had seen since the Civil War, at one time numbering 60,000 soldiers. The soldiers of 1898 had the unique experience of serving with Civil War veterans from both the North and the South.

Camp Thomas training was intense and grueling. Reveille was at 4:40 a.m., and a dress parade, where uniforms had to be in tip-top shape with brass buttons polished, was held every evening.

Conditions at Camp Thomas were less than adequate. Supplies were limited, and personal cleanliness was virtually impossible. A soldier could only wash his clothing when not wearing it. Consequently, clothing was frequently not washed for four months at a time. In one instance, an entire outfit of soldiers was marched to the creek where everyone stripped and washed their clothing using the creek bed as washboards. The clothing was hung to dry and, of course, did shrink to some extent. However, it wasn't of particular concern as the clothing was poorly fitted to begin with anyway.

Tents available at Camp Thomas were also in short supply, and the men of Company D crowded seven to nine men in a tent measuring seven feet by nine feet. Obviously, these were extremely tight conditions. The tents had no floors, there were no cots or beds, and each man had a single blanket.

There were no regular cooks or well-equipped kitchens or mess halls. Crude cooking was done over open fires, and the soldiers themselves had to be self-sufficient in finding and cooking their own meals. They then had to wash their own dishes, often without water, which was quite scarce at that time.

Sanitary conditions at Camp Thomas were extremely unfavorable. A shallow, open pit was dug a few feet back of each of the crude company kitchens. All the refuse and waste from the men was dumped into these unenclosed pits, which became literal cesspools. Flies multiplied wildly, and the stench could be smelled for miles away. In addition, the refuse from horses and mules also piled up in those areas.

The cootie, known to the men as the "grayback," became quite prevalent in the camp. They were actually said to be in greater number in the camp than the flies and, of course, were very annoying to the soldiers.

Obviously, disease was a great concern under these unclean conditions. Company D suffered severely, but no more so than the rest of the members of the camp. Typhoid fever, dysentery, and malaria were the prevalent diseases. Typhoid was especially severe and caused the majority of deaths at Camp Thomas.

There was an inadequate supply of hospitals, doctors, and nurses. Consequently, care and treatment was woefully scarce and little could be done for most of the sick. There was what was called an "incurable ward," in which it was said that it was nearly impossible to distinguish the living from the dead.

A Soldiers Relief Society was formed in Fairmont and was very active in forwarding supplies and other comforts to the sick. A public meeting was also held in Fairmont and resolutions adopted demanding the men be discharged or at least be moved to a more sanitary camp.

In August, Company D was moved to another area of the park that was considered uncontaminated. The men were there but a few days when orders came for them to move to Camp Hamilton in Lexington, Kentucky. Then, on September 15, the men left for Minnesota to be mustered out. The Spanish–American War ended without any of the Company D soldiers seeing action.

Upon reaching Fairmont on September 23, they were met with a resounding welcome home that included a band and a large crowd of well-wishers. The public meeting and grand reception for the soldiers included a banquet held at Daniels Hall.

Following their discharge, the men quickly and quietly resumed civilian life as best they could at that time. They came home with no money, jobs were scarce, and winter was soon upon them. However, many worked on farms, returned to school, or convalesced after contracting illnesses at Camp Thomas.

Firsthand information on this event is from Major Arthur Nelson's book Martin County in the Spanish–American War. *Nelson was a member of Company D.*

The Nonpartisan League

The Nonpartisan League is a term that may not be very familiar today; however, during World War I, it significantly affected some residents of Minnesota as well as Martin County. Sedition, patriotism, Liberty bonds, and the Commission of Public Safety were terms that became widely used and accepted at that time in our history.

Initially, the Nonpartisan League was an agrarian effort that started in North Dakota in 1915 and spread to Minnesota shortly thereafter. It developed as a result of poor market conditions for farmers, and it promoted economic reforms that were alleged to aid the farmers who considered themselves exploited by middlemen in the grain elevators, packinghouses, stockyards, and cold storage industries. Opponents labeled it as socialist; however, the league did not attempt a third-party approach but rather endorsed candidates who pledged to support their goals. With the onset of World War I, leaguers were viciously attacked as disloyal pacifists, and the Commission of Public Safety was eventually instrumental in dismantling the League in 1918. At that time, the NPL had over 50,000 members in Minnesota and had endorsed Charles A. Lindbergh, Sr., as their candidate for governor. He and league members faced brutal opposition during the campaign.

The Commission of Public Safety was created by the Minnesota Legislature. It had what appeared to be limitless latitude and authority in essentially trampling civil rights in the name of patriotism at that time.

As a result of America's entry into World War I, a climate of suspicion arose around anyone who seemed different. This was not limited to Minnesota's long-established German population but included all immigrants, those who spoke a foreign language, those who belonged to unions or supported strikes, and those belonging to suspect organizations such as the Nonpartisan League.

Then, with the establishment of the Alien Registration Act of 1918, all aliens were required to register, to declare their holdings, and to state why they had not become citizens. Consequently, many schools discontinued the instruction of foreign languages and even foreign language speakers were considered unpatriotic. Homes and businesses of those considered unpatriotic were given coats of bright yellow paint by loyalty enthusiasts. This heralded a rather dark chapter in the history of Minnesota, a state generally considered to be quite progressive.

Nonpartisan League Meeting Barred by Carver and Allen

OFFICERS NOTIFY ORGANIZATION NO GATHERING CAN BE HELD HERE WHILE OFFICIALS ARE UNDER DISLOYALTY INDICTMENTS—SPEAKERS WELCOME UNDER OTHER AUSPICES.

So how did this play out in Martin County? Editions of *The Martin County Sentinel* from January through June of 1918 gave front page accounts of incidents deemed "unpatriotic." Included in the articles were the alleged crimes, the perpetrator's names, and their penalty. Some examples of headlines making the news at that time were: "Guilty Traitor in Drunken Talk Defames Country—Fined $200;" "Waverly Farmer Questioned on Loyalty and Why He Has Bought No Liberty Bonds;" "3 More Arrested on Disloyalty by Deputy Roepke;" "War Safety Board of 23 To Be Named—A Countywide Organization Formed to Quell Sedition in Advance of the Nonpartisan League's Expected Invasion;" "Nonpartisan League Manager Spends Night in County Jail, Then Taken Back to St. Paul escorted by the Martin County Attorney;" "Loyalty Teaching Opposed, Five Homes Get Coat of Yellow Paint;" "Nonpartisan Meeting Banned by Sheriff Carver and County Attorney Allen;" and there were many more described throughout this time period.

Liberty bonds were being sold at that time in an effort to support the Allied cause in World War I. The purchase of these bonds was considered a symbol of patriotic duty. Citizens of Martin County were expected to purchase Liberty bonds and the county, as well as each township, had an allotted quota they were expected to fulfill. County

Chairman Frank Wade stated that there was a small army of Liberty bond solicitors in every township in the county.

The names of Liberty bond participants, including the amounts each participant purchased, were also listed in the newspaper. This was called the "Liberty Loan Roll of Honor." Those not participating at all or failing to purchase what was considered their allotted amount were considered disloyal and were persecuted and prosecuted. They were brought before the War Board to explain their reasons. In addition, there was a movement gaining momentum to confiscate the property of those deemed to be disloyal for refusing to purchase Liberty bonds. From these accounts it would appear that people had little choice but to purchase Liberty bonds or face the consequences determined by the War Board.

In 1918, Sheriff Carver and Deputy John Allison arrested Charles Lindbergh, Sr., the candidate for governor endorsed by the Nonpartisan League that year. The arrest took place on a farm in Martin County where Lindbergh was to address an estimated 1,000 persons gathered for a league picnic. When law enforcement arrived, Lindbergh denied membership in the NPL. His statement was printed in the June 11, 1918, edition of the *Martin County Sentinel*: "I am not a member of the Nonpartisan league, but am running as a republican. The league merely endorsed me. I have not spoken of the league in any of my addresses and did not know that the gathering today was billed as a league meeting." Lindbergh was later released on $1,000 bail.

Historical documentation shows that many of the events taking place during that era against the Nonpartisan League, although considered by many to be patriotic in nature, may actually have reflected something other than patriotism. The Commission of Public Safety had broad and sweeping authority that seemed to hold all citizens accountable to the Commission's definition of patriotism and the requirement to purchase Liberty bonds. Furthermore, anyone speaking against the war was charged with sedition or contributing to the incitement of discontent or rebellion against the government.

Additional sources for this story include www.mnopedia.org/group/nonpartisan-league and Patriot Hearts *by Frederick Johnson, 2017.*

MIA: The Drip B–24 Liberator Bomber

We live in a free country as a result of the investment and sacrifices of many young men and women over the course of America's notable history. One brave individual who helped secure and guarantee our freedom was Martin County-native George Winzenburg, the youngest of George and Catherine Winzenburg's children, born in Granada on May 7, 1918. The family moved to Fairmont two years later where young George attended parochial school at St. Paul's Convent School and later graduated from Fairmont High School in 1936.

Winzenburg was drafted into the Army in 1941. He was assigned to the Air Corps and was trained as a navigator. Upon completing his training at Pocatello, Idaho, Winzenburg and his crew "buzzed" Fairmont on August 9, 1943, while on their way to their assignment at Wendling Air Base in England. While buzzing Fairmont, Winzenburg dropped a note to his parents inserted in a shell casing attached to a homemade parachute. The note was found on Lake Park Boulevard in some bushes by Walter Kasper who in turn delivered it to Winzenburg's parents. The note read: "Dear Folks, Just Buzzing the Town. Signed, George."

Lieutenant Winzenburg served as a navigator on a B–24 Liberator bomber, one of the most famous American-built aircraft of World War II. Winzenburg's plane was known as The Drip. He was in the 579th Bomber Squadron out of Wendling in Norfolk, England. He flew on two missions during September and October that perhaps might be considered somewhat routine and quite successful; however, his good fortune was soon to change.

George Winzenburg, 1943

The third mission took place on November 3, 1943. They werc to fly to the German city of Munster and bomb the weapon factories in and around the city. The silver B–24s were easily spotted in the sky and were soon attacked with anti-aircraft fire. The Drip was hit after dropping its bombs, causing it to lose two engines and drop out of formation. It was then attacked by Messerschmitt fighters and subsequently shot down by one of Germany's ace pilots, Heinz Knoke. However, as a result of the gallant efforts of the crew, they were able to shoot down ten enemy aircraft, including Knoke's plane, before they ran out of ammunition.

Several of the crewman parachuted to safety, later to be taken prisoner by the Germans. The remaining crewmen were killed either before or during the crash into the North Sea near the Netherlands. Their navigator, Winzenburg, had been hit by exploding shrapnel from under the plane's nose. Winzenburg's status was MIA for nearly two years until he was declared dead by the war department after his body was found washed up on the shore of the Netherlands. He is buried in the Ardennes U. S. Military Cemetery, Neuville, Belgium. He was posthumously awarded the Purple Heart.

In August 2007, a wreck diver and underwater photographer, Vic Verlinden, discovered the wreck of the aircraft and began salvage operations. Through serial numbers and data plates, he was able to identify the plane. It had disintegrated upon crashing, so no bodies were salvaged; however, they were able to salvage part of one landing gear, a machine gun, a large piece of wing, pneumatic gauges, dynamos, and a number of 50-caliber shells.

As Americans remember the fallen on Memorial Day and celebrate our independence on July 4, it's important for every citizen to remember that our freedom didn't happen by accident. It took the bravery, courage, and persistence of those daring young men and women, some of whom, like Lieutenant George Winzenburg, gave the ultimate sacrifice in order to protect and preserve the freedoms we in the United States of America enjoy today.

Information on Winzenburg's mission for which he received the Purple Heart is from http://www.b24.net/MM110543.htm. Other sources for this story include the August 9, 1943, Fairmont Daily Sentinel*; Dear Folks–Love George, Family Genealogy 87 and George Winzenburg, Family Geneaology 88 at MCHS; and Frank Winzenburg.*

Freedom

Freedom is a term that may be defined in more than one way, depending upon the source of the definition. Earl Nolte, who had thirty-five relatives who served in World War II, succinctly defined it this way: "To me, freedom is doing what we ought to do—what is right, not what we want to do."

The thirty-six Nolte cousins who fought in World War II

Those Nolte relatives can be traced back to 1885 when Carl and Louise Nolte moved to Martin County from Downers Grove, Illinois. They bought 200 acres of land west of Fairmont and raised twelve children, including a set of identical twin boys.

All of those who served during World War II were sons, sons-in-law, or grandsons of Carl and Louise.

With that many relatives serving in the military at the same time, one might think their paths would eventually cross at some point, as was the case with Paul Nolte. He was stationed in Naples, Italy, and, while walking down the street one day, he encountered Elmer Haertel who was on leave after landing on Anzio Beach. Paul was also stationed in Rio de Janeiro, the Suez, and Durban, South Africa.

Earl joined the military at age eighteen. He served in the 1st Cavalry Division of the 7th Cavalry Regiment, General George Armstrong Custer's regiment. He handled heavy weapons and machine guns. He was quoted as saying, "We had horses until we went overseas. I think they expected us to carry as much as a horse." He was wounded twice in different campaigns and was sent home by the time he was twenty-one. Earl also served as the first World War II commander of the Lee C. Prentice American Legion Post 36 in Fairmont.

Herb Haertel joined the Army in 1941, serving for four years and eight months. He was a clerk in the Air Corps in the states before being sent to Okinawa in 1945.

Gordon Oltman of Fairmont served in the Navy in both the Atlantic and Pacific. His ship was torpedoed out from under him twice. The first time he was in the North Atlantic and wasn't injured but spent about four hours in the frigid water before being rescued. After the second sinking where he said he "hardly got his feet wet," he was sent to the Pacific. He was aboard what were called Liberty ships that carried cargo and were not known for their sturdy construction.

Vern Nolte served in the Navy as a pilot from 1941 to 1945. He flew from an aircraft carrier. Some of the places he visited in raids or in support of landings included Wake Island, Baker Island, Tarawa, Kwajalein, Truk (the aforementioned were all atolls, or coral reefs, in the Pacific Ocean that saw WWII action), New Guinea, Saipan, and Guam. In addition, Vern participated in the "Mariana's Turkey Shoot," a battle in which about 360 Japanese planes were shot down. It marked the end of Japan's naval air power. The ship and air group also participated in the first Philippine Sea Battle which basically destroyed the remaining Japanese fleet.

Mark Nolte, Vern's brother, served in the Marines as a Navy doctor. He was the physician who signed the death certificate of Ernie Pyle, the nationally-known war correspondent who wrote about the average American soldier's daily life while at war. Pyle was killed instantly by Japanese machine-gun fire.

Truman native Loren Wessel joined the Army in 1942. He was sent from Fort Roberts in California to Port Adelaide, Australia, to join Company D, 128th Infantry, 32nd Division. He went to Papua, New Guinea, as a machine gunner to help Australian forces clear the island of the Japanese enemy. This campaign was a crushing defeat for the Japanese army. Loren's faith and love of God helped him survive the trauma of World War II in the South Pacific Theater during some of the bloodiest fighting of the war.

Walter Wessel, although not in combat, served in the military and was headed to India on a ship when the war ended.

Reinhardt Wessel entered the Army in 1944 and was assigned to the 56th Armored Infantry Battalion of the 12th Armored Division as part of General Patton's Third Army. His unit advanced rapidly through Germany, taking many German prisoners. The Germans used horses for transportation at that time, and Wessel would frequently unhitch the German horses so that they were free to run off. He was hit by shrapnel and was flown to a hospital in France to recover. His decorations included the Combat Infantry Badge, the Purple Heart, and the Bronze Star.

Freedom, the state of being at liberty rather than in confinement, is what the aforementioned cousins fought for and helped to preserve.

"To me, freedom is doing what we ought to do—what is right, not what we want to do" more precisely defines the true meaning of freedom. That's a powerful message in but a very few words!

Sources for this story include the November 11, 1997, Sentinel, *including Earl Nolte's quote; and Nolte family members.*

Martin County's Battery H in WWII

"Coming just two decades after the last great global conflict, the Second World War was the most widespread and deadliest war in history, involving more than thirty countries and resulting in more than fifty million military and civilian deaths (with some estimates as high as eighty-five million dead)," reads information on the war from History.com. "Sparked by Adolf Hitler's invasion of Poland in 1939, the war would drag on for six deadly years until the final Allied defeat of both Nazi Germany and Japan in 1945."

The Martin County contingent of Battery H was mobilized at the Fairmont Armory at 7:30 a.m. on January 6, 1941. It included 153 men and five officers who were assembled and sent to train at Camp Haan, California, ten days later.

In July of 1941, they received orders to move to the state of Washington where the Fourth Army was holding maneuvers. They left Camp Haan by motor convoy for the 1,474-mile journey to Camp Murray, Washington. Upon arrival at Camp Murray, they received orders for Fort Greely, Alaska, located on Kodiak Island. They were among the first troops to arrive at Fort Greely, and their initial mission was to build up Alaska's defense. Battery H remained at Fort Greely until March of 1944 when they were ordered to Fort Bliss, Texas, for reorganization and training for service in Europe.

In November of 1944, Battery H left for England. It was eventually deployed on the mainland of Europe where it took part in the Rhineland and Central Germany Campaigns with the Third Army. In 1945, when the war was over, members of Battery H received replacements which allowed longer-serving personnel to be sent back to the states to be discharged. Some of these soldiers had served for nearly five years from the time they initially left Fairmont.

Sources for this story include history.com/topics/world-war-ii and the Service Record Book of Men and Women in World War II in Martin County *sponsored by the DAV, VFW and American Legion of Fairmont, Minn., page 15.*

POWs in Martin County

When we think of prisoners of war, or POWs, what most likely comes to mind is our soldiers being held in a prisoner-of-war camp in some foreign country. However, Martin County was at one time the site of a POW camp, which provided a fairly colorful picture of local history during the WWII era.

The POW camp was at one time located next to what is now Fairmont Foods along Highway 15 in Fairmont.

POWs were housed in Fairmont in the 4H buildings at the county fairgrounds from early June 1944 through sometime in July of that year. The fairgrounds were located where the Five Lakes Centre now stands.

Strict orders from the U.S. Government were given regarding how the POWs should be treated by local people. It was made clear they were enemies of the United States and that it would be a high crime for any civilian to converse, pass written messages, or receive gifts from them. Anyone giving aid to the enemy would be considered guilty of treason.

Regardless, the June 15, 1944, *Sentinel* stated that "giddy females who have been trying to carry on a flirtation with the Nazis through the fence are also due for summary discipline."

"These prisoners like it here and haven't given us any trouble," said Lieutenant Orff who was in charge of the guards. "But the other day we had to throw two females out who crawled through the fence to get to them."

Soon after the camp was established, the commander was replaced due to improper association with local women, and two enlisted men were returned to Algona, Iowa, for allowing prisoners to sneak out of camp to visit young women and carrying notes between POWs from Fairmont to Algona. In addition, two POWs escaped from the Fairmont camp in July. The Fairmont POW camp was known as Algona Branch Camp Number 2.

The camp closed for a short time in July and August and then was relocated.

A notice sent to the Fairmont newspaper on September 5, 1944, said that, because it was "faced with a critical labor shortage, Fairmont Canning Company and the United States Army have brought in a group of German war prisoners to work in the Fairmont factory."

The group arriving in September included approximately fifty POWs who were part of German Field Marshal Eric Rommel's Africa Korps. Some prisoners were also housed at Interlaken Park in both the cottages and the Interlaken Inn, which had been surrounded by a barbed wire enclosure "to protect the prisoners from predatory females and other wild animals," according to Dean Simmons' book *Swords into Plowshares*. The public was warned to stay away from the compound. The local deputy sheriff also was on duty at the camp to prevent civilian interference.

Most of the POWs were employed by the Fairmont Canning Company and worked in the factory and on the viners in the fields. They were also permitted employment on farms in the area during what was called the "in-between" season at the canning company.

A special barracks was erected on the canning company site for the POWs, and they were allowed twelve hours away from the camp to work. They were required to return at night. Newspaper accounts of that time indicated there were requests from Windom, Storden, Okabena, and Brewster for prisoners to work on farms. Some of the POWs also worked at the Pioneer and DeKalb seed companies. Accounts indicated they were considered very good workers by those in the area who employed their services.

The prisoners were paid seventy cents per hour which was turned over by the canning company to the United States government, and they also received directly ten cents per hour which they could spend on items of their choice. They had access to a camp exchange to purchase these items, such as candy or tobacco.

It was made quite clear that the POWs were used only because there was a labor shortage due to the war and that they would not be used when American labor returned.

Further newspaper accounts indicate that the prisoners appeared quite docile, seemingly glad to be out of the war. They were initially accompanied by several guards when they were moved from one location to another. However, as time passed and they were assigned to individual farms, they were simply entrusted to the farmer hiring them who was in turn responsible for their return to camp.

In addition, they had their own mess hall and cooks, and it was said that their selection of food was quite good. Under no circumstances, however, were they to be allowed leave or liberty.

There were approximately 600 POWs housed in Fairmont between 1944 and 1945. They provided what was a rather interesting and unique bit of local history before the camp closed its doors in December of 1945.

The Cooties Are Coming

"Fairmont to host Cootie Convention," read a headline in the April 5, 1984, edition of the *Sentinel*. That would probably get the attention of more than a few people.

The term cootie most likely brings to mind something rather "lousy" and unpleasant. However, the term also can be a reference to a non-profit veterans service organization known as the Military Order of the Cootie of the United States. According to the Veterans of Foreign Wars, membership in the MOC is comprised of officers and leadership of the VFW and comes with recognition of outstanding service to the VFW and its programs.

Cooties greeting one another in Fairmont

Founded in New York City on September 17, 1920, MOC is based on the principles of good humor and fun. Over the past ninety-five years, the Cooties have provided social and entertainment programs to members of the VFW as an ancillary unit within the organization. Since 1923, their first year as a part of the VFW, the Cooties have worked hard to further the aims of the VFW while adding to it the frivolity, known as military humor, to offset the serious work of their parent organization.

What would ultimately become known as the VFW National Home for Children, a sprawling campus of homes located in Eaton Rapids, Michigan, started out as the brainchild of the MOC. They firmly believe in caring for the widows and children of our Armed Forces.

Consequently, the convention held in Fairmont in 1984 was a noble event dedicated to very positive activities and outcomes. According to the *Sentinel* article, the twenty-eight Fairmont Cooties had spent time visiting the Crippled Children's and Veterans' Hospitals in Sioux Falls, South Dakota. Among those planning to attend the Fairmont convention were from 500 to 1,000 Cooties in addition to the state and national commanders of the Cooties as well as the national Supreme President of the MOC Auxiliary. This was obviously a fairly significant convention at that time.

Martin County Sports

The Boynton Ranch and Dan Patch

The Boynton Ranch was a landmark in Martin County at one time, and it's been said that Dan Patch, the famous harness-racing horse of the early 1900s, had a connection to this ranch.

The Boynton Ranch, located in Section 12 of Waverly Township, was at one time very well known in the Truman area. The ranch, or farm, was perhaps most famous for its race track and its large white barn, which was built around 1903. Apparently, there was no expense spared in building the barn as lumber was shipped from northern Minnesota and a Wisconsin lumber company for its construction.

Its owner in the early 1900s was Carlos N. Boynton of St. Paul, a capitalist who owned 1,200 acres of land in Waverly and Westford Townships. Although Boynton seldom visited the farm, which even included a school, he always insisted on maintaining the property in a respectable manner. He took great pride in his stable of race horses. The ranch was managed by Jack Yaeger and his wife. Other employees included approximately a dozen hired hands and "Cap" Nelson, the trainer who provided a daily workout for the race horses on the one-mile track.

"Back in 1913, the ranch was probably the largest piece of land under single ownership and management outside of the Dakotas and Montana. At least it had that reputation ever since 'Muletown,' near Sherburn, faded from the picture," wrote Claude Swanson in a *Sentinel* story.

The Boynton Ranch was devoted primarily to the raising of small grain and corn. All the work was done with horse-drawn equipment, and there was said to be as many as forty workhorses on hand at all times.

Boynton had both race horses and draft horses; however, they were kept in separate locations on the farm. The race track was located just north of the barn. There is conjecture that the great Dan Patch exercised or perhaps even raced at the Boynton Ranch track.

Dan Patch was a record-breaking horse in harness racing, where a jockey rides behind the horse in a sulky. His unofficial record of 1:55 minutes for the mile was set at the Minnesota State Fair racing grounds in 1906. His official record was one-quarter of a second slower. In his lifetime, he earned more than $1 million for his owner, Marion

Savage, who owned property in what is now Savage, Minnesota. Eventually, other horse owners refused to race against Dan Patch. The horse's record was equaled in 1938 but not actually broken until 1960 by Adios Butler.

Although the claim that Dan Patch did actually appear at the track located on the Boynton Ranch can't be corroborated with historical documentation, I believe it happened.

By 1921, 800 acres of the ranch was sold for $200,000, but it was not until 1983 that the barn, which had badly deteriorated, was finally torn down.

The Boynton Ranch was certainly a unique and significant part of the history of the Truman area and Martin County in the early 1900s. The aura of Dan Patch only adds to the mystique of its memory.

Other sources for this story include unidentified county newspaper accounts from 1900–1978.

Big League Baseball Played at Hand's Park

Although it's hard to imagine today, in 1924, a major league baseball team actually scheduled a game in Martin County.

The Brooklyn Robins were in a tight pennant race with the New York Giants. Brooklyn had a record of 92–62 and fell just short of the Giants who won with a record of 93–60.

Brooklyn v. Fairmont 1924

The September 27, 1924, edition of the *Fairmont Daily Sentinel* reported that Major League's Baseball National League runner up, the Brooklyn Robins, were to play a baseball game against Fairmont's baseball team at Hand's Park. The Robins were later re-named the Brooklyn Dodgers.

At the time, Brooklyn featured the National League's most valuable player, Dazzy Vance. He was an all-star pitcher who led the league in wins, strikeouts, complete games pitched and earned run average. Vance spent ten years in the minor leagues before finally breaking into the major leagues at age thirty-one. Vance earned $9,000 for the 1924 season. He was elected to the Baseball Hall of Fame in 1955. In comparison, Justin Verlander of the Detroit Tigers signed a contract in 2017 that gave him an average of $27 million annually for six years.

Several promoters were involved, including J.M. Wolf, Einer Nelson, L.C. Meyer, and Ernest Hand as well as the Fairmont baseball team which had made contact with the Brooklyn team, guaranteeing them $750 to appear. The game was scheduled at Hand's Park on October 7, 1924, while the Brooklyn team was on their anticipated barnstorming tour from September 29 through October 26. The date was initially tentative as they were in a tight pennant race with the Giants, and should they have won, they would play in the World Series rather than at Fairmont, probably not a difficult decision to make.

Subsequent *Sentinel* accounts indicated the event was being advertised in all the Twin Cities and southern Minnesota daily papers and that record attendance was expected. Fairmont's manager Ray Barr had letters from fans fifty miles away requesting tickets be held for them. They expected it to be a sellout before the first pitch was thrown. An October 6 *Sentinel* account stated the game would "tax the capacity of the stands to the limit." The weather forecast was good and tickets were going fast at the Strand Cigar Store in Fairmont.

The Brooklyn team arrived in Fairmont by train the day of the game at 9:40 a.m. from La Crosse, Wisconsin, and checked into the Hotel Fairmont. They spent the remainder of the day before the 2:30 game playing golf or fishing on the Fairmont lakes.

The game was witnessed by 1,200 excited fans at Hand's Park. It was scoreless until the fifth inning when Brooklyn's pitcher hit a home run. The game was very close with Fairmont actually outhitting the big leaguers eight to six. Finally, the future hall of famer Dazzy Vance came in to pitch the ninth inning, much to the delight of the local fans who were calling for him to get into the game. Vance allowed a hit to Barr before retiring the side. In spite of Fairmont's efforts, the Brooklyn team won the game by a score of 3–1. Incidentally, the only run scored for Fairmont was also by their pitcher, Lee Venemon.

The following day, the October 8, 1924, edition of the *Fairmont Daily Sentinel* had a number of positive quotes from the Brooklyn players, including centerfielder Ed Brown who said, "Your team is the best we have been pitted against since we started on this trip…Not only did they do good work in the field, but they showed up remarkably strong at bat. Fairmont has a team it can well be proud to back."

That venture, although not a financial success, proved to be very popular. The promoters were applauded for their efforts, and it was heralded as an event dearly appreciated by everyone in attendance.

The Brooklyn Dodgers, established in 1883, became the Los Angeles Dodgers upon their move to Los Angeles in 1958. During their years in Brooklyn, they had a number of names and nicknames including the Robins, Superbas, Trolly Dodgers, Bridegrooms, Grooms, Grays, and Atlantics, according to baseball-almanac.com. They were playing under the name Brooklyn Robins in 1924 when they came to Fairmont; however, the paper listed them as the Brooklyn Nationals.

It is truly amazing that a major league baseball team that included a future hall of fame pitcher came to Martin County to play a baseball game at Hand's Park against a local baseball team. What would be the chance of that happening today? One can only imagine what it would be like to have the 2016 World Champion Chicago Cubs come to Fairmont, or the runner up Cleveland Indians? What about the Twins, the Yankees, the Red Sox, or any other major league team? However, in 1924, it actually happened right here in Martin County at Hand's Park!

Fairmont Town Ball

Back in 1930, the Fairmont Cardinals amateur baseball town team played in the Minnesota–Iowa League. Their season was divided into two parts with divisional champions for both the first and second half of the season. Their players and manager were not necessarily just local talent; some came from the surrounding Midwest states as well as from Minneapolis and St. Paul.

The Fairmont team was made up of "Scrub" Anderson, Jack Connolly, Marty O'Neill, Dick Wade, "Lefty" Wienke, Harry Strong, "Poss" Owens, Wally Swanstrom, Eddie Deal, Ronny Golden, and player/manager Elmer Miller. Golden and O'Neill were graduates of St. Paul Central High School, Wienke was also from the Twin Cities, Connolly was a left-handed pitcher from Waseca who joined the team after pitching for Albert Lea, Miller was from Ohio, and Deal was from Jamestown, North Dakota, but apparently lived in Elmore.

Miller had a stint in the major leagues before coming to Fairmont, most notably with the New York Yankees where he played in the same outfield as Babe Ruth and Bob Meusel. Miller batted .267 and appeared in the 1921 World Series against the New York Giants as a lead-off batter, according to baseball-almanac.com. His efforts in the 1921 season were perhaps a bit overshadowed by fellow outfielder Babe Ruth who managed 59 homers while batting .378, although Miller did contribute four home runs. His professional career also included playing for the St. Louis Cardinals and the Boston Red Sox.

After O'Neill's amateur baseball career, he officiated high school and college football games and then went on to become a play-by-play sports broadcaster. He was inducted into the Minnesota Baseball Association's Hall of Fame in 1963 and the Museum of Broadcasting Hall of Fame in 2010.

The "Little World Series" of 1930 pitted the Fairmont Cardinals against the Estherville Eagles. It was comprised of a five-game series that would determine the Minnesota–Iowa League champion. This was to be followed by the Minnesota state amateur baseball tournament. Estherville wouldn't qualify for that as they were an Iowa team, and the Fairmont team had never previously made an effort to go to the tournament as they considered the cost prohibitive.

The Fairmont Cardinals had a less-than-stellar performance in that series. The hitting and pitching of the Eagles, combined with some bad breaks for the Cardinals, were too much as Estherville took the series three games to one, making them the champs.

Nonetheless, the Fairmont team decided to enter the Minnesota State Amateur Baseball Tournament and was slated to play at Lexington Park in St. Paul. The Twin Cities media carried stories on Miller, Golden and O'Neill. Miller was called an old favorite as he was known from his St. Paul Saints days. Golden and O'Neill were also well known as former St. Paul Central High School stand-out athletes.

In the state tournament, the Fairmont Cardinals went up against the Northern Pacific Railroad team for the state championship. Although Northern Pacific managed seventeen hits off of two Fairmont pitchers, it just wasn't enough. The Cardinals heavy-hitting Strong, a former Mankato Blue Sox and Sioux City Stockyards player, coupled with Connolly's pitching and timely hitting proved more than the Northern Pacific Railroaders could handle as the Cardinals prevailed by a score of ten to eight. This win gave them the Minnesota State Tournament Class A title.

The era of those barnstorming, independent, town baseball teams has evolved over the years as has the game of baseball. The likelihood of a former major leaguer managing or playing for a Minnesota town team today is highly improbable. Nevertheless, the lore of baseball's past involving those players, their travels, and their experiences are what make baseball aficionados continue to follow and love the game.

Sources for this story included stories from the Fairmont Daily Sentinel *in 1930, including September 2, 3, 4, 5, 6, 8, 9, 12, 15, 19, 20, and 22;* Fairmont Town Ball *by Peterson and Tomashek; baseball-almanac.com/teamstats/roster.php?y=1921&t=nya; pavekmuseum.org/oneill.html.*

A Sunday Afternoon in Martin County—Many Years Ago

Sunday afternoon entertainment today might consist of watching sporting events on TV, attending a Twins game, golfing, going to a movie, swimming at the aquatic park, shopping at your favorite mall, surfing the internet, or other options too numerous to mention. Many of these options were not available to our Martin County residents seventy-five years ago.

However, the entertainment options of that long ago era were in fact as much, and maybe more, satisfying than the multitude of choices we have at our disposal today. The following is an example of a Sunday afternoon at Hand's Park and the entertainment it provided to county residents of that time.

The year was 1932 and Harry J. Earle, perhaps one of the few black residents of Martin County at that time, was the sports reporter for the *Fairmont Daily Sentinel.* A story in the sports section of the June 10 edition featured an article that the Donaldson All Stars, a noted and skilled black baseball team, would be playing against the St. Cloud Ramblers on the following Sunday afternoon at Hand's Park. Game time was scheduled for 3 p.m. The cost of a ticket was forty cents, and grandstand seating was free.

The 1932 Donaldson All-Stars as they appeared in the June 10, 1932, Sentinel. *John Donaldson is in the top row far left.*

Earle stated in his column, entitled "Sports Notes," that "Friendly enemies is the term we'd apply to Harry Strong, the pilot of the St. Cloud Ramblers, and John Donaldson, manager and star flinger of the Donaldson All-Stars, the two clubs that are slated to tangle at Hand's Park Sunday afternoon at 3 o'clock." The two managers were apparently veterans of numerous diamond battles, and they in turn made a fifty-dollar wager as to the outcome of the upcoming game. The bet came up after the All-Stars won the previous game against the Ramblers in the tenth inning. Apparently many of the fans watching believed that the All-Stars simply became tired of playing and decided to win in the tenth. This did not bode well with the Ramblers and was said to "get Harry Strong's goat."

As there appeared to be no ill will from either team toward the other, the wager suggests a bit of "theatrics" on the part of the teams of that era in an attempt to create additional fan interest in the game. The article further stated that "unlike the wrestling show ballyhoo, the players are not going to run around the field shaking their fists in each other's face and telling the world how good they are." Earle went on to state that "win or lose, there will not be any ill feeling, that's a cinch."

The Donaldson All-Stars were due at Hand's Park following a trip in which they played in Iowa and Garrison, South Dakota.

After the game, the headline read, "Ramblers Lose to Donaldsons." Earle wrote in his coverage of the game, "The Ramblers are having their troubles these days. Last week the city of St. Cloud emphatically refused to own the Ramblers and left them—just plain 'Rambling Orphans,' but they were still happy. Yesterday they came to Hand's Park with blood in their eyes, all set to atone for their defeat of the previous week."

"So sure were they of winning, Harry Strong, the manager, made a little wager and had the check half spent."

The Donaldson All-Stars once again prevailed as Donaldson, manager and pitcher for the All-Stars, held the Ramblers to five singles and a shutout until there were two out in the eighth inning when the Ramblers scored their lone run.

The following Sunday's game featured Elmer Miller's Fairmont Travelers in a game against Donaldson's All-Stars at Hand's Park. And, guess what? In his column in the June 20, 1932, *Fairmont Daily Sentinel,* Earle wrote, "Elmer Miller's peppery bunch of youngsters known as the Fairmont Travelers invaded Hand's Park yesterday afternoon and truly upset the dope pot by returning to the City of Lakes with a 6 to 5 victory over John Donaldson and his All-Stars. To make the win cherished all the more, it was the famous John who took the walloping."

And so it goes. The perception of "good entertainment" evolves from generation to generation. There is little doubt that baseball and Donaldson's All-Stars were enjoyed immensely by county residents in the 1930s!

Earle's coverage also added a great deal to the flavor of the sports section of that era with his ability to inject commentary that in and of itself created entertainment and interest.

Play Ball!

Baseball is affectionately referred to as America's Pastime, but how many of you recall what some might refer to as the "glory days" of baseball right here in Fairmont?

After World War II, from the late 1940s to 1960, baseball might have been called Fairmont's Pastime. The Fairmont Martins semi-pro baseball team was very popular. They played a very good brand of baseball and had about twelve to fifteen players on the team. They played at Martins Park, which was located in the vicinity of the current U.S. Post Office parking lot at Five Lakes Centre, with the 315-foot right field line aiming out toward Willow Street.

The Fairmont Martins were a class AA team and were in Class A during the 1959 and 1960 seasons. They started in what was called the Western Minny League and then joined the more prestigious Southern Minny League in 1955. The Martins were the state champions in 1955 and 1957, and the class A champs in 1959.

The 1956 Fairmont Martins

The ball club was one of the biggest promotions Fairmont had during those years. The team would draw over 25,000 annually, averaging about 1,100 to 1,200 spectators per game. As the oft-quoted Yogi Berra, famed New York Yankee of that era, might have said regarding the attendance for Martins games during that time in local history, "If the people don't want to come out to the ballpark, nobody's going to stop them."

Many of the players at that point in time came to Fairmont by word of mouth, and they came from all over the U.S. Some were attracted by the opportunity it presented. They were actually able to make more money than they did playing for the minor league teams, and they had regular jobs in the community. Many of them stayed here after their playing days, making Fairmont and Martin County their permanent home.

So, who did the Martins have for baseball players? Were they local players, perhaps some former high school baseball stars? Well, not really. Based on information in the *Western Minny 1954 Yearbook,* they appeared to have talent from across the nation. Based on my readings, people I've talked to and my own personal observations as I had a chance to watch some of these games, the Fairmont Martins of the 1950s were a solid baseball club with skilled players and an excited fan base. Their players were professionals coming from all parts of the U.S. while some even sported credentials from the "Big Leagues."

According to a *Sentinel* article from May 11, 1976, building a team was truly big business in those days. "They would run ads in 'The Sporting News,' the big league baseball newspaper, in hopes of gleaning players who might be looking for a nice place to settle down." Sometimes one player would get an offer and bring a couple of his buddies along, which was the case with Don Dahlke. He signed with the Martins in 1955 and convinced his friends and former teammates Harry Pritts and Loyal Bloxam to play for the Martins too. They had previously played minor league baseball in Denver where they played with Baseball Hall of Famer Earl Weaver and against Baseball Hall of Famer Sparky Anderson.

After playing for the Martins, Weaver went on to manage the Baltimore Orioles, winning a World Series title in 1970. Anderson went on to win three World Series titles, two while managing the Cincinnati Reds in 1976 and 1977 and one while managing the Detroit Tigers in 1984.

For Pritts, whose career had taken him all the way up to the big leagues for a brief stint with the Pittsburgh Pirates, it served as an opportunity to continue his career as a star pitcher for the Martins.

Anyone following the Martins teams of that era would surely recall their spunky manager, Jim McNulty, a former Marine who coached the team for nine of their ten years and also played a mean second base. He turned a 13–22 record into Western Minny Pennants in 1953 and 1954 and won the "Little World Series" in 1954.

He was a Brooklyn native who spent much of his time hanging around Ebbets Field and was in the Dodger's chain for years. He truly was "Mr. Baseball" in Fairmont during the Fairmont Martins heyday.

Employment for the players during the off-season was often solved by the community and their efforts to keep the players in Fairmont. Salaries during the season were good; in the case of one Fairmont player, it was $500 per month, and one pitcher was paid $1,000 per month, which was good money during the mid-1950s. However, the pay was only for three months, and of course, that left nine months in which to live, eat, and make mortgage or rent payments.

During the off-season, some of the players worked on city crews, some found jobs on their own, and some enlisted the help of the team's board of directors. Pritts worked for an electric motor business that he later owned, Dahlke became a guidance counselor for the Fairmont Public Schools, Al Thune worked for 3M, Bob Yankovich was a car dealer, Spike Gorham, who managed the team during its first season, worked for Anderson Beverage and stayed in baseball as an umpire.

That era in the major leagues boasted such names as Sandy Koufax, Stan Musial, Ted Williams, Mickey Mantle, Warren Spahn, and Willie Mays. Although the names that will forever be coupled to Fairmont Martins baseball of that time are not necessarily the household names recalled, they will be forever ingrained in Fairmont Martins history. Some of those names include Joe Colasinski who returned to plumbing in Detroit, Emil Restino who settled in Florida, Jim King from the Chicago area, and Hank Workman who became an attorney in Los Angeles. Other names include Herb Banton, Bill Dudding, Don Neuenfeldt, Bloxam, Dick Eaton, Sid Langston, Grady Wilson, Bill Spaeter, Tom Palmer, Tom Idstrom, Myron Hoffman, Hal Snyder, and Dave Ramnes. Another Martin's player, catcher Ken Staples, went on to be a third-string catcher with the Dodgers behind Roy Campanella and was considered by McNulty to be the best player he managed in Fairmont.

That era of baseball in Fairmont has passed, but the memories, as well as some of the players, still remain today. It was a different time and, in many ways, a different sport than today's "contemporary" style of baseball with its designated hitters, middle inning relievers, and closers, not to mention the astronomical salaries. To make reference to another Yogism that might have held true to that time, "The future ain't what it used to be." However, that epoch in baseball history will always be nostalgically remembered as Town Ball in those communities of the Western Minny, the Southern Minny, and other similar leagues throughout the country.

Sources used for this story include the August 31, 1982, Sentinel, *page 2A.*

Some members of the 1954 Martins included:

Jim McNulty, a 5'10", 190-pounder, who played four years in the Brooklyn Dodger organization. The player/manager of the Martins lured many professionals to play in Fairmont and was so effective that, at one time, he was threatened with legal action by minor league baseball to stop recruiting minor league players.

Jim King, played left field, batted and threw left-handed. He came from Waukegan, Illinois, and played with Wichita in the Class A Western League. He batted .363 for the Martins in 1953.

Bruce Frank, from Fairfax, Minnesota, graduated from the University of Minnesota in 1948. In 1954, as a veteran of the league, he was playing in his twelfth season. He batted .287 and drove in thirty-three runs for New Ulm in 1953.

Herb Banton was a pitcher and an outfielder. Born in Scottsville, Virginia, this six-foot, 190-pounder was in his second year in the league with a pitching record of 8–3 while hitting .387. He previously played for Elmira, a Brooklyn farm club, in the Eastern League before coming to Fairmont.

Bob Jaderlund, center field, was twenty-six years old and had six years of professional baseball experience. He hit .328 for Fairmont in 1953 and set the league home run record of twelve. He previously attended Central State Teachers College in Washington.

Grady Wilson from Columbus, Georgia, was thirty-one years old and married. Before coming to Fairmont from Charleston, South Carolina, he played two years of AA baseball and also played with the Pittsburgh Pirates in the National League.

Joe Colasinski was the Martins right-handed batting catcher. He was from Detroit, Michigan, and had three years of professional experience before coming to Fairmont in 1952. He batted .215 with the Martins in 1953.

Irv Burton was a twenty-five-year-old pitcher from Belle Rose, Long Island. He was previously in the New York Giants organization and joined Fairmont after playing with Wilkes Barre, Pennsylvania, where he had a 7–14 record with a seventh place team.

Roland (Red) Malcolm was a right fielder in his fourth year in the league. He was a graduate of Gustavus Adolphus College in St. Peter, Minnesota, where he was also a Little All-American fullback. He batted .288 for the Martins in 1953.

Gerry Orleman played both the outfield and infield. He was twenty-five years old, single, and from Brooklyn, New York. He had six years of experience in professional baseball in both Class A and B in the Brooklyn Dodger organization.

Sources for this sidebar include Town Ball *by Armand Peterson and Tom Tomashek, and the* Western Minny 1954 Handbook.

Yank

Bob Yankovich was from Mason City, Iowa. He was an all-state Iowa high school football player and played baseball at the University of Iowa and Luther College after graduating from Mason City High School.

Bob Yankovich

World War II interrupted his life in 1942. He served in the Army in the 45th Infantry Combat Division and participated in the African Invasion, and the invasions of Sicily, France, Germany, and Austria. In all, his military service took him to sixteen countries.

After his military service, he played baseball for the Denver Bears, which was at that time part of the New York Yankees chain. He was "farmed out" to Quincy, Illinois, of the 3-I league, and played there until 1947.

Yankovich came to Fairmont as a result of Scrub Anderson who played with him at Decorah, Iowa. Anderson informed him of an opening on the Fairmont Martins baseball team.

Yank sold cars for his brother in Mason City during the off-season;

consequently, upon coming to Fairmont in 1948, Yank worked as a used car salesman for Pannkuk Nash. He also worked for Red Mackey TV and Refrigeration.

In the fall of 1949, he decided to go into business for himself and rented a space at the fairgrounds. He had $1,800 in cash, enough to buy one good used car. Yankovich did all the business himself, from trading cars, to bookkeeping, to sales. As time went on, he became successful, and by 1960, he had bought and sold approximately 5,000 cars. He could get almost any make and model of automobile a customer wanted.

Sources for this sidebar included the October 22, 1960, Sentinel.

Jim McNulty

Before the Minnesota Twins, interleague play, and the astronomical salaries of today's professional baseball players, there was something called Town Ball. The Fairmont Martins of the 1950s epitomized the Town Ball era as their "Boys of Summer" built somewhat of a dynasty, winning state championships in 1954, 1955, 1957, and 1959.

Jim McNulty

Their manager through much of the 1950s was a former Brooklyn, New York, native named Jim McNulty. A previous member of the Brooklyn Dodger organization, McNulty, the colorful second baseman and manager, spent thirteen seasons playing a significant role in Minnesota town team baseball.

He arrived in Minnesota in 1948, spending three summers in Fergus Falls and one summer with Estherville in the Iowa State League. From Estherville he went to Fairmont and carved out 197 regular season wins, six pennants, and five playoff championships in the Western Minnesota and Southern Minnesota Leagues, at that time considered the state's two premier leagues.

McNulty's baseball career began on the streets of Brooklyn, New York, playing "sewer-to-sewer ball," a form of stickball. He eventually became a baseball star in high school, earning all-city as well as all-state recognition in soccer. Then he quit school and enlisted in the Marines. While in the military, he participated in the invasion of Iwo Jima.

McNulty played on a Marine divisional team where he met Dick Durrell, a Minnesota native who was influential in McNulty's coming to Minnesota.

McNulty wanted to play professional baseball; however, after an unsuccessful tryout with the New York Giants, he decided to enroll at Colgate University. At that same time, the Brooklyn Dodgers offered him a signing bonus of $1,800 to play in their organization. He accepted and thus began his professional career in the Class D Georgia–Florida League while earning a salary of $125 a month plus a couple of dollars daily for meal money.

He had limited success in the minor leagues; consequently, he decided to come to Minnesota in 1948 following a telephone conversation with his Marine friend, Durrell. He was offered a position with the Fergus Falls Red Sox in the North Central Minnesota League. His first game in Elbow Lake was quite a culture shock for the Brooklyn native.

Eventually the North Central Minnesota League collapsed, and McNulty then spent a year managing Estherville of the Iowa State League. The Martins at that time had just finished their first season in the Western Minnesota League with a very disappointing 13-22 record. They contacted McNulty and offered him a contract to become their player/manager for $300 a month. He accepted and additionally was provided a sporting goods sales position in a local store. He also eventually purchased a bar and restaurant he named the Martin's Nest located in the 700 block of North North Avenue. McNulty's life at that time, although not exactly the major leagues he had hoped for, seemed to be sailing along quite smoothly.

McNulty was known as a winner, but his skill in recruiting players was also impressive. He recruited more than two dozen professional players, many with Triple A experience, in addition to several players with major league credentials such as Pittsburgh shortstop Grady Wilson, Hank Workman, and Cleveland outfielder Milt Nielsen. The Martins under McNulty won two Western Minnesota titles before moving to the Southern Minnesota League in 1955. They won the 1955 Southern Minny pennant, playoffs, and Little World Series. They finished second in 1956, they won the 1957 Southern Minnesota title, and in 1958 they won the pennant but lost to Austin in the playoffs. In 1959, they won the Southern Minny pennant again.

By 1960, the quality of competition had diminished, the players were playing for a share of the gate, and the Minnesota Twins would soon become Minnesota's baseball team. It was obvious that things were rapidly changing what was known as town ball.

McNulty moved to the Twin Cities and remained in Minnesota for three more years. However, as a result of financial problems, he returned to Brooklyn where he drove a taxi for a time before establishing a limousine service. He later retired to the Poconos in Pennsylvania. He passed away in 2011.

A number of the Boys of Summer from that golden era of the 1950s Fairmont Martins stayed in Fairmont including Bill Dudding, Don Dahlke, and Harry Pritts. They recall that era and Jim McNulty fondly. Dudding, former Martin's second baseman who eventually moved to Bancroft, Iowa, said, "He was a fun manager to play for and he expected us to win–and we did!" Former Martins pitcher Pritts said, "Jim McNulty was as good a manager as I've ever played for and one of the best competitors ever." Martins shortshop Dahlke said of McNulty, "He was always a players' manager. He took care of his players very well."

The Jim McNulty era had a lasting effect on Fairmont and Martin County. Many of those athletes who came to play for the Martins stayed in Fairmont and Martin County, raised families here, and contributed to the local area in many positive ways.

The primary resource for this article was Town Ball–The Glory Days of Minnesota Amateur Baseball *written by Armand Peterson and Tom Tomashek.*

The Ageless Pitcher

"I ain't ever had a job, I just always played baseball," said Leroy "Satchel" Paige, a man considered the greatest player in the history of the Negro baseball leagues. And play he did for about five decades.

Paige was estimated to have been born in 1906 in Mobile, Alabama. He finally got a chance to play in the big leagues in 1948 when the Cleveland Indians called him up to pitch for them in their run for the American League pennant. The famed New York Yankee slugger Joe Dimaggio praised Paige, calling him "the best and fastest pitcher I've ever faced." Paige rounded out his major league career playing for St. Louis and Kansas City. He was elected to the Baseball Hall of Fame in 1971.

In 1959, the Fairmont Martins had Bill Dudding, Herb Banton, Jim McNulty, Milt Nielsen, Don Dahlke, and other quite accomplished players in their lineup. In July of that year, they played an exhibition game against the Havana Cubans featuring the illustrious Paige as one of their pitchers. Although Paige may have been in the twilight of his career, his appearance continued to attract large crowds whenever he was slated to pitch. Such was the case when he appeared in Martin County.

There was a great deal of publicity leading up to the game. Tickets were available at every drugstore in Fairmont in addition to Fairmont Furniture. Advance ticket prices ranged from $1 for adults and fifty cents for students. Ticket prices increased to $1.50 for adults and seventy-five cents for students. In addition, a sports story in the local newspaper several days in advance of the game featured Paige's picture and a brief history of his memorable career.

About 1,100 local spectators came to watch the game that evening in July in hopes of seeing the renowned Paige pitch. According to the July 14, 1959, *Sentinel* article account of the game, Paige was held out until the fourth inning so that anyone arriving late to the game would still have the chance to see him pitch his two innings. When he came to the mound to face the Martins, the Cubans were trailing one to zero. The first batter he faced, Dudding, was safe on an error. Don Saatzer walked, McNulty grounded out, and Ray Rosenbaum hit a sacrifice fly which brought in a run. Paige got out of the inning without any additional runs being scored.

In the fifth inning, there were two out when Milt Nielsen hit a home run over the right field fence. Following successive singles by Dahlke and Dudding, Jim Saatzer hit a fly ball out to end the inning. The Cubans managed a lone run off Harry Pritts in the eighth inning, ending the scoring at three to one in favor of the Fairmont Martins.

Dahlke later recalled that "after Nielsen hit the home run, Paige jokingly shook his finger at him in saying, 'You shouldn't do that.'"

"He (Paige) thought we were nobody," said McNulty in an August 31, 1982, story in the *Sentinel*, "until Milt Nielsen ripped a three-run homer to beat him. He was making $100 an inning to pitch and walked off the mound and out of the ballpark after that happened." Nielsen had been an outfielder in the Cleveland Indians organization and eventually owned an auto dealership in St. Peter.

It was estimated that Paige made approximately $200 for his brief appearance and that, incidentally, a drove of mosquitoes hovering over him during his stint on the mound was said to have caused him as much concern as the Martins baseball players.

The game of baseball, from the local level to the major leagues, has evolved significantly since the 1950s. The quality of local baseball at that time, and the fact that a player the caliber of Satchel Paige actually pitched in a baseball game in Martin County is certainly noteworthy and worthy of remembering.

Additional information for this story (along with other fascinating facts about Paige's life and career) was found at satchelpaige.com.

Although Underdogs, Raiders Were Decisive Winners

The term March Madness was originally coined in 1939 by Henry V. Porter, a teacher and coach in Manito, Illinois, to capture the spirit of high school basketball state tournaments. The term is actually a registered trademark held jointly by the NCAA for the collegiate level and the Illinois High School Association on the high school level.

In 1970, the Sherburn Raiders, undoubtedly characterized by many as the quintessential underdog and led by Coach Dennis Christofferson, crafted a perfect 18–0 record in the regular season followed by an astonishing 8–0 record in the district, region, and state tournaments. Their state championship is remarkable in that it occurred during a time when it was a single class tournament; only one Minnesota state basketball champion emerged, whether it was a big school or a small school.

The Raiders' starting five included seniors Tom Mulso, Jeff McCarron, and John Tirevold accompanied by sophomores Pete Eiden and Paul Krohn. They started the season by literally annihilating Jackson by a score of 74–38. They continued by beating Butterfield, Mapleton, Truman, Trimont, and Mankato Loyola. They entered the holiday break with a 6–0 record.

Following the Christmas break, the Raiders defeated Madelia 98–65 with Jeff McCarron scoring forty-five points, a new school record previously held by Joe Eiden. They continued their winning ways throughout the regular season; however, they were challenged by Lakefield, having to come back from a ten-point deficit in the second quarter to finally win by thirteen.

Tom Mulso | Jeff McCarron | Pete Eiden | Paul Krohn | John Tirevold

The 1970 Sherburn Raiders State Basketball Champs

The Raiders entered the District V tournament as a number one seed facing Fairmont in their first game. Fairmont, an archrival, had defeated them in district play each of the preceding three years. However, Sherburn handily beat them with a final score of 73–57. They went on to win the district by defeating Delavan and Wells; and in Region II, they defeated Luverne 76–63 and Jackson 48–38, thus earning them a spot in the state tournament in Williams Arena at the University of Minnesota in Minneapolis.

In the first game of the state tournament, the Raiders defeated Melrose 65–54 and then defeated Marshall 71–60 to qualify for the championship game against South St. Paul.

Although decidedly underdogs, the Raiders were agile, could run, and had three players in the 6'5" range. South St. Paul was heavily favored, undoubtedly as a result of their supposed tougher schedule in the metro conferences. In addition, they were rated number one in the state for much of the year.

More than 18,000 fans, including most of Sherburn, packed Williams Arena for the tip-off of the championship game. As the game progressed, Sherburn opened up a thirteen-point lead in the first half. South St. Paul staged a comeback in the second half, but were humbled by the Raiders who took home the trophy with a decisive sixteen-point victory, 78–62. In addition, the Raiders also featured the tournament's leading scorer in Tom Mulso who averaged 27.7 points per game which totaled 83 points for the three games. Ironically, the championship trophy was presented to them by a South St. Paul resident, Governor Harold Levander.

Although the Raiders were undeniably a talented and well-coached team, they also had an intangible of sorts that, to some extent, may have helped them achieve their championship status. That intangible was the character of George Packard, an ardent fan dedicated to the hometown team who also fit the role of the town outcast. According to a Minnesota Public Radio story on the Raiders' season, "Packard liked to play up Sherburn's underdog status by calling them 'the hicks from the sticks.' By the time the team reached the championship game, a tight bond had formed: the small-town basketball team, underdogs in the state tournament. And George Packard, underdog for life," wrote Mark Steil. Packard's analysis of opposing teams and their players seemed to have a grounding effect on the team, keeping them focused. Packard, 67 at that time, passed away in 1983.

The Sherburn Raiders proved their skills by prevailing in 1970, the final year of the single class era dating from 1913–1970. Their victorious season exemplifies the role of the underdog, not only in sports, but also in life. Their accomplishment gives hope and meaning to anyone feeling like an underdog aspiring to be successful in whatever endeavor in life they might contemplate. Their success put the Sherburn Raiders forever in the annals of Minnesota State High School basketball history.

Sources for this story include npr.org/2015/03/15/392764016/five-fun-facts-about-march-madness-fan-culture; the March 23, 1970, Sentinel*; basketball.org/march-madness-history/; Minnesota. Publicradio.org/display/web/2012/03/21/sherburn-high-school-basketball;* A Centennial History of Sherburn, *page 62; MSHSL Boys' Basketball State Tournament 1913–2012; chicagotribune.com/sports/college/ct-flashback-march-madness-spt-0315-20150314-story.html.*

Martin County's Ski Resort

Jackson Hole, Aspen, Squaw Valley, Vail, and even Mount Kato are all popular destinations for winter skiing enthusiasts. Ironically, Martin County at one time entertained the possibility of developing a recreational area for winter sports aficionados. However, a number of obstacles facing the project created a slippery slope that eventually created a blizzard of concerns during the course of this rather short-lived venture.

This local ski resort was named Fair Mount. Its location was to be about two miles east of Fairmont on what was at that time the old Fairmont dump site. In 1975, the Fairmont Park Board appointed a committee to determine the feasibility of constructing a hill that could be used for sledding and skiing on that site. In 1976, the project got the go-ahead. This created a flurry of activity including earth moving machines piling up dirt to form a ski slope slated to be as tall as the incinerator's smoke stack.

The project progressed and the slope was completed and ready in December of 1978. However, several obstacles impeded its progress. The first was the liability the city had if someone got hurt on the site. The second concern involved getting adequate supervisory help to maintain and groom the slope and to oversee the renovated warming house that included a fireplace built to keep skiers and sledders warm. Although other ski slope operators were contacted for assistance, it became crystal clear that their rather frigid responses demonstrated their unwillingness to help. That was likely as a result of being busy at their own facilities in addition to the fact that Fair Mount was no doubt seen as competition for their courses.

The final roadblock encountered by the developers was a result of Old Man Winter. He failed miserably to provide any blizzards, snow storms, snow squalls, or even good old snow flurries. Consequently, with such a meager amount of snow available for their inaugural season, city plows were utilized to truck snow out to the site in an attempt to provide a base for skiing. Eventually, the entire project was found to be impractical by the city council and, with less than a snowball's chance in July of surviving, plans for the Fair Mount ski slope drifted away.

Sources for this story include the January 7, 1984, Sentinel.

Martin County Mysteries and Legends

The Legend of the Sisseton Oak

Legends, or stories that may or may not have happened but have become accepted by most as historical, have made their way into local lore. The following account is based on a story in the April 12, 1895, edition of *The Martin County Sentinel* entitled "Tradition of the Sisseton Singer" and "Legend of the Sisseton Oak" by Major Arthur M. Nelson which describes a legend associated with our local history.

The setting for the legend of the Sisseton Oak, sometimes referred to as the Singing Oak, was described as an ancient oak tree which measured nearly four feet in diameter, having gnarled, decaying, and broken branches. It once stood in the northwest corner of Sylvania Park in Fairmont. The article went on to state that at one time, when the area was wilderness and inhabited by the Sisseton Sioux, there was a famous singer among them. He was known throughout the whole Sioux nation and considered extremely talented in song and poetry and thus greatly admired by the Sioux people. Although his songs frequently ridiculed war and bloodshed, which often incensed the tribal leaders, he still maintained his immense popularity with the people of the Sioux nation.

One August evening, as the legend portrays, the Sisseton warriors returned from an expedition with but one captive, a Caucasian girl about three years of age. The Sisseton Singer befriended the child, and they soon became very attached to each other.

All was well for a time, as the child was seemingly happy and the Singer's songs delighted the many listeners, some of whom referred to the little girl as "the little child of the pale moon—a star dropped down into the Sisseton Village."

Later, a fatal epidemic, likely smallpox, appeared in the tribe. As a result, a council of the wise men was called regarding the outbreak. It was their unanimous decision that the Great Spirit was displeased with them due to the presence of the white child in the tribe. Therefore, in order to regain the approval of the Great Spirit, they believed the child must be put to death. The day was set for the sacrifice, and runners were sent to inform the villages along the lakes.

The news was initially met with jubilation among all with the exception of the Sisseton Singer. He went to all the villages pleading for the life of the young white child through his songs. His message carried in song so influenced the people that they soon openly condemned the action to be taken by the wise men of the tribe. This in turn so enraged the tribal leaders that they met once again and, as a result of the singer's actions, condemned the singer to die with the child the following evening.

The subsequent evening, the child was bound to the singer, and they were led to the large oak tree in what would later become Sylvania Park. They were fastened to a large limb that extended out over the lake and dry fire wood was placed beneath them and ignited. What happened next, according to the legend, is that the singer met a heroic death by continuing his song above the hiss and crackle of the fire, telling of war and bloodshed as being hateful to the Great Spirit and telling of coming peace among all tribes when violence and torture would be unknown. The singer's tragic death and words of his song so influenced the people that from that time on, they no longer engaged in war and massacre. Nelson wrote, "And it is a matter of history that at the time of the great Sioux uprising in '62 the Sissetons under their aged chief, Standing Buffalo, were the only ones that remained passive and did not make war on the whites."

The remains of the two victims were gathered and buried in the sand near the water's edge of Sylvania Park. The Sioux believed that when standing at the foot of this oak tree at dusk, the voice of the singer and the cries of the child could be heard. As a result of this, they moved their village north to Buffalo Lake.

The white trappers and hunters of that time also believed the legend and avoided the area, and others unaware of the history of the event claim to have heard the voice of a man singing and a child sobbing. A historical marker at the entrance of Sylvania Park quotes Major Arthur M. Nelson as he reflected on visiting the site, "I am free to admit that a feeling of indescribable dread, if not fear, crept over me when there came in my ears much more distinctly than ever before a man wildly singing, mingled with the agonizing cries of a child." Nelson said he came away believing that there is much in life and beyond that natural causes cannot explain.

The oak tree, which no longer stands, was mysteriously destroyed by fire in June of

1908. Nelson's article states that evidence would seem to indicate that it was struck by lightning or that perhaps it had been smoldering at its heart ever since the cremation of the singer. An engraved marker on field stone is located in the northwest section of Sylvania Park identifying the location of the Singing Oak tree. This local legend lives on in. Is it real, or merely a fictional account of history? Perhaps your decision can be reached by visiting the site in the northwest corner of the park at dusk.

Where's the Mayor?

The world of politics never seems to be lacking for interesting, and sometimes controversial, happenings whether locally, or at the state or national level. This appears to have also been true in the past.

The year was 1905, and Mr. William W. Ward was the newly-elected mayor of Fairmont. The April 7, 1905, *Martin County Sentinel* stated that "Mr. Ward is a natural-born diplomat, enterprising and up to date and will make Fairmont a first class mayor." He was reelected in April of 1907.

Mayor Billy Ward

Ward was the third mayor of Fairmont after it became a city. Known as Billy to his friends, Ward came to Fairmont in about 1900 from Peoria. He worked for a short time with his uncle, Thomas Gleason, in the saloon business before opening one of his own. He also partnered with H.C. Keck in the drainage business, owned a plumbing business, and was one of the organizers of the Fairmont Telephone Company, serving as both president and manager. He was apparently quite an entrepreneur.

The October 18, 1907, headline of the *Martin County Sentinel* announced "Mayor Ward Disappears." The article said Ward had left Fairmont about six weeks prior and hadn't been seen since September 30 in St. Paul.

Newspaper accounts indicate that Mrs. Ward soon began taking active steps to locate her husband. She initiated a search through her attorneys. A flyer was sent to law enforcement agencies relating what little was known about Ward's disappearance and included pertinent information like his appearance, such as height, weight, a smooth shaven face with a "florid complexion." The printed circular went on to say Ward had been expected to leave Fairmont on official business and that he was "somewhat involved financially, but not enough to warrant his leaving for parts unknown, as most of his creditors were secured and his unpaid bills were few and in small amounts."

Further reports stated that "there has been nothing dishonorable in his business transactions."

Apparently, Ward left for St. Paul in early September on business and was last seen by a Fairmont resident there at the end of that month. Many speculated he had met with foul play; some thought that he had committed suicide. Others suggested that he had quietly left rather than face the certainty of business failure.

In any event, Fairmont was without a mayor. The city council was at work attempting to find a viable solution as the public was becoming concerned that there was no mayor of Fairmont, and the city charter of that time provided that vacancies shall be filled whenever they occur.

Three months later, the January 17, 1908, *Martin County Sentinel* reported that Billy Ward had been spotted in Tacoma, Washington, by a Fairmont resident. In addition, other reported sightings of Ward were in Peoria, Illinois; Indiana; Des Moines; Chicago; Texas; Seattle; and Alaska.

The editor of the *Sentinel* reportedly received a letter from J.R. Dalton, referred to as a reliable man formerly of Martin County, stating that a Mr. William Hartley, another reliable man also formerly of Martin County, had spoken to Mr. Ward. He said that the ex-mayor had just come from San Francisco and was on his way to Tacoma. Either Ward did a considerable amount of traveling or he had a number of doubles.

At last, the January 31, 1908, *Martin County Sentinel* read, "Lost Mayor Is Located!"

Mrs. Ward had finally received a letter from her missing husband. In his letter, he wrote that he left St. Paul for San Francisco and that he became sick and grew worse along the way. He said he lay sick in Oakland for two weeks. He then spent a short time in San Francisco and later went to Portland to visit an old friend for a couple of weeks. After that, his journey led him to Seattle, his location at the time he sent the letter to his wife.

Ward apparently gave no reason for his disappearance except that he was "all in financially, and saw no hope of bettering himself here." The article speculated that he would eventually send for his wife and family to come west to live.

Ward, the third mayor of Fairmont, was considered as being one of the "good fellows" of early Fairmont. He ultimately settled in Santa Ana, California, and ran a cigar store. He passed away at age 65 in February 1932.

The Tale of the Disappearing Pastor

Disappearances seem to make headlines and talking points in today's news media. This was also true in the past. After William Ward disappeared in 1907, a Fairmont pastor mysteriously turned up among the missing in 1914. The following is based on a series of articles from the *Fairmont Sentinel* dated January 12 through February 16, 1915.

What was referred to at that time as a "baffling mystery" took place in mid-December of 1914. It captured the public's attention, as well as the attention of the national media. The disappearance was of twenty-eight year old W.R. Burton, pastor of a local church, who was married and the father of a four-year old boy. On December 15, 1914, he was said to have boarded an eastbound Milwaukee train to preach at a funeral in Austin. Upon establishing the fact that he never arrived in Austin, there ensued wild speculation and gossip, including scandalous stories, as to his disappearance and whereabouts.

Ten days after his disappearance, Burton's wife received a letter from him stating that he was "fully aware of his condition, and that he would seek relief in a sanitarium, the location of which he did not disclose." It was also later discovered that, prior to his disappearance, he had been taking treatments for a "nervous condition" that he was fearful of, and that he had a mania in which he would purchase anything he saw without any regard or concern as to how he would pay for the purchases.

The next communication from the missing pastor came in January of 1915 from a New York hospital in the form of a telegram. It read, "At New York Hospital. Here since Jan. 10. Was picked up unconscious in street. Remember nothing since Dec. 15th. Severe pains in head then. Don't know where I have been."

Adding to the mystery, a New York newspaper printed a story about how Burton had, while suffering from amnesia, enlisted as a musician in the U.S. Navy under the name of Richard Hudd at Key West, Florida, on December 26, 1914. The newspaper account further stated that he had been transferred to the Navy Yard in Brooklyn and had been living at the YMCA since January 2, 1915. This account went on to describe Burton's collapse after which he was hospitalized.

The article stated that on January 10, a man in the afternoon throng of Fifth Avenue onlookers clapped his hands to his head, uttered a cry, and collapsed on the sidewalk of Forty-second Street. After being taken to the hospital, unconscious, his identification revealed that he was Richard Hudd, a musician with the U.S. Navy, and that he was waiting for a uniform and assignment to a ship's band.

In fact, the name Richard Hudd was actually his given name; however, he had adopted the name of Burton from his stepfather, who was his mother's second husband. In addition, the *New York Times* sent a telegram to the Fairmont postmaster requesting information about Burton. It read, "Rev. Walter R. Burton found here with memory gone, enlisted in Navy. Please wire at once at our expense the story of his disappearance."

When the unconscious Mr. Hudd, a.k.a. Pastor Burton, opened his eyes, he said: "Where am I, why am I here, and what happened?" Burton had no idea as to how he had ended up in New York. His mind had apparently been a blank from the time he left Fairmont, traveled across the United States, and enlisted in the Navy.

Dr. Ray M. Jones, a Fairmont osteopath who had previously treated Burton, said in the January 12, 1915, edition of the *Fairmont Daily Sentinel,* "The medical term for his case is circular insanity with mixed forms. There are some interesting facts to be noted in connection with these symptoms and characterizations as applied to the case of Rev. Burton. You will note that the disease is most prevalent among women. I should say that Mr. Burton is one of the most effeminate men I have ever known. While he is an athlete, yet he is not of the physically strong construction usually attributed to athletes and his temperament is decidedly feminine." So much for patient privacy in 1915.

After eventually obtaining a discharge from the Navy, which took several weeks, he encountered more problems in that he was then unable to locate his wife. She apparently had gone to the home of a sister in Boise, Idaho, following his disappearance. She was later found to be at the home of another relative. Finally, Burton returned to Fairmont, was reunited with his family, and his congregation was very supportive in unanimously asking him to come back to serve as pastor at his church. He continued his ministerial duties until the fall of 1915 when he and his family left for Idaho, presumably on a vacation to visit his wife's family. However, while in Idaho, he resigned from his church in Fairmont, never to return.

Burton's disappearance was given national publicity to some extent, and his medical condition attracted the attention of some of the nation's most highly respected physicians and surgeons of that era. He was never able to fully explain how he traveled from Fairmont to Key West via Kansas City and then to New York as he had only $8 to $10 in his pocket when he left home, and a mere $1.33 in his pocket when found on the streets of New York.

As to why he resigned from the church, conjecture was that he could no longer take the scrutiny, stares, and curious questions from local citizens, even though he wrote an account of his experience for the *Sentinel* that took almost a full page of space. In addition, his story was carried by a Chicago newspaper. He was apparently tired of explaining and felt it better to go somewhere else and get a fresh start.

So ends the mystery of the disappearing pastor, in some ways quite similar to the disappearing Fairmont mayor of 1905. Both instances were somewhat puzzling, both attracted a degree of national attention, and both were, to some extent, unexplainable.

One could only speculate as to the attention and the media coverage these two mysterious events from the past would attract in today's world of around-the-clock news channels and the internet.

Sources for this story include the Daily Sentinel *Martin County Centennial edition, July 19, 1958, page 8.*

Shrouded in Mystery: The Museum Table

When entering the research library in the Pioneer Museum in Fairmont, one of the first things to catch your attention will no doubt be the large table located in the north central part of the room. It seats twelve, is very ornate, and measures twelve feet in length and forty-two inches wide. So, what's the history of that table?

Based on an article about the table written by Claude Swanson in the February 1, 1967, edition of *The Sentinel*, it has a very lengthy and interesting history. According to Swanson, it was donated to the city during the tenure of Mayor W.L. Nicholas and served as a table for the Fairmont City Council for decades. Some of the mayors presiding over the table included John Gorman, E.J. "Tech" Edwards, Julius Simon, Frank E. Wade, Harold E. Wade, Nicholas, K.M. Brown, John Brandenhoff, and

Dr. W.L. Webb. Those names in and of themselves are significantly interwoven into the fabric of our local history.

The detailed, white oak table now resides in the Pioneer Museum.

In addition, a number of justices of the peace used the table during and shortly after World War I, including J.A. Everett, E.A. Luedtke, Arthur M. Nelson, and Nicholas.

But where did the table come from? According to Swanson, it was in the possession of Harry Serle, former Fairmont Justice of the Peace, fire chief, and mayor. But, how did it come into Serle's possession?

In a February 11, 1967 segment of "The Lake Breezes Whisper . . . ." in *The Sentinel*, Swanson quotes Ralph Parker, a clerk in the Fairmont Post Office in the early 1900s, regarding its origin. Parker stated, "A Chicagoan, an actor and politician of sorts, told Rudy Henry about the table...I met the man–his name was O'Hara–several times in the company of Henry. He is the one who told Henry about the table, and Henry told Serle, who 'just couldn't rest' until he obtained possession of it. What Serle paid for the table, whether or not he saw it before it was shipped from Chicago, I can't recall. But, this I do remember: O'Hara told Serle that the table had been used by the city council in Chicago for many years, until the council became too big for the table to accommodate all the members around it." Henry was a Fairmont saloon owner in the early 1900s.

Swanson estimated the table was well over 100 years old, perhaps dating back to the Iroquois Theater fire or the time when Mrs. O'Leary's cow kicked over the lantern causing the fire that all but destroyed Chicago. Additionally, he stated, it was handmade, was priceless, and that if displayed in a Chicago museum, it would attract thousands of visitors.

Although Swanson's analysis can well be considered subjective in nature, whether it is completely accurate or not, it certainly adds to the mystique surrounding the history of the table. Nonetheless, Swanson's accounts regarding the table reflect the most authentic documentation available.

The table was acquired by the Martin County Historical Society from the city of Fairmont in 1996 after being used in the office of the city clerk. It now serves as a meeting table for the Martin County Historical Society Board of Directors, individuals conducting research, and any other groups needing a table of that size for a meeting in the museum.

KKK in Martin County

Martin County's lush farmland, well-kept communities, and law-abiding citizens were at one time home to some 3,000 Ku Klux Klan members. According to newspaper accounts, the Ku Klux Klan invaded Fairmont and Martin County in the 1920s with memberships selling for $10 each.

An article written by Claude Swanson that appeared in the October 23, 1965, *Sentinel* regarding the Klan states that "its emergence into the community in the 1920s was not heralded by brass bands, or advance advertising. It came silently."

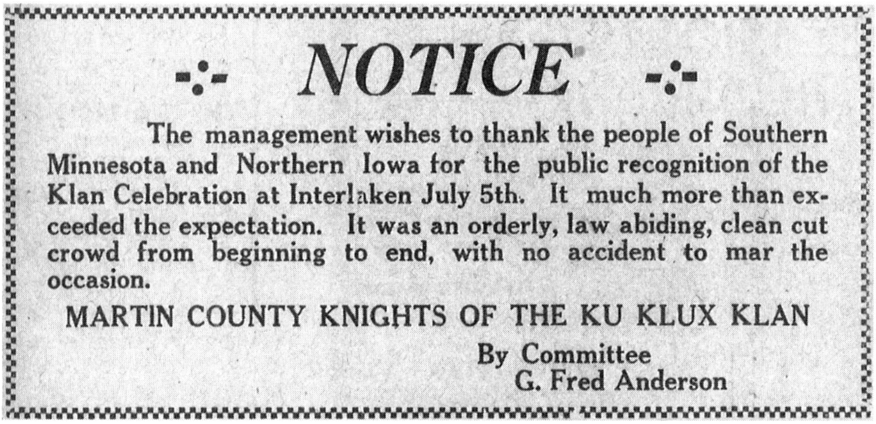

NOTICE

The management wishes to thank the people of Southern Minnesota and Northern Iowa for the public recognition of the Klan Celebration at Interlaken July 5th. It much more than exceeded the expectation. It was an orderly, law abiding, clean cut crowd from beginning to end, with no accident to mar the occasion.

MARTIN COUNTY KNIGHTS OF THE KU KLUX KLAN

By Committee
G. Fred Anderson

Apparently, it wasn't until the Klan had 70 carefully chosen members in the city of Fairmont that anyone else even suspected it was here. Although its presence gradually became known, its membership remained very secretive. Many guesses as to who actually belonged were apparently quite inaccurate.

The *Sentinel* article further stated that "at the peak of power, the Klan membership in Martin County stood at more than 3,000 with a klavern (meeting place) and a King Kleagle (head klansman) of its own." The King Kleagle was at one point provided a voluntary token of appreciation by the local membership due to what they considered his outstanding Americanism and leadership. This "token" happened to be a new automobile.

The Klan membership was originally confined to what they considered to be the "cream" of local citizens, as only those individuals thought to be reputable and trustworthy were given the opportunity to join. There was a membership fee plus an additional charge of $5 for the ceremonial robe. The local organization also included a women's auxiliary which had a membership that numbered in the hundreds.

Their meetings were often held in the country, frequently in a cow pasture, where candidates for membership were sworn in as new Klansmen before a flaming cross. The meetings were apparently always held at night. In addition, no one knew of the exact meeting time or location until a few minutes prior to the meeting, when the time and location was finally revealed. Armed "Kluxers" patrolled the meeting sites and challenged anyone nearing the meeting location. When membership reached about 300, the organization began to bring in speakers from the outside for their public meetings.

A June 29, 1923, *Sentinel* article read "Ku Kluxers Here." The article elaborated on the fact that "Twilight" Orn, "thinker, orator, man, a happy combination," would be giving a free lecture on the courthouse lawn to understand "the most powerful, secret, nonpolitical, militant, Christian organization the world has ever known." Another account read "100 at Ku Klux Klan Gathering Six Miles West," as evidenced by an individual out for a ride who noticed flashlights and white robes. County newspapers also reported numerous Klan happenings at that time.

Moving forward to 1924, a newspaper article entitled "15,000 Pack Fair Grounds for Klan Meet," stating that 600 candidates from three counties were initiated at the public "Klonklave."

The *Truman Tribune* also published an article referring to this Klan meeting at the Fairgrounds. It spoke of a Klan band from Sheldon, Iowa, several floats, and that few Martin County Klansmen were seen in the parade as it's a policy of the organization to keep the membership secret. The ceremonies that followed involved fiery crosses formed by electric lights, speakers, and the initiation of an estimated 300 to 600 new Klan members. At the conclusion of the initiation, various fireworks were set off, one forming a fiery cross.

In 1926, the July 6 headline of the *Fairmont Daily Sentinel* proclaimed "66,000 Celebrate in County, 1 Accident." This involved a three-day county celebration of our nation's sesquicentennial, the largest crowd ever assembled to date in Fairmont at one time.

While the public event was held at Interlaken, it was said the "Kluxers" attending began entering early in the day. The crowd was estimated to be from 20,000 to 25,000 people, of which half were thought to be Klan members. They apparently took an active part in the festivities.

The Klan appeared to be rather well-organized and quite powerful locally, as it was said that at one point they elected both a mayor and city council in Fairmont. Its membership continued to grow for about a year.

Also in 1926, the *Fairmont Sentinel* did a series of four articles with an individual calling himself the Nighthawk. The Nighthawk provided the newspaper with a confidential account of his experiences from the time he originally joined the Klan until that point at which he became disillusioned and decided to leave the organization.

The Nighthawk stated that it began for him in the summer of 1923. He went on to say that getting into the Klan was considered quite an accomplishment and that only the "best men" belonged. The campaign for new members was waged secretly, only cash was accepted for membership, and their oath, taken in a cow pasture, in part said "… to disobey means dishonor and death." He found that to be a good "Kluxer," you also had to be a good liar, finding that he eventually started to believe his own lies.

The Nighthawk's account indicated that the first few weeks were happy as he was one of the chosen few. At that time, the membership was less than 100 and included lawyers, doctors, preachers, and business leaders. They were referred to as the "flowers" of the male population.

However, as reported by the Nighthawk, this vexing organization seemed to be taking a turn for the worse. He was surprised that one candidate for membership was widely known as a swindler. He was further perplexed by the fact that bootleggers, women chasers, and pool hall bums had now infiltrated the membership. In addition, the Kleagle was driving a new car thought to be partly financed by his forty percent take of the $10 membership dues.

It seemed the organization had become less selective and had begun to accept anyone with the membership fee. This apparently led to what Klan members referred to at the time as "crooks, bootleggers, and renegades" joining the organization. It seems that this was a factor which led to the demise of the local organization.

In general, it was felt that the local members of the Klan were misinformed and misled by claims about the Klan made to them by Klansmen. Eventually, after a number of southern orators were summoned to this area to preach hate and vengeance, the local membership became quite concerned.

Although originally motivated by what the locals considered to be good intentions, they soon became fearful of involvement in an organization of this nature and quickly relinquished their memberships.

In a short time, the KKK in Martin County was a thing of the past. The King Kleagle returned to Minneapolis with his new automobile, and he was never heard from again. Local citizens were said to feel that he got out just in time.

It Was a "Doggone" Miraculous Tale!

We've all seen those movies and TV programs about dogs and their heroic deeds: *Lassie, Old Yeller, Rin Tin Tin, Benji, 101 Dalmations,* and *White Fang,* to name but a few.

They all seem to relate the intuitive nature of what has often been characterized as man's best friend. Their roles might include that of being the protector of their master, the diligent watchdog, the crime solver, or merely the "davenport terrier" serving as a faithful companion around the house. It would seem like these animal escapades only happen in the movies. However, back in 1938, a Truman dog named Jiggs provided its owners with a Hollywood-like adventure!

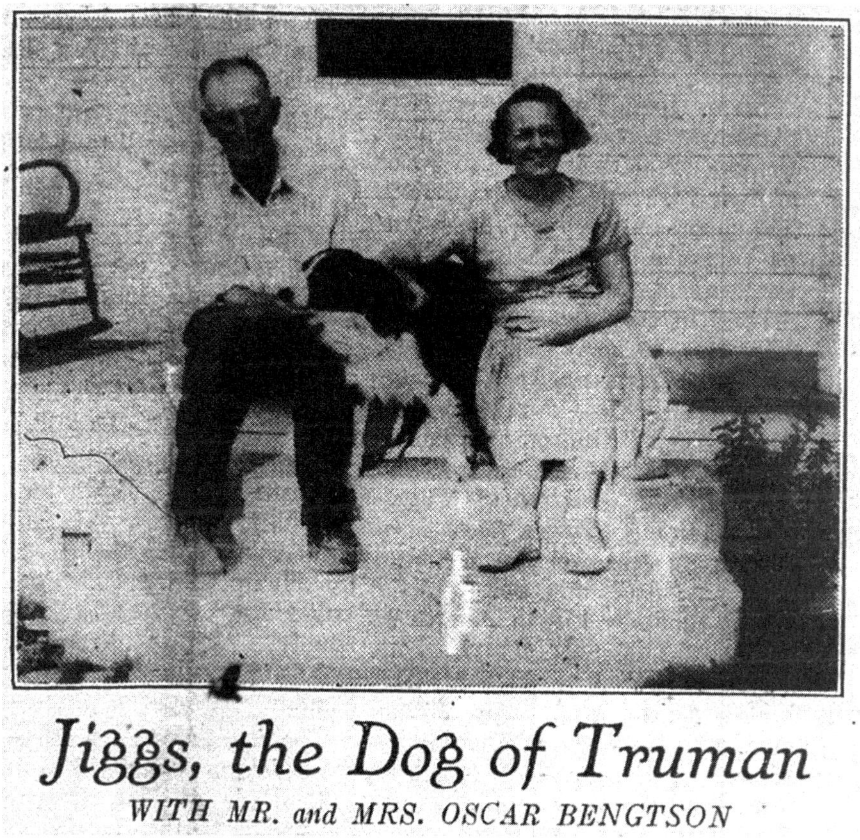

A story on Jiggs' journey appeared in the October 27, 1938, Truman Tribune

Based on stories in the *Truman Tribune* and the *Fairmont Daily Sentinel* editions from 1938, it all started back in 1935 when Mr. and Mrs. Oscar Bengston of Truman boarded a train to move to California. They decided that Jiggs, their pet Shepherd and St. Bernard mix, would be better served by staying behind with a friend since they were unsure at the time as to where they might settle and were concerned that the dog might not be welcome. Consequently, Jiggs did not make the trip to California with the Bengstons.

Although the intentions of both the former and the new owner were in the best interests of Jiggs, it soon became obvious that Jiggs wasn't happy with the arrangement.

He spent days moping around the house, scarcely moving, and appearing forlorn. He had never before been left this long by his owners and was constantly watching for their return to no avail. As a result, Jiggs decided in his canine mind to take matters into his own paws. About a month after the Bengstons left, Jiggs mysteriously disappeared.

Fast forward three years to 1938, since we really have no record of those three years in view of the fact that Jiggs apparently did not keep a diary. According to the *Santa Ana Register*, now the *Orange County Register*, "On the morning of September 6, footsore and weary, he dragged himself to the door of the Bengston home here, 2,000 miles and nearly three years from the starting point. He was flea-bitten and his toenails were worn to the quick. But he was happy. His quest was over." Jiggs had finally arrived at the Bengston's home at 128 South Vine Street in Anaheim, California, albeit very hungry and tired. After having his ravenous appetite finally satisfied, Jiggs was so exhausted that he slept for the ensuing three days.

However, the Bengstons weren't so easily convinced it was Jiggs. They at first actually refused to believe that it was their dog and, in fact, tried to persuade themselves that this was really not Jiggs. After a month had passed that involved the exchange of photos and the examination of peculiar markings, they finally satisfied themselves that the dog that came to their door in California was in fact their long-lost dog. What eventually proved to be the most convincing piece of evidence was a scar on his nose from a puppyhood indiscretion back in Truman. Temptation caused him to chase a cat that resulted in his ending up on the wrong end of the cat's claws which left an indisputable scar on his nose.

After what must have been a truly remarkable and amazing journey lasting nearly three years, Jiggs had finally arrived in California at the home of his Truman family. What could have easily culminated as a disastrous pilgrimage ended as both a truly happy tale and a happy tail. One can only speculate as to the exciting adventures Jiggs may have encountered on his harrowing expedition.

Could this seemingly impossible journey have really taken place? The Bengstons, and probably many others, were undoubtedly more than a little skeptical. Nevertheless, at least three newspapers carried the story in 1938, and the Bengstons finally appeared absolutely convinced. Was it a factual account or merely an embellished attempt at a human interest story meant to appeal to dog lovers? You be the judge.

The Noteworthy of Martin County

A Salty Martin County Pioneer known as "Colonel"

Throughout the course of Martin County's early history, there were many individuals whose contributions proved significant. As a result, they became quite well known, such as William Budd, Lorraine Swearingen, and Henry Martin. However, there are also those who greatly impacted the development of the county but did not become as well known. One of those lesser recognized individuals was "Colonel" James Andrew Everett, a colorful individual who made his mark on the history of Martin County in his own unique manner.

Colonel and Mrs. Everett

Colonel is noted as a prominent Martin County pioneer; however, little can be found about him in the archives of the Pioneer Museum. What is known of him paints a picture of a decisive, impetuous, radical individual with an adamant devotion to his country.

Everett served in the Civil War, enlisting when he was eighteen years old. His leadership qualities earned him an officer's commission. However, prior to receiving that commission, he had a few bumps along the way. He was promoted to corporal twice, and twice reduced in rank to private. Following that, he was promoted to sergeant, and then reduced in rank again. Then he was promoted again to sergeant, next to first lieutenant, and finally promoted to the rank of captain, all in the short period of three weeks.

Ironically, on the day that he was promoted to captain, during the battle that took place at Charleston, West Virginia, he suffered wounds that would haunt him for the rest of his life. How he got his nickname Colonel was not documented in his military records. Those experiences appear to reflect his character and how it may have shaped his future endeavors.

Everett arrived in Martin County in 1869 and farmed in Manyaska Township. He was instrumental in organizing the township and also served on the town board as clerk. He later moved to Fairmont and was involved in a number of activities, including various civic duties. At one time, he was elected justice of the peace, served as city treasurer of Fairmont, was commander of the Phil Kearny Post of the GAR, and held the position of clerk of the Fairmont School Board. Beyond his local service, he was elected to one term in the Minnesota Legislature, served as state commander of the GAR in 1911, and was on the board of trustees of the Minnesota State Soldiers Home. In addition to these accomplishments, he was appointed deputy oil inspector for the county by the governor of Minnesota. Everett also served as the newspaper editor for the *Fairmont News* for eight years.

Everett was described as salty, staunch, uncompromising, never on the fence, radical, intense, loyal and patriotic. He was depicted as one of those "characters" you will never forget. His obituary in the March 19, 1919, edition of the *Sentinel* concluded that, as a result of his "outspoken radicalism, Mr. Everett never occupied public positions commensurate with his abilities but he nevertheless performed important service by his public utterances." In spite of his uncompromising nature, his obituary further stated that as a result of those previously mentioned traits, he would nevertheless be missed by all of Fairmont and Martin County.

While Colonel J.A. Everett's legacy does not take up a great deal of space in the archives of the Pioneer Museum, it is apparent he made an impact on Martin County. Consequently, his efforts were appreciated, and his salty persona undoubtedly provided for some lively discussions among Martin County residents during that era of our local history.

Sources for this story include Everett's obituary in the March 19, 1919, Fairmont Sentinel, *and the* Sentinel's *Martin County Centennial edition, 1858–1958, page 6.*

The Forgotten County Commissioner

There are many ways in which to be a public servant, county commissioners being but one example. Sometimes public servants are remembered for their accomplishments, and sometimes they are remembered for their lack of accomplishments. The following is an account of one highly respected county commissioner who served Martin County during the early 1900s while the current courthouse was being built. Ironically, as a result of his integrity, honesty, and capabilities, he might be considered the forgotten county commissioner.

Fred Miller was born in Hanover, Germany, in 1851. When he came to America, he lived in the La Crosse, Wisconsin, area and later moved to St. Louis to learn the bricklaying and stone mason trade.

Fred Miller, the forgotten commissioner

While in St. Louis, he married Pauline Rettke. They moved to Fairmont to farm in the early fall of 1885. They purchased land from Pauline's brother, Carl Rettke, for $5.50 per acre. Fred and Pauline had 13 children. While the children helped with the farm work, the men would drive to Fairmont every day by buggy and build homes and other buildings.

Miller began his first term as a commissioner of Martin County in January of 1905. For this duty, he received a salary of $142 annually. During his term, the commissioners made the decision to condemn the courthouse and seek bids for a new courthouse. On December 12, 1905, bids for the new building were accepted. Because Miller was acknowledged as being one of the best builders and contractors in the area, he was appointed as superintendent of construction for the new facility and was to receive $4 per day while employed in this capacity.

Although the construction of the courthouse was progressing favorably, Miller handed in his resignation at the March 29, 1906, meeting of the county commissioners. Why resign when everything seemed to be progressing smoothly? Apparently, at some point following Miller's appointed term as superintendent of construction, it was determined that, according to state statute, no county commissioner could be appointed by the board to any position of trust or be a party to any contract made by the board. At the time of Miller's appointment, neither the board nor Miller was aware of that state statute, and as soon as Miller learned of the law, he tendered his resignation as county commissioner.

The board regretfully accepted Miller's resignation, considering it a public misfortune that he could not remain a county commissioner while simultaneously acting as superintendent of the project. However, following his resignation, the commissioners reappointed him as superintendent of construction of the new courthouse. He was to receive $5 per day for his services.

Unfortunately, Miller passed away at his home on December 9, 1907, just one week before the dedication of the Martin County courthouse. His unexpected death came as a shock to the county's citizens. As stated in the December 13, 1907, edition of the *Martin County Sentinel* reporting his passing, he was regarded as "one of the most intelligent, honorable, and reliable citizens of Martin County having held many positions of honor and trust in his town and country, and in every instance his good judgement and integrity were to be relied upon."

In the December 18, 1907, edition of the *Martin County Independent*, A.L. Ward paid tribute to Miller. "To Superintendent, Frederick Miller, who gave unsparingly of his time and watched with a scrutinizing eye every piece of material used in its construction, commendation is also due. It is regretted that he did not live to partake in the ceremonies of today. Called by the Supreme Architect to the other land a few days ago, he has left a monument in this edifice, which will exist longer than any marble that can be erected at his grave," Ward said.

As a result of the aforementioned circumstances, Miller's name does not appear in the courthouse as a county commissioner, although his name is inscribed as superintendent of construction of the project.

Fred Miller is but one example of the many rugged individuals who were influential in shaping the early history of Martin County. Did he get the proper credit and recognition for his accomplishments? Probably not, but based upon what appears to have been his intentions, he was no doubt more concerned with doing the right thing in all his endeavors and less concerned with recognition for his accomplishments. Miller and his wife Pauline are buried at Lakeside Cemetery.

A.G. Crooker—Pioneer Jeweler

Albion G. Crooker was a jeweler and watch maker who was born in Stockton, Maine, in 1856. He came to Fairmont when he was nine years old from Cannon Falls with his parents in a covered wagon. His father, Dr. Crooker, had taken a soldier's homestead and was one of the founders of Rutland Township. At that time, the courthouse was the only frame building and Fairmont's population numbered about fifty. There was a log hotel located in what is now Ward's Park. It was later owned by E.M. Hyatt and called the Lakehouse.

Crooker attended school in Fairmont and worked for Colonel C.A. Lounsberry, editor of the *Martin County Atlas*. He taught school in Rolling Green Township and at Handy, now known as Granada. One of Crooker's star students in Granada was Archie Handy. He also spent a year at Carleton College in Northfield, Minnesota, where he witnessed the notorious Jesse James Gang robbing the Northfield Bank.

Crooker studied the jeweler's trade in the east and returned to Fairmont in 1883 and worked for George Chapman. In 1899, Crooker and Frank Canright bought out Chapman and continued in partnership until 1908. Then, Crooker bought out Canright.

A.G. Crooker

He established his jewelry store at 108 North North Avenue, across the street from what is now Dee's Floral. By 1950, he was acclaimed as Fairmont's eldest businessman. When he was in his 80s, he said he had no intention of applying for "old age pension," as he didn't consider himself old enough yet. He also said he didn't think the "guvment" owed him a living! Crooker was known to be kind and generous, and he provided a college education to his eight children.

Although considering retirement by the time he reached ninety-four, he still spent his time shoveling snow from his sidewalk and walking to the store to handle bills and write checks, and to expound on his view of world affairs. He gave his opinion on the U.S. involvement in Korea and the Chinese Communists, and wrote three letters to Joseph Stalin asking him to use his influence to rid the world of war-making equipment of all kinds. Crooker planned to remain active. After all, "Who wants to quit altogether just at 94."

Crooker never owned an automobile, never used liquor, walked to work every day, and had tuberculosis in his 40s and was told he wouldn't last. He was obviously a survivor with a positive attitude.

Sources for this story include Jan Dickinson's compiled research of newspaper articles 1920–1924 at the Pioneer Museum, and undated newspaper articles in the Crooker display at the Pioneer Museum.

Henry Ledebur—A Martin County Pioneer

As was the case for many hardy individuals who settled this region in the 1800s, Henry Ledebur was an immigrant. He came to the U.S. from Germany at the age of 14 in 1871. He at first stayed with relatives in La Crosse, Wisconsin, for two years working as a hired man before moving to Wycoff, Minnesota, where he operated a farm. It was there that he met his future wife, Caroline Niemeyer, a widow with two sons.

Niemeyer had relatives in Martin County, and they encouraged her and her husband to move their family to the Fairmont area, which they did in 1883. They purchased 160 acres of farmland in Section 34 of Fraser Township for $12.50 per acre. The farm was purchased from Edwin Berry, also known as "Elder" Berry because he was an ordained Baptist minister.

Ledebur operated the farm, designated as a Century Farm in 1983, for thirty-three years. The Ledeburs built a ten-room brick home in 1895, the first brick home built in the rural area of Martin County by Welcome. It is presently occupied by Jonathon Meschke, a descendant of Ledebur. In 1915, the Ledeburs moved to Fairmont and, in

1926, they built a home at 409 South Park Street.

Ledebur was one of the organizers of the Citizens National Bank of Fairmont that opened for business in 1918. He served as president of the bank from its inception until it was purchased by Fairmont National Bank in 1931. He also served as treasurer of the Farmers Insurance Company, was an officer of elevators in Fairmont and Welcome, and served on both the school board and the Fraser Township Board. He also was an assessor in Fraser Township at one time. In addition to these many activities, he found time to serve as president and deacon of the Lutheran Church in Welcome and later as treasurer of St. Paul's Lutheran Church in Fairmont as well.

Henry Ledebur

Henry Ledebur was considered an individual of foremost integrity who could always be depended upon to do the right thing. His obituary read, "No one more square ever lived." He was a long-time Martin County resident, a truly civic-minded individual, and a beloved citizen. He passed away on June 21, 1938, at the age of eighty-one and was preceded in death by his wife, Caroline.

The Ledebur legacy has extended its influence to present day Martin County not only to his descendants, but also to the room that the Martin County Genealogy Society occupies in the Pioneer Museum named in honor of the Ledeburs. The Ledebur descendants have made significant financial and volunteer contributions to this endeavor which affords both the Martin County Genealogy Society and the Martin County Historical Society the opportunity to more efficiently and effectively serve its patrons.

Consequently, the impact that a fourteen-year-old immigrant had on Martin County did not end with his death. Rather, his influence, as a result of the numerous contributions of his many descendants, has continued well beyond his death by positively affecting Martin County and its citizens of today and the future.

Ed Smellie Prides Himself on Cleanliness

Ed Smellie is a name that may well evoke smiles, laughter, and perhaps the insinuation of an unpleasant odor. However, his name was perhaps oxymoronic in and of itself, because he was actually a fanatic on cleanliness! So, you may wonder, just who was Ed Smellie?

Smellie came to Martin County as a ten-year-old orphan in 1880. As a homeless, undersized child all alone in the world, his prospects seemed bleak at best. However, a serendipitous encounter with I.G. Swearingen and his wife, Lorraine, proved very beneficial for him as they took him into their farm home in Rutland Township. They treated him as if he was their own child, and he lived with them until he was twenty-one years old.

Ed Smellie

Then, in 1891, he moved to Fairmont. He worked for Rudy Henry in a saloon called Rudy's Place. Henry was a well-respected individual, a "gentleman's gentleman." Henry came to Fairmont from Chicago and was known as a very "dapper gentleman" and appeared to have limitless financial resources. Ironically, although Henry owned a saloon, he did not drink.

Smellie eventually went on his own and opened a billiard hall. According to a 1925 Fairmont telephone directory, it was located at 112 West First Street, currently the location of Agency Tax Service. That first billiard table in Fairmont, an English table measuring six feet by twelve feet, was established to "indulge the tastes of the English Colony, many of whom were addicts to the imperial game of billiards." It was considerably larger than the standard billiard table of today which measures seven feet by three and one-half feet.

Smellie's establishment, a "soft drink" bar, was considered a gentleman's resort with not the slightest complaint ever lodged. In spite of his name, one of his idiosyncrasies was his insistence on cleanliness. He prided himself on an immaculately kept establishment and two of his employees, known as the "Gold Dust twins," were constantly on the job, ensuring that everything was spotless and tidy.

Smellie's presence apparently suggested a hint of royalty in spite of his humble past. As a result, to all his friends, he was known as Duke. In addition, due to his early years in the county and his keen interest in history, he was also considered to be the "final authority" on Martin County history at that time.

Ed Smellie, although his name may suggest something less than pleasant, was in fact noted for his irreproachable attitude towards an absolutely impeccable standard of cleanliness. His establishment proved quite successful. Perhaps, as a result of the influence of caring foster parents and an accomplished business owner giving him a chance in life, he was able to capitalize on those opportunities presented him and to in turn create a positive endeavor for the local society of that era.

Sources for this story include Jan Dickinson's compiled research of newspaper articles, 1920–1924.

The 1898 Klondike Gold Rush and Martin County

The Klondike Gold Rush of the late nineteenth century was a frenzy of activity after gold was discovered along the Klondike River near Dawson City, located in the Yukon

Territory of northwest Canada. This set off the Klondike Stampede which caused the population of the Klondike to approach 40,000 inhabitants and threatened to cause a famine by 1898.

Martin County has a direct connection to the gold rush through Henry Huttemeier who made two trips to Alaska.

Huttemeier was born in Fraser Township on June 18, 1872. His family, being true pioneers, hauled lumber by ox team from Wells to build their home. Huttemeier stayed on the home place in Fraser Township until he was twenty-six years old. Then, in 1898, his Klondike venture to the gold fields began in earnest.

Of course, news of the Klondike gold rush took months to reach Martin County and the Midwest. Soon after learning of the potential riches to the north, the decision was made to participate in the gold rush. Jack Johnson, who had previously staked a claim, was considered the instigator of this proposition. In addition to Johnson, the prospecting party included Huttemeier, M. Johnson, Ed Viesselman, Fred Wolter, Sylvan Tonne, Charles Rademacher, George Noben, Fred Farnholz, and J.B. Colton. They left this area by rail in February of 1898 and didn't arrive in Alaska until early June. Although the boat trip from Seattle to Skagway, Alaska, took only four days, the rest of the trip to the Dawson area was extremely slow, difficult, and dangerous. The dangers of this venture was evidenced by the fact that two members of the group died in their search for gold: Tonne from drowning and Farnholz from pneumonia.

Each member of the prospecting team was required by the government to pack 1,800 pounds of food and equipment for their lengthy trek. They first packed their supplies on sleds when traversing the mountain range. Steps had also been chiseled out to make the mountain climb easier. However, when the spring thaws caught up with them, their journey became more difficult as they actually had to stop and build boats in order to transport their supplies and themselves to the inner region of the Yukon.

Upon arriving at the gold fields, they surprisingly found things quite commercialized. As a result, they sought a new gold mining field of their own. They had prospects of becoming millionaires by staking a claim about 200 miles from the main gold field. Eventually, however, this turned out to be somewhat of a wild goose chase. After nearly eighteen months, their equipment wore out, and the prospecting party was basically left penniless.

Huttemeier returned to Dawson and looked for work. He eventually landed a job with a hunting expedition about 125 miles up the Yukon and Steward rivers. Being quite successful at moose hunting on this expedition, the hunting party returned to Dawson and sold the three moose they shot for forty-six cents a pound. This happened to be the first fresh meat brought to Dawson in nearly eight months. Ironically, they finally realized some gold dust income, albeit from hunting moose and not panning for gold.

Huttemeier explained that during the gold rush, gold mines were bought, sold, and traded freely. However, he said the original owners usually retained half interest in the gold rights. He purchased a mine, and it did prove to be rich. However, after ten months of work and finding the other owner quite uncooperative, he sold his one-sixth interest for $10,000.

During his time in the Yukon, Huttemeier also uncovered a cache of prehistoric ivory that measured over nine feet in length and weighed more than 300 pounds.

He returned to Fairmont and married Sadie Diehl in 1907. He then purchased an interest in the Star Corner Saloon, which was located at the present site of Farm Bureau Insurance, 201 Downtown Plaza. He ran the tavern for a number of years with partners Jim Trainor and later a Mr. Lindstaedt. When he began to experience failing health, he went to Rochester to seek medical advice. While there, he was told by a doctor that outdoor life was the only thing that would help him. As a result, he went into farming for twenty-nine years in Westford Township. He and his wife retired in 1943 and moved to Fairmont.

Perhaps one of the most significant and lasting possessions in his gold mining experience was a large gold nugget that Huttemeier mined in the Dawson area. He wore this on his watch chain for some time. This nugget evolved into a Klondike nugget necklace that was eventually handed down from Huttemeier to his sister, Mary Reinke. She then gave it to her daughter, Lennie Reinke Niss, who in turn gave it to her daughter, Erma Niss Rosen. The Klondike nugget necklace was recently handed down to Erma Rosen's granddaughter, Karen Marie Rosen, on her eighteenth birthday as a graduation present.

Again, the hardy pioneers and prospectors of the past, including those from Martin County, have provided us with vivid examples of times gone by. Our heritage, and the history it represents, is truly an important aspect of the present, and it should never be lost or forgotten.

Sources for this story include MCHS History File 863 "Klondike Nugget Necklace Originally Owned by Henry Huttemeier;" Wikipedia.org/wiki/Klondike_Gold_rush; and writeyukon.com.

The Major

The man known as Major, Arthur M. Nelson, was a significant and colorful figure in the history of Martin County. Born in Iowa in 1876, he came to Martin County in 1888 and worked in farming, railroad construction, and education as a teacher in rural schools in the county until 1904. Then he began his career in journalism with the *Sentinel.* This was where he made his mark in life until his death in 1947.

The title Major relates back to Nelson's military experience. Nelson enlisted in the army in 1898 and served during the Spanish—American War. He also enlisted in WWI in 1917 and attained the rank of Major. From that time forward, he was called Major Nelson, even as a civilian. In 1941, at the onset of WWII, he attempted again to enlist. However, because of his age, the military refused to accept him. In his desire to serve, he then took on the job of chairman of the Martin County Selective Service Board. He also served this area in a number of other civic positions and was instrumental in the founding of the American Legion at the national level.

An avid historian, Nelson was known as a stickler for accuracy and would only record facts and not conjecture. This was particularly evident in reference to local history. He was especially concerned that schools of that day didn't devote enough time to local history and geography. As a result of his intense interest in history, particularly local history, it comes as no surprise that he was one of the organizers of the Martin County Historical Society and that he was also a member of the Minnesota Historical Society.

Major Arthur Nelson

However, Nelson's work at the *Sentinel* is undoubtedly his greatest contribution to local history. Nelson was known as an excellent journalist. Consequently, his work was reprinted throughout the state and in some national periodicals as well. He was also known as an entertaining speaker and was sought after for his speaking ability. It should be noted that he left little doubt in his audience's minds regarding the authenticity of his remarks.

Nelson wasn't one to waffle, and once he found a cause, he was relentless in supporting it and wasn't the least bit concerned as to whether or not it was popular or whom he might offend. He would typically draw the line and let the chips fall where they may. Being a staunch Democrat, there was more than one instance when his beliefs regarding politics clashed with others. He was also very definite about his beliefs regarding alcohol consumption. Being a teetotaler, he was credited at that time as being the most influential individual in keeping Martin County dry. In his opinion, anyone that took a drink of alcohol was considered to be an alcoholic.

Another somewhat colorful illustration reflecting his strong personality, as reported in the April 10, 1947, edition of the *Fairmont Sentinel*, involved the manner in which he dealt with those who came into the *Sentinel* office to "lick the editor," as a result of someone's disagreement with an editorial column.

More than once it was necessary to rebuild the front door where some hapless individual was forcibly ejected by the major after he had stood a certain amount of abuse. Only on one occasion did he show any regret over having to throw out an obnoxious patron. That was a woman canvasser who insisted the major run an ad on fortune telling. When she became insistent, he told her to get out. She became incensed and gave him a tongue lashing. Before either he or she realized what had happened, she was picking herself up off the outer edge of the sidewalk outside the *Sentinel* office. "The Major chuckled as he noted she was unhurt, but her dignity and millinery sadly askew. 'I wonder where I grabbed her," he chuckled, "and how did she land so far away?'"

Nelson also had no time for doctors or medicine. Once when suffering from the flu, he was influenced by his family to see a doctor. "Gimme several kinds of colored medicine and pills, Doc," he reportedly told the doctor. "I won't take 'em, but Sadie will feel a lot better if you leave me some medicine."

Nelson's family consisted of his wife Sadie, who had been a former pupil of his in country school, and one son, Uno. Nelson passed away unexpectedly of a heart attack at the age of seventy-one in April 1947.

In reflecting upon the history of any community, there are invariably certain individuals who stand out as instrumental, influential, and some perhaps a bit eccentric in their contributions to local history. The Major would certainly seem to fit that characterization. He conveyed his message through the media in a decisive manner, he was a civic-minded individual who truly cared about his fellow man, and his colorful words and actions seemed to exemplify his personality.

Sources for this story include the April 9, 1947, Sentinel, *and Family Genealogy File 97 at MCHS.*

Hoop and the Orphan Train

The Orphan Train movement from the late 1800s to the early 1900s was a result of concerned, social-minded people in New York City who were appalled at the thousands of neglected and orphaned children roaming the streets. This movement became the forerunner of modern day foster care programs. The people organized trains to transport many of these children to Midwest farm states in hopes of finding them permanent homes. Over the course of several decades, thousands of children were relocated.

There were two delegations of orphans sent to Martin County totaling forty-seven children aged four to eighteen. Boys were in biggest demand because they could help with the farming. Fred "Hoop" Hoover arrived with the second group sent by the Children's Aid Society. He later was referred to as "The *Sentinel's* man of mystery whom everybody knew, but whom nobody knew."

Hoop never knew his real parents and never spoke of his early life in Brooklyn. Hoover's foster parents, Mr. and Mrs. Marion Hoover, finally adopted him when he was thirty-nine years old after having raised him from a young child.

Hoover was characterized as being dependable and a man of few words with a somewhat gruff exterior. However, he was quick to correct anyone providing erroneous facts regarding local history.

He was also remembered as being the father of the rural fire truck. When there were fires in the country, townspeople didn't want the fire truck leaving in case a fire happened in town. As a member of the Fairmont Fire Department with a keen interest in fire prevention, Hoop proposed the idea that farmers buy a fire truck which the local fire department would operate. That idea was well accepted and the concept quickly spread to other communities.

Fred Hoover

He was involved with a number of avocations during his lifetime. Hoop loved military life and served on the Mexican border in 1917. He served several terms with the local National Guard, was a patrolman on the Fairmont Police force, and was also very active in the Veterans of Foreign Wars organization.

Hoop was employed by the *Sentinel* as a janitor following World War I. While there, he also worked as an assistant pressman, helped with mailings, and did some carpentry work.

Regarding his personal life, Hoop never married and kept mainly to himself. His "home" was in the firemen's quarters in city hall.

Many of those children of the Orphan Train era overcame tremendous hardships to become quite successful people in society. Although he might be considered somewhat of a recluse today, history dictates that Fred Hoover was one of the Orphan Train success stories.

Hoop passed away in 1948 at the age of sixty-nine. He had a full military funeral and was buried, as he wished, in his U.S. Army uniform. What estate he had was left to charities.

Sources for this story include the April 3, 1948, Sentinel *and childrensaidsociety.org/about/history/orphan-trains.*

Ahead of Her Time—Mabel Hall

In today's society, women have opportunities unheard of a generation ago. Today, women hold positions in medicine, engineering, business, and government. Although it may still be questioned, legitimately so, that women still don't have equal opportunities to their male counterparts, compared to the past, they have made giant strides.

In that respect, there are many individuals who have contributed to the rich heritage of Martin County. If asked to name some of those individuals, the names first mentioned will likely be male. However, there have been a number of women who have made very positive contributions to the history of Martin County. One woman who was undoubtedly ahead of her time was Mabel Hall, and her accomplishments well preceded the days of women's lib.

Hall was born in Fraser Township, Martin County, in 1886. She attended country school and worked for her room and board while attending Fairmont High School. Following graduation in 1905, she taught in a country school for one year. She then took correspondence courses from the University of Minnesota and the University of Wisconsin before obtaining her teaching certificate from Mankato State Teachers College. Following college, she taught in a number of country schools in Minnesota and then became a principal in Bricelyn, Minnesota. While in Bricelyn, she organized their first athletic team, "in self defense," the diminutive, five-foot-tall Hall once said.

Mabel Hall

In 1920, she became assistant superintendent of Martin County Schools. When the superintendent retired in 1923, she ran for superintendent of Martin County Schools which at that time was an elected position. She was elected and served in that capacity for twelve years.

During her tenure as superintendent, she was required by law to visit each of the 125 country schools in the county at least twice annually. She fulfilled her duty, and more, by visiting each country school at least four times annually. Considering road conditions and transportation at that time, that was certainly a feat in itself!

Then, in 1935, she assumed the position of Martin County Clerk of Probate Court. She held that position until she retired in 1973 at the age of 87.

She was also very civic-minded, playing an instrumental role in the Fairmont chapter of Business and Professional Women. She remained active in that organization for thirty-nine years. During that time, she held all local and a number of state offices, including state president for two years. Hall's 100th birthday was designated National Mabel Hall Day by the National Federation of BPW. She was also a Sunday school teacher, superintendent at the Fairmont Congregational Church, and volunteer with Campfire Girls groups.

Hall, the last living member of her high school graduating class, passed away on April 11, 1991, at the age of 104.

It seems that she never outwardly advocated for women's liberation or equal rights. Rather, she simply modeled what could be accomplished in her day-to-day life, not allowing any form of "glass ceiling" to limit her achievements. She is but one of many women who have played an important role in the development of Martin County and who have been positive role models for younger women to emulate.

Sources for this story include various editions of the Sentinel *including* Hometown Legends 2007; *July 14, 1975; February 1, 1973; October 25, 1968; August 19, 1986; and October 17, 1957.*

Mr. Fairmont

It is truly amazing the number of individuals who have influenced and shaped the Martin County area from William Budd to the present time. Their achievements and civic-minded ideals have influenced the direction our city and county have gone, from the early years in their histories to what still exists and thrives yet today as a result of their endeavors.

One of those entrepreneurial spirits that has made our area a better place is Einer Nelson, at one time referred to as Mr. Fairmont.

From rather humble beginnings, Nelson eventually gained a prominent place in Martin County's history. He was born in Albert Lea in 1888. His father died when Nelson was only six years old, and his mother was then left to care for five children under the age of eight, which was no small task. As if these hardships weren't enough, he was forced to join the workforce before he could graduate from eighth grade. However, a positive attitude permeated his personality, and events that might have proven insurmountable to others did not seem to affect Nelson, as he went on to become a highly successful businessman, public servant, politician, and significant contributor to the good of our local area.

He married Emily Lien in 1910, and they moved to Fairmont in 1920. It was here that he owned and operated the Nelson Ice Cream Company for thirty-seven years.

In addition, he also operated a locker business that was once the largest in the United States. However, in addition to being a successful businessman, he was also very civic-minded and contributed greatly to Fairmont and Martin County with his time and money.

Einer Nelson

He served Fairmont as mayor, city council member, school board member, and member of the Public Utilities Commission. He also served on the Salvation Army board and was involved with KSUM radio, cable TV, Madsen's Super Valu, the Fairmont Chamber of Commerce, the *Sentinel*, the hospital, the United Fund, the Methodist church expansion funding, and more. A staunch Republican, he was also sometimes referred to as "Mr. Republican."

When Nelson passed away in 1984, Ray Stougaard said in his obituary in the *Sentinel* that Nelson "teamed up with Ed Duffey to bring 3M to Fairmont and keep it here." Then, when 3M later needed more space, Duffey and Nelson sat in on the negotiations. Apparently things weren't going well when Duffey brought about a successful conclusion to the meeting by saying "me and Einer will build you a building." It would appear that as a result, 3M remained in Fairmont and has been a significant factor in the local economy ever since.

Before Nelson passed away in 1984, he accomplished a great deal, and his legacy lives on today. He likely served as a role model inspiring others in our local area, as many individuals and organizations have quietly followed that civic-mindedness that characterized Nelson's life.

Sources for this story include various editions of the Sentinel *including the March 19, 1984 editorial by Ray Stougaard; March 20, 1984; June 9, 1956; September 24, 1959; February 3, 1956; and* Hometown Legends 2007, *page 49.*

The Four Horsemen of Martin County

The term "The Four Horsemen" may bring to mind the biblical account regarding the four horsemen of the Apocalypse who symbolize war, famine, conquest, and death. On the other hand, you might also think of the Four Horsemen of Notre Dame, those talented athletes who played football under the venerable Coach Knute Rockne during the 1920s. In any event, the Four Horsemen of Martin County are in no way comparable to either of the previously mentioned four horsemen. Their popularity was based on attributes that were neither frightening nor athletic in nature but rather were based on social qualities that made them highly sought after.

Four Horsemen

Back during the latter 1890s in the Martin County communities of Sherburn and Fairmont, there were four, dapper young men described as the Beau Brummels of their day. They wore "plug hats," a hat that is round and hard with a narrow brim. In addition, they sported mustaches or beards and wore fancy shoes, fine shirts, vests, and flashy gold-braided watch chains. The members of this trendy and rather flamboyant group included George A. Sutherland, D.S. Pingrey, C.L. Everett, and his brother, C.E. "Gene" Everett. They were truly the fashionable trendsetters in men's wear of their day.

This fun-loving group apparently experienced their fifteen minutes of fame in Martin County during the late 1890s. They were in demand at basket socials, picnics, cotillions, and celebrations of all kinds. They apparently filled a niche at that time while riding a wave of popularity, cutting a wide swath through Martin County's social life that kept them busy for quite some time.

Little is known about Pingrey and the Everett brothers. However, Sutherland practiced law in Sherburn and later opened a life insurance business in Fairmont that became quite successful. Some of that success came as a result of his somewhat questionable advertising techniques. His sales approach played on the emotions of wives by providing "tear jerker" ads emphasizing the importance of insuring their husbands in the event of an untimely death. During that period of time, Sutherland was making $200 per month from renewals alone, while the average person was deemed fortunate to earn $50 per month.

Sources for this story include Jan Dickinson's compiled research of newspaper articles 1890–1900 at the Pioneer Museum.

A Colorful Character in Our History

Historical research is interesting. It's not unusual to become sidetracked by a story or event unrelated to the original objective. An example of this is the following account of Charlie Potter, with insight from the August 1, 1951, *Sentinel* story about his death which was headlined "C.H. Potter, Colorful Figure In Fairmont Is Taken By Death At 61."

Charlie Potter

Potter was the owner of the Fairmont Novelty Company as well as owner of a considerable amount of real estate. This article said that "his death removes from the community one of its most colorful, yet one of its most unobtrusive, seldom seen characters in business life." This description seems a bit like an oxymoron in that he was described as "colorful" yet "unobtrusive" and "seldom seen."

He had a humble start to his life in a small town in Iowa. He worked on farms, gradually earning enough money to buy a cow for milk and butter. He soon saved enough to buy several horses with which he did construction work. Although eventually becoming quite successful financially, he was said to have lost two or three fortunes to gambling.

After his gambling losses, he made up his mind to practice with dice until he got good enough to win his money back. He went on to prove his ability with dice to a newspaper interviewer by predicting accurately what he would roll.

He moved to Fairmont because he wanted to raise his children "in a good, clean town." At the same time, he decided to quit professional gambling. Consequently, he leased and then purchased a hotel and café. Although he had minimal capital for this venture, he was able to make it successful, barely.

His family life was somewhat tumultuous. He lost a son to a tragic accident between Fairmont and Blue Earth when the boy fell asleep at the wheel of his car and crashed into a concrete bridge. Potter's first wife died when his children were quite young. Although he soon remarried, as a result of disagreement concerning the care and treatment of the children, he divorced his second wife and for many years remained single.

He eventually remarried for yet a third time. This third wife, Lila, looked after his hotel and café while he attended to other business interests, some of which were out of state. However, Lila eventually decided to leave him and return to Chicago to live with her parents. Sixteen years after she left, he brought legal action against her for divorce, charging her with desertion. In turn, she filed a counter suit. After a long and protracted court battle, she was awarded $30,000 in a lump sum as alimony. He appealed, but to no avail.

It seems that he was also the recipient of bad luck on several other fronts as well. There was a warehouse fire in which he lost about $100,000. It housed pinball machines, coin-operated phonographs, bowling games, and other games. Although they were outdated and considered junk machines, the parts were scarce and quite valuable for needed repairs. Regretfully, he carried no insurance.

Another instance of bad luck was the result of a robbery at his home. According to the April 26, 1948, edition of the *Sentinel*, a trio of gangsters slugged and robbed him and his secretary, who became his fourth wife. The money and jewelry stolen amounted to $12,000. The robbers overpowered them and were even able to subdue Fairmont Police Officer Cavers when he arrived on the scene.

Regarding his apparently insatiable interest in gambling, he once had a conversation with someone about slot machines. Potter's friend said, "I thought you told me you didn't have any."

He said, "I ain't, only where they're legal."

"What do you mean 'legal?'" the friend replied. "They are out[lawed] all over Minnesota."

He replied, "Well, I only operate in counties where the sheriff says it's all right. That makes it legal, don't it?"

Although he finally admitted he was wrong in operating slot machines, another gambling issue arose, this time involving the county fair. He felt that the county commissioners should legalize gambling there. "Them suckers wants to get took," Potter stormed. "They come to the fair loaded with $300 and $400, just a achin' to get took, and I don't know why the fair board don't let honest, respectable, taxpayin' citizens take it away from 'em legal." He felt very strongly that he had been denied a right and that those in opposition were wrong.

At the time of his death, Potter owned what was described as one of the finest, most luxuriously furnished homes in Fairmont located on the east bank of Hall Lake at 2520 Albion Avenue. His property also included the barn and acreage across the street from his home. In addition, he owned Potter's Café and Hotel at 110 West First Street, the current site of Edie's Restaurant, as well as other real estate in town.

Colorful indeed, and this account characterizes but one more unique and intriguing individual adding to the rich, colorful, and very fascinating history of Martin County.

Remembering Bob Porter

There are many individuals from the past who have contributed significantly to the business and economic development of Martin County. One of those individuals was Robert E. Porter, best known as Bob to his friends.

Bob Porter

Porter was born in Alliance, Nebraska, and moved to Fairmont with his parents at the age of one. When they moved to Fairmont and saw the lakes, they were impressed and decided to make Fairmont their home.

Porter's father, Clayton, and uncle, Fred, wanted to own a bank in Fairmont but needed funding for that endeavor. Consequently, as a result of their honest and hard work in Nebraska, Clayton's employer from Alliance, Nebraska, provided the financial backing necessary. The bank they were associated with was the First National Bank in Fairmont. Clayton was president and Fred was cashier. However, neither Clayton nor Fred were handed their positions. Rather they earned them. Clayton had been a bookkeeper in a crockery store in Alliance, and Fred had worked at a buggy factory.

Porter graduated from Fairmont High School in 1910 and the University of Minnesota in 1914. He returned to Fairmont and began working at the First National Bank as an assistant cashier.

Then, when the United States was involved in World War I, he was accepted into officer candidate school at Fort Snelling in 1917. He served overseas as a first lieutenant during the Army occupation of Germany. After his military service, he returned to his job at the bank.

In 1929, the Porters sold their bank to the First Bank Corporation. After they sold the bank, they formed two corporations. The corporation that Porter was in charge of was eventually named Porter Farms with holdings that represented farmland in Martin

County. In addition to overseeing family interests in that corporation, he also served as treasurer of Fairmont Railway Motors and vice president of Martin County National Bank.

Porter kept himself quite busy in a number of other endeavors as well. Perhaps one of the most notable was in 1921 when he, Dr. Lester Webb, Dr. R.H. Zierke, and Frank Jones bought the Grill Motor Company from J.H. Grill. This became the Park Motor Company in Fairmont, presently known as Fairmont Ford. Porter served at various times as secretary or treasurer for Park Motor Company over the years.

Perhaps one of the more memorable and courageous events in his life came about in 1916 in California. Porter, his father and his sister, were vacationing in the Los Angeles area. They were out for a swim in the ocean when a friend who accompanied Porter complained of being tired and wanted to return to shore to rest. However, the strong undertow kept him from coming to shore.

Porter swam out to help his friend, who then panicked, grabbing Porter around the neck. Porter continued to hold his friend above water as best as possible, but he was also becoming exhausted. Their cries for help couldn't be heard above the roar of the pounding surf.

Fortunately, Porter's sister saw that something was very wrong and called to the lifeguards for help. The lifeguards then threw out a life-saving buoy in an attempt to rescue the two boys. The rope broke on the first attempt but fortunately held the second time as the two boys would have likely drowned from exhaustion soon after.

The Los Angeles papers reported the incident; however, Porter was too modest to admit to any heroic actions. He did, however, qualify for a Carnegie Hero Medal as a result of his valiant efforts, according to a front page story in the March 24, 1916, *Martin County Sentinel.*

Porter passed away on December 15, 1973, and is buried at Lakeside Cemetery in Fairmont.

Sources for this story include the December 5, 1958, Sentinel.

More Than a Dentist

Martin County can be proud of its many attributes. When considering the parks, the recreational areas, the lakes, and the many other community and county treasures available to all of us, it's sometimes easy to forget that they are here because someone had the foresight to develop, promote, and maintain those amenities that today enhance the quality of life in Martin County for everyone to enjoy. The following is a brief account of an individual who was born in the 1800s, made his mark locally in the 1900s, and through his efforts, those of us living in the 2000s are experiencing a better quality of life.

Dr. W. Lester Webb was a dentist who was very involved in the community. He loved and promoted the city in which he lived.

He was born in Amiret, Minnesota, in 1893. He attended the University of Minnesota, graduating from dental school in 1916. He settled in Fairmont as a result of a visit to a college friend who happened to live in Fairmont. He immediately fell in love with the area and decided to open a dental practice here. That practice was shared with Dr. R.H. Zierke for fifty-five years, one of the longest, if not the longest, continuous partnerships in the nation.

Dr. Lester Webb

Webb was instrumental in the acquisition and development of many of the things that may easily be taken for granted today. He was an early activist in attempting to get a junior college built in Fairmont. As a result of his efforts in that endeavor and his friendship with the Day sisters who owned the Day Farm, he was instrumental in their selling that site to the city of Fairmont. This was significant because it was not actually for sale at the time. Although the junior college never came to fruition, anyone familiar with Martin County and Fairmont is well aware of the bike trail, the prairie dogs, the armory, the gardens, and Heritage Acres and how those entities have enhanced the quality of life in Martin County.

Additional civic roles included Webb serving as park board chairman during the time when the city acquired Gomsrud Park and as a library board director. He was mayor of Fairmont from 1963–1971 and was very humble and quick to downplay his role as mayor, stating that most everything was really done by the council. He was also instrumental in helping form the Interlaken Golf Club and charter the Fairmont Rotary Club.

In his professional life, Webb was one of the first dentists from outside the Twin Cities area to serve as president of the Minnesota Dental Association. In addition, he served on the state board of health and was one of the few American members of the English College of Dentistry. Webb was described by those who knew him as a genuine people person who frequently made house calls to ailing dental patients, often receiving payment in the form of vegetables, chickens, or some other commodity.

Webb retired from his dental practice in 1972. Although he and his wife, Valeria, traveled some in retirement, they never had a desire to move away. He and his wife were married sixty years before she passed away in 1976. He passed away on January 31, 1979, and is buried in Lakeside Cemetery in Fairmont.

His legacy, in terms of what he helped to accomplish for quality of life, lives on in Martin County. The foresight and accomplishments of Dr. Webb and others in Martin

County's past affects those presently living here in addition to future generations. It is important to recognize what we have, strive to develop and enhance additional amenities, and to acknowledge and appreciate the generosity and hard work of our predecessors who have made living in Martin County what it is today.

Sources for this story include the February 6, 1979, Sentinel *and that newspaper's* Hometown Legends 2007 *insert, page 52.*

A Community Servant

"Community service is the rent you pay for the space you occupy" was the motto of Albert Niss, a Martin County resident for ninety-two years.

Niss was born on February 15, 1895, in Waverly Township in Martin County. He attended rural schools in Waverly and Fraser Townships and graduated from Fairmont High School in 1915. He then attended the University of Minnesota and graduated from the Minnesota School of Business.

Albert Niss

In 1917, he began working for George Sutherland with New York Life on a part-time basis. Then, in 1925, he became a full-time insurance agent. He worked for New York Life until he retired in 1985, a total of sixty-eight years. However, much of his life's work and accomplishments were not limited to the business world.

Niss was very civic-minded, involved in his community, and obviously dedicated to making a difference in Martin County and the many lives he touched. He served as an assistant scoutmaster in Boy Scouts for fifteen years, was a member of the Fairmont Rotary Club for forty-seven years, served as chairman of the Martin County Republican Committee, and was an office holder and member of the Knights of Pythias for sixty-seven years. In addition, he was a Sunday school teacher, a Sunday school superintendent, and a Fairmont school board member. While serving on the school board, he was instrumental in the building of the Fairmont Middle School. He also served at the state level as president of the Minnesota Game Protective League for two years.

However, he was perhaps best known as Fairmont's unofficial historian. He frequently spoke to various clubs and organizations, using his vivid memory to relate historical events from Fairmont and Martin County's past. The Pioneer Museum holds numerous writings provided by Niss, including his book published by the Fairmont Photo Press in 1987 entitled *80 Years of Change In Downtown Fairmont, Minnesota 1906–1986.* His writings provide readers with the opportunity to picture Martin County's history through his eyes during the eighty years of change he saw as a participant, witness, and documenter.

So, what makes up the fabric of a community? In Niss' lifespan, a partial answer can be seen: civic duty, service to others, and an appreciation for history and heritage. His legacy would be best characterized not by his professional accomplishments, but rather by what he left for succeeding generations through his volunteerism and his careful, thorough documentation of local history. His willingness to serve has had a lasting impact on Martin County.

Sources for this story include the October 6, 1987, Sentinel, *and* Martin County Minnesota History, *Taylor Publishing, 1988.*

Others First, Self Last

One notable individual instrumental in the betterment of her community and county was Pauline Welcome. Her motto, "Others First, Self Last," seems to epitomize her legacy, and provides a valid reason for remembering her, particularly in terms of the positive and lasting influence she had on Martin County.

Pauline Welcome

Pauline H. Luegge was born in Rutland Township, Martin County, in 1896. Her father died when she was fourteen, leaving her mother with eleven children. Because her mother was unable to care for all of them, some of her children went to live with friends and relatives. Pauline was taken in by Mrs. S.H. Merrill, a music teacher. Mrs. Merrill had health problems. Consequently, Pauline attended Fairmont High School several hours daily and spent the remainder of each day helping with housework and cooking for Mrs. Merrill during her ten-year stay at the Merrill home.

Following graduation from Fairmont High School, Welcome worked at Fairmont Railway Motors for one summer. However, she was urged by friends to become a rural school teacher as it paid $50 a month, an inviting sum of money at that time. As a result, she made the decision to attend normal school for two years. Following graduation from normal school, she taught in Martin County schools for six years. Then, in 1928, she married Earl M. Welcome. He owned and operated several farms in Martin County and the town of Welcome was named in honor of his father.

Following her husband's death in 1951, Welcome moved into the town of Welcome.

During the years that followed, Welcome's life exemplified her motto. She was active in the Martin County Public Health Nursing Service and its auxiliary, and she was a charter member of the planning committee for the Lakeview United Methodist Home. In addition, she authored a number of books commemorating local history including *The History of Welcome, Minnesota*; *Manyaska Township; Welcome Methodist Church;* and *The Welcome Village Cemetery.*

Having a keen interest in the Martin County Historical Society, she generously furnished a complete room with displays of artifacts from her home in Welcome and her historical family heirlooms. That room in the Pioneer Museum is aptly named The Welcome Room in honor of her family. Her civic-mindedness also included being a member of Martin County Farm Bureau, the Fairmont Community Hospital Auxiliary, and other organizations in addition to her considerable financial contributions to numerous charitable organizations in Martin County.

In March 1973, Welcome was named Philanthropist of the Year by the National Board of Health. The following year, she was named Martin County's Outstanding Senior Citizen. She moved to the Lakeview Methodist Home in 1976 and passed away in 1978. She is buried in the Welcome City Cemetery.

It would seem that Welcome's motto, "Others First, Self Last," inspired her to leave a substantial and significant legacy that proved instrumental and virtually immeasurable considering the lasting effect it has had on Martin County and its citizens. It's a motto that could certainly be worthy of consideration in today's society.

When considering her start in life, one of eleven children sent to live with someone outside of her immediate family, her accomplishments are truly remarkable. She didn't ask for anything, she apparently didn't feel entitled, yet she was very generous and more than willing to give of herself, her time, and her resources in an effort to contribute to the continued development and evolution of a better Martin County.

Sources for this story include the August 16, 1974, Sentinel.

If The Shoe Fits

Shoe repair shops were at one time quite common. If you went into a shoe repair shop, some of the equipment and tools you might see included foot-treadle sewing machines, stitching machines, leather-cutting machines, riveting machines, shoe anvils, and bins of pre-cut leather, soles, shoe lifts, nails, and rivets. Most people today very likely have no idea what these tools might have looked like or how they were used.

In the past, shoe repair work could be a lifetime profession. One of those individuals who devoted his life's work to shoe repair was Bill Witt who spent over forty years in the business.

Witt was a Martin County native who got his start in the shoe repair business by working at Vossberg Harness Shop in Truman. He joined the army in 1917, but when he returned home, he found that the era of harness-making was coming to an end. Consequently, he opened a shoe repair business in Fairmont in 1921. His skills included dyeing shoes and orthopedic shoe rebuilding, and he obtained at that time modern machinery to work on women's shoes that had spiked heels.

His shop was at one time located just east of the Red Rock Center for the Arts on Blue Earth Avenue in Fairmont. He moved to that site from a downtown location and referred to it as the best shop he ever had. He called it really efficient and stated that the only drawback was that it should have been bigger. He built that shop on Blue

Earth Avenue right next to his home because he thought he would then have time to run home and watch TV when business was slack or when he was between customers. However business was so good, he rarely got the opportunity to go home to watch TV and actually had to start working nights in order to keep up, something he hadn't done before. He had a long and successful career in shoe repair, crediting his many customers for his accomplishments.

IT'S WITT'S FOR WORN SHOES — Bill's new shoe repair shop is on East Blue Earth avenue

Bill Witt's Shoe Repair Shop

Another well-known individual in the shoe repair business was Holger Due. His shop was located on Downtown Plaza just north of the *Sentinel* newspaper offices.

Due came to America in 1924 at twenty-two years of age. For a number of years, he moved back and forth between places in the Midwest and also lived in New York and Denmark before finally establishing himself in Martin County.

Due referred to the shoemaker's trade as being among the oldest known to mankind. He felt that as long as people wore shoes, the shoemaker would be in demand. Although he didn't feel that the shoemaker's trade would disappear, he was concerned that the people in the profession were not being replaced. He said that as shoemakers retired, died, or otherwise left the profession, there were no younger ones to take their place.

Due had an interesting and varied background in addition to his leather work and shoe repair. He operated portable roller skating rinks in Minnesota and Iowa and at one time managed a Gamble's Store. He was also noted for riding his bike to work every day.

It seems that in today's ever-changing society, it may be just as easy to throw away the old pair of shoes and get a new pair rather than to make repairs. Perhaps the era of the easily accessible shoe repair shop in every community is gone and unlikely to return. Perhaps Holger Due's appraisal of the future of the shoe repair profession was quite prophetic.

Sources for this story include Jan Dickinson's compiled research of newspaper articles, 1960–1964, *which included* Sentinel *articles from March 11, 1961, and December 30, 1961.*

Maud Brodt

In the past, professions open to women were often limited to teaching, nursing, and secretarial positions. In today's society, there are many more opportunities for women than were available a century ago. Now, there are many women who have proven successful in medicine, business, law, politics, and many other fields.

However, in the first half of the last century, Martin County had a true pioneer in modeling leadership positions for women of that time: Maud Brodt. Brodt left an indelible imprint on Martin County and was a significant contributor to many of the positive aspects of our county that we enjoy today.

Maud Brodt

Maud Murphy was born near Watertown, Minnesota, in 1880. She came to Martin County in 1899 and taught in District 59, Fraser Township. She met her husband, Herman Brodt, when she was employed as a teacher.

After Brodt and Herman were married in 1904, they built a new farmstead in Section 35 of Fraser Township. Their family eventually included a son, Warren, and a daughter, Juanita. Although primarily a homemaker and mother, Brodt became active in many civic endeavors and became known well beyond Martin County's borders.

Brodt was named one of Minnesota's Master Homemakers by *Farmer Magazine* in 1927. Her work as a homemaker was also publicized in *Picture Magazine* and *Ladies Home Journal.*

In addition, she served as chairperson of the Martin County Safety Council and became well known for her work in promoting farm safety. She was also active in organizing the Fairmont Community Hospital and worked for the county library in an effort to better serve rural residents. She served on the Martin County Fair Board, making her the first woman to serve on any fair board in Minnesota. She also organized the Rural Sunshine Club for World War I work.

Brodt organized the Martin County Farm Bureau Women's chorus. This group had many singing engagements, including an appearance on WCCO Radio.

She served as chairman of the Martin County Women's Democratic Educational Club, was a precinct chairman with the County Jubilee in 1932, and worked to promote 4-H in Martin County. Her work in the area of 4-H eventually led to the construction of a 4-H building at the Martin County Fairgrounds. In addition, she was appointed to a Minnesota State Senate Tax Committee in the early 1930s.

Perhaps her greatest accomplishment, however, was being instrumental in founding the Martin County Historical Society in 1929. She served as vice president of the first board of directors. In honor of her seventieth birthday in August of 1949, Judge Julius E. Haycraft wrote Brodt a letter in which he wrote, "You have done a fine and useful work in your life, particularly in the Farm Bureau and in historical matters. You are the originator of the Martin County Historical Society and should have been its first president." She treasured that letter.

Brodt passed away in May 1950. Although gone for nearly seventy years, Brodt's efforts and actions created a legacy that has undeniably left a positive and long-lasting effect on Martin County. She was a leader and certainly well ahead of her time as an example for women in a wide variety of leadership positions.

Some information for this story was from Brodt's obituary in the May 11, 1950, Fairmont Daily Sentinel.

Gomsrud Park

Fairmont has many beautiful parks, including Gomsrud Park between Budd and Hall Lakes. But how did Gomsrud Park get its name?

Michael Gomsrud was a Norwegian immigrant whose love for children was well known in this area. Affectionately known as "Mike," he was born in Norway in 1893 and came to America in 1914. He served with the U.S. Armed Forces in France for thirteen months during World War I. He came to Fairmont in 1920 and worked as a shoemaker for C.E. Braun.

He became very skilled in this seemingly humble profession and his ability attracted customers from a wide geographic area. He considered himself a "shoe rebuilder" and repaired shoes so that they literally looked like new. He was a very hard worker, and as well as repairing shoes, he also made shoes and boots to order.

In addition to his work, Gomsrud had a number of hobbies, including making hunting knives, and hunting for pheasants, ducks, deer, and rabbits. He also organized raccoon hunts on a large scale, and his "raccoon feeds" became increasingly popular with the locals over the years.

Gomsrud Park

As a result of his solid work ethic and prudent spending habits, Gomsrud was able to purchase a home, a farm, and erect a business building as well as an apartment. He acquired the property that is now known as Gomsrud Park because he was a true conservationist at heart. His goal was to preserve the area for future generations to enjoy.

Gomsrud was a glowing example that America is truly a land of opportunity. His accomplishments were realized through hard work and thrifty habits. He demonstrated that success was achievable even though he initially faced a language barrier and had no capital at his disposal. His success could certainly be considered to be a quintessential example of the fulfillment of the American Dream.

Mike Gomsrud passed away in 1945. Although his wife, Inga, had the opportunity to sell the property for more money, she held onto it in the hopes that the city would eventually want it, which would in turn satisfy Gomsrud's desire for it to become a public park. A decade after Mike's passing, the area now known as Gomsrud Park was purchased by the city for $10,000. Naming the park after him was one of the stipulations of the agreement between her and the city in order to pay tribute to his memory and provide a lasting tribute to the American way of life.

Sources for this story include Sentinel *stories from November 16, 1955; November 18, 1955; April 20, 1956; May 18, 1956; January 25, 1957; June 4, 1958; and June 6, 1958; and Jan Dickinson's compiled research of newspaper articles.*

Local Boy Makes Good!

The catchphrase "local boy makes good" undoubtedly has different meanings to different people. "Making good" as it pertained to Fairmont native Carrol M. Shanks meant rising to the pinnacle of success in American business ventures which eventually resulted in his being featured on the cover of *Time* magazine.

Back in 1954, Shanks returned to town to address the high school's graduating class as commencement speaker. Shanks was then president of the Prudential Life Insurance Company of America, which was the largest company of its kind in the world at the time. Shanks brought with him his aide, Rear Admiral G.A. Eubank.

Carrol Shanks, in the dark suit, as he talks to a group of Fairmont graduates

Shanks was born in 1898 and left Fairmont in 1912 at the age of fourteen. His father was the pioneer Fairmont Postmaster Edgar Shanks, and he lived at 304 Woodland Avenue.

Shanks served in the Army during World War I. He was married, and he and his wife had one son and two daughters. His favorite recreation was big game hunting.

Shanks attended the University of Washington and graduated in 1921. He graduated from Columbia University's law school in 1925. One of his classmates in law school was William O. Douglas, who later went on to become a Supreme Court Justice.

After law school, Shanks joined the law firm of Root, Clark, Buckner, and Ballantine, in New York City. He was with the firm for four years while also lecturing at Columbia Law School. He then became an associate professor at Yale before returning to his law firm in 1931.

In 1932, Shanks joined the Prudential Life Insurance Company of America. He became a vice president in 1944, advanced to executive vice president and director, and became president of the company in 1946.

Shanks was well-respected and served in many capacities. He was a trustee of Rutgers University and Wheaton College and president of the Montclair Public Library. He also played a prominent role nationally in educating the public on a sound national economy through public speaking and interviews with the press. In addition, he received numerous honors and awards in recognition of his accomplishments and contributions.

Shank's commencement address in 1954, entitled "Balance Sheet for a Graduating Class," brought a message of faith in the future and his belief in an era of peace. In visiting friends later, he also spoke of his appreciation for Fairmont, which he considered his home even after his lengthy absence.

Shanks appeared on the cover of the March 18, 1957, edition of *Time* magazine with an article entitled, "Chip off the Old Rock."

Obviously, "making good" is a perception based upon personal values. In that respect, it seems at least reasonable to consider Shanks, a Martin County native, as someone who truly "made good" through his business insight and accomplishments, his willingness to serve and better nonprofit organizations, and his zeal for accomplishment which took shape in many forms.

Sources for this story include the May 29, 1954, Sentinel.

Who's Who of American Women

Claude Swanson, the long time *Sentinel* editor during the mid-1900s, often created columns about interesting people and events. In one of his columns from August of 1959, entitled "Personalities in Our Midst," he wrote about a local woman who was the only Martin County citizen to be included in the first edition of *Who's Who of American Women,"* undoubtedly quite an accomplishment. That woman was Rose Hand, the daughter of Ernest Hand, Sr., who attended rural school in Silver Lake and later graduated from Fairmont High School in 1926.

After graduating from high school, Hand didn't see a future for herself in Martin County. Consequently, she decided to enroll in the Minneapolis Business College and learn typing and shorthand.

Rose Hand

Following graduation, she was employed as a stenographer for C.L. Kaye and Sons in St. Paul. When her uncle, August Saggau of Ceylon, was elected state senator, she took a leave of absence and served as his secretary.

Following that, she then took a position with the U.S. Census Bureau as a stenographer in Washington, D. C., for a salary of $3.95 per day. She felt Washington was a good place to work because it provided a great opportunity to attend night schools that offered a wide array of subjects. After eighteen months with the Census Bureau, she accepted a position with the Veteran's Administration, also as a stenographer. It was at that time that she first felt the urge to study law.

As a result, she pursued her goal and graduated from the Washington College of Law with a degree of Bachelor of Laws and was admitted to the bar in the District of Columbia in 1936. She later furthered her education by graduating from Benjamin Franklin University with a Bachelor of Commercial Science degree.

Her work experience included a stint with the tax division of the United States Department of Justice in the 1930s. Following that, in 1942, she was appointed Assistant to the Assistant Attorney General, U.S. Department of Justice, in charge of the tax division. However, she was gradually developing a desire to leave the big city life and return to the more relaxed pace of Martin County.

On one of her visits home, she inquired about the possibility of joining a law practice in Fairmont. That opportunity availed itself in 1952 when there was an opening in Leo Seifert's law office. She became associated with the law practice of Leo Seifert and Newton Johnson and later as a member of the law firm of Seifert, Johnson, Hand, and Berens.

After returning to Martin County, she became a very active member of the community. She was involved in a number of organizations including the Fairmont Civil Air Patrol, the Fairmont Chamber of Commerce, and The Fairmont Business and Professional Women's Club.

Surprisingly, it appears that the completion of a course in shorthand and typing opened the door and inspired Hand to continue and advance her education. She came a long way from those early years in Silver Lake and had significant accomplishments, especially considering that during her lifetime the opportunities for women were limited at best.

This story was based on Swanson's article in addition to other documents in the archives of the Pioneer Museum.

Georgia on My Mind

When you hear the name Georgia, you might think of the southern state, or perhaps the song made famous by Ray Charles. However, to many Martin County residents the name Georgia brings to mind fashion, a clothing store perhaps ahead of its time, and quite likely a stylish entrepreneurial owner who blazed a trail for other women to follow. That store, of course, was Georgia's, and it was located on North North Avenue in Fairmont. The owner was Georgia Meister, an astute business woman with a flair for fashion that set her and her merchandise apart from others.

Georgia Parker initially came to Fairmont to teach home economics after graduating from the University of Minnesota. She married Charles Meister, an established businessman who was the vice president of the Fairmont Canning Company. After she married, she began working for the Fairmont Canning Company as a home economist. During her tenure in that position, she was instrumental in developing an improved method of freezing foods for the company.

However, in 1957, she made a career change, daring to enter what was considered at that time to be "a man's world," the world of business. She borrowed money and opened a store. The boutique sold furs, gifts, and other high-end women's apparel.

Georgia Meister

She had an eye for fashion, and she traveled to the major metropolitan areas in the United States, including New York City, to purchase clothing for her store. She also shared her knowledge of fashion by holding shows in Fairmont and Spirit Lake, Iowa. In addition, she taught classes on etiquette and wrote a weekly fashion column in the *Sentinel*, entitled "Georgia Says." In her column, which was in fact an advertisement for her store, she would discuss fashion trends, new arrivals in her store, and anything and everything that might be of interest regarding women's fashions of the day. She very effectively used catch phrases, such as "Smocks 'smack' of high fashion, especially those at my store," as stated in one of her ads in April of 1972.

Although Georgia was very smart and ran an extremely successful business, she may also be remembered as flamboyant, fashionable, classy, and perhaps a bit of a mystery. She never revealed her age and rarely allowed anyone to take her picture, even though her picture did accompany her newspaper column.

Nevertheless, those who remember Georgia and her distinctive offerings know that they experienced an exclusive and unique shopping experience. Georgia's kept this area at the forefront of innovating and exciting fashion design in women's clothing for many years.

After Georgia passed away in 1985, her store immediately closed.

Sources for this story include the Sentinel Hometown Legends 2007 *magazine.*

A Memorable *Sentinel* Journalist

The *Sentinel* has had a long and rich history dating back to the memorable Frank A. Day in the latter 1800s. Another notable individual affiliated with the *Sentinel* for many years that longtime residents of Fairmont and Martin County will certainly recall with affection is the late Claude Swanson. He was a popular *Sentinel* editor and publisher who was also well known for his column, "The Lake Breezes Whisper...," which was originally written by Day and then continued by Swanson after Day's death. The column included Swanson's commentary and take on many things of interest, whether they be current or from the past, including personal perspectives drawn from his youth while growing up in Westford Township.

Claude Swanson

Swanson was born on a farm south of Truman in 1895. His education included attending rural school, one year of high school, and a business course at Wisconsin Business University in La Crosse.

He began working at the *Sentinel* in 1914 at the age of nineteen as a printer's devil, a printing apprentice, a job that provided no pay. Initially hired by Day, Swanson was fired the very next day for sleeping through the town's biggest fire. However, Day reconsidered when Swanson turned in a bag of money he had collected walking from farm to farm selling subscriptions to the *Sentinel.* In addition, he was provided room and board at the home of Day, whom Swanson idolized.

During the course of his employment with the *Sentinel*, Swanson worked his way through the departments, becoming a reporter, an advertising salesman, the advertising manager, the managing editor, and finally publisher in July of 1950. He was employed by the *Sentinel* from 1914 up to the date of his death in 1972, with the exception of serving as editor and publisher of the *Truman Tribune* from May of 1916 to August of 1917 and serving as a Secret Service agent for the U.S. Treasury from April of 1918 to July of 1919. This was the forerunner to the FBI, and he was extremely proud of his work with that organization. He also ran unsuccessfully as a candidate for the office of Minnesota Secretary of State in 1922 as a DFLer against incumbent Mike Holm who held the office for fifty years.

Swanson truly loved history which was reflected in his work of authoring the *Sentinel's* 1958 Centennial Edition. That, for Swanson, was a labor of love that became a historical compilation of events covering Martin County's first 100 years of existence.

In a farewell tribute to Swanson that appeared in the May 25, 1972, edition of the *Sentinel* entitled "History buried with Swanson," Ray Stougaard said about Swanson's writing style, "In copyreading his editorials in the earlier days, I would run across words I'd never heard of and swear he had made them up. But there they were, in the dictionary, and he had used them correctly."

Swanson was also very civic-minded and involved with many organizations. He was a member of the Minnesota Safety Council and served on the Governor's Commission on Mental Health. Concerning statewide journalism affiliations, he served as secretary-treasurer, vice president, and president of the Minnesota Second District Editorial Association and was president of the Minnesota Associated Press in 1952. Locally, he was secretary and one of the organizers of the Fairmont Planning Commission, organizer and president of the Fairmont Safety Council, and publicity chairman for defense bond sales, scrap drives, Red Cross, USO, and other war-related activities.

From his semi-retirement in 1962, he continued as a contributing editor for the *Sentinel,* writing occasional editorials and the weekly "Lake Breezes" column until the time of his death.

Swanson, a newspaperman from the "old school," could perhaps best be characterized as a highly respected and endeared individual in Martin County's past.

About Swanson, Stougaard said, "We buried Claude N. Swanson today. And with him went one of the final ties to the early days of the *Sentinel*."

"Claude was among the last of the old-time editors, full of fire and brimstone, bumptious, positive, and feeling his oats."

Obviously, Claude Swanson was someone who was held in high esteem by his colleagues, he was a civic-minded servant to our area, and through his writing he undoubtedly touched the lives of many who read the *Sentinel* during his nearly sixty years with that newspaper.

Memories of Christmas Past

Christmas comes but once a year. We all have vivid memories of past Christmases from our childhood. In looking back over 100 years, it's interesting to consider what Christmas was like at that time as compared to the present. One means of accomplishing this "backward glance," is to look through the eyes of a memorable *Sentinel* editor and publisher as he vividly and eloquently related his memories of Christmas as a child in Martin County during the early 1900s.

Claude Swanson, a native of Westford Township by Truman, was a venerable *Sentinel* editor and publisher who was especially well known for his celebrated column entitled, "The Lake Breezes Whisper . . ." that he took over for Frank Day upon Day's death in 1928. Swanson wrote about a multitude of topics including Christmas. The following are several selected excerpts from his December 17, 1945, column descriptively relating his reflections of Christmas during his childhood in the early 1900s. His eloquent accounts may well bring to mind other long-lost memories of Christmas past as well.

Swanson began by restating what he overheard from a local professional man of that time. "I'm glad I was born poor. I know what it means to get a thrill out of Christmas. Christmas has a different meaning for every individual. But really, it is the poor who get the real joy out of Christmas giving and Christmas receiving. Little things make them happy beyond description. The recipients know what they receive involves real sacrifices on the part of the giver."

He then recalled some Christmas presents he received as a child. "We recall the Christmases of the early 1900s in Westford. There was one thing we could count on—a bran' new mouth organ every Christmas from Uncle Andrew. Then there'd be a ball, a sack of candy, peanuts and nuts, and one Christmas–joy of joys, a toy locomotive about two feet long, the gift of the hired man. There was a bell on it and the drivers 'rolled' just like on a big locomotive. Then there was the monkey with green cap and tassel, which would climb a string, the gift of Aunt Sophie. A book, *Hans Brinker of the Silver Skates,* from Miss Burner, our teacher."

He went on to tell of the food and how it differed as compared to the time of his writing in 1945. "Even the food was different in those days. Mush and milk at supper time, with perhaps 'salt herring.' 'Johnny cake' and milk. Home-churned butter and buttermilk. Salt pork. Potato pancake, baked in the oven with a cut of fresh, lean side-pork on every piece. Vegetable sour cooked in an iron kettle, over a wood fire."

He portrayed the attire of the day in great detail. "Those were the days of wasp waists, seven petticoats, bustles, and long underwear. Rats in the hair, red faces, rugged complexions. Any girl that appeared with a peaches and cream complexion risked the chance of the he and she gossips saying 'she used corn starch to powder her face.'"

There was also, of course, the ever present repudiation of the younger generation and what they don't know by the old duffers, of which he himself was included. "Of course we old duffers know all about these things, but the younger generation perhaps doesn't know that we used real candles—red, white, blue and green ones for the Christmas tree. That we trimmed the tree largely with strings of popcorn and popcorn balls. The top place was usually a glass star or trumpet. Used to smash one about every year gettin' the dang thing down."

Finally, Swanson summarized his feelings referring to his interpretation of the real meaning of Christmas in terms of the personal satisfaction in harking back to those many fond memories of Christmas past. "So we didn't get much for Christmas? Well, 'mebbe' not. But fellas, you'd have to pile up a pretty tall stack of stuff to equal in personal satisfaction, the joy we find in reminiscence. The toys of long ago are long since gone. But memories of those halcyon days grow richer, brighter with each passing year."

Swanson's colloquial descriptions depicting his childhood memories of Christmas point to a very different time, a much simpler time, and a far less extravagant time. Imagine, no iPods or iPhones, no computers, no cell phones, no video games, no big screen TVs, no lavish Christmas parties, no expensive gifts, and the unthinkable—no Black Friday. How could they have possibly survived? Yet, those memories of Swanson's, as well as Christmas memories for those of us who may recall some of those somewhat simpler times from the past, are very likely indelibly etched in our minds as being remarkably happy.

Helen Jagodzinske—In a League of Her Own

In today's world, the goal of many women is to shatter the so-called glass ceiling in an attempt to advance in their professions and attain their career aspirations. As most are well aware, this accomplishment does not happen overnight, if at all, and was significantly more difficult to accomplish during the previous century. However, there were those women who achieved a great deal during that period of time in spite of the many roadblocks they faced.

One of those women was Martin County native Helen Jagodzinske. She was born in 1917. She then attended and graduated from Welcome High School and furthered her education at Mankato Commercial College. After college, she moved to Chicago to work.

Helen Jagodzinske

When Pearl Harbor was attacked in 1941, she decided to enlist in the Women's Auxiliary Army Corps, later renamed the Women's Army Corp. She was stationed at Camp Grant in Rockford, Illinois. While there, she became a member of Camp Grant's WAAC softball team through which she had the opportunity to play at Wrigley Field in Chicago facing the Fort Sheridan softball team. It's interesting to note that women's leagues were made popular during the war years in an attempt to remedy professional baseball's wartime decline. The accomplishments and popularity of those teams was instrumental in inspiring the 1992 movie *A League of Their Own,* which characterized, and perhaps glamorized, the teams and players from that era. Consequently, this Martin County native was conceivably making history in ways that she likely had no knowledge of at the time.

Her military experience continued by taking Signal Corp training. Following her instruction, she was eventually stationed in New Guinea and served out her tour of duty there until the war ended. She was discharged in 1945.

Upon completing her military service, she embarked on a career in the Federal Civil Service. In 1946, she moved to Washington, D.C., and was assigned to the Adjutant General's Office in the Pentagon. She spent her career there and received numerous awards and commendations reflecting the quality of her accomplishments during her employment. She retired in 1973 as a security specialist.

Not one to sit idle, she then embarked on what might be considered a second career at the Smithsonian Institute. She worked there for another thirty-eight years and was honored in 2011 as being their oldest working employee.

This Martin County native was certainly a part of making history that was exemplified by her role in the military, her career in civil service, her many years at the Smithsonian Institute, as well as the unique opportunity she had to experience playing softball at Wrigley Field in Chicago. Welcome native Helen Jagodzinske is but one of the many individuals born and educated in Martin County who have gone on to make their mark in a positive manner, thereby contributing to the betterment of our society in a wide variety of ways and professions.

Sources for this story include the Jagodzinske family scrapbook of clippings and photos in the Military Room of the Pioneer Museum.

A Newspaperman

Martin County has had a number of interesting and colorful journalists throughout its history, including the locally iconic names of Arthur "Major" Nelson, Frank Day, and Claude Swanson, to name a few. Another journalist to make a mark on Martin County's newspapers was James F. Cavers.

Cavers was born in North Dakota in 1906. He moved to Fairmont with his parents and was a 1924 graduate of Fairmont High School. The summer following his graduation, he began to work for the Fairmont Canning Company, earning thirty cents per hour. In the fall of that same year, Cavers' work in journalism began with the

Martin County Independent as a cub reporter making $12 weekly. After two years with that newspaper, he got a job as a reporter for the rival newspaper, the *Sentinel.* However, he left the *Sentinel* in 1926 to work for the *Minneapolis Journal.* It seems Minneapolis, that big city, wasn't to his liking, so he returned to the *Sentinel* in September of that year for a weekly salary of $26.

James Cavers

He stayed with the *Sentinel* until 1943 when he decided to go to Alaska to work on the Alaskan Highway and manage a construction company. This was apparently not something he wanted for the long term as he returned home at Christmas of that same year. At that time, he returned to his first employer, the Fairmont Canning Company, and worked as a labor recruiter, traveling to Texas and the Bahamas to recruit workers. After twelve years with the canning company, he still had the newspaper business in his blood. Consequently, he got back into the profession and split a year between the *Waseca Journal* and the *LeSueur News–Herald.* After that, in 1956, he rejoined the *Sentinel* as a news reporter. He continued at that position until he retired in 1970. During his career at the *Sentinel,* he worked with those renowned figures in local journalism such as Harry Fairley, Day, Nelson, Swanson, and Walter Mickelson, all of whom were colorful and legendary editors of their day.

However, retirement did not seem to entirely suit him. As a result, he began working for the highway department. Apparently this didn't satisfy him either. In 1972, the editor of the *Truman Tribune*, Don Peterson, asked him if he would be interested in writing a few stories for his newspaper. Cavers took the offer and, upon arriving at the *Tribune* office, found he would be in charge of writing the front page news, not merely an article or two from time to time. Obviously, this was to his liking as before long he was filling in in all departments. He soon became a popular figure with readers; they especially enjoyed his "I Was There" column which cited interesting places and people. He had the ability to get the scoop on local breaking news and the talent to relate his stories in a manner that was viewed very favorably by his readers.

Jim Cavers, known for his "nose for news," died unexpectedly on December 31, 1974, at the *Truman Tribune.*

Sources for this story include the January 2 and 15, 1975, editions of the Sentinel.

If at First You Don't Succeed...Try, Try Again!

Success doesn't always happen on the first try. That insistence on continued attempts might seem to serve as a motto for John Livermore, a Martin County resident who was active on many fronts.

Livermore is probably most recently remembered for his Iron Grill Café on North North Avenue in Fairmont and for his opinions stated in advertisements in the local media either supporting or condemning the actions of public officials. Not one to ride the fence, he made his opinions known quite vociferously as evidenced in his 1971 advertisement relative to the Luedtke Slough controversy.

John Livermore

Livermore was born in Swea City, Iowa, and spent his youth on the farm with his parents. After his mother passed away when he was eleven, he moved with his father back to Fairmont which was his father's home. He attended and graduated from Fairmont High School in 1919.

He was involved in a number of business interests in Fairmont, including operating the Livermore Ice Company. He constructed an ice house on the Budd Lake shore at Oak Beach in 1937 and sold ice at the Lake Sisseton boathouses for a number of years.

Other business interests included farming, rental properties, amusement park operations, salvage, and boat livery operations.

Having an interest in education, Livermore headed the citizens' group instrumental in the construction of both Budd and Lincoln Elementary Schools. The initial intent was to build only one elementary school on the south side of Fairmont; however, opposition led by Livermore prevailed and two elementary schools were finally constructed. He was also at one time the director of a campaign to establish a junior college in Fairmont.

In 1949, Livermore headed the movement toward a free-gate fair. His first attempts proved unsuccessful; however, he vowed to "clean out the deadwood" on the fair board. Finally achieving success in establishing a free-gate fair, attendance and participation greatly improved.

Not one to shy away from politics, he made several attempts at getting elected to public office. He unsuccessfully ran for mayor of Fairmont, the school board, and the state legislature before finally being elected to the House of Representatives where he served from 1950–1952.

Whether he was loved or loathed, he was an activist for his era. He stood his ground, made his point, and apparently didn't back down. There was little doubt he was persistent. It would also seem that he would fit into the broad category of those somewhat colorful and interesting characters from the past who add to the lore of our local history.

Sources for this story include the Sentinel Hometown Legends 2007 *magazine.*

"Furrin" Car Specialist and Sports Car Psychiatrist

As we reflect upon individuals we've encountered throughout our lives, there are occasionally some who, for one reason or another, stand out in our minds.

One such interesting person who fits this description is the late Charles L. Nicholas. Charlie had an auto repair shop and dealership specializing in foreign car sales and service at 1410 East Blue Earth Avenue in Fairmont, presently the location of Day Plumbing and Heating. Charlie was the son of W.L. and Mrs. Nicholas, owners of the Nicholas Theater.

Charlie, born in 1921, served during WWII in the Army Air Corp and trained to be a pilot. However, he once refused to fly a particular aircraft as he suspected the plane had a mechanical issue. That decision cost him his wings and launched his new career as a mechanic, initially involving aircraft.

He and his future wife, Ruby, met in the 1940s in Rochester, Minnesota. Their unlikely introduction was a result of Ruby getting her leg caught in the bumper of a car while crossing a street in Rochester. Ironically, the driver of that car was her future husband, Charlie. They later married and lived in the Rochester area for a time.

The automobile business had long been a part of their lives since both of their fathers were at one time car salesmen. Therefore, when they moved to Fairmont in 1946, Charlie opened a Crosley repair shop. He later began working at the Thaine Peck Car Shop. Then, in 1948, they bought the business from Mr. Peck and soon purchased a Volkswagen franchise. In the 1950s, they acquired a Jaguar franchise, possibly the world's smallest, eventually selling only a total of six Jags. One of their chief concerns in the automotive business was the difficulty in obtaining auto parts for their customers; consequently, they frequently drove to Chicago themselves to obtain needed parts.

Charlie could be described as a portly individual who had a rather witty sense of humor; he was fastidious to the point of perfection and was obviously very meticulous with his work. He was also emphatic regarding the proper usage of the English language. He could usually be seen at his shop wearing mechanic's coveralls. He loved and took a great deal of pride in his collection of foreign vehicles, and much of the Lincoln's social life revolved around automobiles and car shows.

Those who knew him over the years more than likely encountered many unique and interesting experiences and conversations. Charlie, who once ran for U.S. Senate against Hubert Humphrey, was known to have an opinion on most any topic. However, he was also known to be very knowledgeable, well-read, and intelligent.

As the owner of a 1974 MG, I had the opportunity to visit Charlie's shop on a number of occasions in the mid-1970s, both for service as well as for automotive advice. On one such visit to his shop, Charlie offered a ride in one of his pristine Jaguars, a very elegant white 1964 Mark II. Of course, I immediately accepted the enviable opportunity to ride in what I considered to be a rare, exquisite and exotic automobile. Charlie drove west on Blue Earth Avenue and turned north on County Road 39 past the fairgrounds. While passing the fairgrounds, Charlie floored the Jag. The speedometer quickly registered 90 miles per hour and continued to climb when Charlie calmly remarked, "Oh, I forgot something!"

CHARLIE NICHOLAS FURRIN CARS

FURRIN CAR SPECIALIST AND SPORTS CAR PSYCHIATRIST
SERVICE ON JAGUAR - TRIUMPH - MG - AUSTIN-HEALEY
SPRITE - MORRIS - VOLKSWAGEN - PORSCHE - CROSLEY
MICHELIN TIRES

1410 EAST BLUE EARTH AVENUE
FAIRMONT, MINNESOTA 56031

CHARLES L. NICHOLAS
SERVICE MANAGER & JANITOR

SHOP PHONE 235-3403
RES. PHONE 235-3703

CHARLIE NICHOLAS FURRIN CARS SERVICE DEPARTMENT

JAGUAR, MG, HRG, TRIUMPH, MORGAN, ROLLS-ROYCE, AUSTIN-HEALEY, SUNBEAM, HILLMAN, BRISTOL . . . .
Our English Mechanic - - Charlie Nicholas

PORSCHE, MERCEDES, VOLKSWAGEN, BMW . . . .
Our German Mechanic - - Karl Niklaus

FERRARI, ALFA-ROMEO, MASERATI, LANCIA, OSCA . .
Our Italian Mechanic - - Carlo Niccoli

CITROEN, SIMCA, TALBOT, RENAULT . . . . . .
Our French Mechanic - - Charles Nicolles

VOLVO, SAAB . . . .
Our Swedish Mechanic - - Carl Nikkolas

PEGASO, HISPANO-SUIZA . . . .
Our Spanish Mechanic - - Carlos Nicollez

Charlie Nicholas' business card gave you a sense of his personality.
And his staff on the back of the card? All variations of Charlie Nicholas!

I asked, somewhat nervously, "What did you forget Charlie?"

Charlie's instantaneous reply was, "My heart pill!"

In the mid-1970s, seat belts were provided in automobiles, but wearing them was neither mandatory nor particularly common. Nevertheless, it undoubtedly took me less than a split second to securely fasten my seat belt after Charlie's comment. In later reflection on that incident, it seemed Charlie's remark was probably more an indication of his subtle sense of humor rather than that of an actual medical condition. Obviously, it had the desired effect, and he undoubtedly had a number of laughs recounting that story to others over the years.

Former Fairmont resident Kim Rock remembers Charlie after having gone to work for him in 1973. Rock, at that time a high school student, was interested in mechanical things and thought the chance to be an apprentice for Charlie would be pretty neat even though Charlie was semi-retired and seldom came to the shop until after lunch.

Rock also recalled Charlie's perfectionist traits. "I remember learning from him that all four slots of screws holding a license plate on were aligned vertically rather than simply tightened. This was a remnant of his aircraft mechanic days," Rock reminisced.

Charlie's invoices were completed in a painstaking manner as well. According to Rock, "A customer could also expect to receive a very detailed, handwritten invoice from Charlie enumerating each repair in agonizing detail. This process might take a half hour or more while the customer patiently waited but was also accompanied by Charlie's wit and storytelling."

"Charlie was frequently known for fixing things the car owner hadn't asked to be repaired 'because they needed fixing,'" said Rock. This, of course, sometimes caused disputes with his customers.

"At the end of the work day, Charlie's friends, many of whom were British sports car lovers, would show up at his shop for a libation and a few stories," Rock said. "This may have been the most important aspect of the apprenticeship."

Gordy Luckow, another local resident, remembered Charlie telling his friends, "If the lights are on in the house, you're welcome to stop." Luckow added, "He was fun to be around, and there were always interesting people stopping by his home."

Charlie was a colorful character indeed. It would seem that he might compare quite favorably with some of those Martin County legends from the past such as Lenny Burton, Sam Carver, and Frederich Wherland. They were unique, interesting, and provided a luster to our local history that would have been missed otherwise.

Charlie Nicholas passed away in August of 1987 at the age of 66.

Fairmont's Music Man

The term "Music Man" may well bring back memories of Meredith Wilson's musical *Music Man* inspired by his boyhood home in Mason City, Iowa. Fairmont Public Schools also had its own music man who served as director of bands from 1950–1981 and could arguably be credited at that time for putting Fairmont's music department on the map.

Richard Scherer grew up in Mankato and graduated from high school there in 1943. He then enlisted in the Marines and served as a sergeant in the South Pacific until 1945.

Richard Scherer

Following his honorable discharge from the military, he attended Mankato State University, now Minnesota State University in Mankato, where he was a principal percussionist for the MSU Bands. He later transferred to the University of Minnesota where he was also a principal percussionist, a marching band leader, an orchestra timpanist and a swing and Dixieland jazz drummer for gigs in the tri-state area. Scherer earned a bachelor's degree in music education from the University of Minnesota and a master's degree in music education from MSU.

During his tenure as band director and head of the music department at Fairmont Schools, Scherer's marching and concert bands, which were sometimes joined by orchestral and choral groups, performed throughout the United States. Some of those appearances included the Orange Bowl, Disney World, Disneyland, and the World's Fairs in Seattle, New York, and San Antonio. His bands also appeared in the Minneapolis Aquatennial, the Minnesota State Fair, a festival parade in Honolulu, halftimes at several Minnesota Vikings football games, and numerous area parades. As a result of the contributions he made to his students and his profession, he was honored by being voted Teacher of The Year by his colleagues in 1979.

During his career, Scherer was also active in professional organizations, musical groups, and educational roles. He served as chairman of the Minnesota Music Educators Association of the Southwest Division, president of the Fairmont Concert Association, and as co-chairman of the Fairmont Bicentennial Festival Committee. He directed the Fairmont City Band and acted as music director and percussionist for the Fairmont Civic Summer Theater. He often played with Al Menke's band under Leo Ortyl's leadership and The Six Fat Dutchmen. Scherer played timpani for a community ecumenical production of the *Seven Last Words* and directed the Methodist Church Adult Choir. He was a percussion instructor at MSU for many years and a clinician for their summer music camp as well as the music camp at the International Peace Garden.

Following his retirement from the Fairmont Public Schools, Scherer continued to participate in a number of other musical organizations. Some of these included the American Legion Band, the Minneapolis Policeman's Band, the Wayne King Orchestra, the Mankato Symphony, the Sheldon Theater Brass Band, and Jay McShann's jazz combo in Kansas City.

Scherer inspired his students with his intensity and his enthusiasm. His manner and methods of instruction exemplified the expectations he had of his students.

Consequently, and very possibly as a result of the passion he exuded for his profession, a number of his students went on to become band directors or professional musicians.

Richard Scherer is but one example of an individual dedicated to a career that inspired and impacted many people in a very positive manner. His dedication, persistence, and attention to every detail in his program provided an outcome that proved positive for his students, his music program, the Fairmont Public Schools, and the community at large.

Richard Scherer passed away at his home in Wabasha, Minnesota, on September 24, 2004.

I would like to acknowledge and thank the family of Richard Scherer for their contributions to this article. Other sources also include the Sentinel Hometown Legends 2007 *insert page 6, and the September 28, 2004,* Sentinel.

They Made a Difference

As we journey through life, we have to make many choices. As a result, our choices may well have a lasting effect on the people we meet, our community, our county, and on our society. A prime example of this might be Bob and Mary Arneson and the positive influence they had on Martin County through their quiet leadership and dedication.

Above: Dr. Bob and Mary Arneson have become closely associated with saving the Fairmont Opera House, but they also gave in many other ways to their community.

Upon graduating from college, Bob accepted a teaching position in Lakefield. Shortly before the academic year started, he met his future wife, Mary. They were married the following summer, and Bob continued in his teaching position. However, during that time, he made the decision to change careers and become a dentist. Consequently, he resigned from his teaching position after his second year in Lakefield and entered the University of Minnesota Dental School.

Bob and his wife moved to Fairmont in 1961, and he opened a dental practice. They quickly became involved in many community endeavors. Mary was active in the Salvation Army and, at one point, received the "OTHERS" award. This is given to someone who is always caring for others and, at that time, had only been given out twice in the then eighty-seven-year history of the Salvation Army. She was also active with the library, the restoration of the opera house along with Bob, and numerous other community endeavors.

Bob was involved with and active in Fairmont-GO, Boy Scouts, AFS student exchange, the United Methodist Church, the American Cancer Society, and the United Fund. He was also honored as the recipient of the Exchange Club's Book of Good Deeds Award in 1983.

Neither Bob nor Mary sought recognition or accolades for their accomplishments. They were considered quiet leaders who dug in and got the job done while inspiring others along the way. They were optimistic and imaginative, always attempting to be involved in a constructive manner and in turn making the community a better place.

Perhaps the one thing that this couple will be most remembered for is their part in the restoration of the Fairmont Opera House. It has been stated that Bob was, in fact, the driving force behind the restoration of the Fairmont Opera House. Without his leadership and dedication, this county treasure might not be in existence today. Undoubtedly, the Arnesons would not want to be credited for being solely responsible for its survival but would likely give credit to many others who were involved along the way. However, it's likely that anyone familiar with the history of that project would credit the Arnesons for the important part they played in that venture and the lasting effect it has had on our area.

Unfortunately, both Bob and Mary Arneson were killed in an automobile accident in November of 1984. Their untimely death was a tragedy that shocked the community and left the entire area grief-stricken. One might only wonder what positive ventures they might have been associated with had their lives not been cut so short.

The Arnesons, as with all of us, made choices throughout their lives. They chose to make a difference in a positive way that was exemplified by their actions and deeds. John Izzo, from his book *The Five Secrets You Must Discover Before You Die*, said "Your checkbook is not your success—the people you meet and influence in your life will be your success." That quote might seem to epitomize the Arnesons and the influence they've had on Martin County. It would seem unlikely anyone would dispute the fact that what they accomplished during their lifetimes left a lasting and enduring legacy to Martin County and all of its citizens.

Sources for this story include the 2007 Sentinel Hometown Legends *magazine.*

Martin County's Astronaut

Youngsters often grow up aspiring to be baseball or football players, actors or actresses, or perhaps even astronauts. These are goals and dreams that will elude most; however, one young man from Martin County actually fulfilled his dream of becoming an astronaut.

The cold war era of the 1950s intensified on October 4, 1957, with Russia's launching of the unmanned satellite, Sputnik. It was the world's first artificial satellite and the first man-made object to be placed into Earth's orbit. Sputnik's launch came as a rather unpleasant surprise to most Americans who considered space to be the next frontier, a natural extension of the innate tradition of American exploration and explorers throughout history.

The U.S. Space Program intensified from that point forward and culminated with Apollo 11 and astronauts Neil Armstrong, "Buzz" Aldrin, and Michael Collins. On July 20, 1969, Armstrong became the first man to walk on the moon's surface while uttering his iconic statement, "One small step for man, one giant leap for mankind."

Dale Gardner

Martin County's connection to the space program is Sherburn native and NASA astronaut Dale A. Gardner. Gardner was born in Fairmont, spent part of his time growing up in Sherburn, and graduated valedictorian of his class from Savanna Community High School in Savanna, Illinois, in 1966. He then went on to receive a bachelor of science in engineering physics, with great honors, from the University of Illinois in 1970.

After graduating from college, he entered active duty with the U.S. Navy Aviation Officer Candidate School. Upon being commissioned as an ensign, he was selected as the most promising naval officer from his class. Then he began Basic Naval Flight Officer training in Pensacola, Florida. He graduated from this program with the highest academic average ever achieved in the history of the squadron at that time.

Gardner was selected by NASA as an astronaut candidate in January of 1978 and reported to the Johnson Space Center in July. He completed the training period in

August of the next year, making him eligible for assignment as a mission specialist astronaut. He later served as the astronaut project manager for the flight software in the shuttle onboard computers leading up to the first flight in April of 1981. He served as a support crew astronaut and a mission specialist, and logged 337 hours in space, including 225 orbits of the earth and two space walks. In total, he logged more than 2,300 hours of flying time in more than twenty different types of aircraft and spacecraft.

Gardner flew shuttle missions in 1983 and 1984 and was also selected to be a member of the first shuttle mission to launch from Vandenberg Air Force Base into a polar orbit; however, this project was cancelled as a result of the Challenger accident. In addition, in 1984, he was involved in a shuttle mission salvaging two satellites that were in the wrong orbits and brought them back to earth. He went on two spacewalks totaling twelve hours, and he was also the first to go outside of a space vehicle by utilizing a backpack while unattached to his spacecraft.

Gardner retired from the Navy in 1990. He worked for TRW, Inc., in Colorado Springs, Colorado, and was later associated with Northrup Grumman's Colorado Springs operations. After that, he joined the National Renewable Energy Laboratory in Golden, Colorado, as the associate director for renewable fuels science and technology. Gardner retired in 2013 and passed away in February of 2014.

Gardner represents another example of a Martin County native who accomplished exemplary distinction in his chosen field. He distinguished himself by being one of thirty-five candidates chosen from a field of 8,079 applicants to the U.S. Space Agency's shuttle program. Gardner was the recipient of a multitude of special honors, he was academically gifted, he achieved significant accomplishments in his chosen profession, and most importantly, he made a positive difference in the lives of Americans and our society as a whole.

For more information on Gardner, you can read his bio on NASA's website. Other information for this story came from the January 19, 1978, Fairmont Sentinel.

The Year of the Revolving Door

While Fairmont has always been a relatively stable community in terms of employment and employee longevity, the year 1973 seems to have been somewhat of an anomaly! A headline in the February 21, 1974, edition of the *Sentinel* reads, "For Fairmont area, '73 becomes the year of the revolving door." While frequent changes, particularly among the higher profile positions in the community, were comparatively rare, that year saw new faces appearing in these roles continually.

So, what were the changes, and who were the new faces? A new school superintendent and a new welfare director, for starters. In addition, Fairmont had no city engineer, no county engineer, and no Chamber of Commerce manager. The changes that took place meant there was somewhat of a youth movement in many of those vacant positions.

The Fairmont Public Schools were faced with finding a new superintendent as their current superintendent, L.H. Baumann, announced he would retire in January of 1974.

The district, with an enrollment at that time of nearly 2,500 students, hadn't faced the challenge of finding a new superintendent in nearly ten years. After interviewing candidates for the position, the board hired a young administrator named Dave Wettergren. He grew up in St. Peter, graduated from Gustavus Adolphus College, obtained a master's degree at the University of Minnesota, and had earned a doctorate. Wettergren was in his mid-30s when he left his position as principal of Kellogg Junior High School in Rochester to come to Fairmont as the new superintendent.

The Chamber of Commerce manager at that time was Wayne Unze. He had come to Fairmont in 1968 as its first full-time chamber manager. During his five-year tenure in Fairmont, he launched the Festival of Lakes. In addition, forty new businesses came, and Fairmont began studying downtown renewal. However, Unze decided to take a position as manager of a cable television operation in Las Vegas and left on August 1.

The person hired to replace Unze began on October 1 and died suddenly of a heart attack on October 10. Finally, after being without a chamber manager for nearly six months, Tom Kucera was hired for the position. He was young, thirty years old, and a very tall six feet, seven inches. He was a former basketball player who had held a similar position at a Chamber of Commerce in Sioux Falls for three years prior to coming to Fairmont.

The county auditor's office went through what seemed like an evolution of change in a relatively short time, too. According to the *Sentinel*, the current auditor at that time, Clement Smith, announced his retirement at the end of July; Roger Wehner, deputy auditor, was promoted to auditor. Two deputy auditors eventually resigned, and Wehner himself also resigned, which left the county with an auditor's office, but no one to work there.

The commissioners then asked a retired deputy auditor from Albert Lea, Mrs. Rachel Holt, to fill in during the interim. She subsequently became the acting auditor. Then, after a short time, the commissioners hired one of the original applicants for the job, Robert Katzenberger, to fill the position. Katzenberger brought a mood of stability to the office and things seemed to settle down. He eventually rehired Wehner as his chief deputy auditor and named Mrs. Dennis Olson as deputy auditor. At that point, things seemed to be back to normal.

Other changes during that era involved a new Martin County welfare director, Robert Sullivan. He began work six months after the resignation of Dennis Johnson.

In addition, Fairmont lost forty-six years of engineering experience when Wesley Youngerman and Arvel Klessig announced their retirements. Consequently, the city selected Gailen Narum, assistant engineer, to be acting city engineer. Eventually, the city hired Bob Witty of Mankato who had been a sales engineer for North Star Concrete. Before that, he had been an associate engineer for Mankato and the state highway department.

Other changes involved LeRoy Krahn replacing Oliver Anderson as county assessor. Anderson resigned to take a similar position in Red Wing. In addition, Gary Hamman was hired as community education director to replace Tom McMullen who resigned to return to college.

That year, 1973, appears to have been a somewhat unstable time; however, it appears that the effects of this relative "instability" seemed to have been constructive for the community and county in the ensuing years, as many of the newly hired individuals remained on the job for many years and, in turn, had a positive impact on our area with their accomplishments.

My Visit with the Vice President

In adding to our archives at the Pioneer Museum, I had thought it would be of interest to include an interview with a well-known Martin County native who became vice president of the United States. That was, of course, Walter F. Mondale, who was born in Ceylon. Consequently, I emailed him in late February 2008 asking if he would agree to an interview. To my surprise, I received a response the very next day stating he would.

It was an early morning in late March; a light winter snowfall didn't materialize to the extent predicted. My wife, Carol, and I left at 7 a.m., allowing extra time due to the weather conditions. We stopped at Gemini Studios to pick up Shelly Abitz who was going to do the videotaping, and we made one more stop in Blue Earth to pick up my niece, Lorrie. Incidentally, she is presently the owner of the former Mondale home in Elmore.

We arrived at the Dorsey and Whitney law firm in downtown Minneapolis at 9:30 a.m. as the roads were in good driving condition. We were early, as my appointment with Mr. Mondale was at 11:15 a.m. I drove up to the third level, pressed the keypad and was asked who I was going to see. I said I had an appointment with Mr. Mondale, told them my name, and immediately the gate lifted so we could drive into the client parking. If we didn't know better, this could have made us feel quite important.

I then called his secretary to let her know that we had arrived. She asked me to hold momentarily, and then asked me to come up to meet her in the conference room on the twentieth floor and get the video equipment ready as Mr. Mondale would see us early.

As we were getting prepared in the conference room, Mr. Mondale's secretary provided us with enough coffee and bottled water for a small army. The hospitality shown to us was most impressive. She also provided two large pictures of Mr. Mondale, one in his army uniform and another with Mr. Mondale as a very young child with his older brother in a little wagon. After getting set up for the interview, we informed his secretary that we were ready. She said she would send him down.

Walter Mondale, left, with Lenny Tvedten as they page through Chain of Lakes Country

As I waited in anticipation, I wondered what to expect. I wondered what he would be like, this individual of humble beginnings born in Ceylon who rose to the pinnacle of power by becoming the vice president of the most powerful nation on the face of the earth. Someone said they saw his secretary walking down the hallway and, thinking he would be coming from that direction, we were all taken by surprise as he came through the opposite doorway.

When he entered the room, any preconceived impressions or uncertainties that I may have had immediately vanished as this smiling gentleman with the warm, welcoming handshake and jovial remarks greeted us. He immediately made us feel most welcome and at ease.

He asked how things were in Fairmont, Ceylon, and Martin County, as I thanked him for taking time for an interview and began showing him our book, *Chain of Lakes Country–An Illustrated History of Martin County*, our 2008 calendar, and our latest MCHS newsletter. He was obviously intrigued by the book and, as he paged through, immediately picked out the house in Ceylon where he had lived nearly eighty years ago. He commented on other pictures as well.

After visiting for what seemed like about fifteen minutes, we sat down at the large conference table for the interview. I planned to discuss his life from his birth in Ceylon, Martin County, through his youth growing up in small towns in Southern Minnesota, to his college experience, his political career, and what he is involved with at the present time. It was more than obvious as our discussion unfolded that he was genuinely sincere in providing me with both a very interesting and a very informative interview involving a man who came from small town America, yet rose to great heights in serving his fellow man in many capacities. As we talked, our discussion involved his parents and family as well as what life was like in Ceylon, Heron Lake, and later Elmore while he was growing up in these small Southern Minnesota communities.

As a high school student in Elmore, it was obvious from his 1946 senior yearbook that he was a leader in every respect. He was a standout in athletics, with the nickname "Crazy Legs" for his ability as a running back in football. In addition, he served as captain of both the football and basketball teams his senior year. He also participated in many other extra-curricular activities and was class president his junior year. Yet when I asked about his leadership roles and athletic ability as a student, he was very modest and said that in a small school like Elmore, if you were a warm body, you just participated in those activities.

We went on to discuss college and law school. As an undergraduate, he majored in political science. He said that he went into the army after graduating from college so that he could then afford to attend law school on the G.I. Bill after being discharged.

I asked how he became involved in politics. He talked about working for Hubert Humphrey's senatorial campaign, being appointed attorney general at a young age, his work in the Senate, and eventually being elected the forty-second Vice President of the United States. I asked him to elaborate on how, as vice president, he was instrumental in expanding the role of the vice president's office from one of being merely a figure head to a functional position that for the first time served as a true presidential advisor, a model that has been followed by subsequent vice presidents. He also discussed his work with Jimmy Carter during Carter's presidency and the fact they still keep in contact with each other.

He spoke of the importance of the values he learned as a youngster from his family, his father being a Methodist minister and his mother a teacher, and the values he acquired growing up in small towns in Minnesota and how they influenced his life. I asked him what advice he would give a young person who had an interest in entering politics. His comments were relative to public service in any capacity. I interpreted this to mean doing something worthy, being of service to your fellow man in whatever endeavor you choose. This might certainly involve politics, but it could also include many other forms of public service. We discussed many things during the forty-minute interview.

In closing the interview, I had planned to ask him about the many interviews he'd had in his lifetime, as well as which ones were most notable, and in turn, I had planned to make a joking reference to where this interview rated compared to the others. However, before I could finish my question, he said none were as good as this one. This was a compliment that I didn't deserve; however, it served to reflect the character of the person I came to know in that short span of approximately sixty-to-ninety minutes.

After the interview, we continued to visit about many things, including politics, as my wife was taking pictures and as he was signing autographs. He was in no hurry to rush off, but rather took plenty of time to talk, reminisce, joke, and make certain we had what we wanted in our interview. It seemed important to him too, as he asked if he could also have a copy of the interview.

As I think back at that visit with the former Vice President of the United States, I remember a truly kind gentleman, a person of integrity and honesty, a sincere individual who hadn't forgotten his roots and someone who considered all citizens of Minnesota and our great nation as important. However, I especially remember a person who was so genuine and pleasant to visit with, a person who had a wonderful sense of humor, and a person who exhibited such a warm and caring personality that he immediately made me feel comfortable and welcome. What an honor, what a gentleman, what a statesman!

Epilogue

Then and Now in Martin County

The year was 1920. The county had a population of about 22,000 and sixty-two percent of it was rural. The ethnic backgrounds then were primarily German, Swedish, Norwegian, Danish, Polish and Irish, according to the *Martin County Plat Book and Livestock Breeders' Guide*. Now the county is estimated to have just under 20,000 people and only twenty-seven percent live in rural areas.

Back then, agriculture was the major industry, and corn was the principal crop. Good farmers of that era considered sixty bushels per acre to be an average yield, and eighty bushels per acre was not uncommon.

Regarding livestock, dairy farming was considered profitable at that time with numerous creameries available. Poultry was also considered a significant source of revenue.

Crop farming then involved oats as the principal grain crop with much of it fed locally. Corn silage was also an important crop in connection with the livestock industry as silos were found on "all the best farms." In addition, sugar beets were prosperous at that time, averaging ten tons per acre with the canning factory in Fairmont serving as a profitable outlet for this commodity. The average price per acre of farmland in 1920 in Martin County was $200, hardly comparable to today's prices.

Fairmont was the county seat with a population of 4,400 "happy, contented, prosperous people," according to the plat book. It was said that the city offered ideal living conditions, was thoroughly modern, and was the "biggest little city in the west." The plat book also said Fairmont "gives an impression of being a place of 10,000. Miles of paved streets and alleys. City-owned water, light, and heating facilities. Splendid $200,000.00 high school." The book makes further reference to Fairmont's fraternal organizations, churches, daily press, three great railroad systems, two gas engine factories, and a canning factory. Interlaken Amusement Park was called one of the largest and finest in the west, costing over $100,000 and having one of the finest golf courses in the country. It also called Fairmont a Mecca for thousands of tourists annually.

In 2016, Fairmont's population was 10,115.

Ceylon, in 1920, had a population of 600. It boasted two banks, a cement block and tile factory, a poultry specialty company, three elevators, a thriving business establishment, and its own electric light plant. Ninety-six years later, Ceylon's population was 350.

Dunnell, with a population of 250 back then, had two banks, two elevators, and a thriving, up-to-date creamery. In addition, it had electric lights, a very good school, a garage, and several other "going business concerns." Dunnell's population was 154 in 2016.

Granada had a population of 425 in 1920. It had two banks, elevators, a garage, a creamery, several other business concerns, and one of the best schools in the area. Its electric light and power was furnished by the dam at Rapidan, Minnesota. The 2016 population was estimated at 290.

Sherburn had a population of 1,100 in 1920 compared to 1,091 in 2016. In 1920, it had three banks, three elevators, and one of the most up-to-date creameries in the state. It had its own electric light plant, excellent schools, a hospital, several garages, and other thriving business concerns.

Triumph, with a 1920 population of 350, had two banks, two elevators, a creamery, a garage, excellent schools, and several more thriving business enterprises. Monterey had a population of 250. It had one bank, one garage, an elevator, and a complete modern school. Triumph and Monterey merged in 1959 to become Trimont. The town's population was 707 in 2016.

Truman had a population of 350 in 1920. It boasted three banks, four elevators, a new creamery, excellent schools, a hospital, two garages, many other up-to-date businesses, and obtained its electric light and power from the dam in Rapidan, also. Truman's population was 1,058 in 2016.

Welcome had a population of 600 in 1920. It had two banks, three elevators, one of the best creameries in the state, a garage, a hospital, several other thriving businesses, and electric lights owned by the city. Its population was 653 in 2016.

The rural landscape of Martin County, as well as Minnesota, has changed significantly from 1920 to the present time. Martin County and the communities that comprise it have evolved as have the economic engines that drive them. Gone from many of these small towns are the creameries, the hospitals, the elevators, and their schools. Perhaps the single most significant change agent in the earlier years for these communities was the loss of the railroad.

It is interesting to note that the county's population has remained relatively stable from 1920 to the present time. Although several communities have lost population since 1920, many are quite stable and, in fact, have grown. The one constant appears to be that our county, like our state and our country, will continue to evolve and change over time.

Statistics provided were taken from the U. S. Census Bureau's American Factfinder website on October 19, 2017. https://factfinder.census.gov/faces/nav/jsf/pages/community_facts.xhtml

Index